MODERN STUDIES IN PROPERTY LAW: VOLUME 9

This book contains a collection of peer-reviewed papers presented at the Eleventh Biennial Modern Studies in Property Law Conference held at Queen's University Belfast in April 2016. It is the ninth volume to be published under the name of the Conference. The Conference and its published proceedings have become an established forum for property lawyers from around the world to showcase current research in the discipline. This collection reflects the diversity and contemporary relevance of modern research in property law. Following a foreword from the keynote speaker at the Conference, Queen's alumnus Lord Kerr of Tonaghmore, the chapters address a range of issues, from the nature of land law and property rights, through claims to the home and digital assets, to the growing debate on the nature of public property. Collectively the chapters demonstrate the vibrancy and importance of property law in dealing with modern concerns across the common law world.

Previous volumes in this series:

Modern Studies in Property Law: Volume 1
Edited by Elizabeth Cooke

Modern Studies in Property Law: Volume 2
Edited by Elizabeth Cooke

Modern Studies in Property Law: Volume 3
Edited by Elizabeth Cooke

Modern Studies in Property Law: Volume 4
Edited by Elizabeth Cooke

Modern Studies in Property Law: Volume 5
Edited by Martin Dixon

Modern Studies in Property Law: Volume 5
Edited by Susan Bright

Modern Studies in Property Law: Volume 6
Edited by Susan Bright

Modern Studies in Property Law: Volume 7
Edited by Nicholas Hopkins

Modern Studies in Property Law: Volume 8
Edited by Warren Barr

Modern Studies in Property Law

Volume 9

Edited by
Heather Conway and Robin Hickey

·HART·
OXFORD · LONDON · NEW YORK · NEW DELHI · SYDNEY

HART PUBLISHING
Bloomsbury Publishing Plc
Kemp House, Chawley Park, Cumnor Hill, Oxford, OX2 9PH, UK

HART PUBLISHING, the Hart/Stag logo, BLOOMSBURY and the Diana logo are trademarks of Bloomsbury Publishing Plc

First published in hardback, 2017
Paperback edition, 2019

A catalogue record for this book is available from the British Library.

Library of Congress Cataloging-in-Publication data

ISBN: HB: 978-1-78225-754-7
PB: 978-1-50993-473-7
ePdF: 978-1-78225-756-1
ePub: 978-1-78225-755-4

Typeset by Compuscript Ltd, Shannon

Foreword

BY LORD KERR OF TONAGHMORE

The chapters in this volume are the product of the Eleventh Modern Studies in Property Law Conference, held at Queen's University Belfast from 5 to 7 April 2016. This was the first time in its 20-year history that this increasingly influential conference had been held in Northern Ireland, and I had the honour to be invited to give the keynote address.

When Heather Conway and Robin Hickey first invited me to speak, I felt a mixture of pleasure and apprehension. Pleased to be asked to address such a prestigious event, not least because it took place at my *alma mater*, Queen's University, but also appropriately apprehensive, since property law is emphatically not my field. As an undergraduate, land law and trusts were the subjects for which I had the least enthusiasm. In the years since, as a practising lawyer and later as a judge, I have had only a fleeting exposure to the intricacies of property law disputes. I thus felt something of a fraud, purporting to contribute something to such a distinguished audience. As it turned out, my apprehension was entirely misplaced. It is a credit to the organisers and participants that I was thoroughly welcomed and engaged throughout my time at the conference. One of the many advantages of sitting as an appellate judge is that one has the opportunity to obtain fresh insight into unfamiliar areas of law. In my address, I commented on the handful of property law cases which I have sat on in the Supreme Court, including *Jones v Kernott* [2011] UKSC 53 and *McDonald v McDonald* [2016] UKSC 28. There followed a lively and illuminating discussion. Speaking to delegates from across the British Isles and the common-law world, I was impressed by the breadth and depth of their interests and research.

I am equally impressed by the range and quality of the contributions to this book. There is something in this volume for everyone. Law reformers would be wise to read Martin Dixon's fascinating essay emphasising 'the reality of how people use and enjoy land' (chapter one); Heather Conway and Sheena Grattan's paper on the challenges posed by digital assets to the law of succession (chapter six); Juliet Brook's chapter on testamentary capacity in disputes involving surviving relatives and a carer (chapter seven); Graham Ferris's paper on combating fraud and sharp practice through land registration (chapter twelve) and Chris Wilmore's study of the shifts in public perceptions of planning policy (chapter fourteen). Land law enthusiasts will enjoy James Fisher's paper on freehold covenants (chapter two); Una Woods' research on adverse possession (chapter four) and Warren Barr's chapter on the contractualisation of leases (chapter five). Human rights specialists will find much of interest in Sarah Nield's paper charting how proportionality is 'creeping into the lexicon of property lawyers' (chapter three) and Susan Pascoe's summary of recent case law on disability discrimination in possession claims (chapter eight). Chancery lawyers will benefit from reading John Picton's chapter on charitable giving and failed gifts (chapter ten), and Simon Douglas and Ben McFarlane's research on the doctrine of 'sham trusts' (chapter thirteen). Public lawyers will appreciate Brian Sloan's examination of home sales under the Care Act 2014 (chapter nine), and Ann Brower and John Page's paper on the nature and theory underlying public property (chapter six). Comparative jurists will learn much from Rod Thomas's chapter on Australian title regimes (chapter eleven) and Jill Fraley's paper on the anti-wilderness bias in US property law (chapter fifteen).

Modern Studies in Property Law: Volume 9 is essential reading for all those with an interest in property law, including students, academics, practitioners, judges and legislators.

I hope that the conference itself will continue to grow and to be a guiding influence on the development of this important area of law.

Brian Kerr
London, 6 April 2017

Preface

This is the ninth volume in the Modern Studies in Property Law series, comprising a revised and peer-reviewed selection of papers from the 11th biennial conference. It was our pleasure to host the conference in April 2016 at Queen's University Belfast, the first occasion on which it has been held outside England. We are very grateful to the MSPL Board for entrusting the event to us, and to Professor Sally Wheeler and our colleagues in the School of Law for generously supporting and encouraging it, providing the foundation for a successful conference which continues to attract property law scholars from around the world. The contributors and delegates embraced the occasion, and the papers in this volume provide a snapshot of the lively and timely debate evident in the proceedings, and the rigorous scholarship underpinning it.

Lord Kerr of Tonaghmore was the keynote speaker at the conference. As his Lordship has been kind enough to remark on occasion, he is the only serving Justice of the Supreme Court to have had the great good fortune to be educated at Queen's University Belfast. It was a tremendous pleasure to welcome him back, and delegates were treated to a lively and insightful discourse on a range of significant property-related judgments. We are honoured that Lord Kerr has been kind enough to contribute a foreword to this volume.

The papers begin in Part A, considering land law and the nature of property rights in land. Martin Dixon opens this section with a wide-ranging contribution, highlighting the organic origins of land law and the realities of land use and enjoyment—commercially, economically and socially—when law reformers are contemplating change. James Fisher's focus is the more specific context of freehold covenants, offering an innovative argument on their positive effect which looks to the content rules and the 'touch and concern' criterion in particular. Sarah Nield turns our attention to the timely matter of the role of proportionality in property law, drawing (inter alia) on the recent Supreme Court decision in *McDonald* to argue that, notwithstanding an apparent constraint of the role of proportionality in home repossession proceedings, the concept remains important for rights-based adjudication and the exercise of remedial discretion. Una Woods considers the ever-popular question of adverse possession, investigating the extension of a qualified veto system to unregistered land in Ireland and the merits of a functionally similar concept to 'colour of title' for curing defects. Warren Barr closes the section with some considered thoughts on the contractualisation of leases, critically exposing and examining the law on repudiatory breach of leases to argue that, while it is proper in many respects to treat leases as contracts, nevertheless they are better regulated primarily as property rights.

In Part B we consider property rights through the frames of life and death. Heather Conway and Sheena Grattan begin with a topical examination of the place of digital assets within succession regimes. The paper argues that to date English law has been ineffective in addressing the estate planning challenges presented by digital assets, and looks to US jurisprudence for a possible set of solutions. Juliet Brook continues on the succession theme, critically examining the law on testamentary capacity in the context of disputes between next of kin and carers, and arguing that the complexity of the concept must remain firmly in view as the Law Commission considers possible reform in the area. Susan Pascoe's paper focuses on disability discrimination defences in landlord–tenant possession proceedings, considering the broader normative implications for the contours of property rights, and perceiving scope for significant litigation. Brian Sloan considers the availability and use of deferred payment agreements under the Care Act 2014 to fund social care, and the broader property ramifications of such agreements, critically assessing the relationship between former co-residents of a now-deceased recipient and the local authority aiming to force a sale of the home. John Picton closes the section with a paper considering the relevance of egoistic intent to charitable giving, particularly in the situation where a gift has failed. The thesis here is that gifts made on the basis of egoistic intent should remain in charity, but the paper argues that deep theoretical and conceptual problems in the underpinning legal frameworks would first need to be addressed.

Part C moves to the theme of fraud and title, opening with a paper by Rod Thomas which offers a comparative analysis of fraud provisions of the Australasian Torrens regimes and the Land Registration Act 2002. The paper agues specifically that the alteration powers under schedule 4 of the 2002 Act offer a more plausible position than can be achieved through the Torrens concept of immediate indefeasibility, though it perceives significant scope for development in the framing of the English provision. Continuing with this broad theme, Graham Ferris discusses how land registration systems should deal with sharp practice and fraud, in ways which oppose and sanction dishonest and oppressive practices. Simon Douglas and Ben McFarlane round off this section with a paper which explores the complex area of 'sham' trusts, examining the conflicting views on the doctrine and arguing that the courts' approach in ascertaining the settlor's intent continues to be an objective one.

Part D draws the collection to a close by looking at the themes of property, place and development. Chris Willmore explores the way in which changes in planning law and policy can reflect changing perceptions of property, and how constructs of place, specificity and locality have been radically altered by recent changes to the complex regulatory structure in England. Jill Fraley follows, arguing that the anti-wilderness bias in American property law did not originate there, but was inherited from the English common law system; in looking at how these biases have been allowed to continue, the paper focuses on the law of waste and surface water liability as modern examples. Finally, Ann Brower and John Page guide us through the four dimensions of public property, traversing a spectrum from the orthodox view that public property is a variant of private property to an end where ideas of ownership are redundant. The paper is critical of the under-theorised nature of public property reasoning and concepts, but optimistic about its underpinning values of propriety, inclusion and egalitarianism, and ultimately about its potential to help us understand, not just claims to public space, but also who we are.

As ever, the full papers were not the only aspects of the 2016 conference. The high number of proposals we received for the 'work in progress' section meant that we were able to run three parallel streams in Belfast; and the dedicated postgraduate event on the final day of proceedings encouraged some lively and enthusiastic debates. This year, for the first time at the main conference, there was also a 'how to' section, which focused on generating research income (something which is increasingly important in the UK context) and an informal mentoring lunch to discuss opportunities here. On the social side, conference delegates enjoyed a drinks reception in Belfast's historical City Hall on the first night of the conference and dinner in the Great Hall at Queen's University on the second evening. We are very grateful to both Belfast City Council and Oxford University Press for their sponsorship of the respective events. Our speaker at the conference dinner was The Hon Mdm Justice Denise McBride, Judge of the Supreme Court of Northern Ireland and one of the first two females to be appointed to this position in October 2015. An alumna of Queen's University and former Honorary Lecturer in the Law School, Mdm Justice McBride shared insights and anecdotes from her time as an advocate specialising in chancery and family law and her new position; we are, as always, indebted to her for her ongoing support and close associations with the Law School. The conference dinner also gave us occasion to pause and remember colleagues sadly no longer with us. In Belfast we honoured the memory of Professor Phil Kenny and Professor Gerwyn Griffiths, each very greatly missed.

The 11th MSPL conference was the first to take place since Lizzie Cooke stepped down from the Board following her appointment as a full-time judge. Lizzie would be the first to point out that the credit for initiating the Reading University conferences from which the series originated was shared with her colleagues. It was, however, Lizzie who nurtured and developed the conference series. She led its transformation into the current MSPL series, hosted the first four conferences and edited volumes 1–4 of the publication. It was on her initiative that the conferences left Reading to be hosted by a different university on each occasion and that a Board (of which she became Chair) was appointed to oversee the development of the series. MSPL would not exist as it does today without her leadership and foresight. Lizzie's contribution was toasted at the conference dinner in Belfast and is recorded in this publication with our thanks.

Finally, we would like to extend our thanks to Nicky Clarke MBE and the hospitality team at Queen's, who thoroughly looked after us during our three days in April; Melissa Kent and the Eventus team for their invaluable conference assistance; and all those colleagues who acted as panel chairs during the event. A sincere word of thanks, also, to Bill Asquith and all the team at Hart Publishing for publishing the collection and dealing with our numerous queries along the way. We hope you enjoy the various chapters, and look forward to seeing everyone in 2018 when Professor Ben McFarlane hosts the conference at University College London.

Heather Conway & Robin Hickey
Belfast, March 2017

Contents

Part C: Fraud and Title

Part D: Property, Place, and Development

Part A

Land Law and the Nature of Property Rights in Land

1

The Organic Nature of the Law of Real Property: Reforming Modern Land Law

MARTIN DIXON*

Striving to better, oft we mar what's well[1]

I. INTRODUCTION

THERE IS A tendency among law reformers to want to change things. Sometimes for good reason. Modern land law in England and Wales[2] is the product of the great legislative reforms of the 1920s, and it is unarguable that these were absolutely necessary to bring the originally feudal law of real property into the modern age. As is well known, those reforms were considerable: the ways in which estates and interests could be held, created and transferred were remodelled and in some cases reinvented.[3] Some things were done away with altogether,[4] and some lived on (and still do) only as a shadow of their former selves.[5] Yet, what is also clear is that much about the granular substance of estates and interests in land did not change. There is nothing in the great property reforms that changed the essence of freeholds, leaseholds, easements, mortgages and so on. Certainly, how these interests might be held, whether they could be legal or equitable and how they might be transferred were the subjects of radical surgery, and there was also some keyhole surgery on the manner in which such proprietary rights could come into

* Professor of the Law of Real Property, University of Cambridge. The motivation for this chapter is a desire to explain to students why land law is as it is, and why I appear to regard all proposals for reform with deep suspicion. I have relied heavily on AWB Simpson's marvellous *A History of the Land Law* (2nd edn, Oxford, Oxford University Press, 1986; hereinafter *Simpson*) for much of the historical detail without which I could not have started. I am grateful for the referee's astute observations and the editors' patience.

[1] Shakespeare, *King Lear*, Act 1, Scene 4.

[2] In this context, the law on and after 1 January 1926.

[3] Registration of matters affecting land is a twentieth-century idea, but the Land Registration Act (LRA) 1925 represented the first comprehensive system in England & Wales. See P Mayer and A Pemberton, *A Short History of Land Registration in England & Wales* (London, Land Registry, 2000).

[4] eg copyhold, frankalmoin, gavelkind, mortgages by assignment.

[5] eg Crown rents, payments in lieu of tithes, fee tails.

being in the first place.[6] But *what* people had was much the same in January 1926 as in December 1925, even though *how* they might conduct dealings in the future would be different.[7] This reform of transactional property law did not stop in 1926, and subsequently there were further changes to how deeds are executed, the validity or otherwise of oral transactions and the mechanics of land registration.[8] This is a process that is ongoing.[9]

The reasons for the 1925 reforms are well known and the successes are with us still. It is indisputable that, for example, the move from unregistered to registered conveyancing that gathered pace after 1950 and the changes to the law of co-ownership in 1925[10] have contributed significantly to the economic and social well-being of much of the general population, as well as the health of our financial and public institutions.[11] This needs little emphasis. Indeed, even though the greatest of the reform proposals since 1926, the introduction of electronic conveyancing, remains out of reach,[12] the adaptation of the processes of land law to the world as it is now, or will become, is an undervalued achievement of those engaged in promoting and implementing law reform.

Yet, land law is not just about the mechanics of buying and selling, mortgaging and registering; it is about use and enjoyment, homes and businesses, relationships and security. Here, too, much has been proposed for the reform of the substance of the estates and interests that are so familiar to us, and some of these proposals have found legislative form and some have been woven into the fabric of the common law through judicial inventiveness. However, while reform of the transactional apparatus of land law has, on the whole, been a success, reform of substantive concepts has been less common, with fewer proposals being taken forward and with less critical acclaim for the legislation that does make it to the statute book. This is despite the fact that it would be ridiculous to maintain that the substance of the law of real property is near perfect. While much depends on where you are standing, only the most optimistic analyst would argue that there is nothing that could be improved.[13]

[6] The Law of Property Act (LPA) 1925 consolidated numerous formality provisions, including those of the Statute of Frauds 1677, the Conveyancing Acts 1881 and 1882, and the Law of Property Act 1922.

[7] This too was not a new phenomenon. The Real Property Commissioners, appointed in 1829 to kick start law reform, noted that 'the law of Real Property seems to us to require very few essential alterations: and that those which we feel it our duty to suggest are chiefly modal', quoted in *Simpson* 275.

[8] Law of Property (Miscellaneous Provisions) Act 1989, Trusts of Land and Appointment of Trustees Act 1996 (TOLATA 1996), Land Registration Act 2002 (LRA 2002).

[9] In March 2016, the Law Commission published a consultation paper on land registration. See Law Commission, *Updating the Land Registration Act 2002: A Consultation Paper* (Law Com CP 227, 2016).

[10] And thereafter by TOLATA 1996.

[11] Although not all have benefited. See, eg L Fox O'Mahony, 'Property Outsiders and the Hidden Politics of Doctrinalism' (2014) 67 *Current Legal Problems* 409.

[12] E-conveyancing as envisaged by the LRA 2002 involves the direct electronic entry of transactions on the register by property professionals without the intervention of HMLR. Such a process would create the interest so entered or actually execute the transaction so registered. This is not the same as e-delivery of services, which are proceeding apace. Full e-conveyancing remains on hold. In *Updating the LRA 2002* (n 9) paras 20.16–20.14 the Commission asks whether it should be re-thought.

[13] The Real Property Commissioners were such: 'When the object of transactions respecting land is accomplished; and the estates and interests in it which are actually created and secured, the Law of England, except in a few comparatively unimportant particulars, appears to come almost as near perfection as can be expected in any human institution', quoted in *Simpson* 275.

A tenant struggling with a landlord who refuses to repair the roof,[14] a developer frustrated by a neighbour's prescriptive right to light,[15] a co-owner forced to sell the family home to facilitate payment of their partner's debts,[16] a squatter evicted from their home of many years,[17] a landowner losing title to a property they are now ready to renovate[18] or a borrower finding their property sold by their lender without much apparent regard for their interests[19] will tell you otherwise. There is much that could be done.

It is not the purpose of this chapter to decry the work of law reform bodies, to decry judicial inventiveness in developing the common law or to dissuade colleagues from thinking the unthinkable and proposing even the most radical of surgeries to both the transactional and substantive aspects of the law of real property. However, in thinking about the reform of land law, in both its transactional and substantive aspects, this chapter suggests that we should heed the origins of land law as a subject that grew from how people used, or needed to use, land, rather than assume that land law was, or ever could be, an orderly imposed and orderly constructed system generated from first principles. By recognising the organic origins of the law of real property—that is, as a system that reflected the reality of land use in a social and economic context and not a system built on a necessarily coherent and rational set of principles—we might better understand what law reform is needed now, what needs to be left alone and what proposals for reform are likely to work. This is not an argument which rejects principle per se, or the protection of abstract rights, be they founded in private or public law,[20] but it is an argument which cautions against law reform for its own sake—for example, to make it 'tidier' or 'simpler'. The way that people use land is multifaceted and the stark reality is that land law is correspondingly, and properly, complex. Hence, the essential point is that reform, or a decision not to reform, should reflect in large measure how people behave when using land, within the bounds of external obligations imposed by the civil and criminal law. Even then, modern land law is entirely at ease with recognising proprietary entitlement, flowing from use if the violation of the criminal or civil law is not central to the proprietary claim.[21] Modern land law is more organic than it is principled.

II. THE ORGANIC ORIGINS AND NATURE OF MODERN LAND LAW

It is a trite point, but a good starting place, to remember that modern land law—in both its transactional and substantive aspects—has its origins in the feudal system

[14] Caveat emptor in operation: *Southwark LBC v Mills* [2001] 1 AC 1.

[15] Law Commission, *Rights to Light* (Law Com No 356, 2014).

[16] eg *Fred Perry (Holdings) Ltd v Genis* [2015] 1 P & CR DG5.

[17] Almost certainly true if the claim to adverse possession falls under sch 6 LRA 2002.

[18] Almost certainly true if the land happens to be of unregistered title.

[19] eg *Horsham Properties Group v Clark* [2009] 1 P & CR 8.

[20] The interplay between real property and human rights is challenging for a system built more on 'use' than principle. It is now accepted that land law must adapt to a rights-based jurisprudence, but the practical implications have been limited. See *Manchester CC v Pinnock* [2010] UKSC 45; D Cowan and C Hunter, '"Yeah But, No But"—*Pinnock* and *Powell* in the Supreme Court' (2012) 75 *MLR* 78. The judgment in *McDonald v McDonald* [2016] UKSC 28 is equally cautious.

[21] *Best v Chief Land Registrar* [2015] EWCA Civ 17, [2016] QB 23; *Bakewell Management v Brandwood* [2004] UKHL 14, [2004] 2 AC 519; *O'Kelly v Davies* [2014] EWCA Civ 1606, [2015] 1 WLR 2725.

based on social and economic need at the time of the Norman Conquest. This was the ultimate expression of law based on the reality of land use, where legal rules were bent to serve the economy and society, and not vice versa. Likewise, even when feudalism was replaced by more complex societal arrangements, the substance of the law continued to reflect how people used land and how they might go about vindicating their rights to land in a society where legal jurisdiction was primarily local and built around demonstrable acts rather than recorded principle. So, for example, *profits à prendre* feature much larger in early land law than they do today because they were more important to the local and village community,[22] while easements, vital today in industrialised and urban society, were considerably less developed in the medieval world of real property. Then, as easements come more to the fore as land use changed, the law adapted and recognised that such intangible rights were essential, and this led to a change in the way these property rights could come into being. Easements could not practically be created by delivery of seisin,[23] so the law accepted that they could 'lie in grant'—a rule still with us.[24] Similarly, there is the much-maligned[25] modern rule that the burden of positive covenants cannot run with a freehold estate. Historically, this was because such obligations would devolve with the heirs of the covenantor as a personal obligation bound up with feudal homage independent of land holding.[26] It was not that the burden was not transmissible—it was that it was not an incident of the land but a reflection of personal bond between grantor and grantee. When the possibility was raised that covenant obligations might be more advantageous as incidents of land ownership rather than as personal obligations sounding in contract, a choice had to be made. The principle of transmissible bindingness was not the issue—it was the impact on land use and the economic value of burdened land that were the deciding factors. This led to the practical, not the principled, conclusion that restrictive obligations might run, but positive covenant obligations would normally not.[27] However, a deeper analysis reveals that the law finds a way to pass on positive burdens when that is essential to the effective use of land.[28]

The point of this brief dip into legal history is not to rehearse where the law was, but to underline that land law has deep roots in practicalities and that this organic base is still with us today. In modern land law, we have the obvious examples of the

[22] *Simpson* 107 *et seq*. For a modern example, see *Lynn Shellfish Ltd v Loose* [2016] UKSC 14, [2016] 2 WLR 1126.

[23] *Simpson* 121 *et seq*.

[24] This was central in *Regency Villas Title v Diamond Resorts (Europe) Ltd* [2015] EWHC 3564 (Ch), [2016] 4 WLR 61, where it was held that there was no bar in principle to an easement for a recreational purpose. This is an example of how the organic nature of our law allows developments reflecting modern land use.

[25] But see P O'Connor, 'Careful What You Wish For: Positive Freehold Covenants' [2011] *The Conveyancer and Property Lawyer* 191.

[26] *Simpson* 140.

[27] *Haywood v Brunswick Permanent Benefit Building Society* (1881) 8 QBD 403 declined to 'extend' *Tulk v Moxhay* (1848) 2 Phillips 774, 41 ER 1143 to positive covenants. *Austerberry v Corporation of Oldham* (1885) 29 ChD 750 settled the matter, overruling *Cooke v Chilcott* (1876) 3 Ch D 694.

[28] So, we have 'mutual benefit and burden', *Goodman v Elwood* [2013] EWCA Civ1103, [2014] Ch 442. Other ad hoc examples also represent the triumph of practical need over principle: eg *Crow v Wood* [1971] 1 QB; *Cardwell v Walker* [2003] EWHC 3117 (Ch), [2004] 2 P & CR 9.

law of adverse possession and prescriptive easements. While the theoretical basis of each is apparently different, the acquisition of a title by possession or the legitimisation of long use through prescription is illustrative of a system of land law based around reality rather than abstract notions of right or entitlement. As the Supreme Court emphasised in a 2016 case,

> in order to identify the nature and extent of the right obtained by prescription, one has to examine the actual use as of right upon which it is said to be based ... The correct question is therefore not what the notional grant would have been likely to be ... it is what is the extent of the user as of right for the requisite period.[29]

A land lawyer, on the whole, finds nothing offensive in the idea of right following reality, even if it means the closing out of another's more abstract right that is disconnected from the use of land. In fact, evidence of the organic nature of land law is not limited to the acquisition of rights based on use. The past has seen much discussion over the nature of licences and their alleged proprietary effect, particularly those encapsulated in contract. However, while this can be viewed as a question of principle, what underlies the current orthodox view of licences is an understanding that how people use land is complex, changing and infinitely variable. The reason why licences are not proprietary is that they perform a vital function in the scheme of property law—they regularise current use without the risk that they will affect the future use of the land. To confuse licences with proprietary concepts is not chiefly to misunderstand the theoretical bounds of property law, but to misunderstand that land law is as at least as much about use as it is about principle. Take *Bruton v London & Quadrant Housing Trust*,[30] about which much has been written analysing its conceptual foundations.[31] However, the real criticism of the decision in that case is that it makes no practical sense, irrespective of theory. If we assume that Mr Bruton has a lease, and therefore benefits from an implied covenant to repair,[32] this being the motivation for the litigation, how does he vindicate this against London & Quadrant, who, as is accepted by all, have only a licence? Mr Bruton cannot compel Quadrant to repair, because they have no right to touch the land itself. If Bruton obtains damages under the implied covenant, he cannot carry out a repair. Damages would, in essence, be requiring Quadrant to pay money they may not have, in respect of an obligation they did not in reality undertake and which they cannot actually fulfil. Most importantly, and entirely foreseeably, the decision generated a practical response from the freeholder, who terminated Quadrant's licence in this and other properties across London, so terminating Bruton's and others' 'leases' and rendering many people homeless.[33] While we can theorise as much as we please

[29] *Lynn Shellfish Ltd* (n 22) para 45.

[30] [1999] UKHL 26, [2000] 1 AC 406.

[31] eg S Bright, 'Leases, Exclusive Possession and Estates' (2000) 116 *LQR* 7; M Dixon, 'The Non-Proprietary Lease: The Rise of the Feudal Phoenix' (2000) 59 CLJ 25; M Lower, 'The Bruton Tenancy' [2010] *The Conveyancer and Property Lawyer* 38; N Roberts, 'The Bruton Tenancy: A Matter of Relativity' [2012] *The Conveyancer and Property Lawyer* 87; A Goymour, '*Bruton v London & Quadrant Housing Trust*: Relativity of Title, and the Regulation of the "Proprietary Underworld"' in S Douglas, R Hickey and E Waring (eds), *Landmark Cases in Property Law* (Oxford, Hart Publishing, 2015) Ch 7.

[32] Landlord and Tenant Act 1985, s 11.

[33] *Kay v London Borough of Lambeth* [2006] UKHL 10, [2006] 2 AC 465.

about *Bruton*, the decision is a prime example of what happens when reform or development of land law (either legislative or judicial) is based on theory—even flawed theory—instead of being based on an understanding of how land is used practically. The failure to understand the practical role that licences play in modern land law resulted in a potential change to our conception of leases that was wholly pointless and which compromised the functional (and different) roles of leases and licences. In similar vein, it is hardly surprising that the entirely unorganic commonhold property regime is near extinction.[34] With no roots in reality, this legislative creature needs a bewildering array of complex regulations simply to exist and provides an object lesson in how not to solve perceived problems in land law.

This organic base is not limited to the creatures of medieval land law, for in the law of estoppel we see the clearest example of modern land law developing and growing organically without the fertiliser of a statutorily imposed scheme. From its origins as a rule of evidence, and then as a defence to an action of right by a landowner, through to its emergence as a self-sustaining cause of action, estoppel typifies how land law can respond to changing legal, social and economic circumstances.[35] It is no surprise that estoppel claims mushroomed when the formality rules were tightened by the Law of Property (Miscellaneous) Provisions Act 1989 because estoppel responds to unconscionably denied expectations about land use. Further, it is unsurprising that estoppel is being used more often—at least by judges—in beneficial ownership claims because the flexibility it brings matches the hugely variable nature of people's actual relationships.[36] These developments are made possible by land law's organic nature and they make it fit for purpose in the modern world. The great reforms of 1922–25 were coloured by the need to ensure the effective use of land in the new social and economic conditions post-1918, rather than being built on a great conception of what the law of property should look like. Nothing has happened since then to suggest a better way of proceeding; in fact, the opposite is true. This is a lesson worth remembering as we contemplate further reform of land law, be that transactional or substantive.

III. LAW REFORM: SUCCESS AND FAILURE

The complexity of land law is a reflection of its organic base because how people use land is complex and not static. So it is that land law must evolve if it is to serve the needs of a changing society. This evolution can be judge-led or the result of a more deliberate examination of the law. The former is usually piecemeal (or at least the response to a single issue of concern), the latter more often a wholesale reform of a discrete area. There are, of course, many aims of law reform: solving injustices or uncertainties, resolving revealed or inherent problems, making things clearer, making

[34] At May 2016, only 16 commonholds existed. I am grateful to Giacomo Mastantuono for this information, obtained via an FOI request of the Land Registry.

[35] *Taylors Fashions v Liverpool Victoria Trustees* [1982] QB 133 gives a review of the development of the doctrine.

[36] Claimants may prefer to plead resulting or constructive trusts—not because these are more certain in application, but because, if successful, they lead to a proprietary interest. Estoppel may not.

things more cost effective, recognising changes in social and economic attitudes or pursuing policies in the public interest. However, law reform, whether by legislation or judicially, that outstrips the reality of how people use and think about land—in the sense of requiring people to change how they actually use land or relate to it because the change would be more in the public interest, or cheaper or 'better'—is a risky business. Principle-led law reform is not doomed to fail, but it risks creating more problems than it solves. This is not a particularly attractive argument—it smacks of complacency and itself risks that the past will throttle the future. But it is a mistake to divorce principle from practice in order to achieve policy goals, and even worse to fix something that is not broken. Not only that, a programme of principle-led law reform can be destroyed by those who do not share those principles, or it can be bent to those who shout loudest about their principles. Reform which 'simplifies' or 'tidies' the law is often misplaced because land use in real life is rarely simple or regular. Proponents of law reform sometimes assume that simplification necessarily leads to clarity and efficiency. It may do, but it might also lead to litigation because the complexity of actual use does not go away just because the law wishes it so.[37] Perhaps this is one reason why the story of land law reform since 1925 has been chequered: a patchwork of success and failure.

A. Land Registration

Taken in the round, the implementation of comprehensive title registration has been a success. However, whereas the Land Registration Act (LRA) 1925 was largely transactional in purpose and effect, in that it provided a recording and guarantee system for rights whose validity existed independently of the register, the LRA 2002 mixes substantive reforms alongside changes to the mechanics of registration. As has been noted often enough, the 2002 Act was designed to change the way that we thought about title: registration was no longer to be merely a record of pre-existing ownership, but was to be constitutive of that fact. This is, in fact, quite different from the 1925 conception because, in many respects, it divorces the law of title registration from the reality of how people perceive ownership and use. But even in this the LRA 2002 is schizophrenic. The provisions concerning adverse possession divorce 'use' from 'right' in a way that, probably, the general population would support—at least if they were landowners. On the other hand, the provisions concerning title guarantee and indemnity seem to favour the formal act of title registration over the 'true'[38] owner, and there is certainly disquiet in some quarters that 'the land registration tail [might] wag the land ownership dog'.[39]

[37] See the Landlord and Tenant (Covenants) Act 1995 discussed below.

[38] This is a loaded word. For some, 'true' means the owner irrespective of title registration; for others, the 'true' owner is the person properly registered. See M Dixon, 'What Sort of Land Registration?' [2012] *The Conveyancer and Property Lawyer* 349.

[39] *Scott v Southern Pacific Mortgages* [2014] UKSC 52, [2015] AC 385, per Lady Hale at para 96. But see *Walker v Burton* [2013] EWCA Civ1228, [2014] 1 P & CR 9, where there was no basis for the proprietor's title except registration.

The organic base of our land law is one of the main reasons why in thinking about updating the LRA 2002, we have to make difficult choices. Currently, the 2002 Act expresses a strong preference for the formal act of registration over and above older conceptions of title based on use or pre-existing right. However, it tempers these with an understanding that the law cannot operate effectively if it completely divorces entitlement from reality. Three examples will suffice. First, adverse possession is largely neutralised if the former 12-year limitation period has not been completed prior to the entry into force of the 2002 Act, but there is an exception in favour of boundary disputes which need to be resolved with finality as evidenced by the position on the ground, and for estoppels, the ultimate expression of protection for unconscionably denied use.[40] Secondly, the title of a registered proprietor is unimpeachable, even if built on a mistake such that they would not have had title if the land had been unregistered, but only if the proprietor is in possession, and possession means a sufficient degree of exclusive physical custody and control.[41] When a proprietor is in possession, the register will not be rectified (save in cases of consent or fraud/lack of proper care causing or substantially contributing to the mistake) unless it is unjust not to rectify.[42] This is not the same as allowing rectification simply because it would be just to do so: it must be positively unjust before a proprietor using the land can be disturbed. Conversely, if the proprietor is out of possession, then rectification *must* be ordered, unless there are exceptional reasons to deny it.[43] In other words, full title guarantee in land registration is welded to land use. Thirdly, the well-known provisions on overriding interests generated by 'discoverable actual occupation' recognise that land use—especially use as a home—is something special to be protected.[44]

Consequently, when deciding whether—if at all—to update the LRA 2002, a wise place to start would be to recognise that the unmitigated and blind assertion that the register should be wholly conclusive is misplaced. Indeed, we should remember that the LRA 2002 guarantees title, but does not make it indefeasible. If we accept that, in our organic system of land law, use and enjoyment both have a part to play in deciding priorities and entitlements, we can stop fretting about the 'proper' or ideal way to structure a land registration system and concentrate on building a system that is effective in practice in light of the policy goals we set ourselves. For example, there is no reason to press on with e-conveyancing (as originally conceived) simply because we live in a digital age. Land is not like shares that are tradeable electronically on a stock market and speed is not always better where the asset is a home or a business that is fixed in time and space. If we recognise that land is a different sort of asset, it is entirely proper to argue for a different system for dealing with it than other forms of wealth—as we now have with our current

[40] LRA 2002, sch 6, para 5. *Zarb v Parry* [2011] EWCA Civ 1306, [2012] 1 WLR 1240; *IAM Group v Chowdrey* [2012] EWCA Civ 505, [2012] 2 P & CR 13. A further exception is where there is 'some other reason' for the claimant's title.

[41] LRA 2002, sch 4, para 3. *Murphy v Lambeth LBC*, 19 February 2016, LTL 22/2/2016.

[42] LRA 2002, sch 4, para 3(2)(b).

[43] LRA 2002, sch 4, para 3(3).

[44] *Credit & Mercantile v Wishart* [2015] EWCA Civ 655, [2015] 2 P & CR 15 is challenging because it represents the triumph of legal theory (that a beneficiary automatically authorises a trustee to deal with the land) over reality (that it was Wishart's home and he knew nothing of the mortgage).

formality requirements. So too questions of title guarantee, rectification and indemnity cannot really be answered by starting with the question 'should the register be absolute?' or 'is there room for the *nemo dat* principle?',[45] because that prioritises a conception of land registration over an assessment of how people use and relate to land. The current formulation of the LRA 2002 may well strike the appropriate balance and recent concerns have been driven more because of HM Land Registry's approach to payment of indemnities than difficulties with the 2002 Act itself. In other words, let us not rush to reform the 2002 Act based on principle, but do so only after a realistic assessment of its practical application in everyday experience.

B. Landlord and Tenant: Leasehold Covenants

One legislative reform which has attracted significant criticism is the Landlord and Tenant (Covenants) Act 1995. The Act had a difficult legislative history and its provisions are not fully reflective of the original Law Commission Report published in 1988.[46] Its enactment, via the Private Members Bill procedure, has resulted in a scheme born of compromise and self-interest. As Lightman J described it in *First Penthouse Ltd v Channel Hotel Properties*, the '1995 Act is the product of rushed drafting and its provisions create exceptional difficulties'.[47] In fact, these difficulties are only partly attributable to the Act's legislative history, because many of the problems stem from the fact that the Act attempts to impose a statutory scheme on top of a system of covenants that had worked well since the sixteenth century.[48] That is not to say, of course, that some reform was not desirable—the abolition of original tenant liability itself reflects the move of the leasehold estate from contract to property and was long overdue—but the Act goes much further than was needed in the misguided pursuit of a simplicity and regularity that just does not exist in practice. The Act, at times, appears to proceed in isolation from the practical world of landlord and tenant in which it is meant to operate, which in turn has led to significant litigation as parties try to make it work in a manner that reflects commercial realities. So, in *First Penthouse Properties* Lightman J decided that whether a covenant was 'expressed to be personal' and so was not automatically transmissible with the freehold reversion had to be assessed by looking at the substance of the obligation as well as the words used—thus preventing covenants which had nothing to do with the land passing by default (and thereby contradicting sensible commercial practice).[49] In *Lee v Sommer*[50] the court refused an interpretation of the 1995 Act (concerning 'problem notices' under section 17) that would have prevented the

[45] *Updating the LRA 2002* (n 9) para 535 *et seq*.

[46] 'It is accordingly not possible to assume that the 1995 Act gave unqualified effect to the recommendations in the Report', per Lightman J, *BHP Petroleum v Chesterfield Properties* [2002] Ch 12, para 14.

[47] [2003] EWHC 2713 (Ch), para 43.

[48] The Grantees of Reversions Act 1540, that eventually became ss 141 and 142 LPA 1925, regulated assignment of the reversion, as did *Spencer's Case* (1583) 5 Co Rep 16a for the lease. The evidence that these were causing *practical* difficulties prior to the 1995 Act was skimpy.

[49] [2003] EWHC 2713 (Ch). See Landlord and Tenant (Covenants) Act 1995, s 3(4).

[50] [2015] EWHC 3889 (Ch).

compromise of landlord and tenant disputes over arrears of rent, and in *UK Leasing v Topland Neptune*[51] a reassignment back to the original tenant who had assigned in breach of covenant was held not to be invalidated by the Act (as made perfect practical sense), despite this being an entirely plausible interpretation of the statute.[52] The alternative result in both of these cases would have made no sense practically, but each was nearly the unintended consequence of a statutory scheme divorced from reality.[53] Then there are the two major decisions in *K/S Victoria Street v House of Fraser*[54] and *Avonridge Property v London Diocesan Fund*,[55] which underline forcefully that the Act has to be interpreted wherever possible so that it operates in the real world of landlord and tenant.

The 1995 Act is, in other words, an example of legislation which concentrated too much on principle and policy at the expense of practice and reality. Of course, it was designed to deal with a number of perceived imbalances in the landlord and tenant relationship, and it does that. But it goes too far and, being divorced from the organic structure of landlord and tenant law, it has led to complexity, cost and criticism. Settled practice, over which there was little litigation, was replaced with unsettled practice and considerable litigation. The central objectives of the Act—that is, protecting against original tenant continuing liability and making liability co-existent with possession of the lease or reversion—was achievable without an elaborate scheme, and this would have resonated with how people understood the landlord and tenant relationship to work. But there was no need to go beyond this and to replace a perfectly clear system with an elaborate statutory machinery whose practical implications had not been thought out. It is no surprise that the Law Commission has flagged the Act as potentially in need of attention,[56] but that reform needs to be light touch and should concentrate on remedying some of the practical problems thrown up by the Act rather than attempting, for a second time, to reinvent the wheel.

C. Landlord and Tenant: Remedies

The Law Commission has struggled long with the question of remedies in landlord and tenant law with little apparent progress. Its report on distress proposed abolition in 1991,[57] but it was not until the introduction of the Commercial Rent Arrears Recovery scheme (CRAR) in April 2014[58] that the old feudal remedy was abolished for all tenancies. It is noteworthy, however, that, given the practical importance of

[51] [2015] EWHC 53 (Ch), [2015] 2 P & CR 2.

[52] Contrast *EMI Group Ltd v O & H Q1 Ltd* [2016] EWHC 529 (Ch), [2016] 3 WLR 269, a decision driven by the words of the Act that flies in the face of commercial good sense.

[53] See also *Ridgewood Properties v Valero Energy* [2013] EWHC 98 (Ch), [2013] 3 WLR 327, where the court determined, entirely sensibly from a practical standpoint, but still debatable on the Act's wording, that s 3 (automatic passing of covenants) only applied when there was a lease per se and not merely a conditional contract to grant a lease.

[54] [2011] EWCA Civ 904, [2012] Ch 497.

[55] [2005] UKHL 70, [2005] 1 WLR 3956.

[56] See *Updating the LRA 2002* (n 9) para 12.48.

[57] Law Commission, *Landlord and Tenant Distress for Rent* (Law Com No 194, 1991).

[58] Tribunals Courts and Enforcement Act 2007, s 71. CRAR was activated by The Taking Control of Goods Regulations 2013, SI 2013/1894, para 1 and part 7.

distress, especially in the case of a tenant's impending bankruptcy, a self-help remedy was provided in its place for commercial leases. CRAR is not quite distress in disguise, but it is close to it.[59] A more depressing picture—if you are a tenant—is the failure to implement any changes concerning termination of tenancies, particularly in relation to forfeiture. This has been the subject of considerable Law Commission activity,[60] and although there have been reforms to the process of forfeiture (both legislative[61] and judicial),[62] the essence has remained the same—landlords can terminate a lease for breach of covenant but tenants cannot (save in truly exceptional cases)[63] bring the lease to an end during the term. Although formally this project awaits a final government response, and one can fairly say that the Law Commission has fulfilled its remit to propose reform, it does not seem likely that any proposals will be taken forward.

The reasons for this lack of progress are well known, but one should also not forget the historical perspective of the forfeiture remedy and its relationship to how land is used. Forfeiture harks back to the days when superior estate owners needed an efficient and effective method of recovering possession—the root of title—against a person whose interest in the land lay somewhere between contract and property. We see even today a widespread common perception that 'tenants' do not really have a stake in the land and that the true owners should be entitled to recover 'their' land if the temporary occupier does not fulfil their side of the bargain, however onerous. The greatest argument for reform is that practically there is no reason for self-help, save perhaps in cases of abandonment, because court-sanctioned remedies are not difficult or (relatively) expensive to obtain. Consequently, perhaps a way forward is not to focus on the remedy of forfeiture/termination itself—because there is no doubt that it has a proven utility—but instead to reform the process by which the remedy may be obtained significantly. Similarly, in relation to the tenant's ability to compel performance of the landlord's obligations, what is needed is a quick and secure method of enforcement, rather than a method of securing a tenant's release from obligations freely undertaken. Perhaps an expansion of the jurisdiction of the First Tier Tribunal, along the lines of the jurisdiction exercised by the Tenancy Tribunal in New Zealand (but not limited to the residential sector), is a way forward.[64] Or perhaps the recent changes introduced by the Deregulation Act 2015 concerning prevention of retaliatory termination of assured shorthold tenancies[65] can provide a template.

[59] Seven days' clear notice must be given under CRAR before seizure of goods can take place, which may make it less effective than distress as a means of recovering unpaid rent.

[60] Law Commission, *Termination of Tenancies for Tenant Default* (Law Com No 303, 2006); *Termination of Tenancies for Tenant Default* (Law Com CP No 174, 2004); *Codification of the Law of Landlord and Tenant: Forfeiture of Tenancies* (Law Com No 142, 1985); *Landlord and Tenant Law: Termination of Tenancies Bill* (Law Com No 221, 1994).

[61] For long leases of dwellings, ss 167–69 of the Commonhold & Leasehold Reform Act 2002 protect tenants from forfeiture for small amounts of rent and inhibits the landlord threatening forfeiture where no breach has been established. See s 81 of the Housing Act 1996 in relation to service charges.

[62] *Billson v Residential Apartments Ltd* [1992] 1 AC 494, interpreting s 146 LPA 1925 to permit relief from forfeiture after the landlord has recovered possession through peaceable re-entry.

[63] Landlord's repudiatory breach, *Hussein v Mehlman* [1992] 2 EGLR 87; frustration, *National Carriers Ltd v Panalpina (Northern) Ltd* [1981] AC 675.

[64] Residential Tenancies Act 1986. See P Howden-Chapman, *Home Truths: Confronting New Zealand's Housing Crisis* (Wellington, Bridget Williams Books, 2015).

[65] In force 1 October 2015.

In other words, rather than a relatively elaborate scheme for tenancy termination, which will be regarded by many as inherently contradicting the very nature of a leasehold, reform should concentrate on securing effective recourse for obligations undertaken and on preventing abuse of such recourse as already exists. Reform which seeks to undermine what is regarded as the essence of the leasehold as an estate held of another person has, it is submitted, only a limited chance of success—with none achieved so far.

D. Landlord and Tenant: State and Condition of Property

In 1996, the Law Commission published a report which set out with great clarity the defects in the current law concerning repairing obligations in leases, particularly as they apply to short-term residential lettings.[66] The Draft Bill would have made a significant contribution to improving the lives of residential occupiers and would have addressed what for many people is one of the great injustices of modern land law—the absence of a widespread basic habitation standard.[67] It is now clear that the recommendations in the Law Commission's report will not be enacted.

There is no immediate prospect of reform of this area of law. The perception is still that the repair of property a matter of contract between the parties, subject to minimal implied obligations, supported by general safety regulations concerning particular aspects of the premises. The feudal history of the lease and our perception that the market will not bear significant repairing obligations (at least, not in short-term residential lettings) are bars to progress, although other jurisdictions have not been so shy of imposing significantly higher minimum standards.[68] Again, however, perhaps the place to start is the development of effective remedies and protection for tenants who are prepared to activate those protections that they do have.

E. Easements and Covenants

Another long-running reform saga concerns easements and covenants. The most recent iterations of the proposals for reform—the 2011 Report 'Making Land Work: Easements Covenants and Profits *a Prendre*'[69] and the 2014 Report 'Rights to Light'[70]—now appear to have a chance of making it to the statute book, or at least those aspects that will facilitate the development of land.[71]

[66] Law Commission, *Landlord and Tenant: Responsibility for State and Condition of Property* (Law Com No 238 1996).

[67] This is not to minimise the importance of s 11 of the Landlord and Tenant Act 1985 for residential leases of less than seven years.

[68] eg Residential Tenancies Act 1986 (New Zealand); Residential Tenancies Act 2006 (Ontario); Residential Tenancies Act 2010 (New South Wales).

[69] Law Com No 327, 2011.

[70] Law Com No 356, 2014.

[71] In May 2016, the government indicated that it would bring forward proposals in response to the easement report. See also Law Commission, *Transfer of Land: Appurtenant Rights* (Law Com WP No 36, 1971); *Transfer of Land: The Law of Positive and Restrictive Covenants* (Law Com No 127, 1984).

A main area for reform concerns the law of prescription, and there are few who would argue that the current law is satisfactory.[72] The value of the ability to claim a right through long use is widely accepted,[73] even in an age of comprehensive land registration, but the technical and fictitious aspects of our current law, and the failure of earlier reform, considerably diminish the utility of the doctrine. It is obvious that something should be done provided, I would submit, that it does not make it more difficult to acquire easements through use. Reform should not amount to de facto abolition of prescription and the Law Commission proposals do appear to be based on a pragmatic assessment of what is needed to make the law work in modern circumstances. However, when it comes to the proposals to change the way that easements might arise by implication, it is not so obvious that reform is necessary or desirable. As we know, most cases of implication, be it by reason of necessity, common intention, section 62 LPA 1925 or now less commonly *Wheeldon v Burrows*,[74] are the result of inattention by those responsible for the relevant sale or lease of the land.[75] Cases are not common. The essential characteristic of these 'methods' is that they enable the grantee[76] to enjoy a previously used activity which benefits the potentially dominant land and which is reasonably regarded as an attribute of it. However, there is no evidence that the current law is uncertain or complex, or has unduly burdened land unexpectedly.[77] The reality is that implication by grant or reservation is easily and commonly avoided. A statutory reformulation in these circumstances may seem harmless, but it risks inadvertently altering the parameters of the current law—that is, of expanding or (more likely) contracting the circumstances when such rights might be impliedly created, thus altering their practical rationale—for no appreciable gain. Likewise, perhaps the proposal to give power to discharge or modify easements, such as currently exists with freehold covenants, needs more careful thought. There is no doubt that owners of servient land would want such a power to exist, principally to disapply or modify easements which impede development.[78] Perhaps public interest and economic advancement should triumph over private right, but the nature of easements is such that they are largely 'single use' limited rights that positively enhance the use of the dominant land. They do not usually curtail the use of the servient land significantly.[79] While the Law Commission Report is not unbalanced, its tone is that easements are inhibitive, rather than enabling, but this is not their purpose or, it is submitted, generally their effect. Given that it is rare for any purchaser to acquire land without at least having the chance to discover all of the binding easements,[80] it is not immediately

[72] Law Com No 327, 2011, para 3.71 *et seq.*

[73] *Lynn Shellfish Ltd* (n 22).

[74] (1879) 12 Ch D 31. *Wood v Waddington* [2015] EWCA Civ 538, [2015] 2 P & CR 11 nearly, but not entirely, assimilates the doctrine with s 62 LPA 1925.

[75] See *Platt v Crouch* [2003] EWCA Civ 1110, [2004] 1 P & CR 18.

[76] And sometimes the grantor. The proposals in Law Com Rep No 327 do not distinguish between grant and reservation.

[77] Law Com Report No 327 recognises the theoretical problem, but that is not the same as evidence of an actual problem.

[78] Abandonment is difficult to establish, *Dwyer v Westminster City Council* [2014] EWCA Civ 153, [2014] 2 P & CR 7.

[79] Save, perhaps, rights to light.

[80] They may be registered, or discovered on inspection or pre-contract inquiries.

apparent why they should later be removed without the agreement of the dominant owner, even if he or she is to be compensated. The proposal seems to prioritise value over use in a way that is at odds with the fundamental basis of our land law. The same might also be said of the proposals concerning prescriptive rights of light. While prescription generally is in need of attention, the case made for changing the way that rights to light are enforced is based squarely on prioritising the needs of one set of landowners—developers—over others. This is out of step with the organic nature of land law as a system which seeks to balance the rights of neighbours and not to artificially enhance one at the expense of the other.

The 2011 proposals concerning covenants revisit an issue long discussed in modern land law—the running of positive obligations with the freehold estate. *Rhone v Stephens*[81] makes it clear that legislation is now the only way to change the law, and the demise of commonhold apparently makes this an imperative. As noted above, there is not universal agreement that this change is desirable, and perhaps it misunderstands the reasons why positive obligations do not generally pass with a freehold estate. It is tempting to think that this is a historical quirk, but the case law reflects clearly the worry that such obligations might overburden the servient land and render it sterile. Given the Law Commission's view on easements generally and prescriptive rights to light in particular, the introduction of a more burdensome obligation such as a positive covenant needs a powerful argument. That positive obligations can run in leaseholds is not of itself persuasive that they should run in freeholds—indeed, one could say that modern land law has evolved to allow landowners to have a choice of how to organise their use of land. Allowing positive obligations to run in leaseholds is consistent with the obligations of two parties who are still connected to each other (via the lease); allowing them to run in freeholds permits one landowner who may be completely disconnected from the other to require their neighbour to take some action. We should not forget that it is not only the fact that a landowner has to spend money that counts against positive freehold obligations, but also that the spending may be required by a person with whom they have no connection. There is a reason why rentcharges are generally no longer possible in modern land law.

F. Co-ownership: Creation and Consequences

Unlike the law of landlord and tenant, the law of co-ownership is radically different today than that pre-1926. But the story is not one of unbridled success. Although there have been significant reforms to the mechanics of co-ownership, it is well known that the evident social changes in the nature of families and intimate relationships has not been recognised legislatively.

The 1925 reforms were designed to free co-owned land from the strictures of settlements and old style trusts, and the success in making co-owned land alienable and marketable is there for all to see. The Trusts of Land and Appointment of Trustees Act (TOLATA) 1996 modernised the 1925 scheme, but in reality only

[81] [1994] UKHL 3, [1994] 2 AC 310.

confirmed what case law had already rendered a reality. However, the replacement of the trust for sale with the trust of land—and the apparent removal of the duty to sell in the event of a dispute—has had no significant effect on the ability of a co-owner to remain in possession if the other wishes to escape or has otherwise alienated their share of the property. Priority is still given to the monetary value of the land rather than its social use. In this sense, the law fails to reflect fully the way that land ownership and use has changed since 1925 and is still fixated with land as an asset that must be alienable.[82] This was vital in 1926, but not in 2016. While significant changes to, say, the overreaching machinery of a trust of land would do much to redress this problem, that might be going too far. A tweak to sections 14 and 15 of TOLATA 1996, reaffirming that sale is not the default position, especially in cases where the person seeking sale does not have priority either by reason of overreaching or under the LRA 2002, would reflect more clearly the way co-owned land is used as a home and is not just an asset. Likewise, there is some unease about whether the joint tenancy is an appropriate construct for dealing with beneficial interests in land because it assumes much about the parties' relationship. However, the real fault here is not with the substantive law—for there is no doubt that the beneficial joint tenancy can be invaluable—it is the failure of property professionals to advise clients properly, if at all. A simple and effective reform, championed by Lady Hale in *Stack v Dowden*,[83] would be to make completion of Land Registry Form JO compulsory on the registration of joint proprietors. Not only would this resolve 'variation' disputes of the *Stack/Kernott*[84] type, it would perforce require property professionals to address and explain the differences between the tenancy in common and joint tenancy, and thus give owners real choice about how to organise their affairs so that they could accurately reflect their relationship with each other and the land they live on.

Perhaps, however, these are but small criticisms when compared with the complete failure of the legislature to deal with the concerns so clearly demonstrated by the Law Commission in *Cohabitation: The Financial Consequences of Relationship Breakdown*.[85] The legislature, for no good policy or practical reasons, continues to ignore the reality of how a significant number of couples choose to cohabit and instead the judiciary has had to develop a jurisdiction to resolve property disputes out of the ill-suited tools of resulting and constructive trusts. This is not ideal for well-known reasons, and perhaps this is why estoppel is gaining in currency in such disputes, as it offers considerable flexibility in fashioning a remedy to deal with the almost infinitely variable situations that can arise.[86] This is at least possible, given

[82] In *Fred Perry v Genis* [2015] 1 P & CR DG5, para 8, the judge noted that the 'authorities demonstrate a recurring tension between these competing claims, but as I understand it, the upshot has been to give precedence to commercial interests rather than to the residential security of the family'.

[83] [2007] UKHL 17, [2007] 2 AC 432, para 52.

[84] *Jones v Kernott* [2011] UKSC 53, [2011] 3 WLR 1121.

[85] Law Com No 307, 2007. See also Law Commission, *Cohabitation: The Financial Consequences of Relationship Breakdown* (Law Com CP No 179, 2006); *Sharing Homes, A Discussion Paper* (Law Com No 278, 2002).

[86] See *Southwell v Blackburn* [2014] EWCA Civ 1347, [2015] 2 FLR 1240; *Arif v Anwar* [2015] EWHC 124 (Fam), [2016] 1 FLR 359.

our organic approach to land law. However, it is extraordinary that the law continues to disregard the position of so many of its citizens, who it has encouraged to 'get on' by owning property, and instead forces them to litigate with all the emotional and financial cost that entails. While a statutory jurisdiction would not prevent all litigation, if it were coupled with a mediation requirement and built around a structured statutory discretion, it is likely that fewer disputes would end up in the county courts. While the judiciary has recognised the reality of changing relationships and how this has changed land use, the legislature is fixed in the past. The criticism here is not that reform has occurred contrary to how people use land, but that a positive choice has been made not to reform despite certainty that land use has changed.

G. Mortgages

The substantive law of mortgage has been largely untouched by law reformers. There have been changes to the processes by which mortgages might be created—which in turn reflects the reality of the modern mortgage market[87]—but most of the activity has been focused on regulating the 'buying and selling' of mortgages rather than the substantive content of a mortgage. There are, however, changes that could be made to reflect more accurately the role of mortgages in today's land law.

The current approach to mortgages is, in essence, to treat a mortgage like a tin of beans. The label on the tin/mortgage must inform the consumer of the ingredients and what they mean, but, essentially, once the customer has decided to buy/execute a mortgage, the law will not intervene unless the ingredients have been mislabelled or the consequences are so severe that this is evidence of some wrong under the general law.[88] There has been recent reform of this regulatory framework,[89] and serious violations can result in compensation for the borrower, but violations of the regulatory code do not generally prevent a lender from exercising its right to take possession and pursue other remedies.[90] In fact, little has changed in the substantive law of mortgage since the intervention of equity in the late nineteenth century. At that time, lending was not generally institutional or on standardised terms, and lenders were not necessarily in the business of lending.[91] Mortgage law reflected this and dealt with the lack of efficient judicial processes for the enforcement of the security by developing the proprietary content of a mortgage—particularly the right to possession. Today, the substantive law of mortgage is out of step with the reality of how a large portion of the mortgage market operates, particularly given the prevalence of residential purchase mortgages. Current mortgage law is firmly rooted in the past. While this holds significant advantages for lenders, it does not accurately reflect the social and economic context in which most mortgages operate. There is,

[87] LRA 2002, s 23(1) and 27(2).

[88] eg so as to vitiate consent.

[89] The Mortgage Credit Directive entered into force on 21 March 2016. This transfers the regulation of virtually all land mortgages to the Financial Conduct Authority, operating the MCOB regime, and modifies that regime.

[90] *Thakker v Northern Rock* [2014] EWHC 2107 (QB).

[91] See, eg, *Noakes v Rice* [1902] AC 24; *Biggs v Hoddinot* [1898] 2 Ch 307; *Kregliner v New Patagonia Meat & Cold Storage Company* [1914] AC 25.

therefore, a case for reform, not simply because of an abstract sense that borrowers need more 'protection', but because the current construction of mortgage law is divorced from its organic context.

Necessarily, there is a need to ensure that a lender has sound and reliable security, for this leads to an efficient, inexpensive and plentiful supply of mortgages. We must recognise that residential mortgages fulfil social and economic functions relating to personal wealth and the funding of small business. But that does not mean that the substantive law is properly aligned with substantive use. For example, at the heart of a mortgage is the fiction that the lender is granted an estate in the land and with it an all too real right to possession. As is commonly known, mortgages of registered titles must be made by a registered charge,[92] which is not the grant of an interest, and even if this is a trivial point, there is little justification today for according a mortgagee a *right* to possession rather than a *remedy* of possession in the event of default. This is not an insignificant matter.[93] To replace this right with a remedy available by court order only (at least in respect of residential mortgages) and to be justified as a response to default would not significantly impact on mortgages but would ensure that all borrowers using a dwelling as security could utilise section 36 of the Administration of Justice Act 1970.[94] There is also no justification today for allowing a mortgage contract, even if created by deed, to be treated differently from any other type of contract in relation to the limitation period on the personal covenant to repay. The 12-year limitation period is a throwback to the days when deeds were treated entirely differently from 'mere' contracts and has no justification in the modern law.[95] Further, there is no longer a good reason to permit a lender to sell residential property without first obtaining possession, thereby sidestepping such safeguards as exist on the granting of a possession order and rendering the borrower a trespasser in their own home.[96] This, too, distorts the reality of how mortgages are used and perceived in the residential market, and making the obtaining of possession mandatory before sale (ideally only by court order) would be to make obligatory a practice which the vast majority of mortgage lenders already observe. With mortgages, there is a strong case for reform so that the law compliments and reflects modern mortgage practice.

IV. CONCLUSION

There is nothing simple nor straightforward about the business of law reform. Competing policies, a complex historical legacy and a temporary and shifting

[92] LRA 2002, s 23. The vast majority of mortgages of unregistered title are made by charge, not least because such an event triggers compulsory first registration.

[93] See *Ropaigealach v Barclays Bank* [2000] QB 263, which confirmed a lender's right to take possession without a court order and without triggering borrower protection under s 36 AJA 1970.

[94] Note that s 36 is not carte blanch for borrowers. The borrower must be 'likely to be able within a reasonable period to pay any sums due under the mortgage'—and payment is, after all, what lenders usually want.

[95] Under s 20 of the Limitation Act 1980, the period is 12 years for capital sums under a mortgage as opposed to six for other contracts. *West Bromwich Building Society v Wilkinson* [2005] UKHL 44, [2005] 1 WLR 2303.

[96] *Horsham Properties v Clark* [2008] EWHC 2327 (Ch), [2009] 1 P & CR 8.

political landscape ensure that even proposals for 'technical' law reform encounter opposition. It is not meant as a criticism of the Law Commission to note that its recent major projects in the field of property law—save the great achievement of the Land Registration Act 2002—have not resulted in reforming legislation. The aim of this chapter has been to highlight the organic origins of land law and to urge those responsible for law reform to ensure that proposals for reform accommodate the reality of how people use and enjoy land today, commercially, economically and socially. Conversely, when deciding which areas of land law to consider for reform in the first place, a good starting point is those areas where the law is out of step with modern land use and practice. This is not a rejection of principle-based law reform, or even principle-led law reform, but it is a rejection of top-down law reform based on a sterile conception of what the law should be rather than an assessment of how the law can enhance the social and economic uses to which land is currently put.

2

Rethinking the Rules for the Proprietary Effect of Freehold Covenants

JAMES C FISHER*

I. INTRODUCTION

THE ENGLISH LAW of freehold covenants is widely acknowledged to be unsatisfactory. In 2011 the Law Commission recommended significant reforms intended to solve the problems they identified with the current law.[1] The government recently announced the intention to 'bring forward proposals to respond to the recommendations of the Law Commission's report' with a draft Law of Property Bill.[2] This stops conspicuously short of a commitment actually to implement the Law Commission's draft legislation. Although the government will probably seek to implement at least some of the Law Commission's recommendations, whether and to what extent the law of covenants will be reformed remains unclear. There is still time to improve on the Law Commission's designs for the mechanism by which the reformed property law will allow neighbouring freeholders enduringly to regulate the use of their respective tenements.

Perhaps the most troublesome aspect of the current law is the rule that positive obligations cannot bind successors to the original covenantor. This chapter supports the Law Commission's moves to abolish the rigid distinction in this respect between positive and negative obligations. However, it argues that reform should also include a significant reworking of the other requirements that an obligation must satisfy in order to operate with proprietary effect. The Law Commission proposes to replace freehold covenants, which arise necessarily out of the law of contract and gain proprietary effect thanks to a patchwork of legal and equitable doctrines, with the 'land obligation', a novel property interest independent of the law of contract.

* Associate Professor, University of Tokyo Faculty of Law & Graduate Schools for Law and Politics. I am grateful for the constructive comments of the anonymous reviewer, and for the insightful questions and comments from colleagues at the conference, all of which brought about many changes to this chapter. Remaining errors and oversights are mine.

[1] Law Commission, *Making Land Work: Easements, Covenants and Profits à Prendre* (Law Com No 327, 2011). This followed the 2008 Consultation Paper: Law Commission, *Easements, Covenants and Profits à Prendre* (Law Com CP No 186, 2008).

[2] Queen's Speech, Briefing Notes, 61, available at www.gov.uk/government/publications/queens-speech-2016-background-briefing-notes (18 May 2016).

But the coherence of this reform is reduced by the substantial retention of the existing rule that obligations must 'touch and concern' the relevant tenements. The touch and concern criterion is bound up with covenants' enduring status as an uneasy hybrid of contract and property law principles. This liminality is shown by the independent running of a covenant's benefit and burden, and the conceptually anomalous requirement of annexation. The criterion is also vague, lax and the cause of practical problems that make it harder to justify obligations' proprietary effect. For all these reasons, retaining the touch and concern criterion as the litmus for the validity of a 'land obligation' is acutely problematic.

Section II of this chapter defines the focus of the argument, identifying the touch and concern criterion and the negativity rule as the content rules currently applicable to covenants aspiring to proprietary effect. In Section III, the chapter demonstrates the inadequacy of the touch and concern criterion as a meaningful content rule. Section IV expands on this analysis, exploring some of the practical and conceptual problems resulting from the touch and concern criterion. Moving on to consider the second content rule for covenants' proprietary effect, Section V argues in support of the abolition of the negativity rule. Section VI draws together the previous two sections, suggesting that, in abolishing the negativity rule, care must be taken to replace the lax touch and concern criterion with something more rigorous in order to compensate for the removal of the only truly exacting (however unprincipled) rule limiting the kind of obligations capable of sounding in property.

II. THE PROPRIETARY EFFECT OF FREEHOLD COVENANTS: THE RULES OF RUNNING

A covenant between freeholders dictating the use of the burdened land is, in the first instance, a contractual undertaking between the covenantor and covenantee that takes effect between the parties on ordinary contract principles.[3] Provided certain requirements are satisfied, the law of property allows the covenant to be enforced by a successor to the covenantee even though he is a stranger to the covenant; the covenant's benefit is allowed to run.[4] Likewise, provided certain requirements are satisfied, the law of property allows the covenant to be enforced against the covenantor's successor even though she is a stranger; the covenant's burden is

[3] The covenantor therefore remains contractually liable for breach of the covenant despite divesting herself of any interest in the burdened tenement. This increases transaction costs for covenantors who sell their land, since they are required to negotiate for indemnities, or otherwise purchase indemnity insurance, to avoid liability in the event of breach of the covenant by their successors in title: Law Com No 186 (ibid) [7.38]. The 'land obligation' would not take effect as a contract, so the creating parties would be affected only while they had estates in the relevant tenements. This replicates the law for leasehold covenants under the Landlord and Tenant (Covenants) Act 1995.

[4] This is in addition to any enforcement rights the successor may have by virtue of the Contracts (Rights of Third Parties) Act 1999. This chapter does not discuss the impact of that Act, or of s 56 of the Law of Property Act 1925, on the basis that these are not intrinsic to the workings of covenants as property interests per se, but are instead aspects of the law of obligations which can be used to circumvent troublesome rules relating to the peculiar limitations of covenants as property interests. In any case, the 1999 Act does not affect the position of successors to the covenantor; unlike benefit privity, burden privity is unaffected by the peculiar departure from contract logic represented by that legislation.

allowed to run. This chapter critically assesses some of these requirements,[5] namely the content rules with which a covenant must comply in order to operate with proprietary and not merely personal effect.

The burden of a freehold covenant will bind a successor only if this effect is triggered, in most cases by registration.[6] However, this chapter focuses solely on the separable and logically prior question: *what kind* of obligations are *capable* of affecting successors if that triggering event occurs? This looks to the content rules that the law imposes on rights that aspire to proprietary effect, rules that are separate from the triggering rules established by the registration regime, which dictate when a right capable of proprietary effect will in fact apply beyond the original parties to the agreement.[7]

In *Tulk v Moxhay*,[8] Lord Cottenham LC held that the conscience of a covenantor's successor with notice of the covenant was bound such that equity would not allow him to violate the covenant. The equity in *Tulk* was eventually reconceptualised as an equitable property interest that came into being upon creation of the covenant itself, not by virtue of a subsequent transfer. As such, its parameters became subject to the scrutiny that necessarily accompanies admission to the *numerus clausus*, mandating the reasoned development of content rules for this new property right.[9] It is 'old' law that the benefit of a freehold covenant will run to the covenantee's successor provided it touches and concerns the dominant land. Likewise, the covenant's burden will run (in equity) provided it touches and concerns the servient land, although only insofar as it imposes negative obligations.[10] So, for a covenant to have full proprietary effect (ie to be enforceable *by and against* the relevant successors) the appropriate content rules are: (i) negativity; and (ii) the touching and concerning of both tenements.[11] The negativity rule is simple enough in

[5] This chapter does not consider all the requirements that must be satisfied for a covenant to apply between the parties' successors. For instance, it excludes the requirement that the covenanting parties had suitable estates in the respective tenements, on the grounds that these are rules of a distinct character. Unlike the touch and concern criterion and the negativity rule, they do not determine what kind of obligations are capable of proprietary effect. It is this substantive question—what the 'content rules' for covenants aspiring to proprietary effect are—with which this chapter seeks to engage.

[6] If the servient land itself is unregistered, the covenant may be registered against the name of the original covenantor as a Class D(ii) Land Charge under the Land Charges Act 1972, ss 2–4. If the covenant is not thus registered, purchasers for value take the servient land unencumbered. Registering the covenant ensures it binds even purchasers for value. If the servient land is registered, the covenant's burden is registerable as a minor interest against the title of the burdened land: Land Registration Act 2002, s 32. If thus registered, the covenant will have priority over a registered disposition. Covenants cannot function as overriding interests.

[7] One cannot make a right bind a successor (through the relevant 'triggering') if that right does not conform to the content rules the law imposes for property rights of the relevant kind, a principle concisely articulated in the Land Registration Act 2002, s 32(3).

[8] *Tulk v Moxhay* (1848) 2 Ph 774, 779.

[9] B McFarlane, 'The *Numerus Clausus* Principle and Covenants Relating to Land' in S Bright (ed), *Modern Studies in Property Law*, vol 6 (Oxford, Hart Publishing, 2011) 321.

[10] *Hayward v Brunswick Permanent Benefit Building Society* (1881) 8 QBD 403; *Austerberry v Oldham* (1885) 29 Ch D 750; *Rhone v Stephens* [1994] 2 AC 310; *Thamesmead Town Ltd v Allotey* (1998) 30 HLR 1052. It is the substance, not the wording, of the obligation that counts: *Shepherd Homes Ltd v Sandham (No 2)* [1971] 1 WLR 1062, 1067, per Megarry J.

[11] If the claimant is suing anyone other than the original covenantor, that claimant must necessarily show that the burden has run in equity, since it cannot run at law: *Keppell v Bailey* (1834) 2 My & K 517. And where the burden is alleged to have run in equity, a claimant who is not the original covenantee

principle,[12] even though, as Section V below will argue, the case for that particular content rule is weak. But what does it mean for a covenant to touch and concern freehold land?

III. TOUCH AND CONCERN IN THE FREEHOLD CONTEXT

It is rare for courts to consider in detail what it means for an obligation to touch and concern servient land. Judicial focus typically gravitates towards the covenant's implications for the *dominant* land, even in cases between the original covenantee and a successor to the servient land, where the relevant question is whether the covenant's *burden* has run, and the running of the benefit is irrelevant.[13] The requirement that a covenant touch and concern the servient land has consequently become difficult to articulate with any real precision, but generally it is taken to demand only that a covenant relate to what is done on the servient land.[14]

More cases turn on the touching and concerning of the dominant land, but even here the criterion has not been rigorously controlled and has become a troublingly lax rule for determining obligations' proprietary effect. The language of touching and concerning originated in leasehold disputes between those in privity of estate.[15] Applying it to disputes between neighbouring freeholders predictably transformed it into an altogether more nebulous enquiry. In the freehold context,

> any 'touching and concerning' … must, necessarily, represent a broader concept [than in privity of estate cases] since land cannot be touched and concerned by what is done elsewhere in quite the same sense as the demised property can be touched and concerned by what is done on the demised property.[16]

In recognition of that reality, the law has come to accept a looser notion of touching and concerning according to which 'protected land can be touched and concerned by observance taking place on the restricted land'.[17] This criterion purports to assess the *nature of the benefit* the covenant bestows:[18] does it benefit the

must correspondingly satisfy the rules of equity, not law, in showing the benefit has also run (*Re Union of London & Smith's Bank Conveyance (Miles v Easter)* [1933] Ch 611), although in fact the rules for the running of the benefit overlap in law and equity; provided a covenant's benefit touches and concerns the dominant land, it will run both in law and equity.

[12] An obligation is negative if it can be complied with by total inaction. Therefore conditional prohibitions that appear to mandate positive acts, such as covenants against building without first seeking permission, are nonetheless negative.

[13] See, eg, *Cosmichome Ltd v Southampton City Council* [2013] EWHC 1378 (Ch); [2013] 1 WLR 2436.

[14] Occasionally there is express discussion about what kind of obligations can have proprietary effect as freehold covenants: see, eg, *University of East London Higher Education Corporation v London Borough of Barking & Dagenham & Ors* [2004] EWHC 2710 (Ch), [28]–[29], per Lightman J. However, this discussion was not about whether specific rules of user touched and concerned the servient tenement, but instead distinguished between user restrictions in general from other obligations, such as purported restrictions on alienation.

[15] The language is generally traced to *Spencer's Case* (1572) 5 Co Rep 16, 77 ER 72.

[16] DJ Hayton, 'Restrictive Covenants as Property Interests' (1971) 87 *LQR* 539, 544.

[17] G Newsom, *Preston & Newsom: Restrictive Covenants Affecting Freehold Land*, 10th edn (London, Sweet & Maxwell, 2013) 60.

[18] ibid 61.

dominant land *qua* land, or merely the covenantee personally? In *Rogers v Hosegood*, Farwell J emphasised that the dominant land itself must be affected by performance or non-performance of the covenant; it is not enough that successive holders of the land each derive personal advantage from its performance.[19]

Nonetheless, many cases reach outcomes that seem to ignore that crucial distinction. In *Wilkes v Spooner*, Farwell LJ accepted that a covenant against selling certain kinds of meat could benefit the dominant land *qua* land, and not merely the business operating there.[20] In *Newton Abbott Cooperative Society Ltd v Williamson & Threadgold*,[21] Upjohn J held that a covenant prohibiting certain (objectively inoffensive) business undertakings on the servient land touched and concerned the dominant land because it increased its value, since upon sale the dominant landowner would be able to offer commercial premises with special protection from local competition. Cases rigorously distinguishing benefit to land *qua* land from mere profitability are rare. One is *Kelly v Barrett*,[22] in which the court insisted that the relevant test is not one of increased land value, although ultimately even that case left the question of whether the covenant benefited the dominant land *qua* land largely to the parties' own determination. Generally, if a covenant makes clear that the parties *intended* it to benefit the dominant land *qua* land, the law assumes it actually does so unless this is entirely implausible. In *Kelly*, Warrington LJ thought the question for the court was whether 'the land to which the benefit purports to be attached *[can] be reasonably regarded as capable of being affected* by the performance or breach of the obligation'.[23] In *Wrotham Park Estate Co Ltd v Parkside Homes Ltd*,[24] Brightman J reasoned that a covenant created on sale of land is presumed to benefit the dominant land *qua* land, such that where the question is open to disagreement, 'it is not for the court to pronounce which is the correct view [but only to] decide whether a particular view is one which can reasonably be held'. Likewise, in *Marten v Flight Refuelling Ltd*, Wilberforce J declined to subject the covenanting parties' presumed belief that the covenant benefited the dominant land *qua* land to any significant assessment, stating: 'Why indeed should the court seek to substitute its own standard for that of the parties?'[25] The answer to that question is that the *numerus clausus* principle requires rights to conform to specific content rules in order to operate with proprietary effect, and that it is for the court, not the parties, to decide whether they have complied with mandatory rules of law.

Some cases do demonstrate an atypical willingness to probe the nature of the benefit the covenant supplies, such as *Cosmichome Ltd v Southampton City Council*.[26] The Council had sold city centre land to the BBC, retaining adjacent land.

[19] *Rogers v Hosegood* [1900] 2 Ch 388. See to similar effect *Re Ballard's Conveyance* [1937] Ch 473, 480–81, per Clauson J.

[20] *Wilkes v Spooner* [1911] 2 KB 473, but *cf* Fletcher Moulton LJ's (more compelling) opposing conclusion on this point at 485.

[21] *Newton Abbott Cooperative Society Ltd v Williamson & Threadgold* [1952] 2 Ch 286, per Upjohn J.

[22] *Kelly v Barrett* [1924] 2 Ch 379, per Tomlin J.

[23] ibid 411 per Warrington LJ (emphasis added) and specifically endorsed in A Francis, *Restrictive Covenants and Freehold Land*, 4th edn (Bristol, Jordan Publishing, 2013) 90.

[24] *Wrotham Park Estate Co Ltd v Parkside Homes Ltd* [1974] 1 WLR 798.

[25] *Marten v Flight Refuelling Ltd* [1962] Ch 115, 137.

[26] n 13 above.

A restrictive covenant provided that the land could be occupied only by the BBC and used only as a broadcasting centre except by consent of the Council, for which a large sum would be payable. The transfer duly described this covenant as being 'for the benefit ... of the adjoining or adjacent land'.[27] The BBC wished to sell the land to a developer, who sought a declaration that the covenant would not bind following the transfer. The judge accepted the presumption that the covenanting parties' declaration that the covenant benefited the dominant land should be upheld unless that were an unreasonable conclusion:[28]

> the question is whether [the purchaser] is able to discharge the burden of showing that, despite the wording ... the restrictive covenant was not intended, at the time it was imposed, to benefit the Council's adjoining or adjacent land or, if it was, that it was incapable of doing so.[29]

The judge nonetheless concluded that, although the BBC's presence might benefit the Council by increasing the prestige of the city centre and its cultural credentials,[30] there was no evidence to suggest that any specific part of the Council's adjoining land would be benefited *qua* land.[31] As counsel for *Cosmichome* put it, the benefit of the covenant was of a 'personal or quasi-personal nature'.

Cosmichome is a welcome example of the courts thoroughly testing whether a covenant satisfies the content rules that the law imposes. But it was also a particularly clear instance of benefit in personal capacity alone, and the very fact that the Council was advised that the covenant *would* operate with proprietary effect suggests that the touch and concern requirement is not regarded as a serious obstacle to the enforcement of covenants against successors. Moreover, *Cosmichome* does not represent the normal use of the touch and concern criterion. It is seldom used to determine whether a covenant is *of a kind* capable of proprietary effect, but rather to determine which parts of what was formerly a single tenement now hold the covenant's benefit. In other words, is *this* particular parcel of land (as opposed to a parcel a little closer to the servient tenement) touched and concerned by the covenant? But, even here, deference to the parties' own estimation is profound. In *Zetland v Driver*, the defendant had opened an apparently offensive fish and chip shop in contravention of a covenant against acts deemed a nuisance by the vendor, the original covenantee. Since the covenant, the dominant land had been divided and sold off. Bennett J at first instance held that the covenant could not plausibly touch and concern the entire (very large) former estate because the greater part of it 'could not be affected in the least by anything done on [the servient land]'.[32] The Court of Appeal, overturning Bennett J's judgment, emphasised the precise language of the covenant, which expressly purported to benefit 'the whole *or any part or parts*' of the dominant land,[33] as opposed to merely 'the whole estate'. The decisive issue

[27] ibid [6].
[28] ibid [14]–[16].
[29] ibid, [17].
[30] ibid, [32].
[31] ibid.
[32] *Zetland (Marquess) and Zetland Estates Co v Driver* [1937] 3 All ER 795.
[33] *Marquess of Zetland v Driver* [1939] Ch 1, 10, per Farwell J (emphasis added).

was not whether the covenant *in fact* touched and concerned each part of the large estate, but whether the parties had insisted that it did so with sufficient conviction and specificity.

With all this in mind, what kinds of covenant are really likely to be denied proprietary effect by the touch and concern criterion? Gardner and MacKenzie consider a covenant against constructing a religious building. While this would probably touch and concern the servient land, the authors note that whether it touches and concerns the dominant land depends in principle on the parties' intentions.[34] If they agreed the covenant to indulge the dominant landowner's militant atheism, then it cannot have been intended to benefit the dominant landowner in his capacity as owner and so does not touch and concern the dominant land. Conversely, if the point was to avoid the inconvenience of frequent Sunday visitors, then the requirement may be met.[35] However, although that distinction is crucial in theory, in practice it is of limited importance because of the dual presumptions the law employs. We have already seen that, where the parties have created a covenant affecting the use of the servient land, it is presumed that they intended it to benefit the dominant land *qua* land and not merely the covenantee personally. Moreover, if it is shown that the parties intended the covenant to benefit the land *qua* land, the law presumes that it really does so unless this is implausible. A survey of the workings of the touch and concern criterion makes it difficult to accept the Law Commission's conclusion that it provides 'a robust control mechanism' for the obligations capable of proprietary effect.[36] It is therefore troubling that the Law Commission has chosen to retain the criterion as the applicable content rule for the proposed 'land obligation'.

IV. PROBLEMS OF THE TOUCH AND CONCERN CRITERION

The law's willingness to give proprietary effect to an extraordinarily wide range of idiosyncratic neighbourly agreements—many with only a remote connection to the land itself—causes numerous problems, both practical and conceptual. The common concern that too wide a variety of covenants sounding in property might inhibit the market in land (by making land too easily encumbered and therefore less attractive to purchasers) is probably misplaced, since individually negotiated adjustments in purchase price will generally mitigate this. Nonetheless, there are wider harms that extend beyond the context of specific land transactions, which therefore cannot be remedied by individual negotiations and market forces. The enormous variety of agreements capable of proprietary effect renders difficult the *ex ante* valuation of the dominant and servient tenements in the abstract, even for specialists in land valuation, due to the particular difficulty of estimating how useful one of an almost limitless range of use-restrictions will be to the majority of potential dominant successors, and how onerous to potential servient successors—the people who comprise

[34] S Gardner and E MacKenzie, *An Introduction to Land Law*, 4th edn (Oxford, Hart Publishing, 2015) 337.
[35] ibid 338.
[36] Law Com No 327, [5.51].

the land market. Because valid covenants are so varied, it is almost impossible to collect sufficient data on which to base reliable estimates. In addition to these practical concerns, there are many conceptual problems attributable to the touch and concern criterion, on which this chapter founds its critique of this unsuitable content rule.

A. The Annexation Anomaly

This chapter's introduction distinguished between content rules (which dictate what kinds of rights can exist as property rights) and triggering rules (which dictate when rights capable of proprietary effect actually exhibit it). This is the usual structure for property law, but for covenants there exist additional and anomalous requirements suspended between these two tiers. For the benefit of a covenant to run, it must in principle have been annexed to the dominant land,[37] annexation being

> the permanent fixing of the benefit of a restrictive covenant to the land of the covenantee at the time of the covenant so that from that time onwards the benefit of the covenant is effectively part of the land and passes automatically when the land is transferred.[38]

Correspondingly, for the burden to run, the parties must have intended it to run with the servient land. Traditionally, it had to be demonstrated in each case that the parties had intended the relevant running to occur.[39] However, the law now presumes that the parties intended annexation to occur,[40] and that the burden should bind successors to the servient land[41] wherever the covenant 'relates to' the relevant tenement.

It is wrong to see annexation as transforming a merely personal right into a property right, because if the parties can be shown to have intended only to create a personal right, then annexation is impossible.[42] Likewise, the annexation requirement cannot remedy a failure to satisfy the content rules necessary for a covenant to

[37] This chapter does not discuss the equitable alternatives to annexation, such as assignment of the benefit to a successor, since this is distinct from the question of a right's proprietary effect properly so-called; it is only a means of transferring a personal right.

[38] N Gravells, '*Federated Homes Ltd v Mill Lodge Properties Ltd* (1979): Annexation and Intention' in N Gravells (ed), *Landmark Cases in Land Law* (Oxford, Hart Publishing, 2013) 103–04.

[39] Express annexation occurred when the covenant stated expressly that the covenantee was intended to benefit in his capacity as landowner, or to benefit the covenantee and his successors. True 'implied' annexation—where the intention to annex was inferred from contextual circumstances alone—was controversial (see, eg, HWR Wade, 'Covenants—"A Broad and Reasonable View"' [1972] CLJ 157, 168–70 in support and PV Baker, 'The Benefit of Restrictive Covenants' (1968) 84 *LQR* 22, 30 against).

[40] Law of Property Act 1925, s 78. In *Federated Homes Ltd v Mill Lodge Properties Ltd* [1980] 1 WLR 594, 605, Brightman LJ concluded that 'if the condition precedent of section 78 is satisfied, that is to say, there exists a covenant which touches and concerns the land of the covenantee, that covenant runs with the land for the benefit of his successors in title'; in other words, annexation is effected by force of statute even where it is not express. The land must still be identifiable for statutory annexation to occur: *Crest Nicholson Residential (South) Ltd v McAllister* [2004] EWCA Civ 410, [2004] 1 WLR 2409.

[41] Law of Property Act 1925, s 79.

[42] The ss 78–79 presumptions are displaced by evidence that this was not what the parties intended: *Roake v Chadha* [1984] 1 WLR 40 Ch D (eg a requirement that the benefit be assigned to successors: *Sugarman v Porter* [2006] EWHC 331 (Ch)). Rebutting the statutory presumptions will also logically preclude a finding of express annexation.

take effect as a property right; if the parties have created a covenant that does not touch and concern the relevant tenements, they have created not merely an unannexed covenant, but an *unannexable* one. It must be then that the law's (notional) demand for annexation accepts that the parties created a right proprietary from its inception, but a property right that is *presumptively ineffective* outside their own relationship, thus requiring some extra process to make it capable of binding successors. If this understanding is correct, then this is highly anomalous; the very essence of a property right is its capacity to affect third parties regardless of privity or consent (although it remains for triggering rules to determine whether specific third parties will actually be affected).

The annexation requirement therefore seems entirely without purpose. On creation, a covenant will exist either as a property right, in which case annexation should be unnecessary, or as a personal right only, in which case annexation is impossible. Gardner and MacKenzie have compellingly criticised the annexation requirement, arguing that to accept covenants as property interests entails that the benefit and burden automatically vest not in the persons with title to the respective tenements, but in the tenements themselves;[43] there is therefore *neither need nor room* for a further act of 'attachment'. The authors do not expressly take issue with the touch and concern criterion, but it nonetheless obstructs their attempt at a rational reconstruction of the law of freehold covenants. Their critique assumes that freehold covenants are indeed most naturally viewed as inhering in the land itself. But that view is less feasible in light of the actual content rules for covenants' proprietary effect, since the lax touch and concern criterion permits idiosyncratic covenants that are far more 'human-centred' than can convincingly be regarded as *automatically and intrinsically* inhering in the land itself. This resonates with the law's continuing demand for some additional demonstration of the covenant's attachment to the land, however anomalous that requirement looks from the perspective of ordinary property law doctrine.[44]

The Law Commission was clearly conscious of the need to insist on a connection of some meaningful kind between the land itself and an obligation aspiring to proprietary effect,[45] correctly concluding on that basis that the law applicable to leasehold covenants would be inappropriate for the freehold context.[46] It is therefore surprising that the Law Commission saw no need to make significant changes to the touch and concern requirement,[47] the criterion that tolerates the proprietary effect of obligations with problematically weak connections to the land in question. In replacing freehold covenants with fully proprietary land obligations (and in so doing ousting the anomalous annexation requirement), we must be wary of retaining the

[43] n 34 above, 350–51. The Law Commission proposals reflect this image in recommending that commonality of ownership and possession of the tenements benefited and burdened by a land obligation should not prevent such obligations' creation or existence: Law Com No 327, [8.33]. Provided there are two distinct tenements, there is no need for two distinct proprietors.

[44] Law Com No 327, [8.24].

[45] Law Com CP No 186 (n 1) [8.70]–[8.75].

[46] The Landlord and Tenant (Covenants) Act 1995, s 3 abolishes the touch and concern criterion for leasehold covenants: the benefit and burden now pass on assignment of the lease or reversion unless expressly personal (s 3(6)(a)), regardless of the covenant's substance.

[47] Law Com No 327, [8.24].

very content rules responsible for keeping covenants a strange hybrid of contract and property, and thus inviting the annexation requirement in the first place.

B. The Bifurcation of Benefit and Burden

In light of its origins, most of the authorities drawn on to establish the meaning of the touch and concern criterion have been leasehold decisions, such as *Mayor of Congleton v Pattison*, in which Lord Ellenborough CJ held that a covenant would run if its content was such as to affect the mode of using the land or its 'nature, quality, or value' independent of collateral circumstances.[48] Bailey J reasoned that the covenant must affect the land itself during the term of the lease (such as its mode of occupation) or the land's value at the end of the term. Such reasoning was adopted in *Rogers v Hosegood* in the freehold context, with Farwell J stating that 'the covenant must either affect the land as regards mode of occupation, or it must be such as per se, and not merely from collateral circumstances, affect the value of the land'.[49]

The role of the touch and concern enquiry in the privity of estate cases lay in testing the degree of connectedness between the substance of the covenant and the demised land. But covenants between freeholders are analytically distinct, necessarily involving two different tenements and the independent relationships that each tenement has with a single covenant. This bifurcated enquiry obviously underlies the independent running of benefit and burden. Since that bifurcation is anomalous for a property interest, there is a temptation to restore normality by treating touch and concern as a single enquiry, much as it functioned in the leasehold context. As noted in Section III, it has become common for courts to assess the touching and concerning of the servient land by considering the benefit to the dominant land.[50] This has been explained on the grounds that 'it is axiomatic that if a covenant confers a proprietary benefit on land, it necessarily involves a proprietary *burden* on the [servient] land'.[51] That claim needs to be considered carefully. If conferring a 'proprietary benefit' on the dominant land means that the covenant benefits the land *qua* land rather than simply benefiting the incumbent proprietor personally, then the existence of a proprietary benefit does *not* necessarily entail a 'proprietary burden' (understood symmetrically, as entailing something which affects the servient landowner *qua* landowner). It is not impossible for the dominant landowner to benefit

[48] *Mayor of Congleton v Pattison* (1808) 10 East 130, 135, 103 ER 725, 727.

[49] n 19 above, 395. See to similar effect Tucker LJ in *Smith & Snipes Hall Farm Ltd v River Douglas Catchment Board* [1949] 2 KB 500, 506.

[50] The reverse is also true. The opinion of Lord Oliver in *P&A Swift Investments v Combined English Stores Group plc* [1989] AC 632 is widely deployed as guidance for evaluating whether a freehold covenant touches and concerns the dominant land. Lord Oliver tested whether a covenant touched and concerned land partially by enquiring whether the burden could affect any occupant. That approach was not objectionable on the facts; *Swift* concerned a leasehold scenario, so there was only one tenement in question that the covenant could touch and concern. However, in freehold covenant scenarios, it is not convincing to assess whether a covenant touches and concerns the dominant land by reference to the effect on servient occupiers. The Law Commission nonetheless considered the *Swift* approach worthy of application to land obligations: Law Com CP No 186 (n 1) [8.78]–[8.79].

[51] M Dixon, *Modern Land Law*, 9th edn (Oxford, Routledge, 2014) 348.

in her landowning capacity from something that does not affect the servient landowner in that capacity; that a covenant touches and concerns the dominant land does not by itself entail that it touches and concerns the servient land.

The Law Commission's proposed reforms would unite the two aspects of proprietary effect, ending the independent running of benefit and burden. The land obligation would be from its inception a legal appurtenant interest, an enduring relationship between neighbouring tenements.[52] To exist as a land obligation in this sense, an obligation must both touch and concern the dominant tenement and describe acts to be done or omitted on the servient tenement.[53] Although it (problematically) retains the touch and concern criterion, the Law Commission's proposals make it commendably clear that the validity of a land obligation depends cumulatively on the obligation's relationship with each tenement. A single test for proprietary effect is attractive in principle, but such a test must consider the obligation's relationship with both tenements, if covenants or their statutory replacements are to be seen as subsisting between neighbouring tenements. The Law Commission's approach is therefore much more legitimate than the judicial tendency wrongfully to conflate two crucially distinct relationships in order to unite the running of benefit and burden, improperly ignoring one of the two tenements.

V. THE EMBARGO ON POSITIVE COVENANTS

The negativity rule has attracted far more scholarly attention than the touch and concern criterion,[54] and the Law Commission has recommended its abolition with the creation of the new land obligation.[55] This represents a desirable reform, since there is no compelling practical or conceptual reason to deny proprietary effect to obligations merely on the basis of their positivity.

A. The Policy Case for Positive Obligations Sounding in Property

The Law Commission is right to conclude that the balance of policy concerns is decisively in favour of positive land obligations. Most arguments against positive proprietary obligations identify worthy concerns, but prove too much, militating equally against the proprietary effect of negative obligations. For instance, there are dangers associated with allowing a broad range of property rights whose onerousness is difficult to assess prospectively. There is also the concern that too many stipulations about the use of land can risk its sterilisation as a useful asset in the long term.[56] But these are mischiefs of which negative obligations are also guilty,

[52] Law Com No 327, [8.24]–[8.25].

[53] Law Com No 327, [8.24] and accompanying Draft Law of Property Bill, ss 1(2) and (3).

[54] A number of these materials will be addressed in the following pages.

[55] Law Com No 327, [8.24] and [8.26].

[56] As noted by Lord Brougham in *Keppell v Bailey* (1834) 2 My & K 517, 536. See also AWB Simpson, *A History of the Land Law*, 2nd edn (Oxford, Oxford University Press, 1986) 257; *cf* Lord Cottenham LC's position in *Tulk*, namely that if successors were not bound, it might deter the profitable alienation (and exploitation) of land because vendors could not safely sell land without risking the remainder.

particularly given the laxity of the touch and concern requirement. On the other hand, many of the arguments supporting restrictive covenants' proprietary effect extend also to positive obligations. Covenants can serve private individual needs for which public zoning laws are unable to cater and with which it would be unrealistic to expect public bodies to engage. They can also indirectly promote wider social goods. By making it safer from a landowner's perspective to dispose of unexploited land, they reduce the incentive to hoard land to preserve one's standard of living. This was particularly crucial in the historical context in which freehold covenants acquired proprietary effect, helping to encourage the breaking up of large ancestral estates and progress towards the democratisation of freehold tenure. That process might be furthered if positive covenants were also capable of proprietary effect; in Scotland, the law's recognition of positive land obligations, such as maintenance duties, has been linked to the increased availability of freehold tenure apartments.[57] Such a development in England and Wales might go at least some way to increasing the number (and therefore affordability) of freehold properties, assisting at least some of 'Generation Rent' onto the first rung of the property ladder.

Some voices have insisted that positive obligations are intrinsically more problematic than negative ones,[58] such that it will always be harder for a holistic cost–benefit analysis to support positive obligations having a proprietary effect.[59] For instance, Rudden identified the risk that a successor bound to perform positive acts could find her liabilities exceeding the total value of the purchased asset.[60] However, certain negative obligations might well end up stripping burdened land of the majority of its value, such as a covenant precluding building more than a small private residence in a burgeoning commercial centre.[61] Moreover, even if positive proprietary obligations are *in general* harder to justify in consequentialist terms than negative ones, this does not support denying proprietary effect to all positive obligations. As soon as one acknowledges that some positive obligations may, on balance, deserve proprietary effect,[62] then English law's current treatment of positive covenants is exposed as unprincipled. If we accept that *some* negative obligations and *some* positive obligations deserve proprietary effect (even if the positive obligations deserving it are less numerous than the negative), it follows that the covenants deserving proprietary effect are necessarily united by some criterion or characteristic that is not negativity—although it is not impossible that this characteristic might occur more often in negative obligations than in positive ones. Therefore, to treat negativity as the legally relevant criterion for proprietary effect is misplaced. Rather than

[57] L Xu, 'Framework for Land Obligations: What Can be Learnt from the Scots law of Real Burdens?' in Bright (n 9) 214. The Law Commission also links the lack of freehold apartment properties in England to the negativity rule: Law Com No 327, [2.41]. Many positive covenants also have full proprietary effect in Northern Ireland by virtue of the Property (Northern Ireland) Order 1997, Art 34. I am grateful to the editors for bringing this to my attention.

[58] P O'Connor, 'Careful What You Wish For: Positive Freehold Covenants' [2011] *The Conveyancer and Property Lawyer* 191.

[59] n 9 above, 327.

[60] B Rudden, 'Economic Theory v Property Law: The *Numerus Clausus* Problem' in J Eekelaar and J Bell (eds), *Oxford Essays in Jurisprudence*, 3rd series (Oxford, Clarendon Press, 1987) 248.

[61] eg *Cosmichome*, where the covenant precluded using prime real estate for anything other than a broadcasting centre occupied and operated by the BBC.

[62] n 9 above, 330.

defending this unprincipled line between negative and positive obligations, our efforts would be better spent in identifying and articulating the characteristic shared by all obligations deserving of proprietary effect, and devising new content rules specifically calibrated to this characteristic.

B. Conceptual Challenges to the Negativity Rule

Ultimately, the future proprietary status of positive obligations will depend on a policy assessment of their utility in consequentialist terms. Nonetheless, it is still worth defending the doctrinal logic of allowing positive obligations to sound in property, if only to demonstrate that such reform will not be simply an ends-focused legislative intervention in the law, but will also represent a refinement of English property law as a rational system.

Many authorities have unsuccessfully attempted to justify confining the doctrine in *Tulk v Moxhay* to negative obligations by suggesting it would be improper for equity to oblige a successor to servient land to spend money.[63] For Farwell J in *Nisbet and Potts' Contract*, '[e]ffect is given to the negative covenant by means of the land itself. The land cannot spend money on improving itself'.[64] It is self-evidently true that land itself cannot 'do' anything, such as spend money on itself, but for the same reason it cannot 'refrain' from doing anything either; the negativity rule cannot be convincingly defended in these terms.

Other attempts have been made to present the negativity rule as a logical necessity. In *Rhone v Stevens*, Lord Templeman (in)famously thought it doctrinally impossible for the burdens of positive covenants to bind successors, due to the established relationship between law and equity.[65] Lord Templeman insisted that equity cannot circumvent the common law's refusal to allow an agreement between two parties to impose burdens on a thirdly, because equity can only supplement, and never contradict, the common law. This reasoning is fallacious.[66] Law and equity frequently diverge in their responses to the same set of circumstances, even though they remain discrete normative systems, in that the internal norms of one do not invalidate or alter the internal norms of the other. Lord Templeman's notion that 'equity supplements but does not contradict the common law' can mean only that some divergences are legitimate equitable 'supplements' to the common law but others are illegitimate 'contradictions'.[67] There is no scientifically deducible answer to whether a specific divergence is one or the other. It is invariably a question of policy, and it is pusillanimous to present the answer as dictated by juristic logic.

[63] In one case, the court refused to allow a repair covenant to bind a successor on the basis that it 'can only be enforced by making the owner put his hand into his pocket, and there is nothing to justify [the court] in going to that length': *Haywood v Brunswick Permanent Benefit Building Society* (1881) 8 QBD 403, 409 per Cotton LJ; see also *Austerberry* (n 10) 774, per Cotton LJ; *Zetland v Driver* (n 53) 8, per Farwell J.

[64] *Nisbet and Potts' Contract* [1906] 1 Ch 386 (CA), [1905] 1 Ch 391, 397, per Farwell J.

[65] n 10 above.

[66] S Gardner, 'Two Maxims of Equity' [1995] *CLJ* 60, 64–68.

[67] ibid 64–66.

For Lord Templeman, enforcing *negative* obligations against successors involves no tension with the common law doctrine of privity of contract; as he observed, 'equity does not contradict the common law by enforcing [the] covenant against a successor … but prevents the successor from exercising a right which he never acquired'.[68] Presenting the rule in *Tulk* as a manifestation of the *nemo dat quod non habet* principle has some support. Indeed, Lord Cottenham LC based his decision in *Tulk* on the logic that '[n]o one purchasing with notice of that equity can stand in a different situation from the party from whom he purchased'.[69] But to see this analysis as inapplicable to positive obligations is to misidentify the 'thing' that a covenant's presence prevents a successor to the servient land acquiring. Succession to the servient land does not bestow *any* rights properly so called, because the covenantor's successor cannot compel anything of the covenantee (or successor). As John Finnis has reiterated, a true claim-right 'can never be to do or omit something: it always is a claim that somebody else do or omit something'.[70] An owner's entitlement to make use of her land is in truth a (Hohfeldian) *liberty*.[71] Liberties can be positive or negative; a landowner generally has the liberty to do a particular action on the land, or not to do so. It is perfectly possible to say that a positive covenant deprives the covenantor's successor of a specific negative liberty, just as a negative covenant deprives her of a specific positive liberty.

The strongest defence of the negativity rule from a logical-doctrinal perspective lies in uniting it with the rule that a covenant touch and concern the servient land in the following way. One might argue that a covenant to cut the hedges of Greenacre (a positive covenant) cannot bind subsequent owners of Greenacre for the same reason that a covenant not to buy non-organic meat (a covenant that does not touch and concern Greenacre) cannot; the *liberty not* to cut the hedges of Greenacre and the *liberty to* buy non-organic meat are not dependent on having any legal relationship with Greenacre, but are instead held by all the world. A covenant can hardly 'withhold' from a successor to the servient land any liberty that was never dependent on the transfer, but was instead a liberty she enjoyed already, independently of any relationship with the servient land.[72] This analysis is compelling for the covenant against buying non-organic meat, and it should make us critically reconsider some commonly approved covenants, such as a covenant not to seek planning permission for development of the servient land (or possibly not to apply for planning permission without the consent of the dominant landowner), which the law regards as a valid covenant with proprietary effect,[73] even though the liberty to apply for

[68] n 10 above.

[69] Supra n 8 at788.

[70] J Finnis, 'Some Professorial Fallacies About Rights' (1972) 4 *Adelaide Law Review* 377, 380.

[71] B McFarlane, '*Keppell v Bailey* (1843); *Hill v Tupper* (1863): The *Numerus Clausus* and the Common Law' in N Gravells, *Landmark Cases in Land Law* (n 38) 22.

[72] I am grateful to Ben McFarlane for identifying this during discussion at the Belfast conference.

[73] For a recent example, see *Re: 89 Holland Park* [2013] EWHC 391 (Ch). Admittedly it is seldom argued that such a covenant does not touch and concern the servient land, so we lack direct authority that it does so, yet, since such covenants are regularly accepted as having proprietary effect, the law impliedly accepts they satisfy the requisite content rules. In this case, the court held that the covenant also touched and concerned the dominant land, because it gave its owner more control over neighbouring development than he would have enjoyed as a mere member of the public confined to opposing planning consent in the normal way.

planning permission is not contingent on title to the servient land. However, the analysis fails to justify the negativity rule. In fact, ordinary individuals do not have a *liberty not* to cut Greenacre's hedges; they have a *duty not* to cut them, and the proprietor has a corresponding claim-right that others shall not cut the hedges on her property. The only person with a true *liberty not* to cut the hedges is that proprietor, just as she is the only person with a *liberty to* cut the hedges. The liberty (properly so called) to cut the hedges of Greenacre does indeed accompany the transfer of Greenacre.

VI. NEW RULES

Whatever the worthiness of covenants as property interests, positive and negative covenants stand or fall together; the negativity rule is unprincipled and entirely deserving of abolition. Nonetheless, such reform must acknowledge that this would remove the only rigorous limitation on what kinds of obligation the law allows proprietary effect, given the extreme laxness of the touch and concern requirement. A new property interest shorn of the negativity rule, with the touch and concern requirement as its sole content rule, would represent a major retreat from the idea of a *numerus clausus* in English law.

The desirability of a *numerus clausus* principle is itself disputed, and its necessity is often assumed rather than convincingly demonstrated. Epstein has advocated abandoning limitations on parties' ability to make their agreements sound in property as part of a sustained attack on the *numerus clausus* principle in American law.[74] For Epstein, such limitations are unwarranted; a strict system of notice is all that is necessary to counteract any resulting market harm because successors will be bound only by private agreements of which they were aware, in which case the price paid for the land will reflect the fact that it is burdened. Against this have been levied a series of arguments defending restrictions on parties' power to create entirely bespoke property rights, on the basis that the creation of property rights is intrinsically more hazardous than the creation of purely personal relationships. Some have stressed longer-term transaction costs; 'when burdened lands have fallen into multiple ownership [through sub-division], strategic individual behaviour or the necessity of multiple transactions will often prevent or delay voluntarily negotiated termination of a bad promise.'[75] Additionally, the market in land is 'loaded with error-prone actors' because it is so much less common for individuals to make real estate transactions compared to normal commercial and consumer agreements.[76] Concerns for inter-generational equity provide another normative reason for scrutinising the extent to which current incumbents' designs are permitted to endure through successive transactions.[77]

[74] RA Epstein, 'Notice and Freedom of Contract in the Law of Servitudes' (1982) 55 *Southern California Law Review* 1353, 1360–61.

[75] JE Stake, 'Toward an Economic Understanding of Touch and Concern' [1988] *Duke Law Journal* 925, 938.

[76] ibid 940.

[77] SE Sterk, 'Freedom from Freedom of Contract: The Enduring Value of Servitude Restrictions' (1985) 70 *Iowa Law Review* 615, 617.

It is beyond the scope of this chapter to offer a thorough defence of the *numerus clausus* principle. However, it is worth noting that many of its critics levy some rather inflated charges against it. American commentators in particular often allege (or simply assume) that the *numerus clausus* principle is contrary to freedom of contract.[78] In fact, the two concepts are not in significant tension. Freedom of contract entails that the law will generally enforce the obligations parties are deemed to have undertaken. A logical corollary is that the law will *not* enforce obligations a party has *not* undertaken—ie two parties are generally unable to impose binding obligations on a third. Most would baulk at the suggestion that our freedom of contract is seriously compromised by our general inability to impose duties or liabilities on innocent bystanders. The law of property provides exceptions to this general inability, but those exceptions are limited by the *numerus clausus*, which actively *promotes* freedom of contract for third parties by upholding the general principle of burden privity.

A. Potential New Rules

The Law Commission wisely decided against specific abolition of the negativity rule and instead preferred the creation of a new property interest to replace freehold covenants entirely.[79] The Law Commission is right to free 'land obligations' from the constraints of the law of contract, but covenants' replacement by a pure property interest will be undermined if the new interest's content rules merely replicate those that originally prevented the organic transition of covenants into normal property rights. The solution is the *de novo* creation of content rules to accompany the creation of the new legal interest in land. How might such content rules look?

The first option might be casuistically to test whether a specific covenant's proprietary effect is desirable in consequentialist terms, holistically assessed; it would benefit and bind successors only if so. There is some support for that approach in other jurisdictions, particularly in the United States, where the relevant Restatement purports[80] to have replaced the touch and concern requirement with 'a much broader and more intrusive test'.[81] Specifically, the appropriate enquiry is now whether the covenant 'violates public policy',[82] assessed in terms of several factors (for instance, whether it unreasonably restrains alienation or trade, or whether its content is illegal or unconstitutional). This has been applauded in American scholarship as reflecting

[78] Assessing the changes to American law reflected in the most recent Restatement, Susan French notes that its rules 'invite, if not require, an explanation of the real reasons why a court is justified in interfering with the parties' freedom of contract': SS French, 'The Touch and Concern Doctrine and the Restatement (Third) of Servitudes: A Tribute to Lawrence E. Berger' (1998) 77 *Nebraska Law Review* 653, 661.

[79] Law Com No 327, [5.50]–[5.51] and [5.69].

[80] Restatement (Third) of Property; Servitudes, §3.2. It has been suggested, however, that most American courts persist in using the touch and concern enquiry: M Allen, 'A Touchy Subject: Has the Restatement Replaced the Touch and Concern Doctrine with an Equally Troublesome Test?'(2013) 65 *Baylor Law Review* 1034.

[81] AD Tarlock, 'Touch and Concern is Dead, Long Live the Doctrine' (1998) 77 *Nebraska Law Review* 804, 810.

[82] n 80 above.

a shift from vain attempts to *define* the touch and concern test to open consideration of the objectives it was supposed to further.[83] However, it is an approach far too prospectively uncertain to be a serious contender for emulation in England and Wales. The American law of covenants is very distinct from that of England and Wales; discretion and flexibility have long been its defining features. Indeed, the dominant 'test' for touching and concerning was the obviously circular approach advanced by Bigelow, namely that a covenant should be seen as touching and concerning the relevant tenement if the value of the owner's legal interest un that tenement is altered.[84] This exercise in question-begging (the land's value is affected only *if* the covenant is held to touch and concern the land) masked the reality, namely immense judicial discretion to decide which covenants should sound in property and which should not, with commentators declaring candidly that American covenants are held to 'touch and concern' the tenements simply if it is fairest to see them run.[85] The American law of covenants, with vagueness as 'its greatest virtue',[86] stems from covenants' involvement in major social and political conflicts. They were, for instance, widely used to maintain racial segregation.

For all these reasons, we need not feel unduly tempted to consider basing our content rules on the American model. Instead, we should seek a general rule, applicable *ex ante* to reliably assess in the abstract whether an obligation will have proprietary effect. That test must be one that mitigates the problems caused by the lax touch and concern rule and restricts proprietary effect to genuinely deserving arrangements, without descending into undue casuistry. Improved content rules should be more intrinsically 'land-centred' and less open to idiosyncratic human agreements than the touch and concern criterion. One possibility is to require obligations to be necessary for the reasonable enjoyment of the dominant tenement. That would doubtless remove the valuation problems characteristic of touch and concern, and it would make it easy to visualise covenant rights as subsisting in the land itself, quite justifying the abandonment of any annexation requirements. Lord Cottenham LC's reasoning in *Tulk* emphasised that successors should not escape covenants lest a vendor be unable to sell part of his land without risking the retained portion being made 'worthless'. Such language might imply that the rule in *Tulk* was itself targeted towards covenants prohibiting acts severe enough to render enjoyment of the dominant land impossible, although that was not the case in *Tulk* itself, and few covenants now operative would satisfy that threshold. Indeed, restricting the behaviour of one's neighbours (beyond the extent achieved anyway by the law of nuisance) is generally *not* necessary for the reasonable enjoyment of one's own land, and insisting on that threshold would be tantamount to the abolition of freehold covenants as property interests.

This chapter concludes by suggesting a *via media*. Freehold covenants or land obligations, whether positive or negative, should be required to affect the use of the servient land in a way of broadly equal benefit to a large number of potential successors to the dominant land, and of broadly equal onerousness to a large number

83 n 81 above, 811.
84 HA Bigelow, 'The Content of Covenants in Leases' (1919) 12 *Michigan Law Review* 639, 646.
85 n 81 above, 829.
86 ibid 834.

of potential successors to the servient land. This is less demanding than a necessity threshold and therefore permits a meaningful range of obligations to operate with proprietary effect, but it is more intrinsically 'land-centred' than the touch and concern threshold, with its manifold shortcomings.

Some approaches have already analysed covenants in terms of their benefit or value to successors, notably in the American scholarship, where the economic analysis of law has found such abundantly fertile soil. In his survey of American case law, Stake argued that 'courts find that a covenant touches and concerns land when the benefit or the burden at issue is more efficiently allocated to the successors than to the original parties to the covenant'.[87] The present chapter is not concerned with the economic efficiency of specific transactions, but with confining proprietary status to obligations of a type that generally justify proprietary effect and can plausibly be regarded as regulating the interactions between two tenements, not two people. The equivalence criterion would also mitigate the random value effect associated with the lax touch and concern rule, which is unlikely to be much improved by the Law Commission's reformulation. It would permit proprietary effect to most of the common restrictive covenants, such as those restricting noise, building height and density, etc, but would exclude idiosyncratic human bargains.

VII. CONCLUSION

It has been observed that '[t]he law of freehold covenants is impossible to defend in its current form; it is overcomplicated, confusing and unhelpful'.[88] The complexity can be traced to a superabundance of piecemeal requirements that must be satisfied for a covenant, born a humble contractual obligation, to gain the indicia of property and affect successors to the relevant tenements.[89] This has seen the problematic adoption of the touch and concern criterion, which has resulted in practical difficulties and perpetuated covenants' liminality between contract and property. Now, however, the case for formalising the transition from obligation to property has become irresistible, as accepted by the Law Commission. Replacing covenants with the new 'land obligation' would be a desirable reform, but it demands changes to the 'content rules' for such a property right that are more significant than those the Law Commission recommends in order to make the new regime altogether convincing. The negativity rule has attracted sustained criticism, and rightly so, but much more attention should be devoted to the other content rule and efforts should be diverted to devising a more appropriate alternative that marks, but does not undermine, the long overdue replacement of freehold covenants with a thoroughbred property right.

[87] n 75 above, 930.
[88] S Clarke and S Greer, *Land Law: Directions*, 3rd edn (Oxford, Oxford University Press 2012) 339.
[89] Law Com CP No 186 (n 1) (Summary), [1.15].

3

Proportionality and the Vindication of Property Rights

SARAH NIELD*

I. INTRODUCTION

PROPORTIONALITY IS CREEPING into the lexicon of property lawyers. It is well known that the proportionality of the repossession of a home by a public authority may be challenged under the Human Rights Act 1998 (HRA 1998).[1] The Supreme Court in *McDonald v McDonald* (*McDonald*)[2] may have rejected the similar application of proportionality to home repossession by a private landlord, but the Equality Act 2010 introduces a proportionality defence where discrimination, based on protected characteristics, is proved upon repossession by either a private or public landowner.[3] In addition, proportionality is appearing as an influence upon the exercise of judicial discretion in the application of private law remedies: for instance, in the grant of relief from forfeiture of a lease and in formulating a remedy in proprietary estoppel. Yet, proportionality is a concept that is relatively unexplored by property lawyers. It is the intention of this chapter to try and fill this vacuum with a view to assessing its potential contribution in the vindication of property rights. It will seek to do so first by exploring the key contested dimensions of proportionality within public law, before examining how the concept has been varyingly employed in challenges to repossession under the HRA 1998 and the Equality Act 2010, as well as within aspects of remedial discretion. It will argue that although, in repossession defences of the home, the courts have constrained proportionality within strict boundaries, property lawyers cannot ignore proportionality as a concept both in rights-based adjudication and within remedial discretion.[4]

* Professor of Property Law, University of Southampton. I would like to thank my colleagues Emma Lauire and Claire Lougarre and the anonymous reviewer for their helpful comments on an earlier version of this chapter.

[1] *Manchester CC v Pinnock* [2011] 2 AC 104; *Hounslow LBC v Powell* [2011] 2 AC 186.

[2] [2016] UKSC 28.

[3] Equality Act 2010, ss 15 and 35(1)(b); *Akerman-Livingstone v Aster Communities Ltd* [2015] UKSC 15. See also Chapter 8 of this book (S Pascoe, 'Disability Discrimation: Recasting the Parameters of Proprietary Rights?').

[4] The concept is pervading other areas of the legal discourse. See N Lacey, 'The Metaphor of Proportionality' (2016) 42 *Journal of Law and Society* 27.

II. THE CONTESTED DIMENSIONS OF PROPORTIONALITY

Proportionality has its origins in German administrative law, where it developed as a basis for the structured analysis of the constitutional validity of legislative and administrative acts.[5] From there, proportionality became adopted within European jurisprudence both by the European Court of Justice and by the European Court of Human Rights (ECtHR). Proportionality in the adjudication of constitutional rights has also found a place in the common law world, most notably in Canada, through the development of a structured approach to the concept. Its origins are thus decidedly within public law and the adjudication of constitutional and human rights, where it plays a key role in balancing competing interests, representing on the one hand public interests and on the other human rights. Controversy swirls around a number of issues: first, whether proportionality has a place at all within the limitation of fundamental rights; secondly, what the role of proportionality as a distinct structured form of reasoning is; thirdly, what the appropriate level of deference within judicial scrutiny of proportionality is; and lastly, upon whom the burden of proof should fall.

A. Balancing Rights and Competing Interests

For some, importing proportionality into human rights adjudication is divisive in itself. It is argued that the concept compromises the special normative force of human rights, which should not be susceptible to balancing with the same weight as conflicting public good, whether through proportionality or some other measure.[6] Alternatively, in Alexy's view, rights are perceived not as rules but as principles or 'ideal oughts', in which proportionality provides a rational tool enabling competing principles to be balanced.[7] The key property related protections found in Article 1 of Protocol 1 and Article 8 are both qualified rights which expressly recognise exceptions within which proportionality plays a key role. The more difficult question is: what role?

Rivers distinguishes between 'state limiting' and 'optimising' concepts of balancing within proportionality.[8] He praises optimising concepts of proportionality as providing a rational, yet institutionally neutral, structure to consider whether a limitation of rights is justified by reference to the strength of competing interests. By contrast, he criticises state-limiting concepts of proportionality as merely pursuing predetermined goals which fall short of the effective balancing of state action

[5] See Lord Reed's account in *Bank Mellat v HM Treasury (No 2)* [2014] AC 700, [68]–[69]; see Lacey (ibid) for its older origins.

[6] For instance, in Dworkin's conception of 'rights as trumps' see R Dworkin, *Taking Rights Seriously*, 2nd edn (London, Duckworth, 1977).

[7] R Alexy, *A Theory of Constitutional Rights*, tr J Rivers (Oxford, Oxford University Press, 2002). Interests may be so disparate that they cannot be balanced: see T Endicott, 'Proportionality and Incommensurability' in G Huscroft, BW Miller and G Webber (eds), *Proportionality and the Rule of Law: Rights, Justification and Reasoning* (Cambridge, Cambridge University Press, 2014) ch 15.

[8] J Rivers, 'Proportionality and the Variable Intensity of Review' [2006] *CLJ* 174.

and individual rights. Young seeks to reconcile the gap between state-limiting and optimising conceptions of proportionality by suggesting that they have different roles in the adjudication of constitutional or human rights.[9] She argues that optimising concepts operate at a more abstract level where there is no clear agreement as to the parameters of the right in question. Thus, although the more abstract nature of a right may lead to its easier engagement, proportionality can provide a rational process to refine the boundaries of that right. For instance, 'home' under Article 8 has a wide meaning based upon the 'sufficient and continuing links test', rather than confined to those who hold property rights.[10] It is also easily engaged by possession proceedings, which are acknowledged to be a severe interference.[11] Proportionality is then employed to articulate more precisely what is demanded by the notion of respect. By contrast, Young suggests that state-limiting concepts of proportionality operate at a more concrete level where there is a clearer definition of the right in question and consequently less room for balancing.

But do these debates about proportionality have any wider place within property jurisprudence? It is important to appreciate two possible and to some extent overlapping roles of proportionality: first, in the balancing of a human right against public interests; and secondly, in reconciling competing rights—for instance, human rights or, indeed, competing property rights.

Kevin Gray, whilst noting that 'land law and human rights have never seemed particularly natural bedfellows',[12] identifies an increasingly evident tension between absolute ideas that 'ownership confers inviolable and exclusive rights of enjoyment and exploitation'[13] against relativist notions of 'property as qualified entitlements based upon social accommodation, community orientated obligations and notions of reasonable user'.[14] It is this latter relativist perception that he suggests is winning through in our 'crowded urban coexistence',[15] which inevitably calls for an assessment of the extent to which property comprises not merely private rights but community responsibility in which proportionality may have a place.

The same tension is evident within American property jurisprudence. Baron characterises this tension between the information theorists and progressive theorists.[16] The information theorists, in their pursuit of efficiency in property dealings, place exclusion at the centre of property rights. They advocate clear and simple processes to vindicate property rights that inevitably seek to minimise the complexity and contextual adjudication in balancing competing interests or rights. Baron uses 'the metaphor of property as a machine' to describe the information theorist's concentration upon the mechanics of how property works to achieve already satisfactory social

[9] A Young, 'Proportionality Is Dead: Long Live Proportionality' in Huscroft et al (n 7) ch 3.

[10] *Gillow v UK* (1989) 11 EHRR 335; *Chapman v UK* (2001) 33 EHRR 318; and adopted domestically in *Harrow LBC v Qazi* [2004] 1 AC 983 and subsequent case law.

[11] *McCann v UK* (2008) 47 EHRR 40.

[12] K Gray, 'Land Law and Human Rights' in L Tee (ed), *Land Law: Issues, Debates, Policy* (Uffculme, Willan Publishing 2002), 211.

[13] ibid 221.

[14] ibid.

[15] ibid 222.

[16] JB Baron, 'The Contested Commitments of Property' (2010) 16 *Hastings Law Journal* 917.

goals and which, with minimal tinkering, can adapt to meet changing demands. This property machine is exemplified, for instance, through the boundaries of the *numerus clausus* principle and the clear signals of registration regimes.

By contrast, the progressive theorists argue that property is not solely about exclusion, but about relationships and the values that should underpin property rules. Baron characterises the progressive theorists through 'the conversation metaphor', in which there is a continual need to question what relational outcomes our property rules produce to promote particular values which they encapsulate within the concept of 'human flourishing'. Progressive theorists see property relationships as necessitating cooperation within and as part of the wider community. Accordingly, self-interest may need to be balanced and constrained by 'a social obligation norm' that requires property owners to consider the effect of their actions upon others. Progressive theorists are thus prepared to embrace the complexity and contextualisation which their 'conservation' demands.

Arguments about the role of proportionality echo elements of the debates between the information and progressive theorists. Proportionality has synergies with the normative conversation that considers the efficacy of the property machine beyond a one-dimensional cost: benefits analysis of efficiency or wealth maximisation to admit the possibility of context, with attendant complexity that is shunned by the information theorists but embraced by the progressive theorists. It acknowledges the relational nature of property, both between rights holders and with the wider community that admits the possibility of the qualification of rights according to context to promote values beyond self-interest.

B. The Structure of Proportionality

Luteran identifies different means of balancing within proportionality.[17] He categorises these within two main groups:[18] first, those who see proportionality as a special kind of legal reasoning that rationally seeks to reconcile conflicting considerations by weighing their respective degrees of importance;[19] and secondly, those who do not recognise proportionality as requiring any distinct form of legal reasoning but as merely providing another guiding principle, much like fairness, in reaching a considered judgment or exercise of discretion.[20]

What is clear is that the courts, in meeting their duties under the HRA 1998, have developed an analytical approach to proportionality which follows other common law jurisdictions and stands in contrast to the more open-textured approach to

[17] M Luteran, 'The Lost Meanings of Proportionality' in Huscroft et al (n 7) Ch 1, 24–26.

[18] See also Christoffersen's distinction between a horizontal general factor-influenced proportionality test and a vertical structured proportionality test in J Christoffersen, *Fair Balance: Proportionality, Subsidiarity and Primarity in the European Convention on Human Rights* (Leiden, Nijhoff, 2009).

[19] Luteran identifies Robert Alexy as a leading proponent: see R Alexy, 'On Balancing and Subsumption: A Structural Comparison' (2003) 16 *Ratio Juris* 433.

[20] Luteran identifies a number of scholars within this group: for instance, S Greer, TRS Allen and T Endicott.

proportionality evident in ECtHR jurisprudence.[21] This approach to proportionality comprises four limbs.[22]

(i) The First Limb: The Legitimate Objective

This limb raises the question of whether the public interest is of sufficient importance to justify limiting a right. Such public interests may be many and various. In the context of repossession cases, centre stage will be the vindication of property rights namely: the right to exclude for instance by landowner or creditor. Other legitimate objectives are also evident in domestic and ECtHR case law including the control of antisocial behaviour,[23] the management of housing resources,[24] planning and environmental conservation,[25] and public health.[26]

(ii) The Second Limb: Suitability

Repossession, as a measure designed to meet the objective, must be rationally connected to that objective in the sense that it is capable of meeting it. Repossession is invariably connected to the vindication of a property right, thus this stage rarely presents any difficulty. The physicality of the subject matter provides the connection and repossession with a powerful incentive to meet a given objective.

(iii) Stage 3: Minimal Impairment

This stage raises the question of whether repossession goes no further than is necessary to achieve the legitimate aim. It thus presses beyond suitability to look at the functionality of the right to exclude in the context of the circumstances at issue. It raises the question of balancing means and ends. Where the right to possession is determining relative claims to possession of the land arising from the vindication of ownership, the connection between means and ends is relatively straightforward; where the right to repossess pursues some other function, however, the connection may be less clear cut. Rights granted by way of security are a case in point. For instance, in *Zehentner v Austria*[27] the ECtHR, though accepting that the sale of the victim's property was a suitable means to meet creditors' claims, did not believe, particularly in the light of Ms Zehentner's incapacity, that it was an appropriate route to recover a relatively small judgment debt. Similar concerns are reflected in

[21] *Bank Mellat v HM Treasury (No 2)* (n 5) [74] (Lord Reed); but see E Brems and L Lavrysen, 'Don't Use a Sledgehammer to Crack a Nut: Less Restrictive Means in the Case Law of the European Court of Human Rights' (2015) 15 *Human Rights Review* 139.

[22] The first three limbs were identified in *de Freitas v Permanent Secretary of Ministry of Agriculture, Fisheries, Lands and Housings* [1999] 1 AC 69, but a fourth limb was articulated in *Huang v Secretary of State for the Home Department* [2007] 2 AC 167 and *Bank Mellat v HM Treasury (No 2)* (n 5).

[23] *Manchester CC v Pinnock* (n 1); *Hounslow LBC v Powell* (n 1).

[24] ibid.

[25] *Chapman v UK* (2001) 33 EHRR 318; *Winterstein v France* No 27013/07 (17 October 2013).

[26] See *Yordanova v Bulgaria* Application No 25446/06 (24 September 2012).

[27] (2011) 52 EHRR 22.

the criticisms levelled at the use of charging orders in this jurisdiction to recover relatively small debts.[28]

(iv) Stage 4: Overall Balance (Proportionality Stricto Sensu*)*

The last stage requires a fair balance to be struck between the right of the individual and the public interest. Inherent within this balancing is a contextual consideration of the individual's circumstances, since no individual should bear an excessive burden in pursuit of the public interest. Balancing thus dictates that the independent tribunal charged with assessing proportionality has sufficient discretion to consider all relevant factors.

It is important to recognise that proportionality can be employed at different levels. For instance, under the HRA 1998, proportionality has a role in assessing the compatibility of legislation with human rights[29] ('legislative review') and also when the decision making of public authorities is challenged for falling short of human rights standards[30] ('applied review').[31] For example, various Supreme Court Article 8 decisions have considered both proportionality of the legislative scheme granting a right to possession of the home and the compatibility of the local housing authority's exercise of that right.[32] The relationship between these two levels of decision making is critical.[33] Indeed, it is this relationship that was at issue in the well-known dialogue between the ECtHR and our highest court[34] which resulted in the final acknowledgement in *Manchester CC v Pinnock*[35] (*Pinnock*) that statutory processes by which a public authority can repossess a home must admit applied review by which the proportionality of the repossession can be tested.

These two aspects of the final stage of the proportionality test exemplify the tension evident in the conflicting perceptions of property displayed by the information and progressive theorists. Clearly admitting contextual factors muddies the crystalline clarity of the exclusionary rules that the information theorists advocate with the attendant need for, and costs of, enquiry,[36] whilst providing a stage for the conversation about the role and values of property advocated by the progressive theorists.

[28] D Capper, H Conway and L Glennon, 'From Obligation to Proprietary Interest: A Critique of the Charging Order System in England & Wales' in S Bright (ed), *Modern Studies in Property Law*, vol 6 (Oxford, Hart Publishing, 2011) Ch 4.

[29] HRA 1998, s 3.

[30] ibid s 6.

[31] As respectively described by D O'Brien, 'Judicial Review under the Human Rights Act 1998: Legislative and Applied Review? [2007] *European Human Rights Law Review* 550.

[32] For instance, *Manchester CC v Pinnock* (n 1); *Hounslow LBC v Powell* (n 1).

[33] A Brady, *Proportionality and Deference under the UK Human Rights Act* (Cambridge, Cambridge University Press, 2012) 18.

[34] For an account of this dialogue see S Nield, 'Clash of the Titans: Article 8 Occupiers and their Homes' in Bright (n 28) Ch 5.

[35] See n 1 above.

[36] Utilising Carol Rose's metaphor of crystals and mud, see C Rose, 'Crystals and Mud in Property Law' (1988) 40 *Stanford Law Review* 577.

C. Deference and the Variable Intensity of Review

The court's role in assessing proportionality has ignited heated debate amongst public lawyers over the extent to which the courts should defer or give weight (being the courts' preferred vocabulary)[37] to Parliament in legislative review or to the relevant public authority in applied review. It thus centres upon the principle of the separation of powers and the need to construe proportionality 'in such a way as to preserve the "proper" roles of the courts, legislature and executive bodies'.[38] The emphasis on objective and transparent rationality in a structured approach to proportionality in some measure seeks to overcome charges that the judiciary is trespassing into the political realm.[39]

This debate has taken place primarily in the context of political and constitutional rights, though it started from the premise that a high degree of deference was appropriate in the fields of social and economic rights. It has moved on to a division between those who advocate a doctrine of due deference and those who do not. The supporters of a doctrine of due deference argue that deference is appropriate where there is good reason, based primarily upon the superior institutional competence and/or the democratic legitimacy of the decision maker. The non-doctrinalists maintain that proportionality, in its accommodation of contextual factors, is already sufficiently flexible. They argue that to acknowledge deference as a doctrinal tool threatens to undermine human rights by allowing the court to hide behind the expertise of the primary decision maker.[40]

In defining the proper boundaries of deference, Rivers calls for a variable intensity of review by the courts dependent upon the seriousness of the right's infringement, taking into account its intrinsic importance and the degree of infringement.[41]

Brady shifts the focus towards '*explaining a process*, not critiquing outcomes'.[42] He develops an institutionally sensitive model to articulate the complex and nuanced relationship between deference and proportionality.[43] He points out that each stage of proportionality calls upon the court to make often complex and uncertain assessments of various factors and deference provides a 'means by which the courts can deal with the limits of their own knowledge and experience'.[44] He builds a more nuanced deference model which looks to the institutional character of the decision maker and the different stages of a proportionality enquiry,[45] each of which can operate differently within legislative and applied review. Thus 'different parts of proportionality connect with different forms of deference in specific cases'.[46]

37 Per Lord Bingham in *Huang v SS for Home Office* [2007] 2 AC 167, [16].

38 Rivers (n 8) 179.

39 See, eg, A Stone Sweet and J Matthews, 'Proportionality, Balancing and Global Constitutionalism' (2008–09) 47 *Columbia Journal of Transnational Law* 72.

40 See, eg, TRS Allen, 'Human Rights and Judicial Review: A Critique of Due Deference' [2006] *CLJ* 671; T Hickman, *Public Law after the Human Rights Act* (Oxford, Hart Publishing, 2010).

41 See n 8 above, 205–6.

42 Brady (n 33) 35 (original emphasis).

43 ibid 31.

44 ibid 21.

45 He utilises Alexy's categorises of structural and epistemic deference: Alexy (n 7) 388–435.

46 (n 33) 32.

D. Burden of Proof

Chan argues that the burden of proof should lie with the appropriate decision maker. Thus, whilst it is for a victim to allege that their rights have been infringed, it should be for the decision maker to prove that a right's infringement is justified.[47] Rivers argues that the proof of proportionality is more nuanced. He accepts that it is for the decision maker to identify the legitimate aim to provide a rational justification threshold. However, he suggests a shift in the burden of proof to the victim within the latter test stages.[48] He argues that it is more efficient for the victim to present just a single less intrusive way to achieve a legitimate aim than for the decision maker to canvas the relative impact of a range of options. Similarly, the victim is better placed to explain his or her personal circumstances that may tip the fair balance within the final stage. In terms of context, Rivers argues that several situations justify a shift in the burden of proof to the victim.[49] For instance, he identifies cases where there is a conflict between protected rights, for instance Article 1 of Protocol 1 and Article 8, or where applied review is conducted pursuant to rules that have been found proportionate pursuant to legislative review. Lastly, there are those cases where the impugned decision has been reached through a procedural rigorous judgment of proportionality made by a well-qualified decision maker.[50]

With these debates firmly in mind, this chapter turns to consider how proportionality has been constructed within the vindication of property rights.

III. ARTICLE 8 RESPECT FOR THE HOME AND PROPORTIONALITY

In *Kay v Lambeth LBC*,[51] *Doherty v Birmingham CC*[52] and *McDonald* our highest courts acknowledged that the compatibility of legislation granting a right to possession of the home is open to legislative review under the HRA 1998—the so-called Gateway (a).[53] They also hinted that common law rules governing possession of the home might be challenged under Article 8. This view was confirmed when the Supreme Court in *Sims v Dacorum DC*[54] (*Sims*) considered the compatibility, both with Article 1 of Protocol 1 and Article 8, of a contractual provision enabling one joint tenant to terminate a joint tenancy by service of a notice to quit. They also commented upon the compatibility of the similar common law rule in *Hammersmith LBC v Monk*.[55]

[47] C Chan, 'Proportionality and Invariable Baseline Intensity of Review' (2013) 33 *Legal Studies* 1.

[48] J Rivers, 'The Presumption of Proportionality' (2014) 77 *MLR* 409.

[49] Rivers suggests six situations where the context of the rights infringement supports a shift in the burden of proof: ibid 427–31.

[50] eg *R(N) v Lewisham LBC: R(H) v Newham LBC* [2015] AC 125.

[51] [2006] 2 AC 465.

[52] [2009] 1 AC 367.

[53] S 3.

[54] [2015] AC 1336. Concerns over the Article 8 compatibility of *McPhail v Persons Unknown* [1973] Ch 447 raises similar common law issues see *Malik v Fassenfelt* [2013] EWCA Civ 798.

[55] [1992] 1 AC 478.

In *Pinnock* the Supreme Court also accepted the need for applied review in possession proceedings by a public authority and outlined how proportionality in such applied review should be structured.[56] This approach was considered in more detail in the conjoined appeals in *Hounslow LBC v Powell, Leeds CC v Hall, Birmingham CC v Frisby*[57] (*Powell*). Possession proceedings by a local authority may thus encompass multi-level proportionality reviews in questioning both the compatibility of the law governing rights to possession and the compatibility of the exercise of those rights to possession by a public authority. However, in *McDonald*[58] the Supreme Court refused to accept that the duties of the court as a public authority to act in a human-rights-compatible manner required an assessment of proportionality within mandatory possession proceedings by a private landlord—at least where the right to possession is conferred by recent legislation.[59] A private landlord's decision to exercise their statutory right to possession may thus be exercised in their own self-interest.

A. Legislative Review

In respect of the compatibility of the legal rules governing possession, the Supreme Court in *Pinnock*,[60] *Powell*[61] and *Sims*[62] read into the mandatory rights to possession conferred by the relevant legal rules[63] a discretion to enable the court to consider proportionality. In so doing, the Supreme Court bowed to the dictates from 'the unambiguous and consistent approach of the ECtHR'[64] that a compliant repossession regime must enable an occupier of their home to question the proportionality of this serious infringement of his or her Article 8 rights within applied review. In *McDonald* the Supreme Court was not prepared to accept that the Strasbourg Court's decisions to date consistently called for the same consideration of proportionality within proceedings brought by a private landlord.[65] Thus a clear divide is emerging between the role of proportionality in the respect due to a home between public and private tenancies and, one suspects, the publicly rented and privately owned home.

However, even in respect of publicly rented housing, the court's assessment of proportionality between the legitimate aim of legal rules and an individual's right to respect for his or her home does not go very much further.[66] The courts have

[56] See n 1 above, [45].
[57] See n 1 above.
[58] See n 2 above.
[59] HRA 1998, s 6.
[60] See n 1 above, [65]–[88].
[61] See n 1 above, [39] and [44].
[62] See n 54 above, [21].
[63] For demoted tenancies, see Housing Act 1996, ss 143D, 143E and 143F; for introductory tenancies, see Housing Act 1996, ss 127, 128 and 129; for accommodation provided by local authorities pursuant to their homelessness duties, Housing Act 1996, pt VII; and in the termination of a joint tenancies by one joint tenant either pursuant to a contractual term or *Hammersmith LBC v Monk*, n 55.
[64] *Pinnock* (n 1) [46] (Lord Neuberger).
[65] See S Nield, 'Shutting the Door on Horizontal Effect' [2017] *The Conveyancer and Property Lawyer* 60.
[66] See A Latham, 'Talking Without Speaking, Hearing Without Listening? Evictions, the Law Lords and the European Court of Human Rights' [2011] *PL* 730.

effectively adopted a state-limited concept of proportionality. Indeed, the Supreme Court has made it very clear that, in respecting the separation of powers, it is not the Court's role to enquire how the housing policy adopted by Parliament may impinge upon respect for the home.[67] Bright challenges this omission in her call for courts post-*Pinnock* to 'not only "take ownership seriously" but also "take home seriously"'.[68]

Whilst the 'sufficient and continuing links' meaning of home has divorced the concept of home from property rights,[69] the courts are yet to articulate the values that are inherent in the notion of respect for the home. At the heart of Article 8 is the autonomy and freedom of the individual to live their own life as they see fit by affording respect to their own beliefs, values and self-expression.[70] Respect for the home thus has important interactions with the right to respect for a person's private and family life that are also protected by Article 8. The ECtHR has identified respect for the home as concerned with 'identity, self determination, physical and mental integrity ... and a settled and secure home and place in community'.[71] Here there are synergies with the 'X factor' values of home that Fox has encapsulated within the concepts of home as territory, identity and a social and cultural unit, but, as Fox argues, these values fare poorly when pitted against property rights that reflect easier to measure financial values.[72] Article 8 should provide a transparent stage for the concept of home to be refined and balanced against competing property interest, but that has not happened. Our highest courts have not moved beyond the faint surprise of Lord Scott in *Harrow LBC v Qazi* at the possibility that home represents something more than 'bricks and mortar and land'.[73]

The cases have been concerned primarily with the compatibility of the legal rules governing mandatory rights to possession where the court has no discretion to consider proportionality.[74] In this context, the courts have shown considerable deference to Parliament in shaping housing policy and the legislation required to implement that policy. In the face of democratic legitimacy and institutional competence, such deference is to be expected. However, that does not mean that legislation or common law rules conferring a right to possession of a home should be glossed over. For instance, one might have expected in *Pinnock* and *Powell* some comment on the proportionality of various schemes to combat antisocial behaviour,[75] or in

[67] See, eg, *Kay v Lambeth LBC* (n 51) 185–87; *McDonald* (n 2) [43]–[45].

[68] S Bright, '*Manchester City Council v Pinnock* (2010): Shifting Ideas of Ownership of Land' in N Gravels (ed), *Landmark Cases in Land Law* (Oxford, Hart Publishing, 2013) 274.

[69] The test was formulated in *Gillow v UK* (1989) 11 EHRR 335 and has been consistently adopted by both the ECtHR and our domestic courts.

[70] See, eg, the discussion by K Moller, 'Two Conceptions of Positive Liberty: Towards an Autonomy-based Theory of Constitutional Rights' (2009) 29 *OJLS* 757; K Moller, 'Proportionality and Rights Inflation' in Huscroft et al (n 7) 155.

[71] *Connors v UK* (2005) 40 EHRR 9, 82.

[72] L Fox, *Conceptualising Home: Theories, Law and Policy* (Oxford, Hart Publishing, 2007).

[73] [2004] 1 AC 983, [145].

[74] The termination of secure tenancies does not present a compatibility problem where the court has discretion to decide if it is reasonable to order possession. See the Housing Act 1985, pt IV.

[75] See the suggestion of Latham (n 66) 740–41, although the victims do not appear to have argued the issue.

McDonald the use of receivers in home repossession whereby the usual mortgage forbearance processes may be sidestepped.[76]

The significance of home as a unique physical and psychological space critical to the occupier's autonomy can only be explored where the court is afforded a degree of discretion in deciding whether or not to order possession and/or sale.[77] However, the nature and width of such statutory discretions vary, and there remains the possibility that a particular statutory discretion is not sufficiently wide to afford an adequate assessment of proportionality.[78]

B. Applied Review

The focus of the Supreme Court in *Pinnock* and *Powell* was upon the proper approach to applied review in social housing repossession cases. They truncated proportionality by concentrating solely upon the first, legitimate aim and the final balancing stages. The suitability and minimal impairment were not considered—largely, it seems, because repossession was presented as the only option. A plea for a structured approach was made in *Powell*, but Lord Hope rejected this plea as 'wholly inappropriate'.[79]

Within the legitimate aims of the statutory grounds for repossession at issue is the vindication of property rights, which 'are of real weight when it comes to proportionality'.[80] Additionally, a social landlord's ownership rights should be exercised in accordance with its statutory duties to manage its housing stock.[81]

It is the victim who must bear the burden of proof to demonstrate that the repossession is disproportionate.[82] He or she faces an uphill task. To avoid summary disposal, he or she must establish that their case passes 'the high threshold of being seriously arguable'[83] before the court will proceed to decide whether eviction strikes a fair balance. This presumption reflects a high degree of deference not only to the decision making of social landlords, but also to the efficiency and contextual issues suggested by Rivers. In *Powell* Lord Hope believed

> it would be demanding far too much of a judge in the county court, faced with a heavy list of individual cases, to require him to weigh up the personal circumstances of each individual occupier against the landlord's public responsibilities.[84]

[76] See S Nield, 'Thumbs Down to the Horizontal Effect of Article 8' [2015] *The Conveyancer and Property Lawyer* 77.

[77] For example, see in respect of secure tenancies the Housing Act 1985, s 84 and regarding a co-owned home the Trusts of Land and Appointment of Trustees Act 1996, ss 14 and 15. In respect of the latter see *National Westminster Bank plc v Rushmer* [2010] EWHC 317.

[78] See, eg, *Pinnock* and *Powell*.

[79] See n 1 above, [41]; but see the approach of Lord Phillips in *Powell* (n 1) [90].

[80] Per Lord Neuberger in *Pinnock* (n 1) [54].

[81] *Pinnock* (n 1) [52]; *Powell* (n 1) [36]; but Bright suggests that the Localism Act 2011, s 1(1) may reduce local authorities' duties not to act for self-seeking reasons: see above (n 68) 259–60.

[82] *Pinnock* (n 1) [53]; *Powell* (n 1) [33] and [37]. This approach is endorsed by the ECtHR: see *Bjedov v Croatia* Application No 42150/09 (29 May 2012), [67].

[83] *Pinnock* (n 1) [61]; *Powell* (n 1).

[84] *Powell* (n 1) [35].

Public lawyers' reactions to *Pinnock* and *Powell* have been mixed. Rivers and Brady endorse the court's presumption of proportionality. Brady believes that the deference displayed is justified by housing policy and attendant high levels of institutional competency and democratic legitimacy.[85] Rivers grounds the legitimacy of the presumption upon the fact that applied review is conducted under a proportionate legislative framework.[86] By contrast, Latham criticises the court's 'managerial approach' for its failure 'to analyse the situation from the point of view of the occupier as rights-bearer'.[87] The focus of attention is concentrated upon the management of social housing and not upon the home values represented by that housing to the victim.[88] The 'sufficient and continuing links test' is easy to pass, but thereafter conceptions of respect for the home sink from view.

C. A Disproportionate Outcome

The reported decisions to date demonstrate that an occupier will rarely be able to rebut the presumption of proportionality.[89] There are two potential indicia of a disproportionate outcome: first, the threshold epitomised by the highly exceptional likelihood of a disproportionate outcome; and secondly, the weight to be given to a victim's vulnerability.

(i) Highly Exceptional

Despite Lord Neuberger's reluctance to use the term,[90] 'very highly exceptional' has been most often employed to describe the likelihood of a disproportional outcome.[91] Walsh challenges the 'pre-weighting' of the proportionality balance by the exceptionality standards imposed. She calls upon the courts to give much clearer guidance as to when that balance may swing in favour of Article 8 rights.[92] In *Kay* Lord Bingham did not think it was either 'possible or desirable to attempt to define what facts or circumstances might rank as highly exceptional'.[93] In his view '[t]he practical experience of county court judges is likely to prove the surest guide'.[94] However, their insight is not easy to discover, unless their decision is appealed; even so, their

[85] See n 33 above.
[86] See n 48 above.
[87] See n 66 above, 740.
[88] See also *R(N) v Lewisham LBC: R(H) v Newham LBC* (n 50).
[89] For a convenient review see I Loveland, 'The Holy Grail as an Empty Chalice? Proportionality Review in Possession Proceedings after *Pinnock* and *Powell*' (2013) 6 *Journal of Planning and Environment Law* 622.
[90] *Pinnock* (n 1) [51].
[91] See, eg, *Powell* (n 1) [92] (Lord Phillips); *R (on the application of N) v Lewisham LBC* (n 50) [65] (Lord Hodge).
[92] R Walsh, 'Stability and Predictability in English Property Law—The Impact of Article 8 of the European Convention on Human Rights Reassessed' (2015) 131 *LQR* 585.
[93] See n 51 above, [38].
[94] ibid.

judgments have frequently been cast aside for failing to appreciate the high evidential standards required.[95]

(ii) Vulnerability

In *Pinnock* Lord Neuberger accepted the suggestion of the Equality and Human Rights Commission that disproportionality is likely to be found 'in respect of occupants who are vulnerable as a result of mental illness, physical or learning disability, poor health or frailty'.[96] Yet such vulnerability has not often made a difference. *Southend-on-Sea BC v Armour*[97] provides one of the few reported instances when the High Court decided that it was disproportionate to evict Mr Armour from his home for antisocial behaviour, attributable to his mental vulnerability, when that behaviour had ceased.

Nevertheless, in Strasbourg jurisprudence a more protective attitude to certain vulnerable groups is growing—with Roma and those suffering from mental disabilities featuring prominently.[98] These developments suggest an emerging positive obligation to take account of the particular circumstances of such vulnerable groups. For instance, in both *Yordanova*[99] and *Winterstein*[100] the respective states were called upon to consider the specific needs, including the risk of homelessness, of the Roma minority groups at issue.[101] Although not constituting a right to a home, the Strasbourg Court emphasised that in determining the proportionality of an eviction a state must weigh the particular needs of a vulnerable group, and even went so far as to suggest that states may be under an obligation to secure shelter to particularly vulnerable individuals within that group.[102] Thus vulnerability appears both as a factor to be considered in meeting procedural standards and as providing more weight within final balancing because of the likelihood that the victim will suffer more acute harm.[103] Along similar lines, in *Zehentner v Austria*[104] there was a call to take account of the specific difficulties faced by the mentally disabled within the debt enforcement process under consideration, whilst in *Bjedov v Croatia*[105] the state's failure, before it resorted to eviction, to try and meet the housing needs of the elderly and frail victim was weighed in the proportionality balance and found to be a violation of Article 8.

[95] See, eg, *Birmingham CC v Lloyd* [2012] EWCA Civ 969; *McDonald v Mc Donald* (n 2); *R (on the application of JL) v The SS for Defence* [2013] EWCA Civ 449; *Thurrock v West* [2013] HLR 5; *Corby v Scott* [2012] HLR 23.

[96] See n 1 above, [64].

[97] [2014] HLR 19. See also in the Scottish Courts *River Clyde Homes Ltd v Woods* Case No SD 122/14.

[98] L Peroni and A Timmer, 'Vulnerable Groups: The Promise of an Emerging Concept in European Human Rights Convention Law' (2013) 11 *International Journal of Constitutional Law* 1056.

[99] See n 26 above.

[100] See n 25 above.

[101] *Yordanova* (n 26) [126]–[133]; *Winterstein* (n 25) [76], [86]–[88].

[102] *Yordanova* ibid [130].

[103] Peroni and Timmer (n 98) 1080.

[104] (2011) 52 EHRR 22, [61]–[65].

[105] See n 82 above, [68]–[72].

The use of the term 'vulnerability' is growing, but the concept of vulnerability is highly contested. Fineman suggests that we are all vulnerable in our dependency upon others and in our universal exposure to harm.[106] She accordingly argues against a group-based conception of vulnerability which may reinforce inequality and discrimination. Peroni and Timmer, in examining the Strasbourg Court's development of the concept of vulnerable groups, recognise this danger but believe that universal and group-based conceptions of vulnerability are not necessarily inconsistent.[107]

They argue that, whilst the whole of human rights is based upon vulnerability, it is anchored upon the universal premise of the rational liberal legal subject. Accordingly, there is a danger of non-recognition and thus exclusion of those who do not fit this narrative. They believe that identification of group vulnerability can help address this exclusionary risk by recognising that some victims are more vulnerable than others. They advocate a concept of group vulnerability that acknowledges three layered characteristics: first, that vulnerability is relational in recognising the situational context in addressing risk within society; secondly, that the particular vulnerability of the individual victim should be recognised; and lastly, that vulnerability should look to the relative harm suffered. They argue that, properly employed, this faceted concept of group vulnerability can promote equality by providing a platform through which difference is accommodated and respect promoted.

It is interesting to look at the employment of these factors by the Supreme Court in *Hotak v Southwark LBC: Kanu v Southwark LBC: Johnson v Solihull MBC.*[108] This case did not concern Article 8 but considered the concept of vulnerability within a local authority's duty to meet the housing needs of those with a priority need who are not intentionally homeless.[109] That duty extends to 'a person who is vulnerable as a result of old age, mental illness or handicap or physical disability or other special reason'.[110] It thus constitutes a positive duty to provide a home rather than a negative duty not to interfere disproportionately with respect to an existing home. Nevertheless, the Supreme Court's comments are of interest since, if an occupier cannot be evicted because their eviction is disproportionate, a landlord is effectively obliged to allow the victim to continue to occupy their home.[111]

The court reinforced the view that vulnerability is a comparative, yet particular, harm-based concept. The harm arising from homelessness suffered by a vulnerable victim needs to be assessed relative to the harm that would be suffered by an ordinary person if they became homeless.[112] Furthermore, that harm should consider the particular circumstances of the victim.[113] The court was divided on whether those circumstances should take into account assistance provided by family members or

[106] See, eg, M Fineman, 'Equality, Autonomy and the Vulnerable Subject' in A Grear and M Fineman (eds), *Vulnerability, Reflections on a New Ethical Foundation of Law and Politics* (Farnham, Ashgate, 2013) Ch 1.

[107] See n 98 above.

[108] [2015] 2 WLR 1341.

[109] Housing Act 1996, s 193.

[110] s 189(1)(c).

[111] See Lady Hale's comments in *Kay v Lambeth LBC* (n 51) 187.

[112] See n 108 above, [51]–[58] (Lord Neuberger).

[113] ibid [62]–[71] (Lord Neuberger).

other support networks. The majority accepted that it should, but Lady Hale provided a spirited dissent.[114] The court was unanimous, however, in its view that the local authority's paucity of housing resources was irrelevant to this enquiry—the focus is on the victim.[115]

(iii) Round-up on Proportionality and Article 8

The combined effect of collapsing the stages of proportionality coupled with high degrees of deference, the shift in the burden of proof and the continued obscurity of vulnerability has frustrated proportionality as a form of rational reasoning in Article 8 cases. The result reflects a state-limiting conception of proportionality identified by Rivers,[116] yet without a fuller definition of the right to respect for the home suggested by Young.[117] Thus we are little nearer appreciating how respect for the home is conceptualised beyond a limited procedural protection in public housing cases. Proportionality offers a foundation for the contextual conversation advocated by the progressive theorists to explore how home values should find expression in our property rules, but its treatment under Article 8 barely opens the contextual door. Instead, Walsh suggests that the information theorists' 'model of property law as a core of exclusion rules, supported by a periphery of governance rules designed to deal with complex cases, can usefully explain the marginal status afforded to art 8 defences'.[118]

IV. THE EQUALITY ACT 2010 AND PROPORTIONALITY

Article 14 may provide a defence based upon discriminatory treatment in the enjoyment of Convention rights, including Article 8. Its target is more often than not legislative or administrative regulation that operates in a discriminatory way.[119] It is the Equality Act 2010 (EA 2010) that domestically addresses individual vulnerability by prohibiting discrimination by both public and private parties. This section thus concentrates on the role of proportionality under the EA 2010.[120]

Part 3 of the EA 2010 prohibits discrimination in the provision of services, including financial services,[121] whilst part 4 of the Act specifically addresses discrimination in relation to premises. For instance, section 35(1)(b) imposes a duty upon those who manage premises not to discriminate directly or indirectly when evicting an

[114] ibid [94]–[101].

[115] ibid [39].

[116] See n 8 above.

[117] See n 9 above.

[118] See n 92 above, 601–02.

[119] See, eg, *Ghaidan v Godin-Mendoza* [2004] 2 AC 557; *R (on the application of H & others) v Ealing LBC* [2016] EWHC 841 (admin). See also the appeals to the Supreme Court on the bedroom tax regulations in *R (on the application of Rutherford and another) v SSWP* UKSC 2016/0029 and *R (on the application of A) (AP) v Secretary of State for Work and Pensions* UKSC 2016/0025.

[120] See also ch 8 of this book.

[121] *South Pacific Mortgages Ltd v V* [2015] EW Misc B42 provides an example, although unsuccessful on the facts.

occupier. The protected characteristics for the purposes of parts 3 and 4 include both physical and mental disability, gender, race and religion.[122]

The protection against direct discrimination is absolute (save in relation to age) and is defined by section 13(1) as arising where a victim is treated less favourably than others. It thus calls for a comparison in the treatment of the victim with an actual or hypothetical person in similar circumstances. Direct age discrimination can be justified where the discrimination is proportionate to achieving a legitimate aim.[123] Nevertheless, such discrimination can only be justified on narrow grounds of public interest, such as inter-generational fairness or dignity, and demands strict and careful scrutiny.[124] It is difficult to think of a circumstance where age discrimination could be so justified in the context of repossession.

Indirect discrimination is also unlawful. It 'attempts to level the playing field by subjecting to scrutiny requirements that look neutral on their face but in reality work to the comparative disadvantage of people with protected characteristics'.[125] Indirect discrimination may be justified where it is proportionate to achieving a legitimate aim.[126] Although requiring less rigorous standards than in the case of direct age discrimination, the courts have adopted a structured approach to proportionality in this context.[127] Thus a landowner seeking possession who is met with a defence of indirect discrimination must establish that not only was the particular reason for possession sufficiently important to justify limiting the fundamental right to equality but also that there was no alternative, less discriminatory, way of achieving that objective.[128] In so doing, the landowner should establish that thought was given to such matters when making the decision to evict,[129] particularly if they are a public authority and thus under a positive duty to promote equality.[130]

In relation to disability, the EA 2010 provides two further protections. First, it imposes obligations to make reasonable adjustments to redress a disadvantage suffered by a disabled person so as to promote their similar treatment to that of an able-bodied person.[131] Secondly, section 15 provides a more general concept of 'disability discrimination', where a disabled person is treated unfavourably because of their disability.[132] Such unfavourable treatment may be justified where the discriminator

[122] See ss 4–12 generally, but age and marriage and civil partnership are excluded characteristics for the purposes of parts 3 and 4. See ss 28 and 32, respectively.

[123] s 13(2).

[124] *Seldon v Clarkson, Wright & Jakes* [2012] UKSC 16; *Horner v Chief Constable of West Yorkshire Police* [2012] UKSC15.

[125] *Horner* (ibid) [19] (Lady Hale), when considering indirect discrimination under s 19 EA 2010 of the need for a law degree to gain promotion within the relevant police department!

[126] s 19(2)(d).

[127] See *Elias v SS for Defence* [2006] 1 WLR 3213, approved in *R (On the application of E v Governing Body of TFS* [2010] 2 AC 728.

[128] ibid.

[129] ibid.

[130] See s 149 and *R (on the application of H & others)* (n 119).

[131] ss 20 and 21. In *South Pacific Mortgages* (n 121) it was unsuccessfully argued that converting the mortgage to interest only was a reasonable adjustment South Pacific should have made.

[132] s 15(1)(a). Hepple suggests that *Malcolm v Lewisham LBC* [2008] UKHL 45 should be decided differently under the EA 2010: see B Hepple, *Equality: The Legal Framework*, 2nd edn (Oxford, Hart Publishing, 2014).

can demonstrate that their actions are 'a proportionate means of achieving a legitimate aim'.[133]

In *Akerman-Livingstone v Aster Communities Ltd*[134] (*Akerman*) the Supreme Court considered proportionality in possession proceedings where indirect disability discrimination was proved. The Court decided that, in contrast to Article 8, a structured four-limb approach to proportionality was required by the 'extra right to equal treatment' that Parliament has provided to the disabled in section 15 of the EA 2010.[135] It is thus necessary, in balancing the reason for repossession against the right to equality, to specifically address the legitimate aim of the repossession before proving both that 'there was no less drastic means of solving the problem and that the effect upon the occupier was outweighed by the advantages'.[136] The Supreme Court found that Mr Akerman-Livingstone's eviction was proportionate in the circumstances despite his mental fragility. Weighing against this vulnerability were the various attempts his landlord had made to provide alternative accommodation and the legal action the landlord faced to enforce the sale of the building in which Mr Akerman-Livingstone lived.

This difference in approach is interesting. In contrast to the deference shown under Article 8, the Supreme Court was clearly happy to enjoy the democratic legitimacy through its adjudicatory responsibilities under the EA 2010, as well as the competency to tackle the proportionality of discrimination—these are 'questions which the court is well-equipped to address'.[137]

The Supreme Court in *Akerman* pointed to a number of reasons why a presumption of proportionality was inappropriate—not least because the legislation specifically places the burden of proof upon the discriminator.[138] The legitimate aim of the EA 2010 is to 'secure equal treatment and thus respect for the human dignity of all people irrespective of their race, their gender, their sexual orientation, their religion or belief, or, in particular their disability'.[139] It thus addresses the vulnerability of particular groups rather than providing a right to protection of the home that is universal. This role of proportionality is thus specific and targeted. The interface between respect for the home and social housing policy is not directly at issue.

The negative duties not to discriminate imposed by the EA 2010 are placed on both private and public parties.[140] These universal duties are particularly significant in the light of *McDonald* and the distinction it draws in the application of proportionality to repossession by public and private landlords. The self-interest of a private landlord, mortgagee or other owner is tempered by their absolute duty not to discriminate directly and by their duty not to discriminate indirectly unless they can prove the proportionality of their actions. In addition, they may be under a positive

[133] s 15(1)(b).
[134] [2015] UKSC 15.
[135] Per Lady Hale, [25].
[136] Per Lady Hale, [34].
[137] ibid.
[138] s 136.
[139] Per Lady Hale, [32].
[140] Per Lady Hale, [24]. The distinction between private and public parties lies in public authorities' additional positive duty to promote equality—see s 136.

duty to take steps to ensure equality of treatment in relation to disability. Thus we find the application of an optimising concept of proportionality to advance equality in what is patently human-rights-inspired legislation. Relativist notions of property are underlined by the moral imperative of equality that echoes aspects of the social obligation norms advocated by progressive property theorists. Even self-interest that may indirectly compromise equality in the exercise of property interests must be justified through the open and structured conversation demanded by proportionality.

V. PROPORTIONALITY AND REMEDIAL DISCRETION

Article 8 and the EA 2010 employ proportionality to balance human rights against public interests, but the language of proportionality is being utilised in the distinctly private sphere in the exercise of remedial discretion.[141] Here the court is seeking to balance or reconcile competing property interests—a task that has long been a concern of the courts. Examples are found in the grant of relief from forfeiture and in measuring a claimant's equity within proprietary estoppel. Whether this use of language is coincidental or marks a cross-fertilisation of concepts between public and private law is difficult to know. Lacey, in mapping the histories of proportionality as a metaphor, suggests its attraction lies in the legitimation of discretionary power by providing a criterion of appropriateness and rationality which in private law is appealing to constrain unbridled market forces within a constitutional frame.[142]

The draconian effects of forfeiture have long been tempered by equitable and statutory rights to relief to transform forfeiture from a right to expropriate to a remedial device affording a landlord security for performance of the tenant's covenants.[143] The court's discretion to award relief from forfeiture is wide and unfettered, but nevertheless is exercised in accordance with principle, in which proportionality plays a part.[144] Examples of the use of proportionality as the guiding principle appears in two recent cases—*Magnic Ltd v Mahmood UL-Hassan*[145] and *Freifeld v West Kensington Court Ltd.*[146] The common features influencing the court's discretion was the deliberate nature of the tenants' breaches and the windfall that would accrue to the landlord upon forfeiture. In granting relief in both cases, the Court of Appeal looked first to the purpose of the forfeiture before weighing on the one hand the nature of the breach and on the other hand the windfall that would accrue to the landlord in a manner that looks suspiciously like a structured approach to proportionality. For instance, in *Mahmood* Patten LJ, giving the leading judgment, stated:

> The starting point for the exercise of our discretion has to be to remind ourselves that the purpose of the reservation of a right of re-entry ... is to provide the landlord with some

[141] Remedial discretion is not the only example in private law. See the employment of proportionality to determine if an agreed damages clause is penal in *Makdessi v Cavendish Square Holding BV* [2015] 3 WLR 1373.

[142] See n 4 above. See also S Shiffin, 'Remedial Clauses: The Overprivatisation of Private Law' (2016) 67 *Hastings Law Journal* 407.

[143] See Law of Property Act 1925, s 146(2) in respect of covenants other than to pay rent.

[144] *Rose v Hyman* [1912] AC 623, 631.

[145] [2015] EWCA Civ 224.

[146] [2015] EWCA Civ 806.

> security for the performance of the tenant's covenants ... There may, of course, be breaches which are so serious and irremediable as to justify the refusal of relief ... But in most cases relief will be granted on the breach being remedied.[147]

After noting that the breach could be remedied, Patten LJ continued: 'It would I think be disproportionate and, to put it bluntly, unjust for the defendants to be deprived of their property for a legal error of this kind.'[148]

Again, in *Freifeld* Lady Justice Arden stated:

> The windfall point is about proportionality. The appellants' egregious conduct is not relevant to the question of the windfall, which was a self-standing consideration to be considered on its own merits and *then* weighed against the appellants' egregious conduct. Once it has been appreciated that the value of the leasehold interest is an advantage which the respondent will obtain from forfeiture, it has to be thrown into the balance with all the other circumstances.[149]

It is not that the circumstances in which relief will be granted has changed significantly; rather, it is the terminology employed that is striking, and suggests that proportionality may provide an explicit framework upon which judicial reasoning can be conveniently and openly structured.

Controversy surrounds the basis of the court's remedial discretion to satisfy proprietary estoppel.[150] Should the court's discretion be expectation based in seeking to satisfy the claimant's expectations or based upon detrimental reliance in compensating the claimant for the detriment they have suffered? In negotiating these different priorities, Aldous LJ in *Jennings v Rice* stated that '[t]he most essential requirement is that there must be proportionality between the expectation and the detriment'.[151] This observation also underlies the Privy Council's statement in *Henry v Henry* that '[p]roportionality lies at the heart of the doctrine of proprietary estoppel and permeates its every application'.[152]

Nevertheless, uncertainty remains as to just how the courts are utilising the concept of proportionality. The Court of Appeal in *Suggitt v Suggitt* appeared to reject a positive framing of proportionality when Lady Arden stated that proportionality 'does not mean that there has to be a relationship of proportionality between the level of detriment and the relief awarded'.[153] She suggested, rather, that

[147] ibid [50].

[148] ibid [52].

[149] ibid [47] (original emphasis).

[150] For the considerable recent academic debate see S Gardiner, 'The Remedial Discretion in Proprietary Estoppel' (1999) 115 *LQR* 438 and 'Remedial Discretion in Proprietary Estoppel—Again' (2006) 122 *LQR* 492; A Robertson, 'Reliance and Expectation in Estoppel Remedies' (1998) 18 *LS* 360; A Robertson, 'The Reliance Basis of Estoppel Remedies' (2008) 72 *The Conveyancer and Property Lawyer* 295; J Mee, 'The Role of Expectation in the Determination of Proprietary Estoppel Remedies in M Dixon (ed), *Modern Studies in Property Law*, vol 5 (Oxford, Hart Publishing, 2009); B McFarlane, *The Law of Proprietary Estoppel* (Oxford, Oxford University Press, 2013) Ch 7; H Biehler, 'Remedies in Cases of Proprietary Estoppel: Towards a More Principled Approach?' [2015] *Irish Jurist* 79.

[151] [2003] 1 P&CR 8, [36], relying on comments made in *Sledmore v Dalby* (1996) 72 P&CR 196 and the Australian High Court in *Commonwealth of Australia v Verwayen* (1990) 170 CLR 394. See also [56] (Robert Walker LJ).

[152] [2010] UKPC 3, [65].

[153] [2012] EWCA Civ 1140, [44]. See also Robert Walker LJ in *Campbell v Griffin* [2001] EWCA Civ 990, [34] and *Jennings v Rice* [2001] EWCA Civ 159, [50].

proportionality should be employed only in a negative sense to pin back extravagant expectations that, if satisfied, would result in a disproportionate outcome in the light of the detriment suffered. By contrast, McFarlane argues for a positive framing of proportionality to guide the court's decision in determining the extent of the claimant's equity.[154] In some measure a negative or positive approach to proportionality in estoppel reflects whether one supports an expectation- or reliance-based justification for proprietary estoppel in the sense of the legitimate aim of the doctrine. As McFarlane points out, we need 'a clear sense of the justification for the doctrine of proprietary estoppel' before we are able to formulate a principled test.[155]

It is not suggested that a structured approach to proportionality is always appropriate within the remedial discretion, but the language of proportionality, as illustrated by these examples, could contribute to a clearer consideration of the principles guiding discretion in the balancing of competing interests. For instance, there is an evident focus on the functionality or legitimate aim of the proprietary remedies in question, whether that be as a security for performance, in the case of relief from forfeiture, or the prevention of unconscionable conduct (however framed) in proprietary estoppel. Minimal impairment suggests a cautious approach to interference with established property interests without clear justification. Thus, within forfeiture there is a concern to avoid a windfall for the landlord and in estoppel there is a desire for the remedy to reflect 'the minimum equity to do justice'.[156] The final fair balance provides a clear platform for the court to explicitly weigh relevant circumstantial factors.

VI. CONCLUSION

Proportionality provides a process to balance competing rights that looks to means and ends rather than the conduct of the parties. It thus seeks to provide a contextual yet rational and transparent exercise of discretion. This consideration of context presents both a procedural imperative and an additional layer of complexity. The nature of the procedural imperative to assess proportionality and the complexity of any such assessment presents a challenge not just for public lawyers, but for private lawyers too. They also need to engage with the meaning and import of proportionality.

The Supreme Court has minimised this challenge from Article 8 in home repossession proceedings by limiting its application to the public sector and by prioritising the simplicity and clarity of the right to exclude in all but exceptional cases. It has done so by marginalising the import of home and its place within the fair balance that lies at the heart of proportionality. Contextual factors, in particular an occupier's vulnerability, are admitted only when an occupier can raise a seriously arguable case that they will suffer greater and unjustified harm or when endorsed by specific legislation beyond the HRA 1998. One such piece of legislation is the

[154] See n 150 above, [7.123]–[7.158].

[155] B McFarlane, N Hopkins and S Nield, *Land Law Text Cases and Materials*, 3rd edn (Oxford, Oxford University Press, 2015) 355. He supports a detrimental reliance based approach. See McFarlane (n 150) [7.35]–[7.38].

[156] Per Scarman LJ in *Crabb v Arun DC* [1976] Ch 179, 198.

EA 2010, which harnesses proportionality to drive the fight against discrimination suffered by certain vulnerable groups.

The place of proportionality within home repossession proceedings may have been constrained, but in its structured reasoning the concept provides a powerful rhetoric which 'opens up valuable new space for debate about the appropriate balance between securing efficiency and other social and individual values',[157] and epitomises the contrasting views of the information and progressive theorist. That rhetoric is also finding an unexpected place in rationalising the judicial exercise of remedial discretion. It may yet provide a stronger and clearer voice in promoting relativist, over absolute, notions of ownership, of which the EA 2010 provides an example.

[157] Walsh (n 92) 603.

4

Adverse Possession, Unregistered Land and Title Defects: A Fly in the Ointment of Irish Reform?

UNA WOODS*

I. INTRODUCTION

OVER THE LAST few decades, concerns have been expressed in law reform circles across the common law world about the fairness of the doctrine of adverse possession. This unease stems, for the most part, from the doctrine's failure to confer adequate protection on owners against the danger of inadvertently losing title by adverse possession and the extent to which the doctrine permits squatters who know they do not own the land (deliberate or 'bad faith' squatters) to acquire title. In England and Wales, the Law Commission purported to address both of these issues by recommending the introduction of a qualified veto system of adverse possession in relation to land which is registered in the Land Registry.[1] These proposals were implemented by the Land Registration Act 2002.[2] Additional protection is conferred on the registered owner, who may veto an adverse possession application. However, the qualifications to the veto system preserve the operation of the doctrine for certain adverse possessors (for example, a good faith adverse possessor of boundary land) in the interest of fairness. In 2005, the Irish Law Reform Commission proposed certain reforms to the law on adverse possession, including the imposition of a mandatory requirement for a court application.[3] These law reform proposals were jettisoned in response to critical submissions made to the Irish government by the Law Society's Conveyancing Committee, mostly related to the workability and increased costs involved in the administration of the proposed scheme. However, the Irish Law Reform Commission plans to revisit this area of law

* Senior Lecturer, School of Law, University of Limerick.

[1] See Law Commission for England and Wales, *Land Registration for the Twenty-First Century: A Consultative Document* (Law Com No 254, 1998; UK LC 254) Ch 10; Law Commission for England and Wales, *Land Registration for the Twenty-First Century: A Conveyancing Revolution* (Law Com No 271, 2001; UK LC 271) Ch 14.

[2] Sch 6.

[3] See Irish Law Reform Commission, *Report on Reform and Modernisation of Land Law and Conveyancing Law* (No 74, 2005; Irish LRC 74), paras 2.04-2.07 and pp 322–39.

in the future.[4] In this event, the introduction of a qualified veto system of adverse possession is likely to be considered for Ireland. A discussion of the substantive arguments in favour of the introduction of such reform has taken place elsewhere.[5] Therefore, this chapter instead investigates the feasibility of extending such a qualified veto system of adverse possession to unregistered land without damaging the current role played by the doctrine in curing defects in unregistered titles.

It is frequently argued that the doctrine of adverse possession plays an essential role in the investigation of title to unregistered land by curing title defects, thereby facilitating transactions in relation to such land. The majority of claims which arise from a conveyancing error are unenforceable following 12 years of adverse possession by the intended grantee, thus providing a 'comfort blanket' to a purchaser's solicitor that a vendor who can establish a chain of title of sufficient length will also have extinguished such claims. This function of quieting men's estates was referred to in the preamble to the Limitation Act 1623 and has long been acknowledged as one of the primary purposes of the doctrine. Ballantine commented in 1918 that its 'great purpose is automatically to quiet all titles which are openly and consistently asserted, to provide proof of meritorious titles, and correct errors in conveyancing'.[6] More recently, the Law Commission for England and Wales noted: 'The fact that adverse possession can extinguish earlier rights to possess facilitates and cheapens the investigation of title to unregistered land.'[7]

In this chapter, it is argued that the function performed by the doctrine in this context could and should be preserved if Irish law is reformed by the introduction of a veto system of adverse possession which applies to both registered and unregistered land. In the case of unregistered land, it is proposed that the qualified veto would be administered by the Property Registration Authority (PRA)[8] on an application for first registration based on long possession or an application for first registration of an unregistered title. Consequently, the reform would become relevant in the lead up to or following a transaction for value which triggers the requirement for compulsory first registration of title. In practice, this reform would mean that a person claiming a title based on adverse possession of unregistered land would be deprived of the ability to engage in a valuable transaction in relation to such land unless efforts were made to identify and protect the owner by allowing them to veto the adverse possession application. However, a qualification to the veto system would operate in the context of an application for first registration of unregistered land based on an imperfect title (or 'colour of title', a concept which this author borrows

[4] Recently in *Dunne v Irish Rail* [2016] IESC 47, [23], Laffoy J commented that the doctrine of adverse possession remains controversial and stated: 'There would seem to be a need for a review of the recommendations made by the Law Reform Commission in 1989, 2002 and 2005 with a view to bringing clarity to the law in this area.'

[5] For such a discussion, see U Woods, *The Irish Law on Adverse Possession: The Case for a Qualified Veto System* (PhD thesis, Queens University Belfast, 2015).

[6] HW Ballantine, 'Title by Adverse Possession' (1918) 32 *Harvard Law Review* 135.

[7] UK LC 254 (n 1), para 10.9; UK LC 271 (n 1), para 14.2. Note that the Irish Law Reform Commission proposals also sought to preserve the doctrine's role in settling doubtful titles—see LRC 74 (n 3), para 2.06.

[8] The PRA was established by the Registration of Deeds and Title Act 2006 to manage the Land Registry and the Registry of Deeds.

from the United States)[9] coupled with 12 years' adverse possession. The extension of the veto to unregistered land coupled with this exception to cater for defective titles represents a fundamental distinction between the qualified veto system of adverse possession which this chapter proposes for Ireland and the system introduced in England and Wales, which applies only to registered land and preserves the old law of adverse possession in relation to unregistered land.

The Law Commission for England and Wales advanced a number of arguments to justify the decision limiting the reforms of the doctrine of adverse possession to registered land.[10] The primary argument was that making it more difficult to acquire title by adverse possession of unregistered land could weaken the security of title to such land.[11] The Law Commission appears to have assumed that extending the veto system to unregistered land could damage the unregistered conveyancing system. It acknowledged that the existing law can produce harsh results, but maintained that they are counterbalanced, in the context of unregistered land, by the essential role played by the doctrine in facilitating conveyancing.[12] It has also been pointed out that, by applying for first registration, unregistered owners could avail themselves of the added security afforded to registered owners and that the disparity in approach could therefore be viewed as playing a role in extending the registered title system.[13] While the Commission's approach encourages the owners of unregistered land to voluntarily apply for first registration of their titles in the Land Registry, it is quite severe on the owners of unregistered land who fail to register and are therefore deprived of the strong protections afforded by the 2002 Act.

This chapter builds on the analysis and critical reflections set out by the author in an article published in 2009.[14] It also revisits and reconsiders one view expressed in that article. It was argued that the introduction of marketable title legislation in England and Wales, akin to that which operates in many jurisdictions in the United States, would allow defective unregistered titles to be cured without reliance on the doctrine, thereby facilitating the introduction of a veto system of adverse possession for the owners of unregistered land. This chapter proposes an alternative approach to achieving the same goal in the Irish context and discusses why it represents a more suitable solution than the introduction of marketable title legislation.

It is beyond dispute that the role played by adverse possession in curing title defects is important, and Part II of this chapter examines its relevance in light of other

[9] This chapter will use the term 'colour', unless quoting from an American source.

[10] The Commission maintained (UK LC 254 (n 1), para 10.19) that while adverse possession runs counter to the fundamental concept of indefeasibility, which is a feature of registered title (a claim which has been refuted by this author elsewhere—see U Woods, 'The English Law on Adverse Possession: A Tale of Two Systems' (2009) 38 *Common Law World Review* 27, 31–38), its role in encouraging the owner of land to guard possession is fully compatible with the unregistered title system, where title is relative and based on possession (UK LC 254, paras 10.6 and 10.11; UK LC 271 (n 1), para 14.3). It is submitted that the reasoning which underpins the Law Commission's argument on this point is circular in nature—the current system of adverse possession is compatible with the unregistered title system, which is based ultimately on possession as ultimately title may be lost by adverse possession. For further discussion, see Woods (n 5) Ch 9, part 1.

[11] UK LC 271 (n 1), para 14.2.

[12] UK LC 254 (n 1), para 10.19.

[13] ibid.

[14] See Woods, 'English Law on Adverse Possession' (n 10).

remedies which may be relied on in responding to the consequences of a title defect. Part III examines the extent to which first registration of title in the Land Registry resolves problems created by title defects which survive the limitation period. This assessment illustrates that the doctrine of adverse possession and the process of first registration represent significant elements of a multifaceted, interconnected system which achieves a delicate but fair balance between the static security of owners and the dynamic security of purchasers.[15] Part IV focuses primarily on describing an important remedy, mentioned above, which is relied on in the United States to quiet title, namely 'colour of title' adverse possession, and discusses the merits of formally recognising certain features of the doctrine in Ireland as a necessary component of a qualified veto system.

As the author has argued elsewhere, the extension of the veto system to unregistered land would ensure consistency in the level of protection afforded to registered and unregistered owners against the risk of squatting.[16] A law which makes it more hazardous to fail to bring an action to recover possession of unregistered land probably makes little sense to the average landowner, who may be oblivious to whether his title is registered or not. Including unregistered land within the scope of a new veto system of adverse possession would also mean that practitioners would not have to be familiar with two different systems and, more significantly, it would make the law more accessible to non-lawyers. Finally, in contrast to the situation in England and Wales, many unregistered titles in Ireland relate to very valuable urban land,[17] making it even more important that the owners of such land are adequately protected by the law in this area.

II. AN ASSESSMENT OF THE ROLE PLAYED BY ADVERSE POSSESSION IN CURING TITLE DEFECTS

In Ireland and elsewhere, adverse possession has carved out a niche in curing title defects, and this chapter explores the parameters of this particular function of the doctrine in Ireland. As a precursor to this discussion, it may be helpful to explain that two mutually exclusive conveyancing systems currently operate in Ireland: the unregistered system (which, to confuse matters, permits the registration of deeds)[18] and the registration of title system (which governs land that has been registered in the Land Registry).[19] Although landowners holding unregistered titles may

[15] The terms 'static security' and 'dynamic security' were originally applied by Demogue—see R Demogue, 'Security' in A Fouillée et al, *Modern French Legal Philosophy* (Boston, The Boston Book Co, 1916) Ch xiii. These useful descriptors have been adopted by other authors—see, eg, P O'Connor, 'Registration of Invalid Dispositions: Who Gets the Property?' in E Cooke (ed), *Modern Studies in Property Law*, vol 3 (Oxford, Hart Publishing, 2005) Ch 3.

[16] See Woods, 'English Law on Adverse Possession' (n 10) 25.

[17] See text accompanying n 22 below.

[18] The Registration of Deeds and Titles Act 2006 facilitated the introduction of simplified and modernised procedures for the registration of deeds.

[19] This system is governed by the Registration of Title Act 1964 as amended by the Registration of Deeds and Title Act 2006. See also B Fitzgerald, *Land Registry Practice*, 2nd edn (Dublin, Round Hall Press, 1995); U Woods and JCW Wylie, *Irish Conveyancing Law*, 3rd edn (Haywards Heath, Tottel Publishing, 2005).

apply voluntarily to register their titles in the Land Registry, it is envisaged that the extension of the registration of title system to the entire country shall occur through compulsory registration. A statutory obligation is imposed on the PRA to promote and extend the registration of title system,[20] and huge efforts have recently been made to extend compulsory registration.[21] Dublin and Cork, which contain the highest numbers of unregistered titles, were the last zones to be designated compulsory first registration areas, from 1 June 2010.[22] Once land is brought within such a zone, on the next sale of the property the purchaser's solicitor is required to apply for first registration of the title to the property. Currently about 93 per cent of the land mass in Ireland is registered in the Land Registry,[23] and it is anticipated that the unregistered system of conveyancing shall eventually become defunct.

A fundamental danger underlying all conveyancing transactions relating to unregistered land is the possibility that the deed from the vendor may not operate to confer good title on the purchaser. The danger of a priority dispute arising, where the vendor has already conferred rights on another party which may trump those of the purchaser, is not the focus of the present discussion. In any event, the purchaser's solicitor can reduce, if not eliminate, this risk by conducting searches in the Registry of Deeds[24] and raising requisitions on title,[25] which are standard steps in a conveyancing transaction. Rather, the focus is on the implications for the purchaser if the deed which the vendor executes in his favour or some other deed forming part of the chain of title is in some way defective. While deeds may be defective for a variety of reasons, for the purposes of this chapter, two of the most likely defects are outlined. One common problem is where a discrepancy arises between the boundaries as delineated on the maps attached to various deeds and the boundaries as they appear on the ground. A second possibility is where a deed purports to act as a conveyance of a fee simple when in fact the vendor was only entitled to a leasehold interest. The further back in the chain of title such mistakes occur, the more difficult they may be to identify and resolve.

A. Conveyancing Remedies

Obviously, if such a defect is discovered before the sale is completed, it may be possible to rescind the contract and the purchaser may also be entitled to claim

[20] Registration of Deeds and Title Act 2006, s 10(1)(b).

[21] Registration of Title Act 1964 (Compulsory Registration of Ownership) Order 1969 (SI 87/1969), Registration of Title Act 1964 (Compulsory Registration of Ownership) Order 2005 (SI 605/2005), Registration of Title Act 1964 (Compulsory Registration of Ownership) Order 2008 (SI 81/2008) and Registration of Title Act 1964 (Compulsory Registration of Ownership) Order 2009 (SI 176/2009) extended compulsory registration to the entire country, with the exception of Dublin and Cork.

[22] Registration of Title Act 1964 (Compulsory Registration of Ownership) Order 2010 (SI 515/2010).

[23] See PRA, 'Frequently Asked Questions', available at www.prai.ie/faqs/what-is-the-difference-between-the-land-registry-and-the-registry-of-deeds-2 (accessed on 8 September 2016). Most agricultural land is registered as the Land Purchase Acts were enacted towards the end of the nineteenth century. These enabled tenant farmers to purchase their holdings from their landlords, but made it compulsory to register the land purchased in the Land Registry.

[24] See Wylie and Woods (n 19) paras 15.42–15.44.

[25] See Law Society of Ireland, *Objections and Requisitions on Title* (2015 edition).

damages.[26] However, if the sale has been completed, the remedies available under the contract for sale are no longer available, because the doctrine of merger provides that the contract is deemed to have merged in the conveyance.[27] If the deed executed by the vendor was defective, the purchaser may be able to rely on certain covenants for title which are implied in a conveyance[28] to protect the purchaser. For example, it is implied that the vendor has full power to convey the property and that the grantee will receive the property freed from incumbrances. The purchaser may be able to sue the vendor for damages if he is in breach of any of these covenants. Another implied covenant provides that the vendor will do anything reasonably requested in order to further assure the property to the purchaser. Therefore, the purchaser may be entitled to insist on the vendor providing a fresh effective deed of conveyance or a deed of rectification. It is important to remember, however, that a conveyance cannot operate to convey title which the vendor does not possess; if the defect arose in an earlier deed, title would not have passed to the vendor and, therefore, he will not be in a position to resolve the problem. Although, in certain circumstances, the benefit of these implied covenants may have passed down through the chain of title so that they are theoretically enforceable by the purchaser against the original covenantor,[29] it may not be practical to seek a remedy against a predecessor in title. Instead of relying on the covenants for title, if the mistake in the vendor's deed meant that the purchaser did not acquire the title he had bargained for, he could alternatively pursue the equitable remedy of rectification of the deed or possibly rescission.[30]

One weak link in the chain of title can have serious repercussions on the marketability of the title as the principle of *nemo dat quod non habet* is applicable to land transactions. Certain defects which arose decades ago may be impossible to correct. It is this danger which makes the investigation of title conducted by solicitors on behalf of purchasing clients so important and where it is alleged that the doctrine of adverse possession plays a vital supporting role.

B. The Role Played by Adverse Possession in the Investigation of Title

The role played by adverse possession in the investigation of title is only briefly outlined in this chapter as it has been explored in more detail by the author elsewhere.[31] The purpose of this chapter is to place this role in context by examining how the various remedies interact to address the most common defects which arise in unregistered conveyancing transactions. In any unregistered conveyancing transaction the vendor is obliged to 'deduce title' or prove that he is in a position to transfer the property he has contracted to convey to the purchaser for the estate he has agreed to sell. However, the vendor is only required to deduce title for the statutory

[26] Note that the rule in *Bain v Fothergill* (1874) LH 7 HL 158, which restricted the purchaser's entitlement to recover damages where the vendor failed to show good title, was abolished in Ireland by the Land and Conveyancing Law Reform Act 2009, s 53.

[27] See Wylie and Woods (n 19) paras 21.02–04.

[28] Land and Conveyancing Law Reform Act 2009, s 80 and sch 3, pt 2.

[29] Land and Conveyancing Law Reform Act 2009, s 80(5).

[30] Wylie and Woods (n 19) paras 21.37 and 21.39.

[31] See Woods, 'English Law on Adverse Possession' (n 10) 15–19.

period, currently 15 years in Ireland,[32] commencing with a good root.[33] The vendor is only required to prove his title for the statutory period as the doctrine of adverse possession provides 'a kind of qualified guarantee that any possible outstanding claims to ownership by third parties are time-barred'.[34] It should be noted that proof of 15 years' title does not provide an absolute guarantee to a purchaser that all prior rights have been extinguished as extensions to the limitation period are provided for in certain circumstances, for example, where the land is subject to a lease or a life estate. As Cretney explains:

> The real threat is, in practice, not the assertion of a claim to the whole of the land in question, but of a claim to a part onto which an encroachment has taken place. The shortening of the period of title unquestionably increases the risk of a purchaser failing to detect discrepancies between plans on earlier conveyances which might raise suspicions. Thus in areas of substantial leasehold or settled estates, the risk is clearly increased by the Act. Such estates are common in areas of high land value.[35]

It is clear, therefore, that certain interests, which may not be revealed by an investigation of title for the statutory period, shall survive the standard 12-year limitation period. It is helpful to illustrate the implications of this limitation of the doctrine by referring to the two common title defects mentioned earlier.[36] A plan attached to a deed which is relied on as the root may include a strip of land which was not owned by the vendor at the time of the transaction. Although the purchaser and his successors in title may have possessed the strip for 12 years, if the title to that strip was held under a lease or subject to a strict settlement, time will not have run against the title of the lessor or the owner of a future interest until those interests fell into possession. Similarly, if the root relied on by the purchaser's solicitor is a deed of conveyance but an investigation of the pre-root title would have revealed that it was leasehold, time will not have run against the lessor's freehold reversion until the expiry of the leasehold term. Finally, no proof of adverse possession is adduced in the average conveyancing transaction which makes the faith placed in the doctrine to bar pre-root rights in relation to the land appear even riskier.

III. THE ROLE OF FIRST REGISTRATION IN CURING TITLE DEFECTS[37]

It could be argued that these gaps in protection need no longer concern the average purchaser or their solicitor in Ireland, as the transaction in their favour will

[32] Land Law and Conveyancing Law Reform Act 2009, s 56.

[33] The definition of a good root provided in T Williams, *Vendor and Purchaser*, 4th edn (London, Sweet & Maxwell 1936) 98 is often referred to as '[a]n Instrument of disposition dealing with or proving on the face of it, without the aid of extrinsic evidence, the ownership of the whole legal and equitable estate in the property sold, containing a description by which the property can be identified and showing nothing to cast any doubt on the title of the disposing parties'.

[34] M Dockray, 'Why Do We Need Adverse Possession?' [1985] *Conveyancer and Property Lawyer* 272, 278.

[35] S Cretney, 'Land and Conveyancing Law Reforms' (1969) 32 *MLR* 477, 481. The statutory period of title was reduced from 30 years to 15 years by the Law of Property Act 1969, s 22.

[36] See text following n 25 above.

[37] The role played by first registration in curing title defects in England and Wales has been explored by Woods, 'English Law on Adverse Possession' (n 10) 19–21.

trigger the requirement for first registration of the title in the Land Registry[38] and this registration will cure any defects existing in the prior title. As has already been mentioned, the entire country is now an area of compulsory first registration. Section 31 of the Registration of Title Act 1964 provides that the register is deemed to be conclusive evidence of the title of the owner to the land as appearing on the register. The first registration of a person as owner with an absolute title operates to vest in the registered owner the estate transferred, subject to any burdens registered under section 69 or recognised by section 72.[39] In the English case of *Argyle Building Society v Hammond*,[40] Slade LJ described registration as operating a certain 'statutory magic' which can reverse the effect of the *nemo dat quod non habet* rule. This suggests that if a pre-root deed included too much land in the plan or purported to operate as a conveyance rather than an assignment of a lease, although subsequent deeds would be defective, first registration on the basis of such deeds would operate to confer a statutory title.

The potential for first registration to cure all title defects is limited for three reasons. First, the requirement to apply for first registration is dependent on a triggering transaction—currently a conveyance on sale of freehold land, or a grant or assignment on sale of a leasehold interest. These triggers could, of course, be extended so that any dealing with the land would make first registration compulsory,[41] but it cannot be ignored that land can remain in families for decades or even generations without formally changing hands. In such circumstances, it seems unlikely that those with current entitlements would voluntarily apply for first registration and so this land may remain unregistered for the foreseeable future.

The second difficulty with relying on first registration to cure defective titles is that the PRA must be satisfied with the title before it can be registered. Currently, if the purchase money does not exceed €1,000,000, registration can take place on the basis of what is known as a Form 3 application. This form includes a declaration that the applicant's solicitor has investigated the title and a certificate that the last instrument on title conveyed (or vested) the fee simple interest or the leasehold interest in the property in the applicant, free from adverse interests, restrictive covenants or incumbrances except those disclosed.[42] The PRA will not investigate the title and will register on the basis of the solicitor's certificate. Certification by the solicitor is not the appropriate route to apply for first registration where anything out of the ordinary is revealed by the solicitor's investigation of the title or any plans accompanying the deeds. In such circumstances, the application should be made pursuant to Form 1, which places the onus on the PRA to investigate the title.[43] The examination of title conducted on behalf of the PRA is designed to ascertain that the applicant has

38 See the Registration of Title Act 1964, s 24.

39 Registration of Title Act 1964, s 37.

40 [1984] EWCA Civ J 1018-1, 8.

41 s 53 of the Registration of Deeds and Title Act 2006 amended s 24 of the Registration of Title Act 1964, and permits the Minister for Justice and Equality to make an order extending the types of disposition which will trigger the requirement to register.

42 Rule 19 of the Land Registry Rules 2012 (SI 483/2012).

43 Rule 14 of the Land Registry Rules 2012.

a good holding title.[44] Generally, the root must be at least 15 years old, although the PRA may accept a root that is at least 12 years old if the market value of the property does not exceed €1,000,000.[45] The PRA has actively pursued a pro-registration policy over the last few decades and if a deed of rectification is not a feasible option, it may be satisfied that certain adverse interests have been barred by the possession of the applicant's predecessor in title and register with an absolute title on that basis. It should be noted that it is also now possible to apply for first registration of a qualified title.[46] This may be appropriate where the period of title shown is too short. With the extension of compulsory first registration, it was recognised that there may be situations where proof of an absolute title simply cannot be obtained. An application may be made to convert a qualified title to absolute[47] when appropriate—for example, when the root is now of sufficient length. Therefore, the investigation of title conducted by the PRA may identify and, hopefully, resolve certain title defects.

However, the defect may have arisen in a deed executed before the deed which is being treated as the root. Also, in some circumstances the defect may not be apparent on an inspection of the title alone—for example, where there is a discrepancy between the identity of the land conveyed on the ground and on the plan attached to the deed. In such circumstances, those with adverse interests may emerge to challenge the title after it has been registered. This leads us to the third difficulty with relying on the register to cure title defects. Section 31 of the 1964 Act, which recognises the conclusive nature of the register, also notes that nothing in the Act shall interfere with the jurisdiction of any court on the ground of fraud or mistake to make an order directing the register to be rectified. Essentially, this preserves the jurisdiction of the court to grant the equitable remedy of rectification.[48] The danger is that the defect may give rise to proceedings to rectify the register. As Gray and Gray note:

> Title plans may be ever so slightly awry; pre-registration deeds and subsequent dispositionary documents may themselves contain inaccuracies; undisclosed interests may suddenly emerge as affecting the land; initial assessments of the reliability of the title offered for first registration may turn out, in the event to have been misjudged.[49]

The statutory jurisdiction of the court to order a rectification of the register in such circumstances appears to be limited to circumstances where it can be achieved without injustice to any person.[50] Fitzgerald notes that this implies that the court would not upset the registration of an owner who was registered on foot of a transfer for value and purchased the lands in good faith.[51] It should also be noted that if an

[44] Rule 18 of the Land Registry Rules 2012.

[45] Rule 19(1) and (2) of the Land Registry Rules 2012.

[46] Registration of Title Act 1964, ss 33 and 40 as amended by the Registration of Deeds and Title Act 2006, ss 56 and 57.

[47] Rule 39 of the Land Registry Rules 2012.

[48] See Woods, 'English Law on Adverse Possession' (n 10) 19–21.

[49] K Gray and SF Gray, *Elements of Land Law*, 5th edn (Oxford, Oxford University Press, 2009) para 2.2.60.

[50] See Registration of Title Act, s 32(1) (as amended by the Registration of Deeds and Title Act 2006, s 55), which sets out how errors in registration may be rectified.

[51] See Fitzgerald (n 19) 446.

order for rectification is made or refused, there may be an entitlement to compensation from the state.[52]

To illustrate the circumstances in which the court may order the register to be rectified, we shall consider the two defects mentioned earlier. First, it should be noted that rectification of a deed is typically ordered where it does not reflect the pre-existing agreement of the parties.[53] Presumably, the same principles apply to the rectification of the register. Therefore, in a straightforward case where the vendor conveyed too much of his own land to a purchaser, who then proceeded to register that deed in the Land Registry, there should be no difficulty in the vendor obtaining a rectification of the register to reflect the true agreement if that agreement can be proved. Matters are less straightforward if the remedy of rectification accrued in an earlier transaction. However, the case law does illustrate that, in certain circumstances, rectification may be claimed by successors in title to the original agreement or third parties affected by the defect who were not privy to the original agreement.[54]

At this point, it becomes necessary to consider the impact of the conclusive nature of the register. If a transaction in favour of a purchaser for value has taken place since first registration, it is generally assumed that the remedy of rectification would not be awarded, as a purchaser is entitled to rely on the register as conclusive. Recently, however, an exception to this general principle was recognised by the High Court in *Boyle v Connaughton*:[55] if the person entitled to the remedy of rectification was in actual occupation of the land in question or in receipt of the rents or profits from the land, this may be construed as an overriding interest which will bind a purchaser, unless enquiries are made and the interest is not revealed. In that case, a discrepancy between the boundaries as they appeared on the ground and on the Land Registry map gave the defendants' predecessors in title a right to rectify the register which passed to the defendants when they bought the land. When their neighbours' land, including the disputed plot, was sold to the plaintiffs, as it was occupied by persons with a right of rectification, this right was held to bind the plaintiffs as an overriding interest. The register could be altered to give effect to such an overriding interest and, as Breen points out, the purchaser in such circumstances has no entitlement to compensation from the state.[56]

What, then, are the implications, in these circumstances, of the other defect which was mentioned—where someone entitled to a leasehold interest mistakenly conveyed a fee simple in a deed executed many decades ago and the vendor was registered as the owner of a fee simple on that basis? Would a court order the rectification of the register if, following a transaction in favour of a purchaser, the lessor appeared on the scene? Presumably, the lessor was not actually receiving or demanding rent in

[52] Registration of Title Act 1964, s 120.

[53] See H Biehler, *Equity and the Law of Trusts in Ireland*, 6th edn (Dublin, Round Hall Press, 2016) Ch 16.

[54] See the *obiter* discussion of this issue by Murphy J in *Lac Minerals Limited v Chevron Mineral Corporation of Ireland* [1995] 1 ILRM 161, 178. See also *Boyle v Connaughton* [2000] IEHC 28 (discussed below).

[55] [2000] IEHC 28.

[56] O Breen, 'Registration of Title and Overriding Interests—Another Crack in the Mirror?' (2000) 5 *Conveyancing and Property Law Journal* 52, 58–59.

relation to the land and therefore it seems unlikely that the court would treat his interest as an overriding one. This would suggest that the registration of the purchaser who relied on the register would not be disturbed, although the lessor may be entitled to compensation from the state.

To summarise, if the person possessing a right to rectify the register was in actual occupation when the (post-first registration) transaction occurred, this right shall constitute an overriding interest which binds a purchaser. However, if the owner of the adverse interest was not in actual occupation, first registration could be viewed as the first step in cleansing any defects in title. The second step is a transaction in favour of a purchaser for value who relies on the register in good faith. Although the extension of compulsory first registration may identify or, in time, resolve certain defects in title, the potential for certain interests to survive a transaction in favour of a purchaser as an overriding interest illustrates the dangers of complacency in this regard.

Issues arising from defects in title tend to be resolved in a satisfactory manner in Ireland through the operation of a combination of doctrines, remedies, conveyancing practices and the requirement for a first registration. Some adverse claims which are not revealed by a standard investigation of title are defeated by adverse possession, while others are not because of the postponement of the limitation period or the inability to prove adverse possession throughout the limitation period. Adverse possession plays a role in curing title defects, but only a complementary one. Some defects may be revealed by an investigation of title by the purchaser's solicitor or the PRA, and may result in a qualified title being conferred on first registration; this qualification may eventually be cured through the passage of time. Other defects may not be revealed by such an investigation and may survive first registration and perhaps even a transaction in favour of a purchaser for value relying on the register. The recognition that a right of rectification may be converted into an overriding interest when coupled with actual occupation of the land in question achieves a fair result, in this author's view, in identifying the point at which the dynamic security of purchasers should give way to the static security of the owner of the interest.

IV. EVALUATING ALTERNATIVE METHODS OF QUIETING TITLE: MARKETABLE TITLE LEGISLATION AND 'COLOUR OF TITLE' ADVERSE POSSESSION

The remainder of this chapter is chiefly devoted to outlining two methods of quieting title which have enjoyed success in the United States and discussing the merits of formally recognising a concept similar to 'colour of title' adverse possession in Irish law as a necessary adjunct to the introduction of a qualified veto system. As has been described elsewhere, the registered title system failed to become established in the United States[57] and investigation of title traditionally required establishing

[57] See T Barnet, 'The Uniform Registered State Land and Adverse Possession Reform Act, A Proposal for Reform of the United States Real Property Law' (2004) 12 *Buffalo Environmental Law Journal* 1, 19–20.

a chain of title back to the original grant from the government. Recording Acts were introduced to provide a public record of conveyancing transactions and to resolve priority disputes. The recording system eventually became cumbersome to navigate; as ownership passed from person to person, the period of search became longer and the number of instruments that made up the chain of title increased.[58] The title examination process became 'dominated by overabundant caution and ultra-meticulous judgments'.[59]

In the United States, lawyers have been more willing to acknowledge the limitations of the doctrine of adverse possession in protecting the purchaser from defects in the chain of title. As is the case in other common law jurisdictions, the limitation period does not run against the owners of future interests or in circumstances of legal disability. However, it is submitted that the most serious shortcoming with the doctrine's role in quieting title in the United States is the requirement for a court application to secure a title by adverse possession.[60]

The difficulties involved in investigating title prompted the introduction of marketable title legislation in many states in the 1940s and 1950s. Although this legislation varies slightly from state to state, it typically provides that any person who has an unbroken chain of title of record to any interest in land for 40 years shall, at the end of such period, be deemed to have a marketable title provided that no other person is in hostile possession of the land.[61] It also operates as a statute of limitations, extinguishing all claims and interests which originate prior to that period of time unless a notice of the relevant interest has been recorded within the period. Even the interests of persons suffering from a disability and future interests are extinguished by marketable title legislation, in contrast to their more privileged position under the doctrine of adverse possession.[62]

In an article published in 2009, the present author argued that a requirement to register certain older interests, which forms the basis of the marketable title approach in the United States, could be successfully adopted in England and Wales to relieve the unwarranted pressure imposed on the doctrine of adverse possession to cure defects in unregistered titles and allow law reformers to contemplate extending the veto system to unregistered land.[63] In the English context, such an approach would provide for the extinguishment of a legal interest which was created or acquired more than 15 years ago and was not referred to in the title deduced by the vendor unless the owner of the interest (or his tenant or licensee) was in possession of the land at the date of the disposition or his estate or interest had previously been

[58] HM Cross, 'Weaknesses of the Present Recording System' (1962) 47 *Iowa Law Review* 245; PE Basye, 'Trends and Progress—The Marketable Title Acts' (1962) 47 *Iowa Law Review* 261.

[59] See Basye (ibid) 265.

[60] In Ireland, of course, it is possible to apply to the PRA for registration of an absolute or good leasehold title on the basis of adverse possession (see Registration of Title Act 1964, s 49), although the decision of the PRA in this regard may be appealed to the court (1964 Act, s 19).

[61] The requirement that no other person be in hostile possession is designed to eliminate the possibility of wild deeds and separate chains of title—see RH Powell, 'Marketable Record Title Act: Wild, Forged and Void Deeds as Roots of Title' (1969) 22 *University of Florida Law Review* 669, 272.

[62] Note, however, that the Act expressly allows anyone to record a notice on behalf of a person under disability, a minor or someone whose identity cannot be established or is uncertain at the time.

[63] See Woods, 'English Law on Adverse Possession' (n 10) 23–24.

registered in the Land Registry. If the older interest in question amounted to a legal estate, the owner would be required to apply for first registration of that estate. Provision could be made for the registration of a caution against first registration or a caveat in the Land Registry to protect (and, in this particular context, to confer priority on) other legal interests not amounting to an estate. An extensive advertising campaign and a transitional period were also proposed to ensure that the holders of the interests affected would be given the opportunity to protect them. It was argued that the extinguishment of unregistered property rights could be justified on the basis that it permits technical defects in conveyancing to be eliminated in a targeted and effective manner. The author has noted that similar measures in the United States have withstood constitutional scrutiny.[64]

On deeper reflection, however, it is submitted that the introduction of a requirement to register certain older interests adds little to the current law relied on to resolve title defects and is not the most pragmatic way to facilitate the extension of the veto system of adverse possession to unregistered land. This becomes apparent once the two title defects discussed earlier are considered. The third party affected by a deed which mistakenly included his boundary strip is unlikely to be aware that his ownership interest is at risk and, consequently, of the need to register. In many states, marketable title legislation does not cure the title defect which arises where a deed in the chain of title mistakenly purported to act as a conveyance rather than an assignment of a lease, as the requirement to register does not extend to the interest of a lessor. It could also be argued that the introduction of such an approach is unnecessary in conveyancing systems which already benefit from a functioning concept of marketability. Titles which can be deduced for 15 years beginning with a good root are regarded as marketable in Ireland. Although certain pre-root adverse interests may not be extinguished by the doctrine of adverse possession and could emerge to cast a cloud on the title of the current owner, it is submitted that the current multifaceted approach to the resolution of such disputes achieves a good balance between static and dynamic security. It also achieves a result in practice that is similar to the result achieved under marketable title legislation which preserves an older unregistered interest if its owner is in possession of the land. As has already been discussed,[65] in Ireland, the right to rectify the register when coupled with actual occupation of the land in question amounts to an overriding interest which will bind a purchaser who relies on the register.[66]

A. Colour of Title Adverse Possession

A second mechanism used to quiet title, which is exclusive to the United States, is the provision made for colour of title adverse possession. According to the Supreme

[64] See 'Constitutionality of Marketable Title Legislation' 47 (1961–62) *Iowa Law Review* 413.

[65] See text accompanying nn 55–56 above.

[66] Note that in England a rectification of the register shall not generally be ordered if the registered proprietor is in possession of the land when the mistake comes to light—Land Registration Act 2002, sch 4, paras 3(2) and 6(2).

Court of the United States, 'The courts have concurred it is believed, without an exception, in defining "color of title" to be that which in appearance is title, but which in reality is no title'.[67] In a similar vein, the Arkansas Supreme Court adopted the following definition:

> Color of title is in law, no title at all. It is a void paper, having the semblance of a muniment of title, to which, for certain purposes, the law attributes certain qualities of title ... It must purport to pass title. In form, it must be a deed, a will or some other paper or instrument by which title usually and ordinarily passes.[68]

The origins of this particular application of the doctrine of adverse possession are interesting.[69] It was the product of legislative and judicial responses to distinctly American economic and geographic realities in the context of the early settlement of the country. The land was wild and uncultivated, and was generally granted by the government and resold in large tracts. In the early days, records of state grants were not well kept and grants were often duplicated or overlapped. Many deeds were defective as few lawyers resided in the back country and speculative trading resulted in land being sold several times over, resulting in a great confusion of land titles.

Colour of title confers a number of benefits on the adverse possessor. Such a claimant may avail himself of a much shorter limitation period, often only five or seven years. The claimant also benefits from the doctrine of constructive possession, which deems a claimant who was only in possession of part of the tract to be in constructive possession of the entire tract as described in the deed constituting colour of title. This doctrine of constructive possession developed as, in the early pioneer days, families lived on such huge tracts of land that it was impossible to actually possess the whole tract. Under the doctrine of adverse possession as traditionally applied, a claimant may only gain title to the land which he or she actually possesses, but this rule was not reasonable in light of the conditions prevailing at the time.[70] The doctrine of constructive possession was later limited so that the constructive possession of the adverse possessor under colour of title could not extend to land in the actual possession of the rightful owner.

It seems to be generally accepted that colour of title requires some written instrument which purports to pass title to a definitely described tract. Private deeds,[71] wills[72] and judgments[73] have all been held to constitute colour of title. Colour of title adverse possession is commonly used in the United States when a tax deed is ineffective in conferring title on the purchaser due to some procedural defect in the manner in which the sale was carried out.[74] Frequently a deed cannot constitute colour of

[67] *Wright v Mattison* 18 How 50 (1855).

[68] See *Bailey v Jarvis* 208 SW 2d (Ark 1948) 13, 15, quoting *State v King* 87 SE 170, 171 (W Va 1915).

[69] See CA Phipps, 'Adverse Possession—Color of Title—Origin of Doctrine' (1942–43) 22 *Oregon Law Review* 188; MC Kalo, 'The Doctrine of Color of Title in North Carolina' (1981–82) 13 *North Carolina Central Law Journal* 123.

[70] The doctrine of constructive possession may also be based on an analogy with real title, which deems the owner in possession of part of his land to be in possession of the entire plot—see Phipps (ibid) 192–93.

[71] *Lofton v Barber* 226 NC 481.

[72] *Chambers v Chambers* 235 NC 749.

[73] *United States v Chatham* 208 F Supp 220.

[74] See eg *Ruark v Harper* 173 NC 249.

title if it contains a defect which is so obviously ineffective that a person of ordinary capacity could not be misled by it.[75] Finally, the deed must be recorded or registered to constitute colour of title, where the dispute involves a purchaser for value or lien creditor who derives his rights from the same source as that asserted by the adverse claimant.[76]

The conditions prevailing in the pioneering days no longer exist in the United States and Phipps has called for the abolition of colour of title adverse possession on that basis.[77] However, Kalo argues that colour of title is not 'an outdated historical curiosity'.[78] He maintains that adverse possession under colour of title represents a significant method of curing defective titles and its potential should not be overlooked. It is interesting to note that in 1995 legislation was enacted in Arkansas[79] which made it necessary to prove colour of title (and the payment of taxes) in addition to the common law elements of the doctrine of adverse possession. This reform was designed to prevent the 'theft' of land without nullifying the positive effects of current adverse possession laws.[80]

B. How Would 'Colour of Title' Adverse Possession Operate in Ireland?

It is submitted that the extension of a veto system of adverse possession to unregistered land could be facilitated by the creation of an exception to cater for the adverse possessor of unregistered land who can also prove a title which approximates 'colour of title' in American terms. This exception would be specifically designed to cure defects or uncertainties in title. Where an application for first registration is made by a person who can prove possession for 12 years which commenced under a defective title, in most cases a person with technical rights in the land due to a defect in title would not be entitled to object to or veto the application.[81]

In the current compulsory registration environment, this facility would operate in tandem with the option for an applicant to apply for first registration with a qualified title if it is not yet possible to prove adverse possession for the limitation period. In due course, most defects would be cured by the passage of time. This approach emulates what is happening in practice in the Land Registry which adopts

[75] See Kalo (n 69) 144–45.
[76] See Kalo (n 69) 145–48.
[77] Phipps (n 69) 197–98.
[78] Kalo (n 69) 157.
[79] Act 776 of 1995, now codified at Arkansas Code Annotated Section 18-11-106. The immediate motivation for the reforms stemmed from reactions to the 'Kiesling litigation', which involved an individual deliberately attempting to rely on the doctrine to acquire title by adverse possession—see SP Raley, 'Color of Title and Payment of Taxes: The New Requirements Under Arkansas Adverse Possession Law' (1997) 50 *Arkansas Law Review* 489.
[80] See the comments of Senator Mike Beebe, Minutes of Joint Interim Committee on Judiciary, 20 April 1994, 2.
[81] Although the deed that included a boundary strip which was not owned by the vendor was defective, this defect could be cured by proof of adverse possession for the standard 12-year limitation period. In the case of a deed which purported to convey a fee simple when the vendor was only entitled to a leasehold interest, the standard 12-year limitation period would not suffice to extinguish the rights of the lessor, who could object on that basis if aware of the application.

a pro-registration approach and where registrations frequently occur on the basis of an imperfect title where the defect cannot be cured if it is accompanied by proof of 12 years' possession.

It is submitted, however, that this analogy with colour of title adverse possession should not be overextended. For example, an adverse possessor with a defective title should only be in a position to apply to be registered as the owner of land in his actual possession; it is not appropriate to adopt the American concept of constructive possession in such circumstances. It is also submitted that the existence of defects appearing on the face of the deed should not preclude proof of a qualifying defective title. As this category of adverse possessor would be subject to a much longer limitation period than in the United States, the more lenient approach in this respect is justifiable. It is important to remember that if the defect could have been rectified in a more expedient manner, that would have happened. The main aim of this exception would be to allow the land in question to be brought within the registration of title system.

C. Practical Difficulties with the Extension of the Veto System to Unregistered Land

The Law Commission for England and Wales has noted that it would not be easy to replicate the new veto system in relation to unregistered land.[82] The most obvious difficulty arises where the paper owner or his address cannot be ascertained. In such circumstances the owner would have been denied the benefit of the opportunity to veto the application, and it may also be impossible to obtain details of the extinguished title. If such a squatter applies for first registration on the basis of adverse possession and the Land Registry proceeds to register him with a fee simple absolute, there is a danger that a lessor or the owner of a future interest whose interest has not been extinguished could emerge at a later date and bring a claim for rectification of the register.

It is important to note that this is a challenge which may currently confront the PRA on an application for first registration based on possession.[83] Typically, the applicant's solicitor would be required to carry out the same searches which are necessary to reconstruct a lost title. A General Valuation Office[84] search may identify the occupiers and immediate lessors, providing names which could be searched against in the Registry of Deeds. In urban areas, knowledge of local pyramid titles (where land is subject to a series of successive fee farm grants and sub-grants and/or leases and sub-leases)[85] may be of assistance. Indeed, it could be argued that in Ireland the prevalence of pyramid titles means that owners are more identifiable than

[82] UK LC 254, above n 1, para 10.45.

[83] See PRA Practice Direction, *First Registration and other Examiner Cases*, available at www.prai.ie/first-registration-and-other-examiner-cases, para 2.1 (accessed on 8 September 2016).

[84] The Valuation Office maintains an archive containing rateable valuation information of all property in the state from the mid-1850s until the early 1990s; and commercial property only from that time.

[85] For an example illustrating the complexity of such titles, see JCW Wylie, *Irish Land Law*, 5th edn (London, Bloomsbury Professional, 2013) para [4.187].

in England in cases where the title has been lost. However, it is not unusual, even in Ireland, for the standard searches to yield no helpful information. If the owner of the property cannot be identified with reasonable precision, the current practice of examiners of title is to insist that the applicant demonstrates 30 years' possession, to ensure that the rights of an owner with a disability would be extinguished.[86] This confers extra protection on the unidentified owner, but the introduction of the scheme proposed by this chapter would mean that such an owner was deprived of his veto. The new scheme should, therefore, require reasonable efforts to be made to identify the owner and obtain details of his title—for example, through the display of site notices and newspaper advertisements. However, if such efforts fail, it is difficult to see how the hazards of registering an applicant with a fee simple absolute can be avoided, particularly if the application relates to land located in a rural area which is unlikely to be subject to a pyramid title. It could be argued that the PRA should register the applicant with only a qualified title in such circumstances. However, without the possibility of converting such a title to absolute in the future (and this could only be facilitated if further evidence of the title came to light), the marketability of such land would be perpetually reduced. As a last resort, for example, where the application relates to urban land and it is more difficult to rule out the probability of a pyramid title, the PRA may register the applicant with a possessory title.[87] However, this title may be converted into a fee simple absolute on the registration of a transfer for valuable consideration when the land has been registered for 15 years.[88]

The existence of these small pockets of land where the owner and his title cannot be identified must be acknowledged, and the problem they pose for conveyancing practice must be confronted. If the registration of title system is to be extended to the entire country, in keeping with the PRA's statutory mandate,[89] the title to such properties will eventually have to be registered despite these challenging 'clouds' or 'stains' on the title. In many cases, the owner may not be aware of their ownership or may have abandoned the property many years ago. If someone has been in adverse possession for the limitation period, it is proposed that a pragmatic approach should be taken: the applicant should be registered with an absolute freehold title in circumstances where the land is unlikely to be subject to a pyramid title, or a possessory title where a pyramid title is a distinct probability. Following first registration, there would be a small risk of a lessor or the owner of a future interest in the land emerging at a later date and seeking a rectification of the register. However, this danger would be eliminated following a registered transfer in favour of a purchaser for

[86] See PRA Practice Direction (n 83) para 2.1.

[87] ibid. See also PRA Practice Direction, *Adverse Possession—First Registration*, available at www.prai.ie/adverse-possession-first-registration (accessed on 8 September 2016). Note that in England the Land Registry has also adopted a policy of registering the applicant with a possessory title in such circumstances—see *Land Registry Practice Guide 5*, para 5.4, available at www.gov.uk/government/publications/adverse-possession-of-1-unregistered-land-and-2-registered-land/practice-guide-5-adverse-possession-of-1-unregistered-and-2-registered-land-where-a-right-to-be-registered-was-acquired-before-13-october-2003#land-registrys-response-and-registration (accessed on 8 September 2016). A possessory title may be upgraded in certain circumstances, see Land Registration Act 2002, s 62.

[88] See s 50(2) of the Registration of Title Act 1964 and PRA Practice Direction (ibid).

[89] Registration of Deeds and Title Act 2006, s 10(1)(b).

value, preceded by the passage of a further 15 years in the case of a possessory title. The proofs submitted in the adverse possession application would eliminate the possibility that such a right to rectify could amount to an overriding interest. Therefore, the title would be immune from challenge at that point in time. However, the lessor or the owner of the future interest may, in such circumstances, be entitled to claim compensation from the state.

V. CONCLUSION

This chapter demonstrates that a qualified veto system of adverse possession, if introduced in Ireland, could be extended to unregistered land in a manner which would not affect the functionality of the unregistered conveyancing system and may even facilitate the extension of the registration of title system. The divergence between adverse possession of registered and unregistered land introduced in England and Wales by the Land Registration Act 2002 is far from ideal, and it is submitted that the reform of the doctrine need not necessarily lead to two different systems of adverse possession. In the context of unregistered land, the veto could not be exercised by someone with rights because of a defect in the chain of title, following an application for first registration of a defective title by someone who can demonstrate 12 years' adverse possession. This approach would allow the owners of unregistered land to benefit from the veto in the face of an adverse possession application, but would also ensure that the registration of title system can ultimately be extended to the most uncertain of titles.

5

Repudiatory Breach of Leases—Hard Lessons for the 'Contractualisation' of Leasehold Law

WARREN BARR*

I. INTRODUCTION

A CONSIDERABLE PERIOD of time has passed since the English courts acknowledged that contractual termination principles could be applied to leases—first frustration in 1981, by the then House of Lords;[1] then repudiatory breach of contract, in 1992.[2] In the intervening years, there have been a handful of reported cases in England and Wales that have sought to clarify the operation of repudiatory breach of contract as it applies to the leasehold bargain, though none at appellate level where the operation of that doctrine has been central to the case presented.

This is, in a very real sense, perplexing. In the intervening years, the property market has felt the effects of numerous financial crises, before and after the deep global recession triggered by the American sub-prime mortgage market. One might have expected a veritable rash of both landlords and tenants seeking to terminate leases in these troubling economic conditions, but this has not happened, or at least the reported cases do not suggest that it has, as they are scant in both number and scope.[3]

That said, a reasonable amount of academic and (extra-)judicial ink has been spilt on the question of whether repudiatory breach (and frustration) should apply to leases,[4] as part of a wider question of what is known as 'contractualisation' of the

* School of Law & Social Justice, University of Liverpool. My thanks are due to Dr David Capper, Dr Juanita Roche and Professor Nicolas Hopkins for their questions and comments at the conference, which have undoubtedly improved the quality of this chapter and led to an alteration of the title in consequence. Any errors or omissions remain mine alone.

[1] *National Carriers Ltd v Panalpina (Northern) Ltd* [1981] 2 AC 45.

[2] *Hussein v Mehlman* [1992] 2 EGLR 87.

[3] One of the reasons might be that there has been a marked increase in the number of tenants going into liquidation or being made bankrupt, with liquidators and trustees in bankruptcy disclaiming leases as 'onerous property' under ss 178–82 or ss 315–21 of the Insolvency Act 1986.

[4] No lesser persons than Lords Millet and Neuberger have clashed on the desirability of repudiatory breach as a remedy for landlord and tenant in the Blundell lectures 2000 (Falcon Chambers).

lease, a concept that, as Bright has neatly expressed it,[5] describes the move to treat the regulation of the lease as more than property, but 'property plus' other obligations. This is to suggest that although the lease involves both contract and property, the fact that it normally creates an estate in land (so-called *Bruton* tenancies aside)[6] is not the sole focus of the relationship in practice, nor should it preclude the application of more general contractual doctrine to the leasehold context. Generally, viewing the lease as a contract has been welcomed, and it appears to be an established process of thinking in Anglo-Welsh law, albeit with some disquiet expressed at times in the developing case law, as will become apparent. Parliamentary intervention has followed the trend of viewing leases as contracts, with residential letting agreements in England and Wales entered into on or after 1 October 2015 now eligible to be regulated in line with other consumer contracts under the Consumer Rights Act 2015.[7] Also, in Wales, housing law has moved away from leases in a proprietary sense to the creation of contractual occupation agreements, regulated under the Renting Homes (Wales) Act 2016.[8]

This chapter will re-examine the impact of the decision in *Hussein v Mehlman*,[9] which introduced the doctrine of repudiatory breach into landlord and tenant law in England and Wales.[10] It will suggest that some of the initial concerns concerning the importation of the doctrine have been assuaged, but that more significant, 'bright line' issues have emerged.[11] The major concern is that the doctrine operates differently depending on whether the claimant is either the landlord or tenant, which is both unprecedented in other common law jurisdictions that allow repudiatory breach of leases and creates serious anomalies in the law. Using repudiatory breach as a case study, the chapter will also consider whether the importation of contract principles has benefited the regulation of leases more generally and suggest that, while it is proper to treat leases as contracts in many respects, it is preferable to regulate them primarily as property rights.

[5] S Bright, *Landlord and Tenant Law in Context* (Oxford, Hart Publishing, 2007) 30–33.

[6] The 'non-estate' or 'Bruton' tenancy, is considered below.

[7] Not only must letting agents now declare all fees upfront (s 83), but the unfair contract terms approach (Part 2) now applies to individually negotiated terms in leases or licences for occupation of property, which used to fall outside the remit of unfair contract terms. Similarly, lettings of furnished premises may well fall within the definition of a contract for the hire of goods (pt 1, Ch 2, s 3(2)(a)), which may lead to the implication of terms as to quality and fitness for a specified purpose (ss 9–14).

[8] This received Royal Assent on the 18 January 2016, and was based on Law Commission, *Renting Homes in Wales* (Law Com No 337, 2013), following *Renting Homes: The Final Report* (Law Com No 297, 2007). English law has not adopted these changes.

[9] One reason for focusing on repudiatory breach is that, at the time of writing, an actionable case of frustration of a lease has yet to be recorded in the law reports, and the particular issues that arise from such an action have already been explored elsewhere—see W Barr, 'Frustration of Leases—The Hazards of Contractualisation' (2001) 52 *Northern Ireland Legal Quarterly* 82.

[10] While the approach in Anglo-Welsh law will be contrasted to key developments in other Commonwealth jurisdictions, where appropriate, it is not within the ambit of this chapter to consider what lessons might be learnt from the treatment of repudiatory breach in other jurisdictions: that has been done elsewhere—see W Barr 'Repudiation of Leases: A Fool's Paradise' in P Jackson and D Wilde (eds), *Contemporary Property Law* (London, Ashgate, 2000); M Pawlowski and M Brown, 'Contractual Termination of Leases: Lessons from the Commonwealth: Part 1' [2009] *Landlord & Tenant Review* 145; 'Part 2' [2009] *Landlord & Tenant Review* 182; 'Part 3' [2009] *Landlord & Tenant Review* 216.

[11] See Barr, 'Repudiation of Leases' (n 10). More generally, see J Morgan 'Leases: Property, Contract or More?' in M Dixon (ed), *Modern Studies in Property Law*, vol 5 (Oxford, Hart Publishing, 2009).

II. THE 'CONTRACTUALISATION' OF LEASES: CONTEXT AND PROBLEMS

Before embarking on re-examination of repudiatory breach, it important to consider the nature of the leasehold bargain and the issue of contractualisation of leases. It is a trite proposition that the lease (or tenancy) has a duality of legal character; that it is a 'hybrid, part contract and part property'.[12] No one denies that the contractual character of a lease is significant, but the key to the contractualisation debate lies in whether the proprietary nature of a lease means that the contract should or should not regulate the agreement in the same way as it would any other contract agreed between parties, giving landlords and tenants the same remedies for breach of contract as other contracting parties.

The arguments for applying contractual remedies to leases have often been rehearsed, but can be summarised in the words of Lord Roskill:

> However much weight one may give to the fact that a lease creates an estate in land in favour of the lessee, in truth it is by no means always in that estate in land in which the lessee is interested. In many cases, he is interested only in the accompanying contractual right to use that which is demised to him by the lease, and the estate in land which he acquires has little or no meaning for him.[13]

To suggest that the proprietary nature of a lease might still preclude the full reach of the contractual arm 'conjures up images of parchment and sealing wax, of copperplate handwriting and fusty title deeds'.[14] Nevertheless, there are very real reasons to argue that the very nature of the leasehold itself should deny these remedies.

A. The Impact of the Estate in Land

The presence of the estate in land, which is central to the concept of a lease, is one element that not recognised in contract law and was, for many years, the reason why it was felt that leases, as property rights, could not be subject to contractual rules to terminate the relationship.[15] It is part of the central distinction between a lease (tenancy), which is a method of property ownership, and a licence to occupy property, which is a permission to use and occupy land, but does not endure against third parties in itself like the lease. For many in the legal world, however, this central distinction between the two forms of occupation is no longer a given.[16] Lord

[12] *Linden Garden Trusts Ltd v Lenesta Disposals Ltd* [1993] 3 All ER 417.

[13] *National Carriers Ltd v Panalpinia (Northern) Ltd* [1981] 2 AC 45, per Lord Roskill.

[14] *Johnston & Sons Ltd v Holland* [1988] 1 EGLR 264, 267j per Nicholls LJ (talking, in that case, about the concept of non-derogation from grant).

[15] The presence of an estate did not impress their Lordships in *National Carriers v Panalpina* (n 13), though no actual consideration of the nature of the estate was undertaken by the majority in reaching their decisions. See Barr, 'Frustration of Leases' (n 9).

[16] Similarly, some commentators feel that the lease/licence distinction creates problems—see H Carr, 'The Sorting of Forks from the Spades: An Unnecessary Distraction in Housing Law?' in D Cowan (ed), *Housing: Participation and Exclusion* (London, Ashgate, 2000) 107, who argues that differentiating occupation agreements (and their legal consequences) creates a great deal of confusion for housing providers, to the detriment of vulnerable groups. This, of course, is no longer a distinction contained in Welsh housing law.

Hoffman's (in)famous speech in *Bruton v London Quadrant Housing Trust*,[17] as later explained in *Kay v London Borough Lambeth*,[18] confirmed that it is possible to have the relationship of landlord and tenant on a contractual level, distinct from a licence.[19] This led a number of commentators to rethink the very basis of the leasehold relationship and the lease/licence distinction, and to suggest that there is no need for an estate. *Bruton* provides, it is argued, a welcome clarification of the law, as it is all about relativity of title and protecting possession.[20] This view of *Bruton* has won judicial acceptance at the highest level; Lord Neuberger said in *Mexfield v Berrisford* that 'Bruton was *about relativity of title which is the traditional bedrock of English land law*'.[21] Some commentators have thus suggested that a licensee in possession is seised in fee, and that 'consensual possession is the root of title'.[22]

This is going too far. While title is relative, it is *adverse* possession, not possession, which explains the root of title. A licensee is not in adverse possession as their occupation is explained by their licence.[23] On this reasoning, 'the licensee's possession merely supports the enjoyment by their licensor of their estate. *Bruton* itself was decided consistently with that approach. It is also one accordant with indications that one can be in possession merely qua licensee'.[24]

The centrality of the lease/licence distinction as the boundary between proprietary and contractual forms of occupation of land therefore survives. *Bruton* tenancies are an anomalous footnote, as the fact that they do not appear to bind third parties, or attract rights that a licence does not, means that it is understandable that the case law has not been swamped with parties claiming that a 'non-estate tenancy' has been created by the document they entered into, rather than a contractual licence. The fact remains that an estate in land is a feature of a lease. This is significant, because one question left unaddressed by the importation of contractual doctrine is how a contractual doctrine would end the lease as a matter of legal theory. The central issue is whether the contractual doctrine of repudiatory breach operates within property law or outside and independently from it. In other words, does repudiatory breach need to make use of property law to bring about the destruction of the leasehold estate or can it do so on simple contractual principles? The consensus is that an integrated approach is required, because of the presence of an estate in land.[25]

17 [2000] 1 AC 406.

18 [2006] 2 WLR 570.

19 This has been classed as a 'non-estate' tenancy by Lord Scott in *Kay* (ibid), and it is clear that, whatever the limits of this type of contractual tenancy, the ability to bind parties outside of the contracting landlord and tenant is no different to a contractual licence.

20 See, eg, J Hill, '*The Proprietary Character of Possession*' in E Cooke (ed), *Modern Studies in Property Law*, vol 1 (Oxford, Hart Publishing, 2001); K Lewison, 'The Nature of a Lease and the Applicability of Principles of Repudiation and Acceptance' [2007] *Landlord and Tenant Bulletin* 2, who argues that 'the creation of the relationship of landlord and tenant will always create an estate in land, but one which may not bind a person having a better right. There is no such thing as a "non-estate tenancy"; but the estate may be a precarious one'.

21 [2011] UKSC 52, [62] (emphasis added).

22 A Baker, 'Bruton, Licences and a Fiction of Title' [2014] *The Conveyancer and Property Lawyer* 494.

23 See *Roberts v Swangroves Estates* [2007] EWHC 513 (Ch).

24 Baker (n 22) 506.

25 Three broad methods have been suggested: viewing the lease as executory, on the basis of the implied covenant of quiet enjoyment (see C Chew, 'The Application of the Contractual Doctrine of Repudiation to Real Property Leases' (1990) 20 *Western Australia Law Review* 86); the use of a fiction of implied

There is still something of a conceptual 'muddle' about the underpinning theory by which an estate is terminated, and it is not revealing too much to note that none of the cases before the courts in England and Wales that have dealt with repudiatory breach have addressed this head on.

B. The Regulatory Framework

The presence of the estate is significant to the definition of a lease, but is just one of the factors that makes the lease distinct from other specialist contracts. In many ways, the more significant issue is that the particular rules and regulations that have built up around the regulation of leases work against the effective operation of broad contractual principles in this specialist context of lettings between landlord and tenant.[26] This context is more than the specialist nature of a particular form of contract, where the operation of rules differs from one contract to another. Leases have distinct features, such as:

> the comprehensive process of assignment of the benefit and burden of leasehold covenants is something unique to the law of leases and is not to be found under general contract law. Leases are also clearly distinguishable from other contracts of hire because engrafted onto them are complex statutory codes, which, often for reasons of policy, seek to confer on tenants additional benefits and advantages. In particular, the complex law relating to the recovery of possession and eviction of tenants (including the law of forfeiture and relief from forfeiture) make leasehold agreements very different from ordinary commercial contracts.[27]

McFarlane has suggested that any tension between the contractual and proprietary aspects of a lease is an 'illusion':[28] the classification of a lease as a property right is one of content (does the right given impose a prima facie duty on the rest of the world not to interfere with the use of a thing?), whereas designation as a contractual right is an acquisition question (does the right arise as a result of a contractually binding promise with the lessor?). It follows that, 'when analysing the practical problems that are often said to depend on a choice between the "proprietary" and "contractual" views, the false opposition obscures the solution to the problems'.[29]

While there is much to commend this as a theoretical perspective, it does not address the concerns raised that the presence of a proprietary estate, and the rules which exist around it, have a fundamental impact on the operation of how the law regulates this extra dimension, which is absent from contracts generally. An analysis which suggests that some contractual doctrines have no place in leasehold law does

surrender (repudiatory conduct supplies the offer, election to terminate would supply the acceptance); and the implication of a condition subsequent, that on the happening of a substantial failure of performance the innocent party may elect to bring the lease to an end (P Luxton, 'Termination of Leases: From Property to Contract' in J Birds, R Bradgate and C Villers (eds), *Termination of Contracts* (London, Wiley Publishing Ltd, 1995). All of these depend on legal fictions, and are unsatisfactory. See Barr, 'Repudiation of Leases' (n 10) 331–34.

26 Barr, 'Repudiation of Leases' (n 10); Barr, 'Frustration of Leases' (n 9).

27 Pawlowski and Brown 'Part 3' (n 10).

28 B McFarlane, *The Structure of Property Law* (Oxford, Hart Publishing, 2008) 697–98.

29 ibid.

not deny the importance of the creative, contractual element of the lease, but instead recognises that the presence of the estate, and the obligations arising from it, present real obstacles to the effective operation of contractual principles in leasehold law. These will be revealed in the consideration of repudiatory breach.

III. CASE STUDY: REPUDIATORY BREACH OF LEASES

A. What is a Repudiatory Breach?

Put simply, a breach of an obligation (or obligations) under a contract is repudiatory when it is so fundamental that it is tantamount to the party in breach repudiating or rejecting the whole contract.[30] The classic formulation is such breach deprives the injured party of 'substantially the whole benefit' of the contract,[31] or goes to the very root of the contract so that damages will not provide an adequate remedy. A repudiatory breach of contract renders the contract voidable, and the injured party has a right to elect to terminate the contract or to continue it and sue for damages for the breach.[32]

The effect of the termination by repudiatory breach is twofold. First, it brings an end to the primary contractual obligations of both parties and releases the parties from any future liability. Liability remains for past breaches of contract occurring before the rescission and for the performance of any obligations so accruing. Secondly, in technical, contractual terms, it creates a secondary obligation on the part of the defaulting party to pay damages to the injured party for the loss sustained by him in consequence of the non-performance of his primary obligations in the future[33] and for the period before rescission. The injured party is thereby compensated for the loss of the contract as a whole.

B. Acceptance of Repudiatory Breach in English Leases: A Tenant Remedy

The acceptance in *Hussein v Mehlman*[34] that a lease might be terminated by a repudiatory breach like any other contract has been considered in detail elsewhere.[35] In essence, the fact that the majority decision of the House of Lords in *National Carriers v Panalpina (Northern) Ltd*[36] treated a lease as any other contract,[37] despite

[30] See *Eminence Property Developments Ltd v Heaney* [2010] EWCA Civ 1168 (CA), where the facts' sensitive nature of repudiatory breach was emphasised in deciding whether the contract breaker in a renunciation case had demonstrated, objectively, that he or she had refused to perform a contact.

[31] *Hongkong Fir Shipping Co Ltd v Kawasaki Kisen Kaisha Ltd* [1962] 2 QB 26, 66 per Diplock LJ.

[32] See H Beale et al (eds), *Chitty on Contract*, 32nd edn (London, Sweet & Maxwell, 2015) vol 1, Ch 24, 24-001–24-017.

[33] See, eg, the facts and decision in *McDonald v Davy Lascelles Ltd* (1933) 48 CLR 457.

[34] *Hussein* (n 2).

[35] Barr, 'Repudiation of Leases' (n 10).

[36] *Panalpina* (n 1). See also Barr, 'Frustration of Leases' (n 9).

[37] Their Lordships expressly approved of the reasoning in *Highway Properties Ltd v Kelly, Douglas & Co Lt* 17 DLR (3d) 710, 721: 'It is no longer sensible to pretend that a commercial lease, such as the one before the court, is simply a conveyance and not also a contract. It is equally untenable to persist in denying resort to the full armoury of remedies ordinarily available to redress repudiation of covenants, merely because the covenants may be associated with an estate in land.'

the presence of an estate in land, meant that repudiatory breach could be applied to leases. Freed from the constraints of precedent, Assistant Recorder Stephen Sedley QC recognised that a tenancy could be ended by repudiation, thereby giving tenants a right to terminate a contract for sufficiently serious breach of covenant by the landlord.[38]

Where a tenant is in breach of covenant, the law of forfeiture provides a means whereby the landlord can seek to terminate the lease, but there is no analoguos system of forfeiture for tenants.[39] Where a landlord is in breach of covenant, absent repudiation, the tenant is generally only entitled to damages for the breach, alongside some limited rights to set off rent where the breach concerned is of a repairing covenant.[40] This 'is certainly no substitute for a right to end the tenancy and find a better landlord elsewhere'.[41] It is easy to understand why the Assistant Recorder felt sympathy for the plight of the tenant before him, not least because English law has no general warranty of fitness for purpose of residential lettings,[42] which would provide a remedy for tenants in jurisdictions such as Canada or the United States.

This is significant, as English law was the first in the common law world to apply repudiatory breach for a tenant. In all other Commonwealth jurisdictions, repudiatory breach was made applicable as a device that only landlords could access.[43] This is more than an arbitrary matter of coincidence as to the type of claimant who happened to bring an action in court, as it has legal consequences, which are explored below. The lack of any proprietary framework, such as the scheme of forfeiture, within which to seat the operation of repudiatory breach when claimed by a tenant against a landlord has led to significant concerns as to how an action to terminate a lease by repudiatory breach actually operates. The significance of this appears not to have impacted on the Assistant Recorder, and what is missing from the judgment in *Hussein v Mehlman* is any analysis of how repudiatory breach should be applied in English leasehold law by tenant or landlord, or whether, indeed, it should be so applied, beyond a tacit recognition that 'the proposition that a contract of tenancy can be repudiated like any other contract has a number of important implications, which it is not appropriate to explore on the facts of this case'.[44]

This is something of an understatement, and while it might have been proper to leave the details of these implications to later cases, it does not cover a failure to

[38] On the facts, the landlord's breaches of the statutory covenant to repair (s 11 of the Landlord and Tenant Act 1985) had been severe: there was no heating, the ceiling of one bedroom had collapsed, water pipes had burst, a flat roof extension was leaking and there was damp in the hall. There had clearly been a substantial failure in performance so as to justify termination through repudiatory breach.

[39] Indeed, statutory efforts to introduce a parallel system of tenant forfeiture have been abandoned. See n 83 below.

[40] See, eg, *British Anzai (Felixstowe) Ltd. v International Marine Management Ltd* [1980] QB 137. Tenants may also have been able to negotiate express break clauses in leases, allowing him or her to escape the lease at an earlier time than the stated expiry date. These are not commonly included in leases. See generally Lewison LJ, N Dowding, Morgan J, M Rodger, E Peters (eds), *Woodfall, The Law of Landlord and Tenant* (London, Sweet & Maxwell, 2016) ch 17, s 14, 17.285–17.301.

[41] Law Commission, *Forfeiture of Tenancies* (Law Com No 142, 1985) para 17.11.

[42] This may now be part of English law, however obliquely, through the Consumer Protection Act 2015—see n 7.

[43] See further Barr, 'Repudiation of Leases' (n 10). In *Highway Properties Ltd* (n 37) for example, the landlord brought the action against a tenant who had abandoned the lease of a unit in shopping premises.

[44] *Hussein* (n 2) 90H.

consider what was, after all, a sea change in the law. So what have later cases made of repudiatory breach of leases?

C. Developments since Hussein: No Actionable Repudiation

There has not been a reported case of successful termination of a lease by repudiatory conduct in a decided case since *Hussein v Mehlman* itself. However, the application of repudiatory breach for tenants appeared to be confirmed in *Chartered Trusts v Davies*.[45] It was assumed at first instance that the lease could end through repudiation and acceptance, and the point was not argued in the Court of Appeal. The case concerned possible non-derogation from grant by the landlords in allowing other tenants in a shopping mall to commit what amounted to a nuisance which interfered with the toy business carried on by the tenant at their demised unit. The tenant alleged that this was a major contributing factor to the driving of the business into bankruptcy. It was uncontested at the Court of Appeal that the action complained of as a nuisance was a substantial interference with the letting and would have fulfilled the criterion for an action in repudiatory breach, if it had been argued.

Similarly, in *Nynehead Developments v RH Fibreboard Containers*,[46] it was confirmed that leases could, in principle, be determined by repudiatory breach following a landlord's breach of covenants. On the immediate facts, there had been clear breaches of the implied covenant not to derogate from grant and an express covenant relating to the landlord's duties in respect of the efficient operation of the estate. However, Weeks QC found that there had been no repudiation of the facts—the breaches were not characterised as sufficiently serious so as to amount to repudiation of the lease. They were an 'irritant and minor interference' with the tenant's business and, though often 'deliberate, prolonged and surreptitious', they were not such as to go to the root of the parties' contract, and damages provided an adequate remedy. Weeks QC also sounded a note of caution in applying the doctrine too readily to allow tenants an escape from what had become a disadvantageous bargain.

In *Petra Investments Ltd v Jeffrey Rogers plc*,[47] it had originally been intended that a shopping centre would have an individual and exclusive image for high-quality fashion retail. However, in order to increase trade and sales revenue, the landlord created a new unit as a Virgin Megastore.[48] The tenant of one of the retail units in the shopping centre, who had suffered a loss of profits, claimed that the landlord's conduct had been repudiatory and also constituted a non-derogation from grant. Hart J concluded that, in a purpose-built centre, there was an obligation on the landlord not to alter or use the common parts of the centre in such a way as to cause it to lose its character as a retail shopping mall. In relation to the letting of units within

[45] [1997] EWCA Civ 2256.

[46] [1999] 1 EGLR 7.

[47] [2000] EGLR 120 (Ch).

[48] This was a successful, international chain store, founded in 1976, specialising in selling music and video products to the public, and was a familiar flagship store in many British city centres. The Virgin Megastore group has ceased trading in most of the world, but continues to trade in the Middle East and North Africa.

the centre, the landlord was required to take account of the expectations of its existing tenants by not doing, or permitting to be done, something that it was reasonably foreseeable would render the premises already demised less fit for the purpose for which they had been let. Having found that there was no actionable non-derogation from grant on the facts, Hart J said:

> In those circumstances, it is unnecessary for me to consider whether, had I come to a different conclusion, the result would have been that the defendant was entitled to accept the claimant's conduct as repudiatory of the lease ... or whether the defendant simply has a claim to damages.

The important decision of *Abidogun v Frolen Health Care*[49] concerned denial of title, so this time it was the landlord alleging that the tenant had committed a repudiatory act: a first in a reported English decision. Space here militates against a full discussion of denial of title as a doctrine, but it was confirmed in this case by Arden LJ that the basis of denial of title is an implied term in a lease,[50] even though it operated by way of repudiation. Significantly, the case also decided that an action for denial of title was an action for forfeiture, which needed to be brought within section 146 to be effective (more on which later).

The repudiation action failed, on numerous grounds. It was by no means clear that either the actions of the tenants in seeking a determination of the court on issues that had arisen between the parties would be seen as repudiatory or that the tenants did not intend to be bound by the lease. Even if there was repudiatory conduct, the acceptance of that conduct by the landlords was lacking, and at trial the case had proceeded on the basis of forfeiture, not repudiatory breach.

Denial of title was also at issue in *Crisp v Eastaugh*.[51] The court found that the actions by the tenant were equivocal and did not amount to a repudiation of the lease, so entitling the landlord to forfeit the lease.

Given the lack of true clarity demonstrated by these cases, which all suggest that repudiatory breach is applicable in principle but not on their individual facts, it is unsurprising that the whole application of repudiatory breach was called into question by Lloyd LJ in the Court of Appeal in *Reichman v Beveridge*.[52] The material facts were straightforward. The tenants took a lease of offices for the purposes of a partnership business. The partnership ceased to practise and vacated the offices. The landlords sued for rent. The tenants alleged that the landlords had failed to mitigate their loss by forfeiting the lease and seeking to relet. In consequence, they said, they ought not to recover the rent. In holding for the landlords, Lloyd LJ cast doubt on the application of the doctrine of repudiatory breach, having considered that 'Since [*Hussein v Mehlman*] other courts in England have held, or assumed, that a lease can be brought to an end by acceptance of a repudiatory breach, *but there is no decision to that effect in this court*'.[53]

[49] [2001] EWCA Civ 1821.
[50] ibid [43] (emphasis added).
[51] [2007] EWCA Civ 638.
[52] [2006] EWCA Civ 165.
[53] ibid [10] (emphasis added).

He added:

> I do not decide whether or not repudiation plays any, and if so what, part in the English law of landlord and tenant. That is not directly in issue before us, and it would be wrong to decide it unnecessarily.[54]

Read together, it is impossible not to feel that his Lordship was severely doubting the application of repudiatory breach to leases generally, but these are, as Lloyd LJ himself notes, *obiter* statements. If they were intended to signal a clear change in direction, it is not one that has been judicially recognised. In *Grange v Quinn*,[55] Jackson LJ clearly felt that repudiatory breach was applicable to leases, as he said, also *obiter*: 'Although there were earlier indications to the contrary, it is now clear that a lease may be brought to an end by repudiation and acceptance.'[56]

At the very least, these cases collectively suggest there is a palpable sense of unease still permeating judicial acceptance of repudiatory breach as a remedy, available both to landlords and tenants, in dealing with termination of leases.[57] This might explain the paucity of case law, legal advisors being equally unaware or uncertain of the efficacy of pleading repudiatory breach of a lease, or it may simply be a coincidence of a multiplicity of factors. Rather than engage in simple speculation, attention now turns to what else these cases have revealed about the operation of repudiatory breach within the landlord and tenant sphere and to see whether any of the implications of the action operating in the leasehold context have been addressed.

D. The Impact of Repudiatory Breach

(i) Landlords Claiming Repudiatory Breach by Tenants: Creating Anomalies

Assistant Recorder Sedley recognised in *Hussein* that introducing a right to terminate on behalf of the tenant meant, inexorably, that the same action would be available to a landlord. Indeed, *Abidogun* appeared to remove any doubt about this, and in so doing brought English law into line with the other jurisdictions that accept repudiatory breach as a landlord remedy. One of the issues considered in *Abiodgun* was the manner in which a landlord may bring an action for repudiatory breach. If, as with the tenant's right to terminate by accepting repudiatory conduct by the landlord, the action is based purely on contract, would it allow the landlord to avoid or escape the requirements of forfeiture? This would give landlords an additional method of terminating leases, and one that would not allow an opportunity for

[54] ibid [42].

[55] [2013] EWCA Civ 24, which considered the quantum of damages recoverable following unlawful eviction of the tenant.

[56] ibid [70].

[57] *Chitty* (n 32) itself is unhelpful here—see 24.001, fn 2, where it is said that repudiatory breach 'would appear to apply to leases'. It is worth noting that in Wales, in residential leases, the Renting Homes (Wales) Act 2016, s 154 permits a tenant to sue for repudiatory breach by the landlord without a possession claim where the breach has led the tenant to give up possession of the home. This is in line with the adoption of 'occupation contracts' to replace the multiplicity of statutory and common law concepts applicable to leases (and licences) of the home.

any remedy by the defaulting tenant, as there is no concept of remediable breaches in the operation of repudiatory breach—it is the acceptance of a repudiating act (or acts) that terminates the contractual bargain.[58] An action in forfeiture, by contrast, activates a discretionary system of relief (equitable and statutory) against the forfeiture action, which permits the tenant to apply to court to allow him to remedy his breach without the landlord repossessing the demised premises.[59] This is because the real purpose is to secure compliance by the tenant with his covenants, not to allow the landlord to get the demised premises back early for breaches of covenant which could be compensated through an award of damages. The attraction of a purely contractual method of termination open to the landlord would be that it avoids the complexity of the forfeiture action where the breach complained of by the tenant was sufficiently serious to merit a finding that it was repudiatory in character.[60]

This concern would appear to have been addressed. Arden LJ made it clear in *Abidogun v Frolen Health Care Ltd* that a repudiatory breach by a tenant through denial of a landlord's title would only be actionable if it was brought within the forfeiture system:

> If it were not so, it would be possible to bring a lease to an end by a means which is wholly outside of section 146, with significant consequences for the law of landlord and tenant and the fact that such repudiatory conduct may only arise occasionally does not seem to me to diminish the significance of the contrary conclusion.[61]

Buxton LJ went further and, in addressing counsel's argument that repudiatory breach operated as a purely contractual doctrine and did not operate with the forfeiture framework, said:

> I can well accept the first point in [the appellant's] argument that relations between a landlord and his tenant, under a lease, are governed by the ordinary law of contract as well as by the more specific doctrines of the law of landlord and tenant. It does not, however, follow from the interaction of those two parts of the law that the protection for a tenant, as has been provided by Parliament in section 146, can be avoided by recourse to a purely contractual doctrine such as that of repudiatory breach.[62]

It is now without doubt that, if repudiatory breach exists as an action for the landlord, it must be brought under the existing statutory forfeiture provisions. Thus, the window of opportunity for landlords was apparently closed and the courts would appear to have found a way to make the doctrine of repudiatory breach work in a sensitive manner in the particular context of the lease.[63]

[58] The fact that the breach is one of sufficient seriousness to be classed as 'repudiatory' does not mean that such a breach is, by its very nature, irremediable—see n 64 below.

[59] Forfeiture is also complex and stands in need of reform, as, for example, in the need for a landlord to determine whether a breach is remediable or irremediable in serving a valid Law of Property Act 1925, s 146 notice on a tenant for breach of any covenant other than rent. The question is not one, as in repudiatory breach, of whether the breach is sufficiently serious as to go to the 'root' of the contract. If an incorrect determination is made, the notice may be invalid—see, eg, *Akici v LR Butlin Ltd* [2006] 1 WLR 201; *Anders v Haralambous* [2013] EWHC 2676 (QB).

[60] See further Barr, 'Repudiation of Leases' (n 10) 323–29.

[61] Above (n 49) [49].

[62] ibid [52].

[63] See in support M Pawlowski, 'Denial of Landlord's Title: Forfeiture or Repudiatory Breach' [2002] *The Conveyancer and Property Lawyer* 399.

The solution is not as sensitive to context as it first appears. There are 'significant consequences for the law of landlord and tenant' in the approach adopted by Arden and Buxton LJJ, tied to the inescapable fact that repudiatory breach is also available to a tenant, while forfeiture is not. What appears to emerge are two separate actions of repudiatory breach operating in the leasehold context. First, there is tenant's right to accept repudiatory breaches committed by the landlord, which, by necessity, must operate independently of any forfeiture system. This operates as a purely contractual right, and in the same way as repudiatory breach of any other type of contract, with the tenant electing to end the lease and the landlord having no right to make good the breach. Secondly, there is a landlord's right to accept repudiatory acts committed by the tenant, which must be brought as an action for forfeiture so that any mechanisms for relief operate to allow the tenant to make good the breach before the lease can be terminated. The fact that the breach is sufficiently serious to amount to repudiatory conduct on behalf of the tenant does not mean that such breach would be irremediable.[64] The landlord's right to repudiatory breach is, in practice, little more than an additional method of forfeiture for serious breach and 'the doctrine of repudiation adds nothing at all to a landlord's ability to recover possession from a tenant in the usual way'.[65]

It is cold comfort to suggest that the landlord's ability to accept repudiatory conduct from a tenant is curtailed by an existing statutory framework, particularly when it is known that the existing system of forfeiture is unnecessarily complex and in desperate need of reform. Indeed, is there any compelling reason why a tenant should have a 'better' right than a landlord, in the sense that a tenant is protected by relief against forfeiture whereas a landlord committing serious breach is not? Consider a repairing obligation in a lease. If it lies with the landlord, who commits a repudiatory breach of the obligation, in theory the tenant has only to elect to end the lease to terminate it, as there are no equivalent statutory provisions for forfeiture.[66] Where the repairing obligation is on the tenant, matters differ considerably for the landlord, who must make sure that they serve an appropriately worded section 146 notice, and the tenant will probably have the chance to make good the breach under the relief against forfeiture provisions and keep the lease, something the landlord would be denied if in breach of the same obligation.[67]

The practical difference, of course, is that the threat of forfeiture is what might compel the tenant to remedy the lack of repair; the tenant, having no such threat, would, without an action for repudiatory breach, have no way of forcing a landlord

[64] The question of whether a breach is remediable or not is not simply a question of seriousness. In essence, the issue is whether the harm that has been done to the landlord by the relevant breach is, for practical purposes, capable of being retrieved within a reasonable time—*Savva v Hussein* [1996] 47 EG 138. See further Woodfall (n 40) para 17.132.

[65] A Oakes, 'Repudiatory Breach in the Leasehold Context: Some Unresolved Issues' [2012] *L&T Review* 95, 97.

[66] The breach must, of course, be sufficiently serious to amount to a repudiatory breach, and simple breach of a repairing obligation would not fulfil that requirement, otherwise tenants would be walking away from their tenancies in droves. There is no evidence to suggest that this is the case.

[67] If the breach is remedied, the landlord suffers no loss in a sense. A breach of repairing obligation may be serious enough to be classed as a repudiatory breach but still be classed as remediable in terms of forfeiture, as the harm can be made good within a reasonable period of time—see n 64 above.

to remedy the breach, other than suing for breach of covenant. It is easy to have sympathy with the tenant, particularly in a residential context, as they have more to lose than a landlord from the loss of the leasehold estate, and repeated action for breach of covenant when premises are rendered uninhabitable seems repugnant. In the more commercial sphere, such sympathy is harder to conjure, as the playing field is often more level between landlord and tenant. Either the landlord or the tenant may want to use the serious breach of the repairing obligation in the example provided as a trigger to end the lease for other reasons. The tenant might be a serial defaulter on rent, for example, only paying when threatened by court action; the market conditions may have changed since the tenant agreed a lease; or the tenant could obtain a (re-)letting at a much lower market rent. In such situations, only the tenant would be able to end the lease by election through repudiatory breach; the landlord would not, due to the relief against forfeiture provisions.

In closing the door on potential injustice to tenants by landlords, the decision in *Abidogun* has created a quandary, however well-intentioned the motives, in that the efficacy of an action for repudiatory breach, and its baseline operation, varies greatly depending on the party accessing it, and has moved the injustice from the landlord to the tenant. This also takes English law further away from some of its Commonwealth cousins. In Australia, for example, the landlord's right to accept a repudiatory breach by the tenant is seen as a contractual means of ending the lease, alternative to a right of forfeiture, in which any question of serving a forfeiture notice 'becomes an irrelevance'.[68]

(ii) A Right to Prospective Damages Post-Termination for Loss of Bargain?

A second, significant issue identified with termination of lease via repudiatory breach concerns the availability or otherwise of prospective damages on the termination of the lease. This is an alien concept if the lease is viewed simply through a property lens, as once the estate terminates all future liability ceases.[69] Prospective damages, as a secondary action for loss of bargain damages throughout the duration of the original contract, are, however, a feature of contract law, as identified above.[70]

The attractions of prospective damages, particularly to landlords, are twofold. First, landlords may make the tenant essentially an 'involuntary guarantor of the rent'[71] upon ending a lease by repudiatory breach. Although the estate would have ended, the tenant has contracted for the original period of the lease, so that the secondary obligation to pay damages would remain. Hence, if the landlord was unable to relet the premises at all or for a period of time, or agreed a new tenancy at a lower rent than the original tenancy, a claim could be made in damages for the rent

[68] *Marshall v Council of the Shire of Snowy River* (1994) 7 BPR 14, 447, per Meagher JA. See also A Dowling, 'Case Comment: Contract Law and the Termination of Leases' [2006] *Landlord and Tenant Review* 12.

[69] This is the effect where the landlord accepts an offer of surrender of the lease by a tenant or successfully terminates the lease through forfeiture action.

[70] See n 33 above.

[71] T Effron, 'The Contractualisation of the Law of Leaseholds: Pitfalls and Opportunities' (1988) 14 *Monash University Law Review* 83, 90.

owing or the diminution in the value of the rent. In Commonwealth countries such as Canada and Australia, the availability of such contractual damages was an accepted consequence of the application of contractual principles to leases.[72] Secondly, and relatedly, the availability of prospective damages would avoid the landlord retaining property which could otherwise be relet as, even where a tenant has abandoned the premises and has no intention of performing the contract, a landlord could, without the cushion of loss of bargain damages, elect to keep the lease alive and simply sue for rent as it became due.

Reichman v Beveridge[73] would appear to have put an end to the availability of prospective damages in English law on termination of a lease by repudiatory breach. There is a general principle that where a repudiatory breach of contract occurs, the innocent party who elects to continue with the contract is under a duty to mitigate the loss.[74] In *Reichman*, the tenants asserted that the landlord had failed to mitigate his loss by forfeiting the lease and seeking to relet it. Their argument thus depended on establishing that: (i) if the landlord terminated the tenancy and took steps to relet, he could recover any loss by way of a claim in (loss of bargain) damages; and (ii) it would be unreasonable for the landlord not to terminate the tenancy but instead continue to sue for rent as it became due. Lloyd LJ disagreed with both of these points, despite having been referred to Commonwealth authorities supporting these arguments:

> There is, however, no case in English law that shows that a landlord can recover damages from a former tenant in respect of loss of future rent after termination … In those circumstances, either damages are not an adequate remedy for the landlord, or at least the landlord would be acting reasonably in taking the view that he should not terminate the lease because he may well not be able to recover such damages.

Lloyd LJ noted that a landlord would, of course, forfeit and relet where market conditions were favourable, but, given that there was no right to sue the tenant for any loss of rent on a reletting at a lower rate, the landlord's option of keeping the existing tenancy alive and suing for rent as it became due was sensible and practical. There was no duty to mitigate damages here, as rent was a debt, not damages.

Later in the same judgment, he put the matter of prospective damages beyond doubt:

> It may be a logical development to hold that a landlord, having forfeited the lease, can recover damages for the loss of future rent, at least if the breach which led to the forfeiture was fundamental and repudiatory, but it does not seem to me that English law has reached that stage.[75]

It follows that, since the action is phrased in terms of repudiatory breach, loss of bargain damages for breach of a continuing covenant in a lease would also be denied

[72] See, eg, *Highway Properties v Douglas & Co* [1971] 17 DLR (3d) 710; *Progressive Mailing House Property Ltd v Tabali Property Ltd* (1985) 157 CLR 17. These cases are considered in Barr, 'Repudiation of Leases' (n 10) 324–27. See also *Gumland Property Holdings Ltd v Duffy Bros Fruit Market (Campbelltown) Property Ltd* [2008] 82 ALJR 576.

[73] *Reichman* [2006] EWCA Civ 165.

[74] See, generally, *Chitty* (n 32) Ch 26.

[75] *Reichman* [2006] EWCA Civ 165, [27].

to a tenant.[76] Though Lloyds LJ's reasoning is open to criticism,[77] and the impact of it is that a landlord must pursue the questionable line of keeping a contract alive purely to sue for non-performance,[78] it has not been judicially doubted. It again places English law out of step with other common law jurisdictions, both in law and in practice. The High Court of Australia, for example, reaffirmed that loss of bargain damages are available to the landlord on termination through repudiation and acceptance in *Gumland Property Holdings Pty Ltd v Duffy Bros Fruit Market (Campbelltown) Pty Ltd*.[79] The court felt it was desirable that the landlord ought to be able to determine a lease by repudiatory breach, as the ability to recover damages for a contractual action, not available on forfeiture, protected against the movement of the market.[80]

The net effect, then, of *Reichman* is to further bolster the idea that there is little utility in an action for repudiatory breach in Anglo-Welsh law. It operates subject to forfeiture when accessed by a landlord and it does not give a landlord a right to prospective damages; as a consequence, it does not provide a tenant with a right to escape from the obligation to pay rent, even where they have abandoned the premises and the landlord would be happy to be rid of them. This is not just a matter of context; of contractual principles operating in a particular way to accommodate the relationship of landlord and tenant. It is, instead:

> the fashioning of an entirely new legal construct to enable one party to a contract to terminate it on breach by another and yet to deny him the right to compensation. Moreover, it would differentiate leases from all other kinds of contract, a differentiation whose existence the proponents of repudiation deny.[81]

Here again is an example of a set of problems unresolved by the importation of contractual principles into the landlord and tenant relationship. It calls into question the very efficacy of their importation.

(iii) Loss of Alternate Remedies

There is, as demonstrated, a disconnection between the need for repudiatory breach in English law—which was to give tenants a right to terminate on serious breach—and the impact of the operation of the doctrine. The irony of introducing the remedy has been to preclude discussion of, potentially, something better through the creation of the Tenant Termination Order Scheme.[82] Broadly, this would introduce a

[76] Lewison (n 20) 3.

[77] See, eg, Dowling (n 68), who argues that there are at least three English decisions which support the proposition that a landlord could recover damages for loss of bargain on the termination of a lease, which were themselves considered and approve in the Northern Ireland case of *Rainey Brothers Ltd v Kearney* [1990] NI 18; none of which were cited in *Reichman*.

[78] See further J Morgan, 'Case Comment: *Reichman v Beveridge*' [2008] *The Conveyancer and Property Lawyer* 165, 173.

[79] (2008) 244 ALR 1.

[80] ibid [64]. See, however, D McGill, 'Anti-Shevill Clauses and Statutory Protection of Tenants from Forfeiture: What's Left After *Gumland Property Holdings Pty Ltd v Duffy Bros Fruit Market (Campbelltown) Pty Ltd*?' (2009) 17 *Australian Property Law Journal* 326.

[81] Lewison (n 20).

[82] Law Commission, *Termination of Tenancies for Tenant Default* (Law Com No 303, 2006).

right for tenants to apply to terminate the lease for persistent breach of covenant by the landlord. The right would be subject to the same relief provisions as the landlord's order scheme, and would therefore introduce the concept of an ability to remedy a default by a landlord, which is missing from repudiatory breach. However, the scheme has been dropped from the Termination Order Bill as, with a due sense of irony, the Law Commission felt able to abandon the Tenant Termination Order because the availability of repudiatory breach covered the same ground.[83] It was clear on consultation that the creation of this statutory right was met with hostility by landlord interest groups. However, given what has since happened to repudiatory breach as an action for landlords, and if that position was fully appreciated by landlords, that hostility might not be as evident if the Commission were to look at this area again.

IV. CONCLUDING REMARKS: LESSONS FOR THE FUTURE

Given the forgoing re-examination of repudiatory breach, it is difficult to see the increasing contractualisation of the lease as a useful addition to the law regulating leases, or for the parties concerned. The use of contractual principles in these contexts has not been sensitively handled and has, in effect, caused serious anomalies in the law. It is judicial legislation, occasioned to meet a perceived need, that has led to unexpected results.[84]

It has created a bright line distinction, for no defensible reason, between the operation of the doctrine as used by a tenant against his landlord and that used by the landlord against his tenant. Only in the former case can it be said to operate as a contract lawyer would recognise repudiatory breach; and even then it has proved of dubious utility and requires some complex (and fictional) legal reasoning to explain the action. In relation to landlords, the remedy adds little, other than additional complexity, to an action for forfeiture and, in denying any entitlement to loss of bargain damages following termination through repudiatory breach, there is little point in pursuing a repudiatory breach by the tenant. It also means that landlords can face termination of a lease if they are in default of a covenanted obligation such that it classes as a repudiatory breach, without any real chance to remedy that breach. However, if the same obligation sits with the tenant, the tenant will likely have a chance to remedy the breach before the lease can be terminated, thanks to the fact that a landlord's claim to repudiatory breach must proceed by forfeiture. With the

83 See Law Commission, *Landlord and Tenant Law: Termination of Tenancies Bill* (Law Com No 223, 1994); Law Commission Consultation Paper, *Landlord and Tenant Law: Termination of Tenancies by Physical Re-entry* (Law Com No 303, 2006).

84 This type of action is not unknown in English property law. Lord Templeman's intervention in *Street v Mountford* [1985] 2 WLR 877 to establish an objective approach to the creation of leases is a case in point. This was designed to address issues caused by landlords seeking to avoid rent protection legislation by creating licences instead of tenancies. The need for intervention was removed shortly afterwards by the removal of rent protection from most residential lettings via the Housing Act 1988, yet the impact of the decision is still being felt by those seeking to create licences rather than leases for perfectly defensible purposes—see, eg, W Barr, 'Charitable Lettings and their Legal Pitfalls' in E Cooke (ed), *Modern Studies in Property Law: Property 2000* (Oxford, Hart Publishing, 2001) 239.

very best of judicial motives, serious anomalies have been created in the law which are difficult to stomach, particularly when, as is apparent, the English version of the importation of contractual principles differs greatly from that of our common law cousins.

At the very least, this re-examination of the area suggests that any fervour for contractual remedies should be receding, as the realities of the impact of their importation begin to reveal themselves through the case law—a point recognised by the Court of Appeal in *Reichman v Beveridge*. The application of contractual principles has been an ill-advised example of law reform by the judiciary.[85] In importing remedies without any clear thought as to how they might operate in the particular context of the landlord and tenant relationship, more problems have been created than solutions. Perhaps of greatest concern, these attempts have allowed attempts at substantive law reform to be sidestepped, as evidenced in the Law Commission's abandonment of the Tenant Termination Order—something which would have given tenant's a right akin to forfeiture and which would have operated in a similar way to the proposed reforms to the landlord's right of forfeiture.

While the distinction between leases and licences as proprietary and personal rights persists, it is suggested that it is high time that English law retracted from allowing contractual remedies to terminate leases; instead, time would be better spent on reducing the complexities of the existing system. At the time of writing, it is uncertain whether, in fact, repudiatory breach is part of English law. What is needed is a decision of the Supreme Court, once and for all, to settle the matter. It is the author's hope that any such settlement suggests that repudiatory breach forms no part of English law.

In fact, the Supreme Court should go further and reconsider the nature of the regulation of leases, and 'contractualisation' more generally. The proprietary nature of the lease has been much maligned, yet it does not represent archaic thinking to suggest that leases should be regulated primarily as property rights, not contracts. It should be remembered that the estate is the essential element which transforms a contract into a 'lease'. The relational contractual element is the creative subsidiary which works within the discipline of the estate and controls the use to which the parties may put the estate. This is so even though the contractual element may seem more important to the parties as it contains the regulatory and commercial provisions of the bargain. It is the distinction between the perceived and the legal reality of what has been created. This does not ignore the commercial realities of the leasehold transaction; indeed, it gives effect to the ultimate commercial reality, which is that the parties have agreed a lease, not a licence, and as such the tenant has become the property owner for the duration of the term (something which is likely to have been reflected in the price paid by premium or rent for the grant of the lease). There is no difficulty in a licence being repudiated or otherwise terminated by any contractual means, since it is a pure creature of contract. There is no anomaly in allowing a licensee to repudiate and not a tenant—the licensee has no proprietary asset to lose.

[85] This is to be contrasted with legislative intervention, as has happened in Wales with renting homes, which follows careful consideration of operational issues and context arising from the work of the Law Commission.

This is a central distinction between the protection of proprietary rights and personal rights. There is therefore no need to resort to contractual remedies to terminate leases; they are not the panacea they may at first appear to be.

When added to the concerns of the special context in which regulation of the landlord and tenant system operates, as demonstrated by repudiatory breach, it is clear that the time has come to learn hard lessons. Those hard lessons, at heart, are that changes to regulation should really be within the purview of the legislature, not the judicial evolution of our common law system. That is an important lesson to learn, and one which may have much wider import beyond the contractualisation of leases. To do otherwise is to create unforeseen anomalies, as demonstrated here, or, at best, not to improve the law in any meaningful or defensible way.

Part B

Life and Death in Property Law

6

The 'New' New Property: Dealing with Digital Assets on Death

HEATHER CONWAY* AND SHEENA GRATTAN**

Death has become more complicated than it used to be, in large part due to the digital age ... Yet, the law, still set in the pen and ink era, has failed to keep pace with technology in many contexts, including one's digital footprint at death.[1]

I. INTRODUCTION

OVER THE YEARS, the law of succession has not been immune to the challenges posed by changing circumstances, whether social, economic or familial. In 1981, Professor Mary Ann Glendon published *The New Family and the New Property*,[2] chronicling, inter alia, the move away from traditional property and family forms. Three years later, Professor John Langbein's seminal article entitled 'The Nonprobate Revolution and the Future of the Law of Succession'[3] highlighted the challenges posed to traditional succession law rules by alternative wealth forms such as insurance and life policies, joint assets and pensions. More than three decades later, succession law continues to grapple with both changing family structures and the issues posed by so-called 'will-substitutes'.[4] However, it now faces another 'New Property Probate Revolution': the legal challenges generated by the so-called 'digital footprint' that virtually every citizen (old and young) leaves behind on death.

At the time of writing, statistics indicate that more than 3.5 billion people worldwide (around 46 per cent of the global population) are internet users.[5] With the advent of the digital age, we spend increasing amounts of our time in the virtual

* School of Law, Queen's University Belfast.

** Barrister at Law.

[1] S Varnado, 'Your Digital Footprint Left Behind at Death: An Illustration of Technology Leaving the Law Behind' (2014) 74 *Louisiana Law Review* 719, 719.

[2] MA Glendon, *The New Family and the New Property* (London, Butterworths, 1981).

[3] J Langbein, 'The Nonprobate Revolution and the Future of the Law of Succession' (1984) 97 *Harvard Law Review* 1108.

[4] Many legal issues in respect of will-substitutes remain unresolved, including their interplay with traditional succession law doctrines as to the burden of debts and liabilities and estate disputes of any kinds, including claims on foot of the Inheritance (Provision for Family and Dependants) Act 1975.

[5] 'Internet Users in the World' statistics, available at www.internetlivestats.com/internet-users/ (accessed November 2016).

world,[6] creating not only an online persona, but leaving a trail of digital assets in our wake. But what actually happens to digital assets when someone dies?[7] This basic question raises a host of legal issues around ownership, privacy, access to usernames and passwords, and the duties of personal representatives when administering estates which do not fit neatly within traditional succession law and property law concepts. The location of digital assets also leads to complex multi-jurisdictional legal issues, yet there is currently no 'joined-up' international law on the subject.

This chapter looks briefly at digital assets and how they are defined, before examining the challenges posed by this (apparently) new form of property from an estate planning perspective. Arguing that English succession law has so far failed to address these issues, the chapter draws on the approach taken in the United States under the Uniform Fiduciary Access to Digital Assets Act and signposts some of the potential issues which any concerted attempt at law reform will have to embrace.

II. DEFINING 'DIGITAL ASSETS': THE INHERENT PROBLEMS

A major difficulty in this area is one of nomenclature: defining 'digital assets' is not straightforward,[8] and there is no current definition in English law.[9] Outside the legal context, standard definitions are equally hard to find; what we have instead are collective descriptors of what typically falls within the realm of digital assets.

Obvious examples include things like emails and email accounts, blogs, social media profiles and accounts (Facebook, Twitter, MySpace and LinkedIn), digital music collections (downloaded from iTunes or similar stores), repositories of digital photographs and videos (beyond those which have been uploaded onto social media sites), and online bank accounts and other financial investments. Online billing arrangements, subscriptions to magazines and gyms, Amazon accounts and eBay seller profiles, as well as other registered shopping sites and loyalty schemes, are also digital assets, as are business information lists (for example, client details and

[6] See, eg, J Miller, 'Britons Spend More Time on Tech Than Asleep, Study Suggests', *BBC News Online*, 7 August 2014, available at www.bbc.co.uk/news/technology-28677674 (accessed September 2016). As in other countries, internet use in the UK varies according to a range of socio-demographic factors, including age, gender and geographical location, with the 16–24 age group spending most time online: Office for National Statistics, 'Internet Users: 2015', available at www.ons.gov.uk/businessindustryandtrade/itandinternetindustry/bulletins/internetusers/2015 (accessed September 2016). However, a significant proportion of older adults are now internet users, with around 33% of adults aged 75 and over recorded as regular internet users during the first quarter of 2015 (a figure that has been steadily increasing): ibid. Of course, these are the most likely social group to have made a will, which raises the succession law issues we are focusing on in this chapter.

[7] The legal challenges created by digital assets are not, of course, restricted to their transmission on death. The same issues, as well as some others, arise when an individual loses capacity; indeed, the problems with incapacity are arguably more acute in that privacy and confidentiality rights are already fully established for the living. More general forfeiture by non-use of digital assets is another issue that will have to be addressed, as is the application of taxing statutes. However, the focus here will be on death and estate planning.

[8] The same difficulties arise when trying to define what constitutes an individual's 'digital estate'.

[9] This may change in the future, in the same way as a broad legal descriptor has been introduced in the United States—see Section V below.

purchasing profiles) and domain names which an individual may have registered.[10] In effect, any files stored or generated on digital devices[11] are treated in this way. Several problems are immediately apparent. First, there is the seemingly endless list of things that can constitute a digital asset.[12] Secondly, the value attached to specific types of digital assets will differ immensely; some (for example, bank accounts, financial investments and domain names) will have an obvious monetary worth, while others (such as photographs, emails and social media profiles)[13] have a purely emotional or sentimental value to the deceased's surviving relatives.[14] Thirdly, there is the issue of how to categorise digital assets, and the implications that this has. These problems all come to the fore in the succession law context, and are discussed at various stages throughout the following sections.

III. DIGITAL ASSETS IN THE SUCCESSION LAW CONTEXT: THE CONCEPTUAL CHALLENGES

Hopkins has noted that '[t]he digitalization of traditional assets has resulted in large amounts of wealth … being stored online, on digital devices, and in the cloud'.[15] When we think of generating wealth, an instinctive thought of a common law property lawyer is its transmissibility on death. However, digital assets pose a unique set of conceptual challenges, which succession law—in its current guise—may struggle to deal with. At the outset, it must be stressed that we cannot conceptualise all of these as succession law issues; yet, it is in this particular legal setting that the question of what happens to digital assets comes to the fore.

While there are multiple ways to categorise digital assets,[16] the most fundamental distinction for present purposes is what constitutes property (since this is what succession law channels between individuals and across generations) and what

[10] Other, slightly more esoteric, examples include online gambling accounts and digital memorials. The latter raise all sorts of issues around who 'owns' and controls someone's post-mortem identity when it comes to memorialising the dead—see H Conway, *The Law and The Dead* (Abingdon, Routledge, 2016) Ch 8.

[11] Usually computers, tablets, mobile telephones, smartphones and any similar digital device—though more examples will doubtless emerge as technology develops. At the risk of stating the obvious, however, the actual device on which the asset is stored or generated is not a digital asset.

[12] As Beyer and Cahn have pointed out, '[t]he list of what a client's computers can hold is, almost literally, infinite'—GW Beyer and N Cahn, 'Digital Planning: The Future of Elder Law' (2013) 9 *National Academy of Elder Law Attorneys Journal* 135, 138.

[13] Unless they belong to high-profile individuals, such as celebrities or leading politicians.

[14] 'Most digital assets are not inherently valuable, but are valuable to family members who extract meaning from what the deceased leaves behind': Beyer and Cahn (n 12) 140. However, a recent report published by The Co-operative Funeralcare suggests that the average UK adult has accumulated personal digital capital worth £275 (though this seems like a rather conservative estimate!), creating a total of £17 billion left in cyberspace when we factor in the 500 million online accounts and assets which currently exist throughout the UK. See 'Death in the Digital Age: Three Quarters of UK Adults Unprepared for Life After Death Online' (February 2015), available at www.co-operativefuneralcare.co.uk/about-us/our-news/death-in-the-digital-age/ (accessed September 2016).

[15] JP Hopkins, 'Afterlife in the Cloud: Managing a Digital Estate' (2013) 5 *Hastings Science and Technology Law Journal* 209, 221.

[16] For example, Beyer and Cahn (n 12) 137–38 suggest four broad categories: personal, social media, financial and business.

does not. Not all digital assets are property in the traditional sense of the word, a fact that is often lost on both lawyers and non-lawyers alike. Instead, the single most important factor will be the terms of the individual service agreement that the account holder entered into with the relevant service provider. The original contractual arrangement may have generated a digital asset in the sense of a distinct item of property which is transferable or, alternatively, a mere licensing agreement which expires on the death of the individual.[17] If the former, it is simply a new variant of intellectual property, albeit one that does not necessarily 'behave' according to a specific set of legal rules.[18] If the latter, the 'asset' does not fall within what is traditionally understood as the jurisdiction of a testator.[19] Individual service providers will also have different policies about what happens to an individual's online persona and digital assets on death: there is no standard distributional model,[20] and (under the terms of the agreement) the same policies can be reviewed and unilaterally altered by the service provider without prior consultation.[21]

In short, what sets digital assets apart from other types of property is the fact that the account holder, the person who we would class as the 'owner' of the digital asset, does not necessarily control their ultimate fate. Attempts to bequeath such assets (or, more likely, authorise access) ignore the fact that the private contractual arrangement with the online service provider, which the individual in question agreed to with little thought for the post-mortem implications, may prohibit this. In an article written in 2014, Natalie Banta noted that digital assets 'all have one striking similarity': their 'inheritability' is controlled the terms of service contract, which typically 'limit the descendability and devisability of digital assets'.[22] According to Banta, this 'threatens the very nature of … succession law by allowing parties to opt out of one of the most fundamental rights of property—the right to devise',[23] and in doing so strikes at the heart of our traditional understandings of personal property and ownership. Highly critical of this approach, she conceded that provisions limiting the transmission of digital assets were probably not open to challenge on basic

[17] In addition, various subcategories of property can exist within the same arrangement. For example, a person's email account may be maintained under a licensing arrangement with the service provider, but the actual email messages attract the same property and copyright laws as letters written on paper.

[18] And the intangible classification might not be as unassailable as we initially think; as Connor points out, only 'digital assets have the unique potential to change from an intangible asset to a tangible one': J Connor, 'Digital Life After Death: The Issue of Planning for a Person's Digital Assets After Death', Texas Tech School of Law Legal Studies Research Paper No 2011-02, 4.

[19] This is not a new concept; there are obvious analogies with dead hand control over property (see AJ Hirsch and WK Wang, 'A Qualitative Theory of the Dead Hand' (1992) 68 *Indiana Law Journal* 1) and an individual's attempts to control the posthumous fate of their remains by setting out funeral instructions (see Conway (n 10) Ch 5).

[20] We return to this theme in Section IV.

[21] 'In the realm of transmission of assets on death, this is unsatisfactory as it means the "rules" vary from site to site, are unclear to users, fail to take account of stakeholder interests and may change on a whim': L Edwards and E Harbinja, '"What Happens to My Facebook Profile When I Die?": Legal Issues Around Transmission of Digital Assets on Death' in C Maciel and V Carvalho Pereira (eds), *Digital Legacy and Interaction* (Cham, Springer International Publishing, 2013).

[22] NM Banta, 'Inherit the Cloud: The Role of Private Contracts in Distributing or Deleting Digital Assets at Death' (2014) 83 *Fordham Law Review* 799. See also Beyer and Cahn (n 12) 136, the authors also making the point that 'the policies of Internet providers often preclude the exercise of individual autonomy'.

[23] Banta (ibid) 803.

principles around formation of contracts, given the full disclosure of the relevant terms and the user's express agreement when he or she signs up to the service.[24] However, Banta went on to argue that contracts which severely restrict or prohibit an individual's right to transfer his or her digital assets should be void as a matter of public policy because:

> Private contracts controlling digital assets are not aimed at distributing digital assets according to an account holder's testamentary intent. Instead of abiding by the principles of succession law, companies, through carefully drafted contracts, determine whether assets ... are devisable by an account holder or are subject to company control and subsequently deleted or destroyed. We are allowing contracts to divest us of the ability to control our digital property and to redefine our property interests in digital assets.[25]

Whether courts subsequently accept this invitation, if such agreements are challenged on this basis in the future, remains to be seen.[26] Meanwhile, other writers have argued that 'management, ownership, or destruction of these assets [should be] based on the foundational principles of deference to the individual's intent'.[27] In short, the law should extend the same rights and freedoms to digital assets that it does to most other forms of personal property: an individual should have decision-making powers over their ultimate fate. Yet such comments overlook the fundamental point that not all digital assets can be classed as property; and even those that can may be incapable of being passed on.

Not all forms of property are inherently transmissible, a concept which is sometimes difficult for those from a common law property law background to appreciate. Many private citizens assume that because they 'own' something, they have the right to bequeath it.[28] Problems arising from the digital estate have echoes with the situation whereby essentially EU concepts such as milk quotas or the Single Farm Payment (and now the Basic Farm Subsidy) have to be married with common law inheritance concepts. The leading decision on milk quotas, that of the English Court of Appeal in *Harris v Barclay's Bank*,[29] underlines the point that such EU concepts are *sui generis* creatures of EU regulations and that there is little to be gained from the metaphysics of engaging in an analysis which attempts to classify them and from whence they derive according to common law property concepts. To underline a

[24] ibid 821, and even though the 'contracts are not negotiated, the terms concerning inheritance are not clear and conspicuous, and there is little alternative choice for users' (ibid 822), who must signify that they accept all the company terms and policies before they can continue (what Banta refers to as the 'take-it-or-leave-it' nature of digital asset contracts).

[25] ibid 826. See also Hopkins (n 15) 241: 'The right to own and pass property at death has been a vital property right in the US legal system for hundreds of years and should not be destroyed by the digital nature of assets'. Although both authors are writing in the US context, the same basic arguments would apply in the UK and in other legal jurisdictions where the concept of private property embraces the core values of transmissibility and testamentary freedom.

[26] Hopkins (n 15) 241 posits the idea of legislation which simply prevents service providers from any attempt to destroy the right of transmissibility in digital assets on death—arguing that this would also benefit service providers who would have fewer inactive and dormant accounts.

[27] Beyer and Cahn (n 12) 136.

[28] Numerous examples exist in the land law context—for example, life estates and property interests held under a joint tenancy. These are not transmissible.

[29] [1997] 2 EGLR 15.

point made elsewhere in this chapter,[30] those of us from a common law background (where there is often the attendant assumption that English is the only language of legal literature) have to address multi-jurisdictional dimensions more than ever before.

Something else that should be borne in mind is that different types of digital asset will trigger very different types of post-mortem 'need' or preference. While some digital assets fit squarely within the traditional succession law narratives of reallocating property (for example, digital photographs and videos; Bitcoins), transmissibility is not the only option here. With things like email and social media accounts, both the individual and his or her survivors are more likely to be concerned about ensuring post-mortem access or terminating the account on the individual's death[31] than about who 'owns' the asset. This has prompted Brubaker and others to propose a 'stewardship' model for things like social network sites, whereby a nominated steward would mediate the deceased's wishes and their data, as well as moderating the needs and requests of the deceased's family and online friends who have an ongoing and active interest in things like the deceased's Facebook account and virtual persona.[32] Of course, this raises questions of access following the account holder's demise, and the need for forward planning. While failure to disclose passwords and log-in details raises the spectre of digital assets floating around in cyberspace for all eternity (and renders the account holder vulnerable to identity theft long after their demise),[33] disclosing these details can breach the terms of service agreement with the service provider.[34] And even when an individual is encouraged to make an inventory of accounts and usernames to facilitate their access by others, 'it does not necessarily mean that they have passed on the legal right to use the account and all the information contained therein'.[35]

In short, digital assets bring a distinct set of legal rules into play, as we enter the collective realms of intellectual property law and contract law, as well as privacy laws and rights of access. The fact that succession law cannot pass lots of digital assets because they are not regarded as transmissible property is not actually a succession law problem, as we noted earlier in this section. However, it is a problem

[30] See Section V below.

[31] We cannot simply assume that everyone wants their digital assets to be passed on or managed by someone else after that person's demise. An account holder who has digital assets of a private nature may want them to be destroyed and should take active steps to ensure this happens, just in the same way as an individual might ask someone they trusted to destroy physical material of a similar nature. We return briefly to this in Section IV below.

[32] See JR Brubaker, L Dombrowski, AM Gilbert, N Kusumakaulika and GR Hayes, 'Stewarding a Legacy: Responsibilities and Relationships in the Management of Post-Mortem Data' in *Proceedings of the SIGCHI Conference on Human Factors in Computing Systems* (ACM, 2014) 4157. In proposing this scheme, the authors were influenced by the fact that inheritance models presume an heir, which is not necessarily the case here.

[33] Most of the literature highlights the problems which can arise if digital assets are simply floating around, making them accessible to the 'wrong' person and vulnerable to post-mortem identity theft—see, eg, Connor (n 18) 5. Of course, the situation is complicated by the fact that, to guard against identity theft, account holders are encouraged to use different passwords for different services, and to change and update these in the event of any perceived threat (or even on a regular basis).

[34] Likewise, if the person in possession of the password or username simply uses these to access the site and locate the asset, or terminate the service, then that person runs the risk of committing a cybercrime by misrepresenting who they are to the service provider.

[35] Connor (n 18) 6.

for succession lawyers, because even if testators and their families begin to understand that many digital assets are mere licences that cannot be passed on because of the terms of the contract that the testator initially entered into,[36] the issues around distributing, managing and (in some cases) terminating these assets will become pertinent on the death of the account holder. It is naive to suggest otherwise, or simply to advise people that a loved one's financial or personal legacies[37] cannot be passed on or dealt with in an appropriate manner simply because they exist in a digital medium and do not adhere to traditional rules. Succession law may simply have to adapt and develop effective solutions, as the difficulties in accessing digital assets and disputed claims over who controls them following an individual's demise bring these issues into the legal arena and strengthen the case for forward planning.[38]

IV. DIGITAL ASSESTS IN THE CURRENT ESTATE PLANNING CLIMATE

While planning for bricks-and-mortar and tangible personal property is a well-established process, currently relatively few citizens address the devolution or distribution of their post-mortem digital estate or plan for their digital afterlife.[39] Digital assets are gradually replacing stored documents, photograph albums, written letters and music collections as personal mementos which people traditionally pass on to their family and loved ones. Estate conflicts are just as likely here; the locus of the dispute simply shifts elsewhere. Fighting, for example, over digital photograph albums, email accounts and online financial investments or business assets raises the same fundamental issues as other items of personal property; these issues just manifest themselves in a different way.

Even among lawyers it would appear that incorporating digital assets within general succession planning has been the exception rather than the norm.[40] According to Connor, 'the biggest problem facing not only estate planners, but their clients as well, is a general lack of knowledge about how to properly prepare for what will happen to their digital assets after death'.[41] This is not the only obstacle to

[36] In other words, we deal with the 'problem' that succession law does not recognise digital assets as property by tackling and correcting the common perception that it does, and the only way to address this issue is by educating lawyers and private citizens more generally.

[37] As with other items of personal property, digital assets can have both emotional value and monetary worth. We return to this in the following section.

[38] One option might be a legal requirement for service providers to give something more than a licence when the individual pays for specific material (eg, music downloads); another would be to introduce specific rules around management of and access to the asset on death. The first suggestion would be much harder to achieve, because it requires a fundamental change to our legal system and wholescale re-writing of terms of service agreements. The second suggestion, which (as discussed in Section IV) is not just about the passing on of assets but also about dealing with liabilities and other 'loose ends', is a much more realistic goal.

[39] One survey found that of the 94% of UK adults who hold online accounts, 75% had not considered or made arrangements for the management of their digital presence on death: The Co Operative Funeralcare (n 14).

[40] In April 2015 one of the current authors asked the 90 private client practitioners in Northern Ireland who were attending the Society of Trust and Estate Practitioners Probate Day (mainly but not exclusively solicitors) how many routinely addressed digital assets when clients were making a will. None did so.

[41] Connor (n 18) 8.

negotiate. As has been noted already, the concept of digital 'property' is multifarious in nature. The list of digital assets is constantly evolving and mutating,[42] creating its own problems from an estate planning perspective, and any legal structures which are developed will have to be sufficiently flexible to accommodate the rapid changes in technological progress.

From the perspective of the legal practitioner, the most obvious classification is those assets which have an economic or income-generating value, and those with purely a dignitary, personal or non-economic benefit. The second category raises entirely different legal challenges to the first, and generally falls outside the remit of the traditional property or probate lawyer.[43] Moreover, it is perhaps not surprising that these non-commercial aspects of the digital footprint generated so little interest in the early years of the digital age: Facebook, for example, was created by and for young college students, who presumably did not have the death of a network user as a core feature of the development phase. The immutable reality is that practising succession lawyers will give little attention to 'sentimental' assets with minimal monetary value, and will engage with funeral and other 'memorialising' disputes only on an ad hoc basis, as and when they arise. While professional lawyers will continue to give lip service to the platitude that their primary function is to implement a client's wishes, the practical reality is that it is not (and never will be) cost-effective for a lawyer to get involved in disputes about low-value personal chattels and funeral instructions, whether that dispute arises out of the real or digital world. Consequently, it is unlikely that our common law system will ever generate much, if any, jurisprudence on these aspects of the digital footprint and systematic legal regulation will inevitably have to be statutory in nature.[44]

In contrast, there are other problems with potentially catastrophic consequences which could arise out of any digital estate, and which should never be ignored by the reasonably competent succession lawyer. Within the last two or three years there has been some evidence that this truism has now been acknowledged by the legal

[42] As do the virtual mediums in which they 'exist'.

[43] Though it is still something that individual citizens should be mindful of when contemplating the emotional and personal legacies that they leave behind.

[44] Isolated examples have already arisen in the USA, most notably the litigation involving the parents of L/Cpl Justin Ellsworth, a US Marine who was killed in Iraq, and Yahoo! The parents wanted to use emails written by their son while in Iraq to create a memorial to him, but were denied access to the email account because of Yahoo! company policy. A probate judge eventually ordered Yahoo! to hand the emails over: see the analysis in J Atwater, 'Who Owns E-Mail? Do You Have the Right to Decide the Disposition of Your Private Digital Life?' (2006) *Utah Law Review* 397. The case also attracted attention on this side of the Atlantic: see 'Who Owns Your Emails', *BBC News Online*, 11 January 2005, available at http://news.bbc.co.uk/1/hi/magazine/4164669.stm (accessed September 2016). In September 2012, various media outlets erroneously reported that the actor Bruce Willis was contemplating legal action against Apple so that he could leave his iTunes music collection to his daughters: see 'Bruce Willis "Considering iTunes Legal Action" against Apple', *The Telegraph*, 3 September 2012, available at www.telegraph.co.uk/technology/apple/9516636/Bruce-Willis-considering-iTunes-legal-action-against-Apple.html (accessed September 2016). Although the rumours turned out to be false, the legal issues such action would have generated were explored by those writing in the area: see, eg, C Wong, 'Can Bruce Willis Leave His iTunes Collection to his Children: Inheritability of Digital Assets in the Face of EULAs' (2012) 20 *Santa Clara Computer and High Technology Law Journal* 703.

profession,[45] with piecemeal references to the challenges of the digital estate appearing within the standard practitioner texts,[46] even if they do tend to pose more questions than answers or do little more than raise awareness of the issues:

> This is a complex area on which there is little, if any, learning or legislation at present … [A]t the very least a testator should, when making his will, compile a list of all his digital and online involvements to enable his executors to have full information of the assets of his estate and to take the appropriate action (if available) to terminate or otherwise deal with an online account or asset.[47]

The reality is that all of these novel challenges for the legal profession have to be addressed and resolved in a legal vacuum, with neither legislation nor case law to assist.

The editors of *Williams on Wills* are undoubtedly correct in their assessment that, at the very least, testators should be encouraged to 'die tidily'[48] in respect of their digital estate. Lawyers need basic information about their client's online presence, and the current consensus among practitioners is to encourage testators to keep an up-to-date record of digital assets with passwords[49] and security questions left in a physically secure and sealed side letter.[50] Solicitors generally tend to refuse to retain passwords, not least because it may be a breach of the user agreement for them to do so, and for very obvious reasons it is totally inappropriate either that passwords be recorded on the face of a will or that the document in which passwords are noted is incorporated by reference to the will, with the consequence that it becomes part of the probate documentation and is open to public inspection.[51]

Moreover, in a will context it is at least arguable that a solicitor or other professional will drafter has not discharged their duty properly if he or she has not completed (and retained) an inventory of those digital assets which have a monetary value. Contentious probate disputes have increased almost exponentially in England and Wales over the last ten years, and one of the most fundamental tenets of the

[45] No doubt some of this is motivated by self-interest. The demand for expert advice on digital assets will only increase, and those private client practitioners who are reluctant to be involved in estate planning with a digital element will cause their clients to look elsewhere.

[46] For example, RFD Barlow, RA Wallington, SL Meadway and JAD MacDougald, *Williams on Wills*, 10th edn (Butterworths, 2014) 1st Supplement; *Butterworths' Wills Probate and Administration Service*, paragraph 4.7; *Tolleys Administration of Estates* B3.3.

[47] *Williams on Wills* (ibid).

[48] *Which?* magazine first coined the term 'dying tidily' in the pre-digital age, effectively encouraging their readership to keep a personal log of details which would make life easier for those left behind, with a pro forma provided. In 2014 the Law Society of England and Wales published a Practice Note and a form of Personal Asset Log, and the Law Society of Northern Ireland has recently undertaken a similar exercise under the auspices of its Non Contentious Business Committee.

[49] It is important that this is kept up-to-date. The average British citizen has 25 passwords.

[50] There is the theoretical risk that giving the means of accessing an account exposes the estate to an argument that a *donatio mortis causa* (DMC) has been created in favour of the individual to whom the details have been given. It is submitted that this is insufficient indicia of title (even if the other components for a valid DMC are present): see the discussion in N Roberts, '*Donationes Mortis Causa* in a Dematerialised World' [2013] *The Conveyancer and Property Lawyer* 113. It should also be noted that the English Court of Appeal has recently sought to reign in the DMC doctrine substantially: *King v Dubrey* [2015] EWCA Civ 581.

[51] There has also been a growth in the number of proprietary software providers, such as Cirrus, who will store passwords and release them on the production of a death certificate to a specified person (such as an executor).

Banks v Goodfellow[52] test for testamentary capacity is that a testator is capable of knowing the extent and nature of his assets.

When a deceased has 'died tidily' in respect of his or her digital estate, the personal representatives at least start from the baseline that they know what exists and can therefore concentrate their time and energy on the subsequent legal and practical minefield[53] of administering the digital estate. When this is not done, the family or those administering the estate are left to reconstitute the digital estate as best they can,[54] but without the traditional 'clues' of an earlier generation, namely large piles of post-death unopened post or previous correspondence retrieved from the deceased's home or workplace.

For those who do seek to engage in digital estate planning, the most fundamental question is whether the benefit of a particular asset can be transmitted by will at all (or, in the absence of a will, falls to be dealt with by the intestacy rules). As noted earlier, the answer is dependent on the type of asset in question and, irrespective of the content of any will, the terms of the specific service agreement. The most perfunctory review of a miscellany of such agreements discloses a bewildering array of permutations with absolutely no consistency.[55] It is imperative that those seeking to plan their digital estate, and those who advise them, have read the fine print of their service agreement, though, in practice, few actually do so.[56] Most of us are guilty of clicking the 'I accept' button to online terms and conditions without paying close attention to the precise contractual terms!

[52] (1870) LR 5 QB 549. *Banks v Goodfellow* remains the relevant test for testamentary capacity, even since the enactment of the Mental Capacity Act 2005— see further J Brooks, 'The Neighbour, The Carer and The Old Friend—The Complex World of Testamentary Capacity', chapter seven in this volume. The 2005 Act does not extend to Northern Ireland, where the function-specific test for testamentary capacity is also that set down in *Banks v Goodfellow*.

[53] 78% of those who had managed a loved one's online account following their death reported difficulty in winding up the account, with 20% abandoning efforts entirely: The Co Operative Funeral-care (n 14).

[54] There is anecdotal evidence of solicitors dealing with the trail of digital chaos left by certain deceased with informal approaches to providers and 'unofficial' computer experts. Often access has been granted, eventually.

[55] The following list is not exhaustive. LinkedIn: users agree not to sell, trade or transfer their LinkedIn account to another party and LinkedIn will close the deceased user's account and remove their profile on completion of a form provided on the LinkedIn website. Twitter: users own the rights to all of the tweets which they produce but Twitter will not give personal representatives access to a deceased user's account (although it will assist personal representatives to de-activate the account). Amazon: grants a limited, non-exclusive, non-transferable licence to access and make personal and non-commercial use of Amazon, with Amazon closing down an account on being provided with a copy of the death certificate. Apple (including iTunes): the terms and conditions prohibit the account holder from renting, leasing, lending, selling, transferring, distributing or sublicensing the licensed application. The iCloud account is non-transferable and any rights to Apple ID or content within the account terminates on death. Upon receipt of a copy of a death certificate, the account may be terminated and all content within deleted. Bitcoins: these are a form of digital currency which can be transferred on the death of the user and, in order to do so, the password to the user's 'digital wallet' must be available to the deceased user's personal representative. If the password is lost, the bitcoins will be lost forever as there is no mechanism to retrieve a lost password. PayPal: the account holder may not transfer or assign any rights or obligations without PayPal's prior written consent and to close the account of a deceased the personal representative needs to inform PayPal and enclose a copy of the death certificate.

[56] The relevant terms of the agreements in question are not always readily accessible and, notwithstanding the campaign for Plain English, they are not the easiest documents to read, even for a lawyer.

In the absence of legal regulation and notwithstanding the undeniably *sui generis* nature of many digital assets, it is submitted that the least ineffective transitional approach for lawyers (essentially the lesser of two evils) is that they should be dealt with by the deceased in a formal will.

It is incontrovertible that traditional wills are not without shortcomings when it comes to the transmission of digital assets on death,[57] and in the post-*White v Jones*[58] era all professional will drafters are reluctant to purport to dispose of an asset which it may later transpire is not transmissible by will at all. Although there remain many grey areas, and while some terms of service-type agreements try to restrict some of the actions suggested above, it is submitted that the inclusion of specific powers to deal with the digital estate, rather than no express power (or very generalised powers), is more likely to result in some sort of response from the online service provider. One would expect a risk-management-aware practitioner to include the usual caveats as to the ultimate efficacy of the testamentary disposition. If difficulties do arise with the providers, the executors would be justified in applying to the court for directions.[59] Will drafters should not be held to have breached any duty of care in the current legal vacuum so long as they can demonstrate by the will, attendance notes and letter of retainer that they were alert to the potential difficulties. Moreover, in an era when no less than the UK Supreme Court has endorsed a highly intention-centric approach to the construction of wills,[60] it is unlikely that a court will seek to thwart a deceased's obvious intention without good reason.

From the perspective of the deceased's family and testamentary beneficiaries, it is obviously important that assets of value are located and secured for the benefit of those intended by the deceased, and much of the popular press has concentrated on this aspect. The reasons are not simply financial ones; the point has already been made that digital assets are rapidly replacing personal possessions as items of property with a high sentimental value for the deceased's family. Being unable to access these items can be frustrating and upsetting for surviving relatives at what is already an emotionally difficult time, and risks 'the story of the life of the deceased … be[ing] lost forever'.[61] The point has already been made that professional probate lawyers aim to avoid getting involved in non-commercially viable disputes, such as those about funeral instructions and personal effects of only sentimental value. Yet any probate lawyer with even a modicum of experience will be acutely aware that the seeds for some of the most hostile estate litigation are sown immediately after death in the emotively charged atmosphere of loved ones, jostling to secure their new

[57] The requirement for formality; also the fact that digital assets change more frequently than other personality and may fall foul of the traditional doctrine of ademption.

[58] [1995] UKHL 5.

[59] On which see further below.

[60] *Marley v Rawlings* [2014] UKSC 2, [2015] AC 129. The ratio of the decision involves the extension of statutory rectification of wills to the 'mixed up' wills of a husband and wife and an expansive interpretation of the concept of a clerical error. Arguably of even more interest are the *obiter* comments of the Supreme Court to the effect that wills should be construed in the same manner as commercial contracts, and that 'context is everything'.

[61] Beyer and Cahn (n 12) 140, the authors making the point that this is 'not only a tragedy for family members, but also possibly for future historians who are losing pieces of history in the digital abyss'.

role in a differently constituted family, arranging the funeral and memorialisation of the deceased. It is in no-one's interest that the law adds even more heat but no light.

Another important point is that academic lawyers have a tendency to view the law of succession primarily from the perspective of the deceased property owner and the beneficiaries, rather than from that of the personal representatives. However, it is the unenviable position of the personal representative (and his or her lawyer)[62] that has generated the most intractable legal difficulties in practice in respect of digital estates, and the impetus for legislative intervention in the United States[63] came initially from the desire to ensure that personal representatives, trustees and other fiduciaries (such as those acting under a Lasting Power of Attorney or an Enduring Power of Attorney) were in a position to manage assets properly and without exposure to personal or criminal liability.

The role of personal representatives in developing jurisprudence in the field of succession law in our common law system should not be underestimated. It has long been accepted that succession law experienced something of a 'dark age' in the British Isles for a period from the mid-1980s,[64] with a complete dearth of seminal case law. Today, it is heartening that succession law is again appearing on the law reform agenda, even though reported cases that establish new principles (the burgeoning testamentary negligence jurisprudence apart) remain relatively rare. Those that do arise often have their genesis in a neutral personal representative, sometimes an insured professional, seeking directions from the court.[65] One suspects that if England and Wales chooses not to enact legislation but to rely solely on the common law to develop and delineate the scope of the doctrines which govern the transmissibility of the digital estate on death, it is highly likely that much of the jurisprudence will be generated by personal representatives seeking such directions.

It is trite law that a personal representative is liable to the extent that property within the estate comes into his or her hands, or should come into his or her possession if they take reasonable steps in relation to it. Prima facie it falls to the personal representative to identify such assets and then take appropriate steps to secure them where the nature of the asset requires the personal representative to do so. If the personal representative causes unreasonable loss to the estate, he or she will be liable for devastavit, and it takes little imagination to come up with illustrations of such loss in a digital context. Consider the unexpected death of the keyman individual of a small business. Delay in accessing fundamental information which is held online in respect of a small business may sound the death knell for that business's very survival. What of the personal representative who distributes the deceased's

[62] And, in turn, his or her professional indemnity policy!

[63] Discussed in Section V below.

[64] See, eg, the comments made by Professor Gareth Miller in his preface to *The Machinery of Succession*, 2nd edn (Aldershot, Dartmouth, 1956). Professor Miller was one of only a handful of academics who specialised in succession law during this period. As Professor Miller points out, the position in Australasia during this period was in stark contrast, with numerous law reform projects being published.

[65] An English illustration is the important decision on the application of the doctrine of ademption where the asset that has been specifically devised has been disposed of by an attorney: *Banks v National Westminster Bank* [2006] WTLR 1693. In Northern Ireland, the only reported decision on the succession law aspects of the Single Farm Payment Scheme that operated for 10 years between 2005 and 2015, *Crossey v Armour* [2008] NI Ch 4, started life as an executor's application for directions.

estate before becoming aware of the large online gambling debts which render the estate insolvent? Or the personal representative who is facing penalties from HMRC (or the relevant taxation authority) for a negligent inheritance tax return because he or she is considered not to have properly investigated the extent of the digital estate? What if the personal representative's alleged failure to safeguard the digital estate on death has resulted in various losses caused by a consequential identify theft?

Often the personal representative is not the most appropriate person to deal with the digital estate on death, particularly if he or she is not particularly computer savvy. With this in mind, the suggestion has been made by several legal commentators that it may be more appropriate to have a separate 'digital executor'.[66] The concept of specialist executors whose responsibility and authority is limited to a particular type of asset has long been adopted in respect of the literary executor and the administration of a testator's copyright, which shares many characteristics with some components of the digital estate. There is no reason, in theory, why a similar division of function could not operate in respect of digital assets. It is important, however, not to confuse the role of an individual who is merely tasked by a deceased with collating and managing his or her digital information on death (often on the basis of their expertise with computers) with a legal personal representative who carries the full mantle of that office's responsibilities and liabilities. The interrelationship between any so-called 'digital executor' and the individuals to whom the grant of representation has been issued would have to be given careful consideration.

Finally, in common law systems, legal regulation of the transmission of digital assets on death is muddied by the fact that while intellectual property rights uncontroversially transmit to the beneficiaries on foot of a will or to the statutory next of kin, there is little recognition of privacy or reputational rights after death.[67] Terms of service agreements between online service providers and account holders have privacy interests at their core—and these are often cited as the basis for such severe restrictions and prohibitions on the transfer of digital assets on death.[68] One could argue that this rationale is somewhat flawed; privacy interests generally cease on death, removing the prospect of the online service provider being exposed to liability through a potential breach of privacy action (unless the terms-of-service agreement specifically provides that it will maintain the user's privacy in the event of his or her death). Broader privacy interests also come into play when someone is deciding what they want to happen to their digital assets after their own demise. An individual might want sentimental items (eg photographs) to pass on to the family, or surviving relatives to have access to digital assets such as online bank accounts; but the same individual may also want certain things to be permanently deleted (eg secret emails from a lover, personal diaries). As with any other assets, lawyers must ascertain and effectuate their client's wishes.[69]

[66] See Connor (n 18) 15; N Cahn, 'Postmortem Life On-Line' (2011) 25 *Property & Probate* 36, 38.

[67] Most obviously the dead have no reputation and cannot be libelled.

[68] See generally L Edwards and E Harbinja, 'Protecting Post-Mortem Privacy: Reconsidering the Privacy Interests of the Deceased in a Digital World' (2013) 32 *Cardozo Arts & Entertainment Law Journal* 1.

[69] Cahn (n 66) 39.

V. LOOKING AHEAD: LESSONS FROM ELSEWHERE?

When looking at digital assets and the future of estate planning in the UK, two things are striking: a dearth of legal commentary on the topic[70] and the absence of specific laws dealing with the key issues. The contrast with the United States is stark where there is a wealth of scholarship on digital assets,[71] and legislative changes have already been introduced in a number of states. For example, Oklahoma gives the deceased's executor a right to access specific online accounts,[72] while Idaho allows the deceased's executors or personal representatives to access a wide range of digital assets—including accounts on social networking sites and blogs.[73] While undoubtedly viewed as a step in the right direction, these laws are not without their limitations: the pace of technological change and constant emergence of new forms of digital assets renders these statutes obsolete within a relatively short space of time (they have a limited legal shelf-life), and not all of them address the contractual relationship between online service providers and account holders which governs the basic terms of access and transmissibility of assets.[74]

The most recent (and most significant) legislative development, however, is the Uniform Fiduciary Access to Digital Assets Act (UFADAA). Released in 2015, this was intended to give fiduciaries such as personal representatives, executors and trustees the authority and ability to access the deceased's online accounts (and in doing so to perform their basic legal duty to deal with and distribute the deceased's estate).[75] The Act defines digital assets as 'electronic records, not including an underlying asset or liability unless the asset or liability is itself a record that is electronic' (not easy to understand at first glance, at least not for the technologically challenged!), and grants fiduciaries the same rights to access digital assets as the account holder—but only for the purpose of discharging their fiduciary duties.[76] The reasons can range from gathering together the estate assets to preventing identity theft and

[70] There are only passing references in one or two of the leading succession law texts (see Section IV), and specific articles on the topic are hard to find.

[71] See, eg, Beyer and Cahn (n 12); Varnado (n 1); Hopkins (n 15); see also most of the other academic sources cited thus far. Other examples include M Perrone, 'What Happens When We Die: Estate Planning of Digital Assets' (2012) 21 *CommLaw Conspectus* 185; N Cahn, 'Probate Law Meets the Digital Age' (2014) 67 *Vanderbilt Law Review* 1697; MD Roy, 'Beyond the Digital Assets Dilemma: Will Online Services Revolutionize Estate Planning?' (2011) 24 *Quinnipiac Probate Law Journal* 376; E Carroll and J Romano, *Your Digital Afterlife: When Facebook, Flickr and Twitter Are Your Estate, What's Your Legacy?* (Berkeley, CA, New Riders, 2011); and AB Lopez, 'Death and the Digital Age: The Disposition of Digital Assets' (2016) 3 *Savannah Law Review* 77.

[72] See the discussion in Hopkins (n 15) 240–41.

[73] Beyer and Cahn (n 12) 144 (though see 140–46 for an overview of other statutes passed in several US states and how these have evolved over a relatively short period of time (in legal years) to meet the challenges posed by new technologies and the emergence of new forms of digital assets).

[74] Beyer and Cahn (n 12) 146–47.

[75] For an overview, see V Blachly, 'Uniform Fiduciary Access to Digital Assets Act' (2015) 29 *Probate & Property Magazine*, available at www.americanbar.org/publications/probate_property_magazine_2012/2015/july_august_2015/2015_aba_rpte_pp_v29_3_article_blachly_uniform_fiduciary_access_to_digital_assets_act.html (accessed September 2016). See also J Lee, 'Death and Live Feeds: Privacy Protection in Fiduciary Access to Digital Assets' (2015) *Columbia Business Law Review* 654; N Cahn, C Kunz and S Brown Walsh, 'Digital Assets and Fiduciaries', GWU Legal Studies Research Paper No 2015-18.

[76] The Act does not grant personal access, nor does it allow fiduciaries to 'impersonate' the account holder: Cahn et al (ibid) 19.

(apparently) consoling grieving relatives.[77] Obstacles still remain: fiduciaries need to have the deceased's passwords to gain entry, copyright and privacy laws might restrict what they can do with the asset (if they access it) and service providers can still unilaterally remove or destroy individual entries.[78] Approved by the Uniform Law Commission in the USA,[79] individual states must actively decide whether or not to enact the UFADAA, though initial signs are encouraging, with several states already having adopted the measure or enacting something substantially the same. Cahn, Kunt and Walsh explain the Act's success in the following terms:

> UFADAA seeks to place the fiduciary into the shoes of the account holder through a variety of provisions, resolving as many of the impediments to fiduciary access to digital assets as possible: it defines digital assets, provides default rules, defers to account holder intent and privacy desires, and encourages custodian compliance. It (1) specifies that the fiduciary is deemed to have the account holder's lawful consent …; (2) clarifies that if any digital material was illegally obtained by the decedent, then the fiduciary's attempt to take control of it will not 'launder' it to pass clean title to the heirs; and (3) sidesteps contentious issues about whether a fiduciary can challenge restrictive terms of service precluding transfer or specifying choice of law.[80]

Whether a similar legal framework is introduced on this side of the Atlantic remains to be seen, though the European Law Institute is currently establishing a joint study group with the Uniform Law Commission in the USA to see if the UFADAA could be used as a model for European legislation.[81]

Within the UK, the Law Commission for England and Wales may address the issue of digital assets as part of a forthcoming wills project, which probably means that legislative reform is some way off.[82] Much will depend on the succession law implications of digital assets capturing the respective legal and public imaginations in the years to come. Social pressure will come from surviving family and friends who are unable to access digital assets following the account holder's demise;[83] this may have financial consequences, but is more likely to result in the loss of the deceased's personal (and historical) legacy. Within the legal profession, the initial impetus for reform will come from lawyers who, faced with a confusing array of user policies

[77] See the discussion in Blachly (n 75).

[78] ibid.

[79] The Uniform Law Commission was established in the USA in 1892, and provides states with 'non-partisan, well-conceived and well-drafted legislation that brings clarity and stability to critical areas of state statutory law'—see www.uniformlaws.org/Default.aspx (accessed September 2016).

[80] Cahn et al (n 75) 18. Lee (n 75) also suggests that the Act's success is largely down to its 'asset neutral' approach in that it treats digital assets in the same way as physical assets for estate administration purposes, though she is ultimately critical of this approach.

[81] The objective is to explore a model law for Member States; for an overview of the initiative, see P Szulewski, 'Digital Legacy—Is it Possible to Transfer Digital Assets in Case of Death?' (6 October 2015), available at https://ec.europa.eu/digital-single-market/en/content/digital-legacy-it-possible-transfer-digital-assets-case-death (accessed September 2016). We are grateful to Prof Dr Sjef van Erp of the European Law Institute for drawing our attention to this initiative.

[82] As with any law reform process, stakeholder engagement will be essential, given that online service providers will have their own concerns around the intended usage of data and allowing others (beyond the account holder) to access it.

[83] Examples have already been publicised: see 'Father Told by Apple to Get Court Order for Dead Son's Data', *BBC News Online* (29 July 2016), available at www.bbc.co.uk/news/uk-england-coventry-warwickshire-36926812 (accessed September 2016).

and virtually no legal authority on the subject, are struggling to advise clients on the post-mortem fate of their digital assets. There is some movement here already, and one of the most active proponents for reform globally has been the Society of Trust and Estate Practitioners (STEP).[84] STEP's Mental Capacity Special Interest Group created a Digital Assets Working Group in 2013[85] with a view to clarifying the issues relating to the access and ownership of digital assets following the death or incapacity of the registered owner. The ultimate aims are to create a best-practice template policy protocol, to be consistently adopted by online providers, to assist in the management of digital assets by fiduciaries and to consider the creation of legislation for adoption and harmonisation by all state and national parliaments where STEP is active. Judicial calls for reform are also likely, when courts are eventually tasked with the interpretation and enforcement of terms of service agreements which restrict inheritance rights.

The UFADAA is one possible model, though other options for reforming the law may yet emerge. Two considerations will be paramount when drafting any new legislative scheme: sufficient flexibility to deal with an array of digital assets and their various uses, while making it easier for personal representatives to access and deal with them by conferring the requisite legal authority.[86] Broader 'territorial issues' will also be an important factor. While 'High Street' succession law had traditionally been insulated from private international law, ownership of holiday homes abroad and increased mobility (together with Brussels IV)[87] have already brought the substantive and procedural laws of other jurisdictions into sharp focus. It will now be virtually impossible for even the most insulated probate practitioner to ignore extraterritorial issues, not least because many providers are based in the United States, where the Patriot Act 2001 and the National Security Agency's Prism Project must be addressed in respect of privacy and confidentiality.[88] The fact that digital assets can be located across an array of virtual places and held by a range of service providers operating through global companies leads to complex multi-jurisdictional legal issues.[89] The traditional starting point of the territory in which the deceased was domiciled at the time of his or her death may be irrelevant if there is an express stipulation about which country's laws apply in the terms of service agreement. The latter would govern post-mortem access to digital assets, making comprehensive and meaningful reform impossible to achieve without a joined-up international approach.

[84] STEP was created in 1991 and now has over 20,000 members and over 100 branches worldwide, including one in Northern Ireland, which was established in 2007. It is represented throughout Europe, North America and the Caribbean.

[85] Chaired by Rod Genders, a senior Australian lawyer.

[86] A consistent set of user policies and standard service provider norms seems unlikely.

[87] Regulation 650/2012 (or Brussels IV, as it is colloquially known) is intended to help with cross-border successions by unifying the succession laws which apply to an individual estate (the default position is that inheritance issues are governed by the law of the state in which the deceased was habitually resident). Both the UK and Ireland have opted out, but the Treaty nonetheless can have implications for testators in both jurisdictions who own assets elsewhere.

[88] For example, the latter is effectively a surveillance programme that allows the National Security Agency to retrieve data directly from major US internet companies (including Google, Microsoft and Yahoo!).

[89] See the general discussion in W Moncur, 'Digital Ownership Across Lifespans' in D Prendergast and C Garattini (eds), *Aging and the Digital Life Course* (New York, Berghahn Books, 2015) ch 13.

VI. CONCLUSION

Succession lawyers are entering new and unfamiliar territory; this, in itself, is not a novel experience, but the pace of change and the rapidly expanding categories of digital assets are leaving little time to catch up. As more people are dying in the digital age, families and estate administrators are starting to realise the digital mess that has been left behind. In 2014, Varnado sounded a cautionary note, warning that 'the problems have not reached epic proportions, but that day is coming, and eventually, the digital footprint issue will become a serious problem'.[90]

Digital assets cross the boundaries between the tangible and the intangible, and between property law, succession law, intellectual property law, contract law and privacy law. They are the 'new' new property and, barring specific legislative changes, succession law will have to encompass them within existing legal frameworks while making the necessary adjustments for the complex regulatory agreements that accompany digital assets and being mindful of the competing interests of all the different parties involved—namely the account holders, their families and beneficiaries, the online service providers, and society more generally. There is a significant degree of uncertainty and confusion around digital assets, and, because of the legal and technical issues they raise, specific laws may have to be enacted in the future. In the meantime, individuals should be encouraged to plan for the future and to leave clear directions for what they want to happen to their digital estates post mortem.

[90] Varnado (n 1) 719.

7

The Neighbour, The Carer and The Old Friend—The Complex World of Testamentary Capacity

JULIET BROOK*

I. INTRODUCTION

THE RELATIONSHIPS MADE by people in their later years are complex and as a result so are the wills they make. Perhaps children have moved away and a bond has grown between the testator and their long-term friend and carer. Perhaps a neighbour has become, over the years, more like family than those with whom they share a blood tie.[1] For these reasons and many others, solicitors are asked to make wills for clients in the last years of their life that break the expectation that the wealth of the older generation will benefit the younger.[2]

Solicitors are reporting a rise in contentious probate litigation[3] and the Law Commission has turned its attention to this issue and will examine it in its forthcoming Wills Project, which has a stated aim of reducing 'the likelihood of wills being challenged after death, and the incidence of litigation'.[4]

Whatever the reasons, the distress caused when 'family' is disinherited by an elderly testator can have expensive consequences and lead to long-lasting rifts within families. This chapter will explore why so many challenges are made to the validity of wills, in particular on the grounds of lack of capacity, and examine whether it is possible to create a simpler, more workable test for capacity that will also provide the protections necessary to preserve the autonomy of often vulnerable testators.

* Principal Lecturer at the University of Portsmouth. Many thanks to Greg Osborne, Caroline Cox and the anonymous peer reviewer for their comments on an earlier draft.

[1] Examples of such changing relationships can be seen in *Cowderoy v Cranfield* [2011] EWHC 1616 (Ch D), [2011] WTLR 1699 and *Cattermole v Prisk* [2006] 1 FLR 693 (Ch D).

[2] Whilst only about half of the population describe themselves as 'likely' to inherit, of those who thought they were 'very likely' or 'definite' to inherit, 91% expect to inherit from their parents—see K Rowlington and S McKay, *Attitudes to Inheritance in Britain* (York, Joseph Rowntree Foundation, 2005) Ch 2.

[3] Whilst court statistics only reflect those cases with sufficient merit to lead to formal court action, these statistics reflect the rise in instructions received by probate solicitors. See, eg, www.independent.co.uk/news/uk/home-news/where-theres-a-will-family-feuds-lead-to-700-increase-in-high-court-disputes-in-five-years-8475962.html.

[4] www.lawcom.gov.uk/project/wills/.

The first part of the chapter will explore the current definition of testamentary capacity and the means by which the testator's lack of capacity is determined. The second part will examine our obligations to those with impaired capacity under the UN Convention on the Rights of Persons with Disabilities. The third part will examine why there are so many legal challenges to wills, before the final part analyses the difference between capacity and autonomy, and considers the inherent difficulties with any simple, singular notion of capacity.

II. OUTLINE OF THE PROBLEM, CAPACITY AND PRESUMPTIONS

A will is seen as an ambulatory document that can be revoked at any time prior to the death of the testator.[5] The testator therefore remains free to change his or her mind, with the will only becoming fixed and unalterable on the testator's death. Until that time, the beneficiaries' potential inheritance is a mere hope—the *spes successionis*. In England,[6] it is accepted that the testator has had testamentary freedom for 500 years.[7] Our common law tradition has none of the 'forced heirship' rules of the kind that exist in many European countries.[8] There are some exceptions to this principle, the most useful of which (as far as disappointed relatives are concerned) is the Inheritance (Provision for Family and Dependants) Act 1975. This enables certain specified categories of persons (for example, the testator's cohabitee) to make a claim for 'reasonable financial provision'[9] if the testator's will or intestacy has not provided for them adequately. However, there are strict rules on who can claim under this legislation and even a successful claimant will only be awarded 'reasonable financial provision', which may still be far less than they were expecting. In particular, despite the success of the daughter in *Ilott v Mitson*,[10] claims by financially independent adult children usually fail.

Other exceptions to the principles of testamentary freedom appear through doctrines such as mutual wills, proprietary estoppel and constructive trusts, but these are beyond the scope of this chapter and will not be discussed further.

If none of these claims are available, the disappointed relative may decide to challenge the will itself. Such challenges will either be made because there was a previous will under which they stood to inherit more or because they will gain under the intestacy provisions. As an example, let us consider Keith and David. Keith (40) is the sole child of David (73). Keith's mother died ten years ago. Under the terms of a previous will, Keith is David's sole heir. However, David has become increasingly

5 *Halsbury's Laws of England*, 5th edn (London, LexisNexis, 2010) vol 102, para 2.

6 A reference to England includes a reference to Wales.

7 R Kerridge, *Parry & Kerridge: The Law of Succession*, 13th edn (London, Sweet & Maxwell, 2016) 183.

8 Law Commission, *Intestacy and Family Provision Claims on Death* (Law Com No 331, 2011) para 1.21, where the idea of forced heirship was described as 'alien to our legal tradition'.

9 Inheritance (Provision for Family and Dependants) Act 1975, s 1.

10 *Ilott v Mitson* [2011] EWCA Civ 346, [2012] 2 FLR 170 (CA).

reliant on Isla (58), a neighbour who provides help and companionship to him. Keith does not get on with Isla, and this has led to rows between him and his father. Following one of these rows, David makes a new will, leaving only a small pecuniary legacy to Keith and leaving the rest of his estate to Isla. David tells his solicitor that this is because Keith has received plenty of help from him in his lifetime, and David is keen to thank Isla (who has little money herself) for her care. Keith is a successful businessman, so a claim under the Inheritance (Provision for Family and Dependants) Act 1975 would be fruitless. However, if Keith can show that the new will in favour of Isla is invalid for any reason, Keith will inherit under the old will. Even if there was no prior will, as David's only child (unless David remarries) Keith will inherit on intestacy. This family situation is far from unusual; if you factor in the large increases in house prices seen by the baby-boomer generation and the likelihood of step-families, it becomes more understandable why contentious probate claims have increased. Although the *spes successionis* does not give any title to property, nor any right to sue for property, it is the tension between the testamentary freedom of the testator and the perceived entitlements of the relatives that is usually the root cause of litigation.

A will is invalid if it does not comply with at least one of the three fundamental requirements for validity: namely, testamentary intention; the testator must have capacity; and the formalities set out in the Wills Act 1837[11] must be complied with. Some challenges are made on the grounds of failure to comply with formalities, but these are relatively few in number. Instead, most challenges are either on the grounds of lack of intention (that the testator did not intend to make that particular will, and therefore did not know and approve of the contents of the will) or lack of capacity. Both claims often incorporate an implicit allegation that the testator was persuaded to make the new will by the new beneficiary, yet to establish either claim there is no need to show any form of undue influence.[12] The substantive allegation is instead that the terms of the new will demonstrate that the testator was so susceptible to suggestions that they lacked sufficient capacity to make a will that reflected their own volition. Challenging a will on the grounds of lack of capacity instead of undue influence may also seem more acceptable to the litigants, who will usually already be very well acquainted with each other.

In stark contrast to most civil litigation, in contentious probate the key witness is always dead, so there is no opportunity for the court to assess capacity directly through the court process. The most acrimonious of these cases are not those where the testator has clearly lost capacity, nor are they the ones where there can be no real doubt cast upon their capacity at all. Instead, it is the borderline cases that are ripe for litigation and where the difficulties for families and solicitors alike arise, and it is these cases that are the main focus of this chapter.

[11] Wills Act 1837, s 9.

[12] Claims are rarely made on the grounds of fraud or undue influence in England, not least because the burden of proof is on the challenger. See also Kerridge (n 7) 77–78 and 85–90.

A. The Common Law Test for Capacity

The test for capacity was originally set out in *Banks v Goodfellow*,[13] the key elements of which are that the testator must:

1. understand the nature of his act (of making a will) and its effects;
2. understand the broad extent of the property in his estate;
3. be able to comprehend and appreciate the claims to which he ought to give effect; and
4. that no disorder of his mind 'shall poison his affections, pervert his sense of right, or his will in disposing of his property'.

It was recently confirmed[14] that this remains the test for testamentary capacity, despite the introduction of the Mental Capacity Act 2005 (MCA 2005). This is because the provisions of the MCA 2005 are to define the circumstances in which living people can and cannot make decisions for themselves,[15] and the provisions of that act 'are inapt to describe a process of evaluating whether a past decision of a deceased person was one which he had capacity to take'.[16] There are a number of consequences of this distinction, but the primary one is that, whilst the MCA 2005 raises a presumption of capacity, there is no such presumption of testamentary capacity. Instead, the initial burden of proof in proving a will lies with the propounder (the person who seeks to admit the will to probate), and this will be discussed further below. As a result, probate solicitors will ensure, as long as there is time available, that they comply with the 'Golden Rule' from *Kenward v Adams*.[17] This rule specifies that whenever there are instructions by a testator whose capacity could be called into question, either due to their age or ill health, the will should be approved or witnessed by a medical practitioner. The record of the medical practitioner's examination of the testator will then stand as evidence of the testator's capacity if required in the future. More pertinently, the existence of such a certificate should dissuade any potential claimants from commencing litigation.[18]

The other differences between the common law and statutory capacity tests are more subtle, but it is arguable that they result in a lower test for capacity than that prescribed by the MCA 2005. The first of these, identified by Nicholas Strauss QC, is that the MCA 2005 requires a person to be able to understand all the information relevant to the making of a decision. In particular, the person must be able to retain that information, and use or weigh it as part of the process of making the decision.[19] In contrast, the *Banks v Goodfellow* test does not require the ability to remember and understand *all* the relevant information, and in *Simon v Byford*, Lewison LJ rejected any capacity test that would amount to no more than a test of the memory.[20]

[13] *Banks v Goodfellow* (1869–70) LR 5 QB 549, [1861–73] All ER Rep 47 (QB).

[14] *Re Walker (Deceased)* [2014] EWHC 71 (Ch D), [2015] WTLR 493. Whilst this has not yet been approved at Appeal Court level, this chapter will not challenge this decision.

[15] Explanatory notes to the Mental Capacity Act 2005 (MCA 2005), para 4.

[16] *Re Walker (Deceased)* (n 14) [27].

[17] *Kenward v Adams*, The Times, 29 November 1975 (Ch D).

[18] See *Re Key (Deceased)* [2010] EWHC 408 (Ch D), [2010] 1 WLR 2020 [8] for judicial comment on the merits of complying with the golden rule.

[19] MCA 2005, ss 3(1)(b) and (c).

[20] *Simon v Byford* [2014] EWCA Civ 280, [2014] WTLR 1097 [39], [40] (CA).

Secondly, in the view of Nicholas Strauss QC, if the MCA 2005 was the test for testamentary capacity, then the effect of section 3(1) together with section 3(4) would be that a testator would lack capacity if he was unable to understand or weigh information as to the consequences of the choices.[21] In contrast, in *Simon v Byford*, Lewison LJ noted that there is only a requirement for the testator to understand the direct consequences of their actions; there is no need for a full understanding of the collateral consequences.[22]

The fact that the common law capacity test seems to set the bar lower than the MCA 2005 capacity test has been noted with approval[23] as it ensures that adults with impaired capacity retain their autonomy. This fits with the general ethos of encouraging people to make wills and therefore avoid the risk of intestacy. Whilst the Court of Protection has the ability to make a statutory will for those lacking testamentary capacity,[24] any such statutory will would only ever be a 'best interests' decision[25] instead of the true will of the testator. The existence of two separate capacity tests could result in some people retaining testamentary capacity yet falling within the remit of the MCA 2005, but this was not considered to be problematical.[26]

The general principle that the autonomy of a testator should be preserved for as long as possible is demonstrated in various ways throughout the case law on this subject. For example, the principle in *Parker v Felgate*[27] enables a testator with quite severe dementia to still have mental capacity if they know that the will they are signing has been drafted in accordance with instructions they gave to a solicitor when they had capacity, even if they are no longer able to remember those instructions. Similarly, a testator who would, in other contexts, be held to have lost capacity may still make a will if they have 'lucid intervals', and the will is made during one such period.[28] These exceptions ensure that the testator has as great an opportunity as possible for self-determination, thereby escaping the need for a distribution in accordance with the 'blunt instrument'[29] of intestacy. As noted in *Gill v Woodall*,

> if the court sets aside a will, the result will be either that an earlier will prevails or that the rules of intestacy apply: either eventuality may result in an outcome that appears to comply with the wishes of the testatrix even less than that produced by the will at issue.[30]

Yet the fact remains that elderly testators can be particularly vulnerable and susceptible to the influence of others. The reality of many situations is that the age of the testator has left them socially dependent on a smaller circle of acquaintances and

[21] *Re Walker (Deceased)* (n 14) [24].

[22] *Simon v Byford* (n 20) [45]. In this case, the collateral consequences could only be understood if the testator could recall not just the extent of her own shareholding in the family company, but also the extent of that of her son.

[23] *Re Walker (Deceased)* (n 14) [32].

[24] MCA 2005, ss 16 and 18.

[25] ibid s 1(5).

[26] *Re Walker (Deceased)* (n 14) [35].

[27] *Parker v Felgate* (1883) 8 PD 171, applied recently in *Perrins v Holland* [2010] EWCA Civ 840, [2011] Ch 270 (CA).

[28] See, eg, *Banks v Goodfellow* (n 13) but also earlier cases such as *Cartwright v Cartwright* (1793) 1 Phill 90, 161 ER 923 (KB).

[29] www.lawcom.gov.uk/project/wills/.

[30] *Gill v Woodall* [2010] EWCA Civ 1430, [2011] Ch 380 [26] (CA).

that, coupled with an increasing lack of confidence arising from physical decline and some occasional confusion, can lead to a 'grey zone'.[31]

The conclusion of Cockburn CJ in *Banks v Goodfellow* is particularly striking:

> The English law leaves everything to the unfettered discretion of the testator, on the assumption that, though in some instances, caprice, or passion, or the power of new ties, or artful contrivance, or sinister influence, may lead to the neglect of claims that ought to be attended to, yet, the instincts, affections, and common sentiments of mankind may be safely trusted to secure, on the whole, a better disposition of the property of the dead, and one more accurately adjusted to the requirements of each particular case, than could be obtained through a distribution prescribed by the stereotyped and inflexible rules of a general law.[32]

Thus the courts have long been aware of the dilemma that everything that preserves the autonomy of the testator will also place the testator at risk of becoming a victim of 'artful contrivance or sinister influence'. In order to try to protect vulnerable testators, the common law response has resulted in a complex set of presumptions and counter-presumptions, to determine the validity of a will as follows:

1. The burden of proof is initially on the propounder, ie the person seeking to admit the will to probate. However, the principle of *omnia praesumuntur rite esse acta* comes into play: if the will is duly executed and appears rational on its face, capacity is presumed.
2. The burden of proof will then pass to the challenger, who will need to adduce evidence to raise a real doubt as to the testator's lack of capacity. If there is no history of mental illness, this will be hard to do and the new will would then be admitted to probate. However, in many elderly testators there are signs of the onset of dementia, no matter how slight. There may have been instances where they were seen to be forgetful, and possibly losing some of their faculties. The more severe these symptoms are, the more likely it is that a real doubt as to capacity can be demonstrated.
3. If sufficient evidence of lack of capacity can be brought forward, the burden of proof will pass back to the propounder to establish capacity. This is often an extremely difficult burden to discharge, as the key witness is dead and the evidence that has already been brought before the court raises questions that are hard to dispel.[33]

From this it can be seen that the starting point is not an investigation into the capacity of the testator but consideration of the terms of the will itself. If we consider David and Keith once more, our father and son whose brief family history was set out earlier, the new will must be examined for rationality. On the facts, a will such as David's new will appears to have a rational explanation (Keith is well off, Isla has little money, Keith and David are increasingly estranged), so a presumption of testamentary capacity will be raised and Keith would need to produce evidence to raise a real doubt as to David's lack of capacity. It can be extremely hard to disprove capacity, especially if the testator was still managing their own affairs in other

[31] MI Hall, 'Equity Theory: Responding to the Material Exploitation' in I Doron (ed), *Theories on Law and Ageing: The Jurisprudence of Elder Law* (Berlin, Springer Verlag, 2009).

[32] *Banks v Goodfellow* (n 13) 564.

[33] This evidential sequence was neatly summarised by Briggs J in *Re Key (Deceased)* (n 18) [97].

aspects of their life. If there has been a recent assessment of the testator's capacity (or, better still, if the Golden Rule mentioned above has been followed), it will be nearly impossible for Keith to bring a successful challenge. In contrast, if David has a history of declining mental health, then it will be easy for Keith to raise the doubt as to David's lack of capacity. At this point the burden of proof would pass back to Isla, who would need to prove capacity—an equally difficult task once real doubt has been raised.

B. The Rationality of the Will

The significance of the rationality of the will had been explained prior to *Banks v Goodfellow* (in the context of lucid intervals) as follows:

> Now I think the strongest and best proof ... is that which arises from the act itself; that I look upon as the thing to be first examined, and if it can be proved and established that it is a rational act rationally done the whole case is proved. What can you do more to establish the act? Because, suppose you are able to shew the party did that which appears to be a rational act, and it is his own act entirely, nothing is left to presumption in order to prove a lucid interval. Here is the rational act rationally done. In my apprehension, where you are able completely to establish that, the law does not require you to go further.[34]

Therefore, for over 200 years the courts have used the rationality of a will as a check and counterbalance to ensure the autonomy of the testator. Whilst it could be argued that this would enable the courts to impose their own view of what the testator ought to have done, there is little evidence in the case law of this occurring. There are passages from the judgment in *Banks v Goodfellow* that indicate a clear link in Cockburn CJ's mind between 'rationality' and theories of natural law, for example when he discusses 'a moral responsibility of no ordinary importance' which goes alongside the freedom of testamentary disposition,[35] but his judgment goes on to emphasise that there are other considerations at play, and suggests that this is at the heart of why England does not have any form of forced heirship law. He explained that the testator's nearest relatives were not the only people to have claims on the estate, and that some relatives may be more in need than others. There was therefore no need for the beneficiaries to be limited to close relatives, nor was there a need to treat all children equally.[36]

Despite the principle of testamentary freedom, most testators follow a predictable path, with relatives being the main beneficiaries,[37] and studies have also shown that most testators do treat relatives of equal genetic 'rank' equally.[38] However, the courts strive not to be prescriptive in their definition of 'rational', emphasising that a rational will is one that distributes property to those whom the testator feels have an

[34] *Cartwright v Cartwright* (n 28), 927 (Sir William Wynne).
[35] *Banks v Goodfellow* (n 13) 563.
[36] ibid 564.
[37] J Herring, *Older People in Law and Society* (Oxford, Oxford University Press, 2009) 314.
[38] J Finch and J Mason, *Passing On: Kinship and Inheritance in England* (London, Routledge, 2000) 77.

entitlement to some of his estate, whether relatives or not, and taking into account their need.[39]

Whilst rationality is a starting point for admitting a will to probate, it is not sufficient to prove capacity; the decision that a will is rational merely raises a presumption of capacity. A recent exposition of this principle was in *Re Key (Deceased)*,[40] in which a fresh will executed within a week of the death of the testator's wife of 65 years was held to be 'eminently rational' due to its fair (ie equal) treatment of the testator's children.[41] Despite this finding, sufficient doubt was raised as to the capacity of the testator and this transferred the burden to the propounders to prove capacity, which they were unable to do. The will was therefore successfully challenged.

Conversely, even if a will is seen to be irrational, that does not necessarily mean that it will be successfully challenged. It has often been stated that there is no need for a testator to leave his estate in a particular way, and no obligation for him to give effect to the moral claims on his estate.[42] Under the *Banks v Goodfellow* test, the testator must simply know and understand the claims, even if he subsequently ignores them. As May LJ stated in *Sharp v Adam*: 'An irrational, unjust and unfair will must be upheld if the testator had the capacity to make a rational, just and fair one.'[43] Notwithstanding this, the resulting shift of the burden of proof onto the propounder to prove capacity does mean that there are few cases where clearly irrational or capricious wills are successfully upheld.[44] Although rationality must not be used as a pretext for ensuring that the testator makes the 'right' will, thereby restricting testamentary freedom, if no reason or justification can be discerned for the terms of the will it seems understandable that the court is likely to find that the testator lacked capacity:

> the ultimate question before the court, when assessing testamentary capacity, is not whether the will is a fair one in all the circumstances of the case. On the other hand, if the provisions of a will are surprising, that may be material to the court's assessment of whether the testator did have capacity.[45]

It should be noted that this test is not dissimilar to the MCA 2005 capacity requirements; whilst section 1(4) states that 'A person is not to be treated as unable to make a decision merely because he makes an unwise decision', the use of the word 'merely' indicates that particularly strange decisions can be used alongside other evidence to conclude that a person lacks capacity.[46]

[39] For examples of dispositions that may be seen as contrary to expectations yet were held to be eminently rational see *Cattermole v Prisk* (n 1); *Markou v Goodwin* [2013] EWHC 4570 (Ch D), [2014] WTLR 605; *Re Watson (Probate)*, sub nom *Carr v Beaven* [2008] EWHC 2582 (Ch D).

[40] *Re Key (Deceased)* (n 18).

[41] ibid [99] (Briggs J).

[42] See, eg, *Gill v Woodall* (n 30) [26]: 'a court should be very slow to find that a will does not represent the genuine wishes of the testatrix simply because its terms are surprising, inconsistent with what she said during her lifetime, unfair, or even vindictive or perverse' (Lord Neuberger MR), although note that in this case the will was found to be invalid because the testatrix did not know and approve its contents.

[43] *Sharp v Adam* [2006] EWCA Civ 449, [2006] WTLR 1059 (CA) [79].

[44] But see *Cowderoy v Cranfield* (n 1) [145], where a 'surprising' will was upheld, and *Parker v Litchfield* [2014] EWHC 1799 (Ch D) [34], where a will that could be understood as 'not fair' was upheld.

[45] *Cowderoy v Cranfield* (n 1) [133] (Morgan J).

[46] Herring (n 37) 56; see also *Re B (Consent to Treatment: Capacity)* [2002] EWHC 429, [2002] 2 All ER 449 (F).

III. THE UN CONVENTION ON THE RIGHTS OF PERSONS WITH DISABILITIES AND THE CAPACITY/AUTONOMY DISTINCTION

The absence of a presumption of testamentary capacity can be criticised, especially now we have a clear statutory presumption of capacity in other contexts through the MCA 2005. Article 12 of the UN Convention on the Rights of Persons with Disabilities (CRPD) requires states to recognise the equal legal capacity of those with disabilities, and to take appropriate measures to provide access for persons with disabilities to the support they may require in exercising their legal capacity.[47] The Committee on the Rights of Persons with Disabilities clarified these 'capacity recognition' requirements by a general comment[48] in which the overarching principles of the Convention (namely individual autonomy and the freedom to make one's own choices) was emphasised.[49] Furthermore, it was noted in the comment that there has been a failure by states to understand that compliance with Article 12 requires 'a shift from the substitute decision making paradigm to one that is based on supported decision making'.[50]

It has been discussed elsewhere[51] whether the provisions of the MCA 2005 comply sufficiently with the CRPD's requirement to move away from the concept of substituted decision making, although the MCA 2005 does clearly require the testator to participate in the decision so far as possible.[52] However, there is a difference between those testators who have clearly lost capacity, and for whom the only solution is a statutory will, and those who have a borderline testamentary capacity. It is the wills of these latter testators that are the focus of this chapter; these are the subjects of most of the litigation, and by the time the will is discovered it is usually too late to apply to the Court of Protection for a statutory will.[53] As Lord Cranworth noted in *Boyse v Rossborough*, 'There is no possibility of mistaking midnight for noon, but at what precise moment twilight becomes darkness is hard to determine'.[54]

The provisions of the MCA 2005 only apply once the testator has lost capacity,[55] but the inherent expense and delays involved in an application to the Court of Protection mean that it is better for all if the testator can be helped to make their own will whilst they still have a residual amount of capacity. As noted above, there will be testators for whom a statutory will would be possible but who would still satisfy the *Banks v Goodfellow* test sufficiently to execute their own valid will, especially if the terms of their will are relatively straightforward, and compliance with the CRPD requires the preservation of these individuals' right to make their own will for as

[47] Convention on the Rights of Persons with Disabilities (adopted 13 December 2006, entered into force 3 May 2008) 2515 UNTS, Arts 12(2), 12(3).

[48] Committee on the Rights of People with Disabilities (2014) General Comment No 1 on Article 12: Equal Recognition Before the Law CRPD/C/GC/1.

[49] ibid [4].

[50] ibid [3].

[51] R Harding, 'The Rise of Statutory Wills and the Limits of Best Interests Decision-Making in Inheritance' (2015) 78 *MLR* 945.

[52] MCA 2005, s 4(4).

[53] See, eg, *Re Key (Deceased)* (n 18), in which the sons had taken steps towards the appointment of a receiver by the Court of Protection once they discovered the presence of a new will.

[54] *Boyse v Rossborough* [1857] 10 ER 1192 (HL) 1210.

[55] MCA 2005, s 16.

long as possible. Indeed, the Committee on the Rights of Persons with Disabilities is critical of the type of functional approach to capacity that is contained within the MCA 2005 whereby, once mental capacity is lost, the corresponding legal capacity is immediately denied. Instead, the Committee argues that support should be provided in the exercise of legal capacity,[56] and the existence of principles such as the rule in *Parker v Felgate* go some way towards meeting this criticism.

It could be argued that the best way to ensure compliance with the CRPD would be to introduce a presumption of capacity, along the lines set out in the MCA 2005, to ensure that only those who have clearly lost capacity need to resort to the Court of Protection. However, whilst this might provide certainty and could enable those with degenerative cognitive diseases to retain testamentary capacity for longer, this would not assuage the criticisms of the functional approach to capacity, nor would it enhance supported decision making.

However, there is a further danger inherent in such a presumption, namely that we would not comply adequately with paragraph 4 of the CRPD, which requires states to

> ensure that all measures that relate to the exercise of legal capacity provide for appropriate and effective safeguards to prevent abuse in accordance with international human rights law. Such safeguards shall ensure that measures relating to the exercise of legal capacity respect the rights, will and preferences of the person, are free of conflict of interest and undue influence, are proportional and tailored to the person's circumstances.

This could be called the 'protectionist' requirement, as it is noted in the general comment on paragraph 4 that there may be increased risks of undue influence for those who rely on the support of others, and therefore safeguards for the exercise of legal capacity must include protection against undue influence.[57] Yet, despite the CRPD's recognition of this risk, the protection offered by states must also 'respect the rights, will and preferences of the person, including the right to take risks and make mistakes'.[58]

Therefore, compliance with the CRPD requires states to enable the individual with impaired capacity to be self-determining for as long as possible through supported decision making, yet at the same time requires sufficient safeguards against undue influence. The complexity of this requirement supports the view that any simple presumption of capacity would exacerbate the risks of testators succumbing to the influences of others, and this would remove the autonomy that the CRPD strives to protect.

Whilst debates about capacity and autonomy arise in many areas of law,[59] in the opinion of the author probate is an area where the legal response to impaired capacity must be particularly astute to the risks of external influences, and therefore the second 'protectionist' part of the CRPD requirement must receive greater weight than in other contexts. The fact that a constant close companionship can alter the

[56] See n 48 above [15].

[57] ibid [22].

[58] ibid [22].

[59] For example, in relation to medical care, where the question arises whether a patient has sufficient capacity to consent to or refuse treatment.

testator's evaluation of family relationships has long been recognised; as Erskine J noted in *Harwood v Baker*:

> [T]he protection of the law is in no cases more needed, than it is in those where the mind has been too much enfeebled to comprehend more objects than one, and most especially where that one object may be so forced upon the attention of the invalid, as to shut out all others that might require consideration.[60]

To understand why there should be additional considerations about the vulnerability of elderly testators it is necessary to explore (briefly) the basic ideas of property ownership.

IV. THEORIES OF PROPERTY

Most theories of property are devised in order to support and justify the notion of private ownership of property. Early Greek philosophers such as Plato and Aristotle (and their predecessors) debated whether private ownership and accumulation of property was justified at all, but the starting point for modern theories of property ownership is, for many, seen as Locke's justification: 'every man has a property in his own person; this nobody has any right to but himself. The labour of his body … are properly his.'[61]

Locke viewed property as a God-given right, but later theorists assimilated the ownership of property with the establishment of law. For example, Hume was an advocate of the utilitarian approach to the state, and argued that property ownership was both useful and beneficial as it encourages industry. Bentham emphasised that '[p]roperty and law are born together, and die together. Before laws were made there was no property; take away laws and property ceases'.[62]

Whilst there remains ongoing debate about the nature of property rights,[63] it is relatively well accepted that property rights and ownership of property are 'a *power relationship*—a relationship of social and legal legitimacy existing between a person and a valued resource'.[64] The complexity of this relationship is demonstrated by the 'bundle of rights' theories of property, and such theories are helpful to justify interventionist legislation such as the Inheritance (Provision for Family and Dependants) Act 1975.

Whilst there is not space within this chapter for a detailed analysis of property theories, the relevance of these ideas to ownership of property on death should become immediately obvious. Hume stated that property produced or improved by

[60] *Harwood v Baker* (1840) 13 ER 117, 3 Moo PC 282 (PC) 290.

[61] J Locke, *The Second Treatise of Government*, ch V [27] (J Locke, *Two Treatises of Government* (CreateSpace Independent Publishing Platform, 2016) 86).

[62] J Bentham, *Principles of the Civil Code*, pt I, ch VIII (J Bentham, *Theory of Legislation: Translated from the French of Etienne Dumont by R. Hildreth* (Boston, Adamant Media Corporation, 2005) 112–13.

[63] See, eg, J Penner and HE Smith (eds), *Philosophical Foundations of Property Law* (Oxford, Oxford University Press, 2013).

[64] K Gray and S Francis Gray, *Elements of Land Law*, 5th edn (Oxford, Oxford University Press, 2009) 87, para 1.5.5 (original emphasis).

man's art or industry 'ought also to descend to children and relations for the same useful purpose'[65] —the notion that the creator of the value should be able to control its destination was seen as a beneficial by-product of property law, and of course the default intestacy provisions rank children second only to the spouse or civil partner of the deceased.

The protection that the law gives to property rights also enables us to plan for future use of our own property without interference from the state. Bentham suggested that 'the idea of property consists in an established expectation'.[66] He continued, '[a]s regards property, security consists in receiving no check, no shock, no derangement to the expectation founded on the laws, of enjoying such and such a portion of good'.[67]

This expectation of future use not only affects our ability to enjoy our property without inference by the state, but also impacts on the relationship between the owner (A) and the non-owners (B, C, D, etc). Convention theories suggest that it is the existence of laws that prevent the non-owners (B, C and D) from challenging A's ownership. Without respect for such conventions, anarchy would arise: 'What must become of the world if such practices prevail? How could society subsist under such disorders?'[68] Whilst such theories of property were originally developed in order to explain and justify political and social power structures, it seems undeniable that '[a]ll property references are, at some level, a statement about the social legitimacy attaching to the claim in question'.[69] Hence personal property rights could not exist without being recognised both by law and by our fellow human beings.

Hume's statement that property should devolve to children and relations was intended as a self-evident fact. No argument was made as to why this should be the case, and although, as noted above, some of the earlier cases talk in terms of natural law,[70] this has never been an established principle. Many of the contentious probate claims that come to court arise in situations where there are no close relatives or there has been a schism between the testator and the obvious close relative(s). In such situations in particular a consideration of these property theories will help to explain why there has been such an increase in contentious probate cases, for it is only if the cause behind the increase is understood that we can hope to counteract it.

If we start by considering the relationship between the owner of the property and the non-owners, the convention theories suggest that 'the limits of property "are the interfaces between accepted and unaccepted social claims"'.[71] The convention principle relies on an expectation of reciprocity: the non-owners conclude that 'I will

[65] D Hume, *Enquiries Concerning Human Understanding and Concerning the Principles of Morals* (first published 1739–40, Oxford, Oxford University Press, 1990) 195.

[66] Bentham (n 62) 112.

[67] ibid p. 113.

[68] Hume (n 65) 203.

[69] Gray and Francis Gray (n 64) 88, para 1.5.6.

[70] See nn 35–36 above.

[71] Gray and Francis Gray (n 64) 88, para 1.5.7, citing *Dorman v Rodgers* [1982] 148 CLR 365, 372 (Murphy J).

not steal from A because I also want A to respect my property'. Now let us consider what the difference would be if A was elderly. Although B would never steal from A, if an expectation is raised in B that A's property will become his on death, then, despite the fact that B only has a mere *spes* in the property, he would develop his own expectation for the future use and enjoyment of that property on A's death. However, unbeknownst to B, C might also have had an expectation raised that the same property would become his on the death of A. C would likewise be developing his own plans for the property. Now, on the death of A, it is discovered that A made a recent will leaving everything to D. Thus both the appointed and disappointed beneficiaries view themselves as being entitled to the property and the situation is rather akin to three people who come across lost or abandoned property at the same time. Although D should become the new owner, both B and C would regard themselves as having socially acceptable claims when judged against societal norms[72] and may feel justified in trying to actualise their expectation of forthcoming bounty by litigating the validity of the will itself. In the context of testamentary claims, property rights will be respected only if all affected parties believe the will truly reflects the testator's wishes.

Even before A's death, the imminence of that death and the ensuing need for A's property to change ownership can encourage all of A's friends and family to 'remind' A of their loyalty and needs. The author does not wish to imply that all such conversations are intended to pressurise A, but there is undoubtedly a greater legitimacy in asking an elderly person what is going to happen to their property after their death and to then plead your case than there is in asking a fit and healthy younger person if you can have their property. The elderly property owner may appreciate advice and guidance on how best to dispose of their property (and be more receptive to it), but the danger is that they also feel pressured by those around them in a way that a younger individual would not.

The hawk/dove analogy that is used in many recent property theories[73] starts to become particularly apt; the phrase 'vultures circling' encapsulates how those who were formerly doves can react when they can see the potential for future proprietary gain. Whilst such comments will not count as undue influence[74] and therefore will not be enough to invalidate the will on this basis, the increased vulnerability and susceptibility of those with borderline capacity to be influenced by others may result in the testator's autonomy being undermined.

[72] See nn 37–38 above.

[73] For example, the works of Robert Sugden, discussed in CM Rose, 'Psychologies of Property' in J Penner and HE Smith (eds), *Philosophical Foundations of Property Law* (Oxford, Oxford University Press, 2013)

[74] A good exposition of the fine line between undue influence and persuasion is found in *Hall v Hall* (1865–69) LR 1 P & D 481: 'Persuasion, appeals to the affections or ties of kindred, to a sentiment of gratitude for past services, or pity for future destitution, or the like,—these are all legitimate, and may be fairly pressed on a testator. On the other hand, pressure of whatever character, whether acting on the fears or the hopes, if so exerted as to overpower the volition without convincing the judgment, is a species of restraint under which no valid will can be made … In a word, a testator may be led but not driven; and his will must be the offspring of his own volition, and not the record of some one else's' (Sir JP Wilde).

V. CAPACITY AND AUTONOMY

At the start of this chapter the aim was to determine whether there could be a simple test for capacity that also preserves autonomy. To answer this question, the relationship between autonomy and capacity needs to be considered. On a simplistic level, those with legal capacity have autonomy; they can decide when and how to do any lawful task. However, it has also been recognised that autonomy is not a simple concept. For example, John Coggon[75] identified three different types of autonomy (ideal desire autonomy, best desire autonomy and current desire autonomy), with the difference between the three being determined by whether the person is acting in accordance with an objective standard of values (ideal desire autonomy), their own long-term values and wishes (best desire autonomy) or their immediate wishes and inclinations (current desire autonomy).

This type of categorisation is very instructive when applied to the writing of a will. The 'rationality' test described above would seem to fit with the principles of 'best desire' autonomy described by Coggon in that a rational will is one that fits with the testator's long-term values and beliefs as opposed to an embodiment of a person's immediate wishes without further reflection. Most testators (quite rightly) deliberate carefully on the terms of their will in order to ensure it properly reflects their wishes instead of acting on impulse without any detailed reflection.

If the *Banks v Goodfellow* test is viewed as being not so much a test for capacity as a test for best desire autonomy, then the complexity criticism that is levelled at the test[76] arguably has a benefit to the testator. A review of the authorities suggests that the courts have always been astute to the different levels of autonomy that may be exhibited in any individual and that the test can operate to assess cognitive function in detail.

As long ago as 1840, following an iteration of an earlier version of the *Banks v Goodfellow* test, the Privy Council gave the direction:

> the question … is not whether Mr Baker knew when he was giving all his property to his wife, and excluding all his other relations from any share in it, but whether he was at that time capable of recollecting who those relations were, of understanding their respective claims upon his regard and bounty, and of *deliberately forming* an intelligent purpose of excluding them from any share of his property.[77]

Thus it was necessary for the testator not only to appreciate the moral claims he ought to consider, but also to have made a conscious decision to exclude them. This change in emphasis usually comes to the fore in cases where there is a concern that the testator might have known the objects of their bounty but may not have been in a position to appreciate the full effects of the new will. In *Re Key* there was no question of the testator failing to understand what he was doing. Instead, as Briggs J recognised, the impairment of his faculties was one that affected his mental energy

[75] J Coggon, 'Varied and Principled Understandings of Autonomy in English Law: Justifiable Inconsistency or Blinkered Moralism?' (2007) 15 *Health Care Analysis* 235.

[76] The *Banks v Goodfellow* test is described as 'difficult to understand and apply' by the Law Commission—www.lawcom.gov.uk/project/wills/.

[77] *Harwood v Baker* (n 60) 290 (Erskine J) (emphasis added).

and therefore the ability to make 'decisions of his own'[78]—the inference being that the testator was lacking the required autonomy.

In *Sharp v Adam*, the Court of Appeal focused especially on the final aspect of the *Banks v Goodfellow* test, namely that that no disorder of his mind 'shall poison his affections, pervert his sense of right, or his will in disposing of his property', which was further expanded in *Banks v Goodfellow* thus: 'If the human instincts and affections, or the moral sense, become perverted by mental disease; if insane suspicion, or aversion, take the place of natural affection … it is obvious that the condition of the testamentary power fails.'[79]

Dementia affects sufferers in different ways, but studies of dementia patients show that 'aversions' are some of the most common cognitive changes.[80] In *Sharp v Adam*, the *Banks v Goodfellow* test was applied to alterations that arise through age-related diseases; although it was acknowledged that the testator's cognition had not been affected, his 'mood' had,[81] and the conclusion of the Court of Appeal that he had lacked testamentary capacity at the time of making his final will was influenced by his decision to exclude his daughters entirely, instead of leaving them a small legacy as his solicitor had suggested.[82]

Therefore, although revised wills can stem merely from the testator's own reflection upon their relationships and obligations in their later years, it is the diminishing ability to retain one's broader focus of all of the testamentary demands that can result in a testator crossing the 'imprecise divide'.[83] The lack of strong presumptions in our current law enables it to reflect the subtleties involved, especially given the fact that many testators with signs of dementia may lose the ability to focus on their long-term beliefs, and instead be driven by immediate desires and wishes. In such situations it is entirely appropriate for there to be a finding of lack of capacity, even though the testator may appear to understand what it is that they are doing.

It is, of course, vital that the courts do not measure wills against an objective standard of values, but a subjective analysis to determine whether the will accords with the long-term wishes and desires of the testator can provide protection for vulnerable testators. Whenever a testator has demonstrated a relatively settled testamentary preference, then it seems uncontroversial to say that a will that corresponds with this intention raises a presumption of capacity;[84] in contrast, a will that runs contrary to the testator's long-term values and wishes suggests a lack of capacity.[85]

Unfortunately many testators do not have such clearly defined intentions, and all attempts to protect vulnerable testators must not inadvertently inhibit testamentary freedom, as to do so would put the testator in no better position than if a statutory will was made for them.[86] Those accustomed to dealing with vulnerable clients

[78] *Re Key (Deceased)* (n 18) [96] (Briggs J).
[79] *Banks v Goodfellow* (n 13) 565 (Cockburn CJ).
[80] N O'Neill and C Peisah, *Capacity and the Law* (Sydney, Sydney University Press, 2012) Ch 2.
[81] *Sharp v Adam* (n 43) [93].
[82] ibid [94] (May LJ).
[83] ibid.
[84] *Bateman v Overy* [2014] EWHC 432 (Ch D).
[85] *Re Ritchie (Deceased)* [2009] EWHC 709 (Ch D).
[86] See, eg, *Dharamshi (Deceased), Re* [2013] EWHC 3917 (Ch D), where an indecisive testator was found to have capacity as he knew what he wanted to achieve when making his final will.

know that it is often necessary to take instructions on multiple occasions to ensure that the testator's wishes are consistently held.[87] It is argued that the complexities of the *Banks v Goodfellow* test can be used to analyse a vulnerable testator's capacity with the care and consideration needed; the various strands of the test allow for a consideration of the type of autonomy the testator has demonstrated and this, coupled with the presumptions and counter-presumptions set out above, provides a mechanism whereby the courts can strive to balance the flexibility of testamentary freedom with the rigidity of testator protection.

The UK approach is in marked contrast to US law, where there is not only a presumption of capacity, but a notable reluctance to declare that a testator lacked capacity even in what would seem the most obvious of cases.[88] The level of testamentary capacity required in the USA has been deliberately kept artificially low due to 'the American commitment to individual preference and autonomy'.[89] The result of this is that the only effective challenge to a will is on the grounds of undue influence.

Although US authorities are often cited with approval,[90] the common law test in England has seemingly always been alert to the influences of those who are close by during the declining years of the testator. In the USA, the ideal of autonomy is seen as an absolute good, yet the presumption of capacity means that the testator could satisfy the capacity test even though they have only the lowest level of autonomy. It could be argued that the English emphasis on the additional capacity requirements of the ability to make decisions[91] and to take control over the testamentary process is overly paternalistic, simply preventing the testator from doing something they might regret. However, if we recognise the particular vulnerability of testators to the claims of others and regard the *Banks v Goodfellow* test as a test for best desire autonomy instead of a test for capacity, a paternalistic approach can be justified as it ensures that the testator's decisions are supported and higher-level autonomous decisions are respected.

If we shift our focus to the differing levels of autonomy, then we can gain a better appreciation of the *Banks v Goodfellow* test. Whilst it does not give the simple clarity that the presumption of capacity in the MCA 2005 provides, the final element in particular allows the will drafter (and subsequently the courts if the validity of the will is disputed) to assess the quality of the testator's autonomy. As Coggon states, a person acting in accordance with their best desires may act against their immediate inclination because the values behind the action are 'settled—although not necessarily permanent—and an agent recognises them as his values'.[92] It is

[87] See, eg, The Law Society Practice Note on meeting the needs of vulnerable clients, available at www.lawsociety.org.uk/support-services/advice/practice-notes/meeting-the-needs-of-vulnerable-clients-july-2015/, which includes (at para 4.6.1) the need to check for consistency in instructions.

[88] See, eg, *Re Dokken*, 604 NW 2d 487 (SD 2000), summarised in LA Frolik, 'The Strange Interplay of Testamentary Capacity and the Doctrine of Undue Influence. Are We Protecting Older Testators or Overriding Individual Preferences?' (2001) 24 *International Journal of Law and Psychiatry* 253.

[89] Frolik (ibid) 255.

[90] See, eg, *Re Walker (Deceased)* (n 14); *Cowderoy v Cranfield* (n 1).

[91] As expounded in *Re Key (Deceased)* (n 18) [96].

[92] See n 75 above, 241.

this sort of comprehension and understanding that the complexity of the *Banks v Goodfellow* test enables the courts to pursue.

Any replacement for the *Banks v Goodfellow* test therefore needs to be considered very carefully if we are not to lose this additional layer. A presumption of capacity would give certainty, but it would also presume only the most basic autonomy and that, this author feels, is a step too far. Such a presumption would also not make our law any more compliant with the CRPD as it would still embed a functional approach to capacity when we should instead be turning our attention to supported decision making, whilst also adhering to the 'protectionist' requirements of the CRPD.

In order to comply better with the CRPD, the Golden Rule mentioned above would seem to be an important element, especially with conditions such as dementia, the effects of which vary on a daily basis. A testator who might not have sufficient capacity on one visit might have improved cognition on a later visit, and the medical certificate of this cognition will help to ensure that the will is able to be proved. However, as simple as this rule may seem, it is not without its difficulties. First, solicitors are under a duty to act quickly when they receive instructions for a will, especially from an elderly testator.[93] In such circumstances they may need to weigh their duty to comply with the Golden Rule against their duty to the client, and sometimes the latter duty may take precedence.[94] Secondly, whilst many probate practitioners take the safe option of obtaining a medical certificate before preparing a will for any elderly testator, this can be seen as demeaning or even insulting,[95] and may deter the elderly from making a will at all—which would be a particularly unattractive side effect of a rule designed to reduce litigation and ensure that the testator's wishes are upheld.

It is worth noting that a significant number of contentious probate cases arise where the wills are written by non-specialist probate practitioners. Under the Legal Services Act 2007, will-writing is not currently a reserved area and, despite calls from the Legal Services Board for it to become one,[96] this seems unlikely to happen. However, if those at risk of losing their autonomy and their capacity are to be supported in their decisions as to where their property goes on their death, it is imperative that the person making the will recognises the dangers. If we really want to support the decision-making powers of the elderly and those with impaired capacity, yet also reduce litigation, then maybe we need to say that this is specialist work for specialist lawyers. This would probably not increase the numbers of those who make wills, but it would hopefully give everyone more confidence in the outcome.

Unfortunately, the author acknowledges that the harder it is perceived to be to make a will, the fewer people will do it, and the distribution of property on intestacy

[93] For an example of a breach of this duty and its consequences, see *White v Jones* [1995] 2 AC 207, [1995] 2 WLR 187 (HL).

[94] See, eg, the comments of Norris J in *Wharton v Bancroft* [2011] EWHC 3250 (Ch D), [2012] WTLR 693.

[95] See *Hill v Fellowes Solicitors LLP* [2011] EWHC 61 (QB), (2011) 118 BMLR 122 [77] (Sharp J).

[96] Two Legal Services Board Consultations from 2012, both entitled 'Enhancing Consumer Protection, Reducing Regulatory Restrictions: Will-Writing, Probate and Estate Administration Activities', concluded that will writing should be added to the list of reserved activities under s 12 of the Legal Services Act 2007.

rules will most likely be even more contrary to the wishes of the deceased than any voluntary will. However, simple wills drafted by those who do not understand the complexities of issues of capacity or the risks of litigation are equally not ensuring that the deceased's wishes are carried out—due to the costs of litigation, it is far worse to have an invalid will than to have no will at all. Furthermore, the mere fact that we permit such wills potentially means that we are in breach of our 'protectionist' obligations under the CRPD.

Even more unpalatable alternatives would be to consider the introduction of forced heirship rules, or alternatively to introduce a limited presumption of capacity with certain common testamentary patterns, but this would impact on non-standard families; given the ongoing battle between the Law Commission and the government regarding rights of cohabitees, it would seem foolhardy to introduce another potential battleground. We must accept and embrace the fact that many people have genuine reasons for wishing to direct their property to some particular friends or relatives at the expense of others.

VI. CONCLUSIONS

The precise identification of testamentary capacity will always prove difficult; our current understanding of mental health means that we are now much more alert to differing levels of capacity, and we are reluctant to deny capacity to those who have been self-sufficient for many years. However, a presumption of capacity would put the vulnerable at risk of succumbing to the influence of others.

Despite the lack of certainty that the existing common law test brings, its complexity enables the evidence to be analysed to establish each testator's capabilities and vulnerabilities on a case-by-case basis. In the more complex and borderline cases, the *Banks v Goodfellow* test can be used to protect the vulnerable by helping to identify the point at which the testator became overly susceptible to persuasion or moves away from best desire autonomy to current desire autonomy. Clearly it would be better for this sifting and analysis of the evidence to be carried out before, not after, the testator's death.

Notwithstanding the principle of testamentary freedom, the underlying social justification for, and acceptance of, testamentary challenges indicates that a certain amount of litigation is inevitable. However, it may be possible to reduce the number of claims being dealt with by the courts if we acknowledge that the complexities of testamentary capacity mean that it should be handled by specialists in the field. This gives us the best chance of supporting the testator in his decision making on a case-by-case basis. The challenge for the Law Commission seems not so much to aim for simplicity and certainty, but to create a rich test of capacity that acknowledges the subtleties of human nature and relationships yet provides scope for supporting the higher-level autonomy of those nearing the end of their lives.

8

Disability Discrimination: Recasting the Parameters of Proprietary Rights?

SUSAN PASCOE*

I. INTRODUCTION

THIS CHAPTER EXAMINES the potential ramifications for proprietary rights of landlords where tenants raise disability discrimination defences under the Equality Act 2010 to landlords' claims for possession. Such ramifications could have far-reaching consequences for both public and private landlords in that such defences will be more extensive than the protection given to tenants under Article 8 of the European Convention on Human Rights as implemented by the Human Rights Act 1998. Disability discrimination defences are contrasted with alternative defences against possession raised under Article 8[1] in order to analyse the breadth and prospects of success of disability discrimination defences under section 15 of the Equality Act 2010 following the Supreme Court decision in *Aster Communities Ltd v Akerman-Livingstone* (hereinafter referred to as *Akerman*).[2] This comparison highlights how the substantive right to equal treatment under the Equality Act differs from the substantive right protected by Article 8 and shows how a proportionate means of achieving a legitimate aim is interpreted and applied in each framework. The potential impact of the breadth of the definition of disability is also considered in this context. In addition, the consequences of section 35 of the Equality Act applying to both private and public sector landlords, the burden of proof on the alleged discriminator and the landlord's duty to make reasonable adjustments under the Equality Act are all analysed.

The Supreme Court in *Akerman* opened new avenues for tenants in possession cases by making it much harder for landlords to obtain possession where a tenant successfully claims discrimination arising from a disability under the Equality

* Associate Professor of Law, Middlesex University; Solicitor (non-practising).

[1] See *Manchester City Council v Pinnock* [2010] UKSC 45, [2010] 3 WLR 1441; *Hounslow London Borough Council v Powell* [2011] UKSC 8, [2011] 2 WLR 287. See also *Thurrock Borough Council v West* [2012] EWCA Civ 1435, [2013] HLR 69; *R (JL) v Secretary of State for Defence* [2013] EWCA Civ 449, [2013] HLR 27; *Sims v Dacorum Borough Council* [2014] UKSC 63, [2014] 3 WLR 1600; *R (N) v Lewisham London Borough Council* [2014] UKSC 62, [2014] 3 WLR 1548.

[2] *Aster Communities Ltd v Akerman-Livingstone* [2015] UKSC 15, [2015] 2 WLR 721.

Act 2010. The Supreme Court agreed unanimously that a disability defence to possession can rarely be decided summarily, unlike the position with a defence raised under Article 8.[3] It was accepted that the defendant was suffering from a disability under section 6 of the Equality Act 2010. He refused offers of alternative suitable accommodation and the landlord claimed possession, which was granted by Judge Denyer QC, who treated the issue of proportionality under Article 8 and under section 15 of the Equality Act 2010 in the same way, following *Manchester City Council v Pinnock*[4] and *Hounslow LBC v Powell*[5] as applied in *Thurrock Borough Council v West*.[6] Judge Denyer QC did, however, grant permission to appeal on the issue of whether the discrimination defence should be treated in the same way as an Article 8 defence. The appeal was dismissed by Cranston J and also dismissed by the Court of Appeal,[7] which held that the approach to proportionality was the same under the Equality Act as it was under Article 8. The appeal was dismissed by the Supreme Court on the grounds that the landlord urgently needed vacant possession of the flat occupied by the tenant in order to comply with its own legal obligations to give vacant possession to the freeholder. The Supreme Court, therefore, felt bound to conclude that the eviction would be a proportionate means of achieving a legitimate aim and that by securing his eviction, the landlord would not be discriminating against him. Nevertheless, the decision is of considerable significance because of the Supreme Court agreeing unanimously that a structured approach to proportionality had to be adopted in cases under the Equality Act and that disability discrimination defences should not be treated in the same way as Article 8 defences.

Section 15 deals specifically with discrimination arising from disability, providing that a person discriminates against a disabled person if he treats that person unfavourably because of something arising in consequence of his disability under section 15(1)(a) and he cannot show that the treatment is a proportionate means of achieving a legitimate aim under section 15(1)(b). Subsection (1) does not apply if A shows that A did not know, and could not reasonably have been expected to know, that B had a disability.[8] Section 15 does not require a comparator, and there is also no need to show detriment under section 15, merely unfavourable treatment. Section 15 applies to eviction due to section 35(1), which provides that 'A person (A) who manages premises must not discriminate against a person (B) who occupies the premises … (b) by evicting B (or taking steps for the purpose of securing B's eviction)'.

II. COMPARISON BETWEEN DEFENCE OF DISABILITY DISCRIMINATION UNDER EQUALITY ACT AND DEFENCE UNDER ARTICLE 8

The values which underpin both equality and human rights are shared values that derive from the Universal Declaration of Human Rights 1948, which states that

[3] See *Pinnock*, *Powell*, *Thurrock* and *Lewisham* (n 1).
[4] *Pinnock* (n 1).
[5] *Powell* (n 1).
[6] *Thurrock* (n 1).
[7] *Akerman* (n 2).
[8] Equality Act 2010, s 15(2).

'All human beings are born free and equal in dignity and in rights'. The values of equality and human rights centre on fairness, equality, dignity, respect, autonomy, empowerment and participation. The European Convention on Human Rights was a response to the Second World War, and its intention was to guarantee a range of political rights and freedoms of the individual against interference by the state. Article 8, namely the right to respect for the home, subject to interference by a public authority for the protection of the rights and freedoms of others, has been the subject of defences in a substantial number of possession proceedings cases. By way of contrast, the Equality Act originated from what Hepple terms 'A history of bits and pieces'[9] deriving from piecemeal legislation. The Equality Act was a major landmark in the long struggle for equal rights and was the outcome of over 13 years of campaigning by equality specialists and human rights organisations.[10] Hepple views the establishment of the Equality and Human Rights Commission and a single Equality Act as 'an historic reunification of equality and human rights law, back to its origins in the Universal Declaration of Human Rights'.[11] The Equality Act 2010 is a significant tool in endeavouring to achieve status equality and prevent status discrimination.[12]

The Supreme Court in *Akerman* had numerous grounds as the basis for its decision that defences under the Equality Act are to be treated differently from defences under Article 8. The differentiating tests for proportionality which have emerged from *Akerman* must necessarily focus on the differentiation in purpose of the provisions.

A. The Consequences for Private Landlords versus Public Landlords

Section 35 of the Equality Act applies to private and public sector landlords, whereas only public authorities and bodies exercising functions of a public nature[13] are obliged by section 6 of the Human Rights Act 1998 to act compatibly with Convention rights.[14] The consequence is that neither a public nor a private landlord can evict a disabled tenant because of something arising in consequence of the disability unless the landlord can show this is a proportionate means of achieving a legitimate aim. Baroness Hale stated that this difference demonstrates that the substantive right to equal treatment protected by the Equality Act 2010 is different from the substantive right protected by Article 8.[15] It is axiomatic that the rights are substantively different, because the legislative requirements of the Equality Act 2010 and Human Rights Act 1998 vary despite the common foundation of values.

Private landlords may be perceived in some circumstances to be performing a social welfare and/or civic duty under the Equality Act, since 'Landlords may

9 B Hepple, *Equality: The Legal Framework*, 2nd edn (Oxford, Hart Publishing, 2014) 11.
10 ibid 1–2.
11 See further Hepple (ibid) 19–20.
12 Terminology used by Hepple (ibid) 22–23.
13 See *R (Weaver) v London and Quadrant Housing Trust* [2009] EWCA Civ 587, [2010] 1 WLR 363.
14 See further *McDonald v McDonald* [2016] UKSC 28, [2016] 3 WLR 45.
15 *Akerman* (n 2) [25].

be required to accommodate, or to continue to accommodate, a disabled person when they would not be required to accommodate, or continue to accommodate, a non-disabled person',[16] which may be particularly onerous for private landlords. For example, if a tenant becomes disabled due to an accident and earns a lower salary due to restrictions on the nature of employment available to such a person with disability, a landlord might be prevented from taking possession proceedings and have to accept a lower rent if the tenant with the disability cannot afford the rent which was agreed at the beginning of the tenancy (subject to the proportionality test, which will be examined later).

An additional question which needs to be analysed as a result of the decision in *Akerman* is whether the Equality Act will impact private landlords seeking to obtain possession under assured shorthold tenancies under the Housing Act 1988, and whether a tenant may raise a defence when a landlord serves notice requiring possession at the end of a fixed-term assured shorthold tenancy under section 21(1)(b) of the Housing Act 1988. Following the Supreme Court decision in *McDonald v McDonald*[17] that a court did not have to consider proportionality under Article 8(2) when considering whether to make a possession order against a residential tenant of a private landlord and that there was no obligation to assess proportionality under section 21(4) of the Housing Act 1988, it is unlikely that a challenge under section 15 of the Equality Act would be successful other than to postpone an order for possession. Lord Neuberger's view in *McDonald* was that even if a proportionality assessment was required, the most a tenant could hope for would be an order for possession in six weeks' time.[18]

B. The Difference in Burden of Proof under Section 15 and Article 8

Another indicator that the position in relation to Article 8 cases and Equality Act cases are to be treated in disparate ways is the differential provision in relation to burden of proof. The Equality Act 2010 contains express provisions relating to the burden of proof. Once a prima facie case of discrimination is made out, the burden of proof is firmly on the landlord to show that there was no discrimination contrary to section 15(1)(a), or that an order for possession is proportionate under section 15(1)(b) of the 2010 Act. The effect of section 136 of the Equality Act 2010 is that if the court could conclude that an eviction was because of something arising in consequence of a person's disability, then the alleged discriminator has to prove that it was not. If he could not do so, the burden would then be on him to show that the eviction was nevertheless a proportionate means of achieving a legitimate aim.[19] If the claim is for indirect discrimination, for example that the landlord has imposed a requirement on its tenants which puts tenants with disabilities at a particular disadvantage, the landlord has to show there was a valid reason for doing so unrelated

[16] ibid [25] (Baroness Hale).
[17] *McDonald* (n 14).
[18] ibid [75].
[19] *Akerman* (n 2) [19] (Baroness Hale).

to the disability.[20] The provisions of section 19 relating to indirect discrimination apply, which will add greater protection for tenants with disabilities.

By way of comparison, the general position under the Human Rights Act 1998 is that once an interference with the protected right is established, the burden shifts to the public authority to prove that the interference is justified.[21] Baroness Hale's summation of the proportionality exercise under section 15 is that

> If it is a claim of disability discrimination under section 15, then the landlord would have to show that there was no less drastic means of solving the problem and that the effect on the occupier was outweighed by the advantages.[22]

Baroness Hale is correct that 'The express burden of proof provisions in the Equality Act cannot simply be ignored because there are some elements in the proportionality exercise which can be taken for granted'.[23] Lord Neuberger confirmed that all that is needed for the tenant is to make out the possibility of discrimination, then the burden of proof is firmly on the landlord to prove that there was no discrimination contrary to section 15(1)(a) or that an order is proportionate under section 15(1)(b).[24] This is a significant improvement for tenants with disabilities, since Article 8 does not offer a substantial defence to or protection from possession claims, and this may be one justification for the divergence in proportionality tests in the two regimes.

C. The Difference in Proportionality Tests under Section 15 and Article 8: Equality Rights versus Convention Rights

The wording of the objective justification test in each provision is different. The question in section 15(1)(b) is whether 'the treatment is a proportionate means of achieving a legitimate aim', whereas in Article 8 the issue is whether interference is 'necessary in a democratic society' for one of the specific purposes listed in Article 8(2).[25] As Baroness Hale recognised, 'they have come to be interpreted the same way',[26] but the Supreme Court held in *Akerman* that they are to be interpreted and applied differently.

(i) Proportionality under Section 15 of the Equality Act 2010

As a result of the decision in *Akerman*, a trial court must undertake a thorough analysis of the proportionality issue,[27] which is a welcome development for

[20] *Woodfall: Landlord and Tenant* vol 3, pt 11, Ch 25, para 25.050.4; *Akerman* (n 2) [34] (Baroness Hale).

[21] *Akerman* (n 2) [33] (Baroness Hale).

[22] ibid [34] (Baroness Hale).

[23] ibid [34] (Baroness Hale).

[24] ibid [55] (Lord Neuberger).

[25] These include 'the interests of national security, public safety or the economic well-being of the country, for the prevention of disorder or crime, for the protection of health or morals or for the protection of the rights and freedoms of others'.

[26] *Akerman* (n 2) [27].

[27] See also S Nield, 'Proportionality and The Vindication of Property Rights', ch 3 in this volume.

equality rights. Baroness Hale explained the three elements set out by Mummery LJ in *R (Elias) v Secretary of State for Defence*[28] and a fourth element set out in Lord Reed's dissenting judgment in *Bank Mellat v HM Treasury (No 2)*,[29] although Lord Neuberger in *Akerman* only referred to the three-stage test. It remains to be determined whether the disparity is substantial and if it may have practical consequences.

As Baroness Hale recognised,[30] the concept of proportionality contained in section 15 is derived from EU law, which is the source of much of the anti-discrimination legislation. The three elements expounded by Mummery LJ in *R (Elias) v Secretary of State for Defence* were: 'First, is the objective sufficiently important to justify limiting a fundamental right? Secondly, is the measure rationally connected to the objective? Thirdly, are the means chosen no more than is necessary to accomplish the objective?'[31] The fourth element identified by Baroness Hale[32] is that 'the disadvantages caused must not be disproportionate to the aims pursued'[33] or 'whether the impact of the rights infringement is disproportionate to the likely benefit of the impugned measure'.[34] This fourth element is the factor most likely to swing the pendulum in favour of the person with the disability, because it acknowledges that 'the ends, however meritorious, cannot justify the only means which is capable of achieving them'.[35]

A helpful overview of proportionality was undertaken in Lord Reed's dissenting judgment in *Bank Mellat v HM Treasury (No 2)*,[36] in which he recognised that 'An assessment of proportionality involves a value judgment at the stage at which a balance has to be struck between the importance of the objective pursued and the value of the right intruded upon'.[37] He undertook a valuable comparison of the approach to proportionality at a national level and at the Strasbourg court, and stated that the Strasbourg court recognises that it may be less well placed than a national court to decide the appropriate balance in the particular national context.[38]

What is notable about Lord Neuberger's judgment in *Akerman* is that in the penultimate paragraph of his judgment, in seeming to agree with Baroness Hale, Lord Neuberger referred to 'the right test' being 'the threefold approach identified by Mummery LJ in the *Elias* case, para 165',[39] but did not refer to the fourth element.[40]

[28] *R (Elias) v Secretary of State for Defence* [2006] 1 WLR 3213 [165].

[29] *Bank Mellat v HM Treasury (No 2)* [2013] UKSC 38, [2014] AC 700 [71].

[30] *Akerman* (n 2) [28].

[31] *R (Elias) v Secretary of State for Defence* (n 28) [165]. These elements were derived from *de Freitas v Permanent Secretary of Ministry of Agriculture, Fisheries, Lands and Housing* [1999] 1 AC 69, 80, which itself was derived from the Canadian case *R v Oakes* [1986] 1 SCR 103.

[32] *Akerman* (n 2) [28], deriving from Lord Reed JSC in *Bank Mellat v HM Treasury (No 2)* (n 29) [68] *et seq.*

[33] Citing from Court of Justice of European Communities in Case C-331/88 *R v Minister for Agriculture, Fisheries and Food Ex p Fedesa* [1990] ECR I-4023 [13].

[34] Citing from *Bank Mellat v HM Treasury (No 2)* (n 29) [74] (Lord Reed).

[35] *Akerman* (n 2) [28] (Baroness Hale).

[36] *Bank Mellat v HM Treasury (No 2)* (n 29). This was undertaken in the context of human rights in the European Convention on Human Rights.

[37] *Bank Mellat v HM Treasury (No 2)* (n 29) [71] (Lord Reed).

[38] *Bank Mellat v HM Treasury (No 2)* (n 29) [71] (Lord Reed).

[39] *Akerman* (n 2) [62] (Lord Neuberger).

[40] *R v Minister for Agriculture, Fisheries and Food, Ex p Fedesa* (n 33) [13].

This may indicate that Lord Neuberger did not consider that this fourth element is necessary or adds to the dynamics of the decision-making process. Alternatively, Lord Neuberger could be advocating a more categorical approach which is less nuanced than that set out by Baroness Hale. By omitting reference to the fourth element, Lord Neuberger has arguably made it easier in future cases for those denying disability discrimination.

Lord Wilson in *Akerman* did, however, state that the court should adopt a four-stage structured approach to the claimant's attempt to show that the steps for securing the defendant's eviction are a proportionate means of achieving a legitimate aim (without citing the authority or case for this).[41] In relation to the fourth element, Lord Wilson stated that

> the eviction may be proportionate to the claimant's objectives without being proportionate in the necessary wider sense. Section 15(1)(b) of the 2010 Act requires the claimant to show that the eviction strikes a fair balance between its need to accomplish its objectives and the disadvantages thereby caused to the defendant as a disabled person.[42]

This introduces the concept of proportionality 'in the necessary wider sense', and it appears that the fourth element is necessary to establish proportionality in the wider sense.[43] However, importing notions of proportionality in a wider sense and a narrower sense encourages litigation due to uncertainty of boundaries and unpredictability of decisions.

(ii) Threshold/Proportionality under Article 8

A completely different approach has been taken to proportionality under Article 8.[44] In *Pinnock*[45] and *Powell*,[46] the Supreme Court rejected the 'structured approach' to proportionality. Baroness Hale in *Akerman* quoted from Lord Hope in *Powell*, who rejected that approach

> in the context of a statutory regime that has been deliberately designed by Parliament, for sound reasons of social policy, so as not to provide the occupier with a secure tenancy [the structured approach] would be wholly inappropriate ... It would give rise to the risk of prolonged and expensive litigation, which would divert funds from the uses to which they should be put to promote social housing in the area.[47]

Baroness Hale, who was a judge in both *Pinnock* and *Powell*, agreed that the two legitimate aims identified by Lord Neuberger in *Pinnock*[48] were valid in Article 8 cases. Making a possession order would '(a) serve to vindicate the authority's ownership rights; and (b) enable the authority to comply with its public duties in relation to the allocation and management of its housing stock'.[49] In relation to Article 8,

41 *Akerman* (n 2) [64] (Lord Wilson).
42 ibid [73] (Lord Wilson).
43 See also *Huang v Secretary of State for the Home Department* [2007] UKHL 11, [2007] AC 167.
44 See also Nield (n 27).
45 *Pinnock* (n 1).
46 *Powell* (n 1).
47 ibid [41].
48 *Pinnock* (n 1) [52].
49 Derived from *Pinnock* (n 1) [52] and supported in *Powell* (n 1) [36].

the position as a result of *Pinnock* and *Powell* is that 'The court will only have to consider whether the making of a possession order is proportionate if the issue has been raised by the occupier and it has crossed the high threshold of being seriously arguable'[50] and would only succeed in 'a small proportion of cases'.[51]

As Lord Neuberger stated in *Pinnock*:

> Unencumbered property rights, even where they are enjoyed by a public body such as a local authority, are of real weight when it comes to proportionality … in virtually every case where a residential occupier has no contractual or statutory protection, and the local authority is entitled to possession as a matter of domestic law, there will be a very strong case for saying that making an order for possession would be proportionate.[52]

The key words are those in the sentence following this quote, that: 'However, in some cases there may be factors which would tell the other way.'

In neither *Pinnock*[53] nor *Powell*[54] did the Supreme Court provide clear guidance on how to balance the occupier's personal circumstances against the local authority's legitimate aims in determining the proportionality of making a possession order.[55] The Supreme Court expressly left it to county court judges to decide, but guidance is needed on the more difficult issues relating to exceptional personal circumstances for the purposes of Article 8. Article 8 defences have not been successful in the vast majority of cases[56] subsequent to *Pinnock*[57] and *Powell*,[58] though there have been cases where tenants have been successful.[59] As a result of *Akerman*, it is likely to be only in a minority of situations that cases under section 15 of the Equality Act 2010 will be dismissed summarily. This will happen if the landlord can show: (i) the defendant has no real prospect of showing he is disabled within the meaning of the Act; (ii) possession was not being sought because of something arising in consequence of the disability; or (iii) bringing and enforcing the claim were plainly a proportionate means of achieving a legitimate aim.[60] The court has to undertake the proportionality exercise itself.[61] Lord Neuberger was realistic in recognising that

[50] *Powell* (n 1) [33] (Lord Hope).
[51] ibid [35] (Lord Hope).
[52] *Pinnock* (n 1) [54].
[53] ibid.
[54] *Powell* (n 1).
[55] S Pascoe, 'Europe, Human Rights and Land Law in the Twenty-First Century: An English Example' [2011] *Property Law Review* 179. See also generally S Nield, 'Article 8 Respect for the Home: A Human Property Right' (2013) 24 *King's Law Journal* 147; I Loveland, 'Horizontality of Article 8 in the Context of Possession Proceedings' [2015] *European Human Rights Law Review* 138; R Walsh, 'Stability and Predictability in English Property Law—the Impact of Article 8 of the European Convention on Human Rights Reassessed' (2015) 131 *LQR* 585; S Nield, 'Thumbs Down to the Horizontal Effect of Article 8' [2015] *The Conveyancer and Property Lawyer* 77.
[56] See, eg, *Corby Borough Council v Scott* [2012] EWCA Civ 276, [2012] HLR 23; *Birmingham City Council v Lloyd* [2012] EWCA Civ 969; *Thurrock BC v West* (n 1); *Ker v Optima Community Association* [2013] EWCA Civ 579, [2013] HLR 37; *Sims v Dacorum BC* (n 1); *R (N) v Lewisham LBC* (n 1).
[57] *Pinnock* (n 1).
[58] *Powell* (n 1).
[59] See, eg, *R (JL) v Secretary of State for Defence* (n 1); *Southend-on-Sea Borough Council v Armour* [2014] EWCA Civ 231, [2014] HLR 23.
[60] *Akerman* (n 2) [36] (Baroness Hale) and [59] (Lord Neuberger).
[61] ibid [38] (Baroness Hale).

these types of cases give rise to disputed facts or assessments, so it would be rare that a landlord would be advised to seek summary judgment.[62]

(iii) Is There a Link between Duty to Make Reasonable Adjustments and the Proportionality Test?

Section 15 makes no reference to reasonable adjustments, but the duty exists in section 20 and is in the background of the proportionality question, because it cannot be proportionate to treat a person in a way which results in a detriment if reasonable adjustments are available to remove a detriment.[63] The duty to make reasonable adjustments arises where a disabled person is put at a 'substantial disadvantage ... in comparison with persons who are not disabled' by 'a provision, criterion or practice'.[64] Six different schedules in the Equality Act 2010 apply to when the duty applies,[65] with schedule 4 being the relevant one for premises. The reasonable adjustment analysis is not the same as proportionality, although there is a likelihood of harmonisation of the reasonable adjustments analysis with the proportionality balancing.[66]

Failure to comply with the duty to make reasonable adjustments constitutes discrimination.[67] As Baroness Hale noted in *Akerman*,[68] it is discrimination under section 21(2) to fail to comply with the specific duties to make the reasonable adjustments which are required by the Act in particular contexts. In *General Dynamics Information Technology Ltd v Carranza*,[69] which was not cited in *Akerman*, there was no issue relating to discrimination arising out of disability under section 15, but the issue concerned the duty to make reasonable adjustments and section 20(3) of the Act. As Judge David Richardson stated, 'Parties and Employment Tribunals should consider carefully whether the duty to make reasonable adjustments is really in play or whether the case is best considered and analysed under the new, robust, section 15'.[70] He continued, 'I have therefore concluded that the majority finding of a failure to make reasonable adjustments cannot stand.[71] If this case had been put forward as a case of discrimination arising from disability, it would have been easier to analyse.'[72] The dynamics of the link between the duty to make reasonable adjustments and the proportionality test are yet to be worked out and may reshape the parameters of the proportionality test. It remains to be determined whether the duty to make reasonable adjustments will extend to modifying policies on rent arrears, for example, or be limited to physical aspects of premises.

[62] ibid [60] (Lord Neuberger).

[63] See I Smith and A Baker, *Smith and Wood's Employment Law*, 12th edn (Oxford, Oxford University Press, 2015) 421.

[64] The Equality Act, s 20 sets out in detail the three requirements which comprise the duty.

[65] See Hepple (n 9) 95.

[66] Smith and Baker (n 63) 421.

[67] Equality Act 2010, s 21(2).

[68] *Akerman* (n 2) [15].

[69] *General Dynamics Information Technology Ltd v Carranza* [2015] ICR 169.

[70] ibid [34].

[71] ibid [46].

[72] ibid [47].

D. Are Human Rights Less Important than Equality Rights?

It is necessary to analyse the reasoning behind the differentiation in approach between Article 8 and claims under section 15. Baroness Hale recognised that in cases where Article 8 is the only defence,

> the court is simply not equipped to judge the weight of an individual's right to respect for her home against the weight of the interests of the whole community for whom the authority has to manage its limited housing resources.[73]

That is well established following *Pinnock* and *Powell*. She then stated correctly that 'No landlord is allowed to evict a disabled tenant because of something arising in consequence of the disability, unless he can show eviction to be a proportionate means of achieving a legitimate aim'.[74] But the next sentence makes a conceptual leap which is not fully justified, when she stated that 'He is thus obliged to be more considerate towards a disabled tenant than he is towards a non-disabled one'.[75] The problem with that statement is that this is not an obligation on the landlord, because the positive action permitted by section 13(3)[76] does not impose an obligation on a landlord.

The other problematic aspect with Baroness Hale's statement is that it has the effect of incorporating the positive action permitted by section 13(3) into a requirement for the proportionality test. Conflating the proportionality test with the desirability for positive action, which is rendered non-discriminatory due to section 13(3), may require a distortion of theoretical analysis. However, it is likely that it is inherent within Baroness Hale's analysis that the proportionality test includes consideration of whether there are possibilities to make reasonable adjustments or alternative ways for the landlord to achieve the legitimate aim which are not as discriminatory against the tenant. Baroness Hale does not make this explicit, but the duty to make reasonable adjustments is a special form of positive action, and treating a person more favourably under section 13(3) could require making reasonable adjustments.

Part of Baroness Hale's justification was a quote from herself in *Lewisham London Borough Council v Malcolm*, that 'people with disabilities are "entitled to have due allowance made for the consequences of their disability"'.[77] She did not deal specifically with the issue of whether section 15 of the Equality Act 2010 enables that to be done and did not explain how 'due allowance' should be interpreted. She circumvented that by justifying that the twin aims identified in *Pinnock*[78] will not invariably trump that right, which is correct. She recognised that the second of the twin aims (to enable the authority to comply with its public duties in relation to the allocation and management of its housing stock) may 'on occasions have to give

[73] *Akerman* (n 2) [29] considering what Lord Hope stated in *Powell* (n 1) [35].

[74] ibid [31] (Baroness Hale).

[75] ibid [31] (Baroness Hale).

[76] The Equality Act, s 13(3) states that 'If the protected characteristic is disability, and B is not a disabled person, A does not discriminate against B only because A treats or would treat disabled persons more favourably than A treats B'.

[77] *Lewisham London Borough Council v Malcolm* [2008] UKHL 43, [2008] 1 AC 1399 [61] in relation to the Disability Discrimination Act 1995.

[78] *Pinnock* (n 1) [52].

way to the equality rights of the occupier and in particular to the equality rights of a particular disabled person'.[79] She did not tackle the problem that the fact that a person is disabled does not magically increase limited housing resources. Personal circumstances are taken into account in making decisions, as is implicit in Baroness Hale's statement that

> The impact of being required to move from this particular place on this particular disabled person may be such that it is not outweighed by the benefits to the local authority or social landlord of being able to regain possession.[80]

This is a very welcome development in equality law for tenants, even though the means by which it is reached may be questionable.

If the example is taken of a tenant who can no longer afford the rent because of having to work fewer hours due to a disability as a result of an accident, the landlord might be terminating the tenancy 'because of something arising in consequence of B's disability' under the wording of section 15(1)(a), although this may be a contestable issue. Even though the tenancy is not being terminated because the tenant has a disability, but is purporting to be terminated as an unfortunate consequence of the disability, this may nevertheless amount to discrimination arising from disability under section 15(1)(a), being a case of unfavourable treatment by terminating the tenancy due to inability to pay rent, which is as a result of the disability, unless the landlord can justify the termination. The problem for landlords is caused by the breadth of the wording of section 15(1)(a), because the consequence of what Baroness Hale stated is that securing equality of treatment would nullify section 15(1)(b) in the vast majority of cases and places landlords at a serious disadvantage trying to justify the proportionality test. If a different example is taken where the reason for eviction is the behaviour of the tenant, if the behaviour arose because of the disability, the landlord will need, for example, to demonstrate that the health and/or safety of neighbours are adversely affected by the tenants' behaviour, so that the eviction is a proportionate means of achieving a legitimate aim.[81]

Baroness Hale stated that the public policy considerations are different in relation to Equality Act claims.[82] There is a change in emphasis and weighting, so that

> When a disability discrimination defence is raised, the question is not simply whether the social landlord is entitled to recover the property in order to fulfil its or the local authority's public housing functions, but also whether the landlord or the local authority has done all that can reasonably be expected of it to accommodate the consequences of the disabled person's disability and whether, at the end of the day, the 'twin aims' are sufficient to outweigh the effect on the disabled person.[83]

[79] *Akerman* (n 2) [31] (Baroness Hale).

[80] ibid [31] (Baroness Hale).

[81] Compare the position in *North Devon Homes Ltd v Brazier* [2003] EWHC 574, [2003] HLR 59, where David Steel J held that the tenant was being evicted because of the disability, which was unlawful, and there was no evidence that the landlord had formed the opinion that discrimination was justified in order not to endanger the health or safety of any person, so her eviction was not justified under the Disability Discrimination Act 1995.

[82] *Akerman* (n 2) [32] (Baroness Hale). This was a point raised by the Equality and Human Rights Commission.

[83] ibid [32] (Baroness Hale).

That is a fair assessment of the position, but raises the question with public authority landlords why its limited housing stock should matter more for human rights cases than equality cases. The justification for this point is not made in the judgments. It is also notable that Baroness Hale stated that 'the court is well equipped to address'[84] these issues with equality cases but not with human rights cases. Again, the justification for this differentiation is not fully substantiated.

The effect on the disabled person has subjective connotations, so if the tenant would be suicidal if the local authority obtained possession, then Baroness Hale's judgment indicates that there should be no order for possession, but if the effect on the tenant is less drastic, an order for possession could be given. Guidance is lacking as to how this should be applied, especially in borderline cases. Because of the comparatively harsh position taken in Article 8 cases, it may be that this approach in *Akerman* offers an olive branch to tenants who fall in the category of disabilities without opening the floodgates in human rights cases.

Lord Neuberger adopts a different line of reasoning and justification from Baroness Hale for equality rights. Whilst following what was stated in *Pinnock*[85] and *Powell*[86] in relation to Article 8, and restating that the vast majority of cases should be disposed of summarily and that 'it will be a very unusual case where such a defence could succeed',[87] Lord Neuberger does not base his reasoning on an obligation to be more considerate towards a disabled tenant. Lord Neuberger's rationale is based on section 35(1)(b) of the Equality Act 2010, that 'the protection afforded by section 35(1)(b) is plainly stronger than the protection afforded by Article 8'[88] and that 'the protection afforded by section 35(1)(b) is an extra, and a more specific, stronger, right afforded to disabled occupiers over and above the Article 8 right'.[89] It is questionable whether Lord Neuberger is as a result marginalising the proportionality test in section 15(1)(b).

Lord Wilson agrees that where a defence is raised under section 35(1)(b) to an action for possession, there should be no presumption that the action is fit for summary disposal. He brings another dimension into the justification, which is that 'CPR r 55.8(2) calls for a careful evaluation at that initial stage whether the claim is genuinely disputed on grounds which appear to be substantial'. As provided in CPR 55.8(2),[90] if a claim 'is genuinely disputed on grounds that appear to be substantial', directions to trial should be given. Lord Wilson does not address specifically the issue of why this is not adopted when Article 8 is the defence. He merely continues that 'when such a defence is raised, the court should adopt a four-stage structured approach'.[91]

[84] ibid [32] (Baroness Hale).
[85] *Pinnock* (n 1).
[86] *Powell* (n 1).
[87] *Akerman* (n 2) [52] (Lord Neuberger).
[88] ibid [55] (Lord Neuberger).
[89] ibid [56] (Lord Neuberger).
[90] Civil Procedure Rules, Rule 55.8(2).
[91] *Akerman* (n 2) [64] (Lord Wilson).

E. Extension of Proportionality in Article 8 Cases?

It was Lord Neuberger himself who raised tangentially the issue in *Pinnock*[92] of whether, where the occupier has certain characteristics (including disability), there will be asymmetrical treatment in those cases and other cases under Article 8. Accordingly, Lord Neuberger opened the door to the proportionality test in Article 8 cases being accorded greater weight and significance in some cases when he stated

> the suggestions put forward on behalf of the Equality and Human Rights Commission, that proportionality is more likely to be a relevant issue 'in respect of occupants who are vulnerable as a result of mental illness, physical or learning disability, poor health or frailty', and that 'the issue may also require the local authority to explain why they are not securing alternative accommodation in such cases' seem to us well made.[93]

Lord Neuberger repeated this in *Akerman*,[94] citing from his judgment in *Pinnock*.[95]

What is salient about this is that Lord Neuberger's statement is broader than the definition of disability in the Equality Act. The statement puts disability on an equal par with mental illness (which may, of course, be a disability, depending on the individual's circumstances) and 'poor health and frailty', which do not necessarily fall within the definition of disability. In such cases, it will be harder for the landlord to satisfy the court on the proportionality issue. Lord Neuberger makes it clear that the statement refers to a defence raised under Article 8 and not under the Equality Act when he states in *Akerman* that 'where the occupier is disabled, it is significantly less unlikely than in the normal run of cases that an Article 8 defence might succeed'.[96] What is surprising, given Lord Neuberger's punctilious attention to detail and accuracy, is that he does not deal with the discrepancy in the definition of disability and has single-handedly opened the door to anyone in poor health or frailty relying on this *obiter dicta* in an Article 8 defence. This a welcome extension of the principle in *Pinnock*[97] beyond the ambit of disability, but encourages litigation by creating uncertainty in the law.

Baroness Hale formulated an interesting twist on what Lord Neuberger stated in *Pinnock*. Lord Neuberger stated in *Pinnock* that

> If domestic law justifies an outright order for possession, the effect of Article 8 may, albeit in exceptional cases, justify (in ascending order of effect) granting an extended period for possession, suspending the order for possession on the happening of an event, or even refusing an order altogether.[98]

It was only two paragraphs later that Lord Neuberger made the statement about the suggestions put forward by the Equality and Human Rights Commission, which, he noted, 'seem to us well made'.[99] Baroness Hale in *Akerman* made a significant

[92] *Pinnock* (n 1) [64].
[93] ibid [64].
[94] *Akerman* (n 2) [56] (Lord Neuberger).
[95] *Pinnock* (n 1) [64].
[96] *Akerman* (n 2) [56] (Lord Neuberger).
[97] *Pinnock* (n 1) [64].
[98] ibid [62] (Lord Neuberger).
[99] ibid [64] (Lord Neuberger).

inversion of the order of what Lord Neuberger stated and consequently extended the law beyond the scope of what Lord Neuberger intended in *Pinnock*. Baroness Hale stated that the consequence of Lord Neuberger's statement is that 'The effect might justify granting an extended period for possession, suspending the order for possession on the happening of an event, or even refusing an order altogether'.[100] The juxtaposition of these two sentences by Baroness Hale achieves a significant shift from Lord Neuberger's judgment. In addition, Lord Neuberger had qualified his statement by declaring that it would apply 'in exceptional cases',[101] but Baroness Hale does not qualify it in this way.[102] Lord Neuberger had also stated that these would be 'in ascending order of effect',[103] but Baroness Hale did not repeat that qualification, rather presenting them as being on an equilibrium and even keel, thus stretching the boundaries of the law further than even Lord Neuberger.[104] The consequence in future cases may be that the boundaries between the proportionality tests in Article 8 and those in disability discrimination cases will be more closely aligned.

III. IMPACT ON PROPERTY RIGHTS OF DEFENCES OF DISABILITY DISCRIMINATION BEING RAISED BY TENANTS

Baroness Hale agreed[105] with what Lord Bingham stated in *Lewisham London Borough Council v Malcolm*,[106] that it may be unlawful to evict a disabled person even though the disabled person had no other claim to remain in the property—meaning that if the defendant succeeds in his defence that bringing proceedings amounts to discrimination by reason of his disability in breach of section 15, then the court cannot make a possession order.[107] The Supreme Court may accordingly be creating new property rights for tenants with disabilities.

A. Is there Positive Discrimination of Those with Disabilities?

A disabled person can be treated more favourably than a person who is not disabled, because section 13(3) of the Equality Act provides that, 'A does not discriminate against B only because A treats or would treat disabled persons more favourably than A treats B'. The distinguishing feature with discrimination, as recognised by Baroness Hale, is that

> Whereas treating a man equally with a woman usually means treating him in the same way as a woman is treated, treating a disabled person equally with a non-disabled person may mean treating him differently from a non-disabled person. This is to ensure that he can play a full part in society despite his disabilities.[108]

100 *Akerman* (n 2) [21] (Baroness Hale).
101 *Pinnock* (n 1) [62] (Lord Neuberger).
102 *Akerman* (n 2) [21] (Baroness Hale).
103 *Pinnock* (n 1) [62] (Lord Neuberger).
104 *Akerman* (n 2) [21].
105 ibid [17].
106 *Malcolm* (n 77).
107 *Akerman* (n 2) [17].
108 ibid [2].

In order to decide whether the eviction is 'because of something arising in consequence of B's disability' under section 15(1)(a) of the Equality Act, the landlord would have to justify the treatment. There is no need for a comparison with how the landlord would treat any other person.[109] Crucially 'it might have to behave differently towards a disabled tenant from the way in which it would behave towards a non-disabled tenant'.[110] In relation to the example of a tenant who earns a lower salary as a result of an accident which causes a disability and who accumulates arrears of rent, the question arises whether a landlord has to take steps to treat this tenant differently from other tenants—for example, allow a much longer time for the tenant to discharge the arrears of rent.

The wording of section 15(1)(a) indicates prima facie that there cannot be negative treatment of a tenant, but to avoid taking proceedings for possession actually requires positive action, which is arguably positive discrimination towards those with disabilities. The only ground on which a landlord will not be obliged to take positive action towards a tenant with disabilities is if the landlord can demonstrate that the unfavourable treatment is a proportionate means of achieving a legitimate aim. A positive duty to advance equality, being proactive, sidesteps many of the limitations of the indirect discrimination provisions.[111] The Equality Act has widened the circumstances in which positive action is lawful. As Smith and Baker point out, the Equality Act is based on a neutral or symmetrical model of equality by giving the right not to be treated less favourably on protected grounds.[112] It is necessary to differentiate positive discrimination, which is usually unlawful, from positive action, which comprises measures to promote equality. Sections 158 and 159 govern positive action, which is a proportionate means of achieving legitimate aims. Section 158(2) permits any action which is a proportionate means of achieving one of three aims: to overcome or minimise disadvantage; to meet the relevant needs; or to enable or encourage participation of those who share a protected characteristic. The provisions are permissive, not mandatory, and important in extending what is permissible.[113] Although sections 158 and 159 are not mandatory, sections 15 and 20 of the Equality Act 2010 may render necessary some form of positive action by landlords in relation to people with disabilities, because otherwise it could amount to discrimination. Time will tell, in the area of possession proceedings, the full extent to which positive action will reshape property rights in landlord and tenant law.

B. Public Sector Equality Duty—Is there an Extension of Duties to Disabled Persons Living with Tenant?

There is no private sector duty to advance equality. The public sector equality duty in section 149 of the Equality Act 2010, which applies to disabilities, requires public authorities to have due regard, in the exercise of their functions, to the need to

109 ibid [18].

110 ibid [18]. The use of the word 'it' in this context refers to the landlord or other provider.

111 Hepple (n 9) 26.

112 Smith and Baker (n 63) 353.

113 Hepple (n 9) 158.

eliminate discrimination, harassment and victimisation, to advance equality of opportunity and to foster good relations between different groups. The duty extends to 'a person who is not a public authority but who exercises public functions'.[114] Specific reinforcement that disabilities must be taken into account is given in section 149(4), which provides that 'The steps involved in meeting the needs of disabled persons that are different from the needs of persons who are not disabled include, in particular, steps to take account of disabled persons' disabilities'. The Equality and Human Rights Commission plays an important role in enforcement of this duty and can issue compliance notices and require specific action.[115]

The duty achieves what Hepple would term as transformative equality, because the provisions of section 149 are important tools in the drive to eliminate discrimination and advance equality of opportunity.[116] McColgan notes that the public sector equality duty 'is a qualitatively different type of provision than those which prohibit discrimination, even discrimination by public authorities'.[117] The duties to advance equality of opportunity in section 149(1)(b) and foster good relations between those who do and do not share the positive characteristic are not limited by the scope of the anti-discrimination provisions. McColgan highlights how this demonstrates 'some movement away from a rigidly symmetrical approach to equality/discrimination even where what is statutorily framed as "positive action" (sections 158 and 159) is not at issue', and rightly notes that the duty is contained with the 'positive action' provisions in part 11 of the Act, entitled 'Advancement of Equality'.[118] Hepple highlights the main defects in the duty as the lack of provision in the primary legislation for engagement with stakeholders and a low standard of judicial scrutiny.[119] He is critical of the approach of governments that if voluntary methods do not work, legislation will be considered at a later date.[120]

It is notable that if the tenant does not have a disability, but someone living with the tenant has one, the public authority will have to take the rights of that disabled person into account in deciding whether to seek possession, because the decision of *Barnsley Metropolitan Borough Council v Norton*,[121] which applied to section 49A of the Disability Discrimination Act 1995, will apply to section 149 of the Equality Act 2010.[122] The Court of Appeal in the *Norton* case held that the duty did not arise only where the rights of a disabled person under other specific legislation were involved, but was entirely general and applied to the council's decision to seek possession of the school house, because the council knew of the daughter's disability and the fact that she could be critically affected by a possession order. The council

[114] Equality Act, s 149(2).

[115] See Equality Act 2006, ss 31 and 32.

[116] See also Equality and Human Rights Commission, 'The Essential Guide to the Public Sector Equality Duty: England (and Non-Devolved Public Authorities in Scotland and Wales)', available at www.equalityhumanrights.com/sites/default/files/psed_essential_guide_-_guidance_for_english_public_bodies.pdf (accessed on 13 September 2016).

[117] A McColgan, *Discrimination, Equality and the Law* (Oxford, Hart Publishing, 2014) 7–8.

[118] ibid 97.

[119] Hepple (n 9) 222–24.

[120] ibid 223.

[121] *Barnsley Metropolitan Borough Council v Norton* [2011] EWCA Civ 834, [2012] PTSR 56.

[122] ibid [34], [37] and [41] (Lloyd LJ).

was under a duty to have such regard as was appropriate in the circumstances to those disabilities at that time and had acted in breach of duty before commencing proceedings and during those proceedings.

The second ground of appeal in *Norton* was that to make an order for possession was disproportionate having regard to Article 8. Lloyd LJ, delivering the judgment of the court, considered that since the first ground of appeal of a breach of duty under section 49A of the Disability Discrimination Act 1995 was successful, it was not necessary to deal with the second ground of appeal concerning Article 8.[123] Lloyd LJ cited from Lord Neuberger's judgment in *Pinnock*,[124] in which Lord Neuberger was referring to Article 8, but which Lloyd LJ stated was also relevant by way of analogy to section 49A of the 1995 Act.[125] Lloyd LJ highlighted the relevance of alternative accommodation from that quote of Lord Neuberger which would be addressed by the council. *Norton* demonstrates how judges find it easier to deal with disability than with Article 8 due to the constraints imposed by *Pinnock*[126] and *Powell.*[127] The Court of Appeal in *Norton*[128] did not, however, quash the judge's decision to make the possession order, because the council could be left to give proper consideration to its equivalent duty under section 149 of the Equality Act 2010 when discharging its housing duties under the Housing Act 1996 to the defendants. Nevertheless, the effect of the public sector equality duty may lead to a reshaping of the scope of proprietary rights.

C. Ramifications of the Breadth of Definition of Disability

Disability has a very broad definition, heralding the possibility that the floodgates may be opened, with thousands of tenants raising defences to possession actions. The definition in section 6 of the Equality Act 2010 is physical or mental impairment, and the impairment has a substantial and long-term adverse effect on the ability to carry out normal day-to-day activities. Schedule 1 part 1 contains supplementary provisions on how disability is determined. The effect of an impairment is long-term if it has lasted for at least 12 months, is likely to last for at least 12 months or is likely to last for the rest of the life of the person affected.[129] An impairment is to be treated as having a substantial adverse effect on the ability of the person concerned to carry out normal day-to-day activities if measures are being taken to treat or correct it and, but for that, it would be likely to have that effect.[130] An example given in

[123] ibid (Lloyd LJ).

[124] *Pinnock* (n 1) [64]: 'that proportionality is more likely to be a relevant issue "in respect of occupants who are vulnerable as a result of mental illness, physical or learning disability, poor health or frailty", and that "the issue may also require the local authority to explain why they are not securing alternative accommodation in such cases" seem to us well made'.

[125] *Norton* (n 121) [29] (Lloyd LJ).

[126] *Pinnock* (n 1).

[127] *Powell* (n 1).

[128] *Norton* (n 121).

[129] Equality Act 2010, sch 1, para 2.

[130] ibid, sch 1, para 5(1).

the government's Explanatory Notes to the Bill for this Act is a man with depression who finds even the simplest of tasks or decisions difficult, for example getting up in the morning and getting washed and dressed. He is also forgetful and cannot plan ahead. Together, these amount to a 'substantial adverse effect' on his ability to carry out normal day-to-day activities. The man has experienced a number of separate periods of this depression over a period of two years, which have been diagnosed as part of an underlying mental health condition. The impairment is therefore considered to be 'long-term' and he is a disabled person for the purposes of the Act. With evidence demonstrating that 9 per cent of the population in the UK had taken anti-depressants in the previous 12 months,[131] even though many of them would not fall within the statutory definition of 'disability', the potential scope and implications are immense.

Some illnesses are specifically provided to be disabilities, specifically cancer, HIV infection and multiple sclerosis.[132] The following also offer guidance on the definition and determination of disability: the Equality Act 2010 (Disability) Regulations 2010 and the Equality Act 2010 Guidance on the Definition of Disability issued in accordance with the Equality Act 2010, section 6(5). Disability is also covered in Appendix A of the EHRC Code of Practice. As stated by Pitt, it is regrettable that, having consolidated everything into one statute, there is still a separate set of regulations on the definition of disability, so that it is necessary to refer to at least three different instruments on the single issue.[133]

In addition, Baroness Hale referred to the obligations which the UK has undertaken under the UN Convention on the Rights of Persons with Disabilities.[134] This may affect the definition of disability in the Equality Act 2010. Article 1 of the Convention states that 'Persons with disabilities include those who have long-term physical, mental, intellectual or sensory impairments which in interaction with various barriers may hinder their full and effective participation in society on an equal basis with others'. The text of the Convention was agreed by the UN General Assembly in December 2006. The UK signed the Convention on 30 March 2007 and ratified it on 8 June 2009. Article 2 defines discrimination on the basis of disability as meaning:

> any distinction, exclusion or restriction on the basis of disability which has the purpose or effect of impairing or nullifying the recognition, enjoyment or exercise, on an equal basis with others, of all human rights and fundamental freedoms in the political, economic, social, cultural, civil or any other field. It includes all forms of discrimination, including denial of reasonable accommodation.

It is the 'social model' of disability which is set out in the UN Convention on the Rights of Persons with Disabilities, and it focuses on the handicaps or obstacles placed on disabled persons by society, so that everyone with an impairment should be protected without the requirement that the impairment is long-term and substantial.[135] Hepple is critical of the 'medical model' of disability in English law in

[131] D Lewer et al (2015), 'Antidepressant Use in 27 European Countries: Associations with Sociodemographic, Cultural and Economic Factors' (2015) 207(3) *The British Journal of Psychiatry* 221.

[132] Equality Act 2010, sch 1, para 6.

[133] G Pitt, *Employment Law*, 9th edn (London, Sweet & Maxwell, 2014) para 2-021.

[134] *Akerman* (n 2) [26].

[135] Hepple (n 9) 44–45.

the Equality Act, which replicates the 'medical model' of disability from earlier legislation, because of the requirement to show a physical or mental impairment which has a long-term and substantial adverse effect.[136]

The UN Convention does not impose liability on either public or private landlords, but imposes obligations on the state party, ie the UK government. The Convention places obligations on the government to take steps to protect and promote disabled people's human rights. While the Convention does not place direct legal obligations on public bodies, they must still act in a way that is compatible with disabled people's human rights. This might include taking positive steps to meet the standards set out in the Convention.[137] While a case cannot be brought directly in the UK courts under the Convention, the Convention can be used as an interpretative tool in relation to the Human Rights Act. When interpreting the Human Rights Act, courts should take account of international law as well as decisions of the European Court of Human Rights.[138] The UN Convention on the Rights of Persons with Disabilities sets out in more detail than the European Convention on Human Rights the steps that the government must put in place to ensure that disabled people's human rights are protected and promoted.

As Baroness Hale stated in *Akerman*, 'This is not an absolute obligation. The landlord is entitled to evict a disabled tenant if he can show that this is a proportionate means of achieving a legitimate aim.'[139] The Equalities and Human Rights Commission published a report in December 2014, 'Monitoring the Implementation of the UN Convention on the Rights of Persons with Disabilities: The UK Independent Mechanism List of Issues Interim Report',[140] which highlights numerous areas of concern by way of recommendations of 66 questions which it recommends that the Convention on the Rights of Persons with Disabilities Committee asks the UK. Apart from concerns about changes to housing benefit, the focus of housing is under Article 9, regarding lack of accessible housing and no mechanism that guarantees accessible housing.

IV. CONCLUDING REMARKS

The Supreme Court in *Akerman* may be creating a new dynamic in property rights for tenants with disabilities, resulting in a paradigmatic shift in proprietary rights and establishing challenging hurdles for landlords to overcome in possession cases. The lack of a horizontal effect of Article 8 has meant that private landlords have

[136] ibid 44.

[137] See Equality and Human Rights Commission Guidance, 'The United Nations Convention on the Rights of People with Disabilities: What does it mean for you?', available at www.equalityhumanrights.com/en/publication-download/united-nations-convention-rights-people-disabilities-what-does-it-mean-you-easy (accessed on 13 September 2016).

[138] See *Glor v Switzerland* (Application No 13444/04, judgment on 30 April 2009), where the European Court of Human Rights referred to the Convention in a decision about whether disabled people were treated unfairly.

[139] *Akerman* (n 2) [27].

[140] www.equalityhumanrights.com/publication/monitoring-implementation-un-convention-rights-persons-disabilities (accessed on 13 September 2016).

escaped scrutiny under Article 8, but the Equality Act 2010 is a net from which private landlords cannot escape. Since Equality Act defences are not suited to be dealt with summarily, the result is likely to be that numerous more possession cases will have to go to trial, and landlords will need to incur considerable expense and time in obtaining possession. Unfortunately, landlords may consequently be reluctant to rent initially to those with disabilities, even though such discrimination is clearly unlawful. Faced with a choice between several potential tenants, it is not difficult to see where landlords' preferences will lie. Whether the floodgates will be opened after the Supreme Court decision remains to be seen.

The structured approach to proportionality is a positive development for equality rights. It would be too simplistic to have a unified approach, especially bearing in mind that the ontogenesis of each provision is entirely different. The Supreme Court rightly rejected a universal test for proportionality which has strengthened rights in the Equality Act. The stringency and parameters of the proportionality test are now dependent on the legislative regime, and there is a need for adequate processes and procedural protections to enable proportionality to be steadfastly determined. The decision is important, because Article 8 and disability discrimination cases will now evolve their own separate jurisprudence without being constrained by each other.

Proportionality in disability cases will necessarily focus on the susceptibility of the tenant to losing possession, and robust contours will be essential to ensure congruity and homogeneity in such cases. The question of whether a claimant satisfies the definition of disability may be a contested issue, especially in borderline cases, as the main weapon in preventing claims under the Equality Act. Those concerned with human rights will wish to see decisions on a par with equality rights. Although different public policy considerations are applicable in human rights and disability discrimination cases, it is highly significant that Lord Neuberger in *Pinnock* opened the door to Article 8 cases being decided differently where very broadly defined disability, which is more extensive than in the Equality Act, is in issue, so that a defence under Article 8 may be much more likely to succeed. This may lead to a slippery slope to confluence between the proportionality tests in Article 8 and in disability discrimination cases, which may over the course of time become more broadly analogous and lead to an overhaul of normative property rules.

9

Charges for Charges: Home Sales under the Care Act 2014

BRIAN SLOAN*

I. INTRODUCTION

HEALTHCARE IS BROADLY provided free at the point of delivery in England by the National Health Service.[1] By contrast, social care (which supports people with physical, cognitive or age-related conditions in carrying out personal care or domestic routines) is subject to a means test that can include the care recipient's home.[2] One principle embodied in the Care Act 2014 is nevertheless the frequent undesirability of a social care recipient being forced to sell her own home during her lifetime to fund her care.[3] It therefore seeks to increase the availability of deferred payment agreements (DPAs), enabling a local authority to make a secured loan to the care recipient in order to fund the care.[4] It seems that there will be 'situations where the local authority is contracting with [a] care home on the person's behalf (and is deferring charging the person)' and also 'situations where the person is contracting with [a] care home themselves and the local authority is effectively "loaning" the person money to pay their care home costs'.[5]

Even if this system is beneficial to care recipients themselves (albeit in an emotional rather than necessarily material sense), it could have profound implications for people (to be termed '(former) co-residents') who wish to remain in the home of a now-deceased recipient. This is particularly true given that the secured loan

* College Lecturer & Fellow in Law, Robinson College, Cambridge. This chapter arises out of the author's project on 'Adult Social Care and Property Rights', begun during an Early Career Fellowship at the Centre for Research in the Arts, Social Sciences and Humanities (CRASSH), Cambridge, in 2015 and supported by a Cambridge Humanities Research Grant. The author is grateful for the comments of attendees at a Centre for Public Law seminar in Cambridge in February 2016 and the MSPL conference, and those of the anonymous referee, on earlier drafts. The usual disclaimer applies.

[1] National Health Service Act 2006, s 1(4).

[2] See generally Commission on Funding of Care and Support, *Fairer Care Funding* (Commission on Funding of Care and Support, 2011).

[3] See, eg, N Hopkins and E Laurie, 'Social Citizenship, Housing Wealth and the Cost of Social Care: Is the Care Act 2014 "Fair"?' (2015) 78 *Modern Law Review* 112, 134–38.

[4] Care Act 2014, ss 34–36.

[5] Local Government Association, 'Deferred Payment Agreements' (7 January 2016), available at www.local.gov.uk/care-support-reform/-/journal_content/56/10180/6522542/ARTICLE (accessed on 29 November 2016.

facilitated by a DPA is due for repayment just 90 days after a recipient's death,[6] and that former co-residents might be vulnerable former providers of informal care.[7] As Hopkins and Laurie put it, the system seeks to preserve 'the paradigm of housing as home' during a care recipient's life, but not to further 'the paradigm of housing as an inheritance'.[8] Former co-residents are affected by a debt owed to the state by a third party and borne out of necessitous circumstances, a debt that would not have arisen had the third party's needs been sufficiently different to be covered by the NHS. The fact that the co-resident has been able to live in the property for the remainder of the care recipient's life and the claim that 'many people choose to use a deferred payment agreement as a "bridging loan" to give them time and flexibility to sell their home when they choose to do so' must nevertheless be taken into account,[9] as must the negative consequences if the social care system were unable to provide for those who require care but lack the means to pay for it altogether.

This chapter aims to evaluate the relationship between former co-residents and home sales forced by local authorities, comparing a former co-resident's position with that of others whose homes are the subject of attempted forced sale by creditors in other contexts, by examining law, guidance and codes of practice. The fundamental question is whether the system of DPAs and related matters governed by the Care Act adequately balances the perceived societal interest in ensuring that those with means contribute towards their care costs and the individual interests of former co-residents in remaining in their own homes both before and after the death of a social care recipient. The chapter begins by considering the relevance of a care recipient's home to the initial assessment of liability to pay for social care. Section III then analyses the law concerning the creation of charges on the home (including via DPAs) both before and under the Care Act, before the last substantive section considers the actual enforcement of debts and sale of homes in the context of social care. The chapter argues that while there are some points of concern, former co-residents are generally in a justifiably stronger position than co-residents of private creditors, and that most prejudice is caused by the underlying policy of means testing for social care.

II. THE HOME AND LIABILITY FOR CARE FEES

A. An Outline of the Social Care Funding System

Before the details of deferred payment agreements and home sales are considered, the system of funding social care and financial assessment must be outlined.

[6] Care and Support (Deferred Payment) Regulations, SI 2014/2671, r 7.

[7] See, eg, *R v Somerset County Council, ex p Harcombe* (1997) 96 LGR 444 (QB); see generally B Sloan, *Informal Carers and Private Law* (Oxford, Hart Publishing, 2013). For discussion of the possible difficulties with dispositions to such carers, see eg B Sloan, 'Reversing Testamentary Dispositions in Favour of Informal Carers' in B Häcker and C Mitchell (eds), *Current Issues in Succession Law* (Oxford, Hart Publishing, 2016).

[8] Hopkins and Laurie (n 3) 135.

[9] Department of Health, 'Care and Support Statutory Guidance' (2016), available at www.gov.uk/guidance/care-and-support-statutory-guidance [9.6] (accessed on 16 November 2016).

Under the social care system pre-dating the full implementation of the Care Act in England, '[v]ery broadly, … people with assets over £23,250 receive no financial state support and need to fund their own care' and '[t]he level and type of state support for people with assets below this threshold depends on their needs and income'.[10] A care recipient's liability to pay is assessed by a local authority (separately to a needs assessment)[11] using an extremely complex set of regulations to determine the existence of relevant capital and income.[12] There is currently a general obligation to charge when the relevant capital limits are exceeded only where care is to be provided in a care home,[13] as distinct from when it is to be provided in the care recipient's own home. The Care Act's Impact Assessment, however, suggests that this obligation will be removed and replaced with a discretion to charge in both contexts when the Act is fully brought into force.[14] Statutory guidance also plays a key role within the social care system.[15]

Inter alia, the Care Act (much of which came into force in April 2015) sought to rationalise the provision of social care[16] and to limit the amount that any one person can be expected to contribute towards her lifetime care costs.[17] That said, the implementation of the cap on eligible lifetime care costs (expected to be £72,000 in the first instance where a person's care needs had developed after the age of 25) has been delayed from April 2016[18] to April 2020.[19] In addition, while the threshold below which means-tested help is provided was to increase to from £23,250 to £27,000 where the person's home was not included in the financial assessment and £118,000 where it was included,[20] there were a number of significant limitations on the cap's effect even before the delay was announced,[21] and many individuals will be expected to contribute a significant sum towards care costs even if the Act's funding provisions are fully commenced.

[10] Commission on Funding of Care and Support (n 2) 11.

[11] Care Act 2014, ss 9–13.

[12] Care and Support (Charging and Assessment of Resources) Regulations, SI 2014/2672, made under Care Act 2014, ss 14 and 17, inter alia.

[13] Care and Support (Charging and Assessment of Resources) Regulations, r 12(2).

[14] Department of Health, *Impact Assessment: The Care Act 2014* (Department of Health, 2014) [1.116].

[15] Department of Health, 'Care and Support Statutory Guidance' (n 9). For analysis of the guidance's legal effect, see B Sloan, 'Trusts and Anti-Avoidance under the Care Act 2014' [2015] *The Conveyancer and Property Lawyer* 489, 499.

[16] See, eg, Care Act 2014, s 13.

[17] ibid s 15.

[18] Department of Health, *The Care Act 2014: Consultation on Draft Regulations and Guidance to Implement the Cap on Care Costs and Policy Proposals for a New Appeals System for Care and Support* (Department of Health, 2015).

[19] Department of Health, 'Letter from Rt Hon Alistair Burt MP: Delay in the Implementation of the Cap on Care Costs' (17 July 2015), available at www.gov.uk/government/publications/delay-in-the-implementation-of-the-cap-on-care-costs (accessed on 29 November 2016).

[20] Department of Health, *The Care Act 2014: Consultation on Draft Regulations* (n 18) [9.7].

[21] See, eg, B Sloan, 'Adult Social Care and Property Rights' (2016) 36 *Oxford Journal of Legal Studies* 449.

B. The Significance of 'Disregards' in Protecting Co-Residents

A fundamentally important means of protecting the care recipient's home (and a co-resident's ability to continue living in it) at the financial assessment stage must be appreciated. This is the fact that a home can in many cases be excluded from a local authority's assessment of the care recipient's capital in the first place. If an adult care recipient is to receive non-residential care in her own home, assessment of her capital must exclude her main or only home.[22] Even if the care recipient is to receive residential care in a care home, the very presence of some of the co-residents with whom this chapter is concerned can prevent a home from being included in the local authority's assessment from the outset, meaning that the care recipient will be assessed as though she did not have an interest in it for these purposes. There is a mandatory 'disregard' not only if the care recipient is in a care home temporarily and intends to return to the main home or is taking reasonable steps to dispose of it, but also if the main home is occupied by a non-estranged partner, a single parent who is an estranged partner, or a relative aged 60 or over or under 18, or who is incapacitated.[23] A 'relative' for these purposes is defined very broadly within the statutory guidance.[24] It is extremely noteworthy that these provisions are based on the occupation of relevant individuals alone, who need not have any entitlement in the home at all.

There is a discretion to disregard the home in other circumstances,[25] such as where there is a co-resident who is not a qualifying relative for the purposes of the mandatory disregard. Forbes J held that when considering whether to exercise the equivalent discretion in the pre-Care Act regulations,[26] it was necessary to 'maintain an appropriate balance between the exercise of that discretion and the need to observe the important underlying principle of the legislative scheme', namely 'to ensure that [care home] residents with assets are not maintained at public expense'.[27]

Cases where a relative moves into the property only after the adult has become resident in a care home are included in the scope of the discretionary disregard. When the Court of Appeal considered the pre-Act disregard relating to occupation of a care recipient's home by family members in *Walford v Worcestershire County Council*, Underhill LJ noted that the new regulations 'deal more explicitly with the issue' than the old ones.[28] There is also a 12-week disregard of the value of the home when the adult first enters a care home or another disregard ends unexpectedly because a qualifying relative dies or goes into a care home himself.[29]

[22] Care and Support (Charging and Assessment of Resources) Regulations, sch 2, para 4; Department of Health, 'Care and Support Statutory Guidance' (n 9) [8.43].

[23] Care and Support (Charging and Assessment of Resources) Regulations, sch 2, paras 1–8; Department of Health, 'Care and Support Statutory Guidance' (n 9) Annex B, [34].

[24] Department of Health, 'Care and Support Statutory Guidance' (n 9) Annex B, [35].

[25] Care and Support (Charging and Assessment of Resources) Regulations, sch 2, para 4(2); Department of Health, 'Care and Support Statutory Guidance' (n 9) Annex B, [42]–[44].

[26] National Assistance (Assessment of Resources) Regulations 1992 SI 1992/2977.

[27] *R v Somerset County Council, ex p Harcombe* (n 7) 456.

[28] *Walford v Worcestershire County Council* [2015] EWCA Civ 22, [2015] PTSR 880 [17].

[29] Care and Support (Charging and Assessment of Resources) Regulations 2014, sch 2, para 4(3).

There is a discretion to disregard in relation to other unexpected changes of circumstance.[30]

As discussed in Section III, a deferred payment agreement is unlikely to be offered where a care recipient has been assessed as liable to contribute towards care costs and has relevant property other than the main home. This, in turn, means that where a home is disregarded, it is unlikely to be subject to a DPA, a state of affairs likely to benefit co-residents. There may nevertheless be circumstances where arrears of care fees have accumulated (perhaps at the time of death) and the home is sold in order to meet the debts of the estate without reference to a DPA or even where a home was disregarded in the initial financial assessment. The enforcement of debts is considered in Section IV of this chapter.

Even if a home is not formally disregarded, the value of a non-care recipient's share of it in principle should not be included in the financial assessment,[31] and it may be difficult for a local authority to justify taking even the care recipient's share in the home into account where someone else has an interest in it given that '[t]he [relevant] current market value will be the price a willing buyer would pay to a willing seller'.[32] Where the property in question is land, the regulations quite properly disapply the general principle that where the care recipient and others are beneficially entitled to capital 'each person is to be treated as if each of them were entitled in possession to an equal share of the whole beneficial interest'.[33] If the care recipient deliberately alienates part of the beneficial interest in order to avoid liability for care fees, however, this is likely to trigger the Care Act's anti-avoidance provisions, which allow a local authority to treat her as though she still owned it (subject to the market value issue just considered) or to pursue the disponee for a relevant amount.[34] Moreover, it will be seen in Section III that where the presence of a co-resident has not prevented the offering of, and entry into, a DPA, the notion of priority for the purposes of the DPA regulations might prejudice the protection apparently given to a co-resident's share.

This sub-section has demonstrated that there are a number of circumstances in which the sale of a home forced by a local authority will not in principle become a realistic prospect because of the existence of a co-resident. These circumstances are notably peculiar to the liability to pay for social care, and are advantageous to such co-residents as compared to (perhaps more familiar) situations involving private-sector creditors. There will nevertheless be cases where a home sale at the behest of a local authority would be possible and could prejudice the interests of a former co-resident, and the remainder of this chapter deals with these. The next section addresses the creation of charges on the home, a highly significant means of facilitating such sales.

[30] Department of Health, 'Care and Support Statutory Guidance' (n 9) Annex B, [45]–[46].

[31] ibid [8.8].

[32] ibid Annex B, [15].

[33] Care and Support (Deferred Payment) Regulations, SI 2014/2671, r 24.

[34] Care Act 2014, s 70; see generally Sloan, 'Trusts and Anti-Avoidance under the Care Act 2014' (n 15).

III. SOCIAL CARE AND THE CREATION OF CHARGES ON THE HOME

A. Deferred Payment Agreements pre-2015 and Charges under the 1983 Act

It has been seen that, aside from the cap on care costs, a major area of funding reform within the Care Act relates to the widespread offering of deferred payment agreements, which allow for the payment of social care costs to be deferred (effectively via a secured loan) until a certain point, such as the death of the care recipient or the (potentially voluntary) sale of her home.[35] Despite their opposition to the cap, Hopkins and Laurie support the new principle of 'universal deferred payment'.[36] As discussed in more detail in the next sub-section, as well as retaining a discretion to offer a DPA, local authorities are prima facie obliged to do so to an adult whose needs are to be met in a care home, who has no more than £23,250 in assets other than any interest in the home and the home is not disregarded.[37] This is significant because of the concern that people could be forced to sell their homes during their own lifetimes in order to pay for their care, although some have questioned the idea that people have been 'forced' to sell their homes in a real sense, and pointed to the advantages of doing so in certain situations.[38] The postponement of sale would bring short-term advantages to a co-resident even if it did not protect their interests in the longer term.

In any case, Spencer-Lane notes several weaknesses in the pre-2015 DPA scheme,[39] which was contained in the Health and Social Care Act 2001.[40] There was no obligation on local authorities to offer DPAs, and the Impact Assessment for the Care Act reported a 'wide variation in both the number of deferred payment agreements offered in local authorities and in the eligibility conditions attached to local schemes', such that only around 4,000 people entered them each year.[41] In addition, local authorities were not able to charge interest until after the relevant person had died.

Moreover, some local authorities apparently preferred to use their general debt recovery powers under the Health and Social Services and Social Security Adjudications Act 1983 because those allowed a charge to be placed on the home[42] but did not require consent.[43] The Court of Appeal in *Walford* was told that

[35] The DPA prima facie falls due for repayment 90 days after the person's death or on disposal of property on which the local authority has a charge: Department of Health, 'Care and Support Statutory Guidance' (n 9) [9.104]; Care and Support (Deferred Payment) Regulations 2014, r 7.

[36] Hopkins and Laurie (n 3) 137.

[37] Care and Support (Deferred Payment) Regulations 2014, r 2.

[38] T Spencer-Lane, *Care Act Manual*, 2nd edn (London, Sweet & Maxwell, 2015) [1-373].

[39] ibid [1-371].

[40] Health and Social Care Act 2001, s 55.

[41] Department of Health, *Impact Assessment: The Care Act 2014* (n 14) [8.3].

[42] Health and Social Services and Social Security Adjudications Act 1983, s 22.

[43] Spencer-Lane (n 38) [1-371] (apparently containing a typographical error).

> in a case where a resident owns property which is not the subject of a disregard but has no significant income it is standard practice for authorities to take such a charge, though they may choose not to seek to enforce it forthwith.[44]

This ability to create a charge unilaterally was detrimental to both care recipients and co-residents, albeit that, as the Land Registry put it, '[w]here the [care home] resident is a joint owner, the charge affects only his or her beneficial interest, not the registered legal estate', and 'section 22(5) provides that the joint tenancy is not severed, but the charge will be for an amount not exceeding the value of the interest which the resident would enjoy if the tenancy were severed'.[45] Section 69 of the 2014 Act, which addresses debt recovery, does not contain an express power to create such a charge, which is beneficial to both care recipients and co-residents, albeit that matters may be different to the situation described by the Land Registry where a charge has been imposed by consent under a DPA. The Act does leave open the possibility of 'alternative financial arrangements' to DPAs, but the section providing for them is not in force at the time of writing.[46] The details of the new DPA scheme, and its implications for co-residents, are considered in the next sub-section of this chapter.

B. Deferred Payment Agreements under the Care Act 2014

The government reported that '[t]he majority of respondents' to its consultation exercise were 'highly supportive of the overall intention to extend the deferred payments scheme' under the 2014 Act.[47] The new DPA scheme is designed to be cost-neutral, such that interest rates and administration charges can be levied. There is a national maximum interest rate specified in a circular, and the guidance suggests a given local authority must use the same rate for all of its DPAs.[48]

On particular issues, 'some [consultation] respondents suggested that the guidance needed to provide further clarity around how to manage issues associated with lack of mental capacity'.[49] There were concerns about 'people entering into deferred payment agreements … inappropriately when they lacked capacity, and what might happen if people lost capacity whilst in DPAs'.[50] It was also noted that

> A number of consultees also pointed out that, given that DPAs may be relatively brief in length, people should be provided with statements of the amount deferred at more frequent intervals, and should be able to request statements as and when they were needed[51]

[44] *Walford v Worcestershire County Council* (n 28) [22] (Underhill LJ).

[45] Land Registry, 'Practice Guide 19: Notices, Restrictions and the Protection of Third Party Interests in the Register' (2016), available at www.gov.uk/government/publications/notices-restrictions-and-the-protection-of-third-party-interests-in-the-register/practice-guide-19-notices-restrictions-and-the-protection-of-third-party-interests-in-the-register (accessed on 29 November 2016) [6.22].

[46] Care Act 2014, s 36.

[47] Department of Health, *Response to the Consultation on Draft Regulations and Guidance for Implementation of Part 1 of the Care Act 2014* (Cm 895536, 2014) 27.

[48] Department of Health, 'Care and Support Statutory Guidance' (n 9) [9.66]–[9.67].

[49] Department of Health, *Response to the Consultation on Draft Regulations and Guidance* (n 47) 27.

[50] ibid 27.

[51] Department of Health, *Response to the Consultation on Draft Regulations and Guidance* (n 47) 28.

and '[s]ome respondents also suggested that the guidance should be clearer that local authorities should signpost people to independent financial advice (including regulated financial advice but only where appropriate)[52] when considering taking out a DPA'.[53] The guidance was amended to reflect all of these concerns. The guidelines on the equity limit (explained below) have also been simplified. While 'the majority of respondents were supportive of the suggestion to incentivise rental by allowing people to retain a proportion of any income they generated from letting their property',[54] this will not always be feasible where there is a former co-resident.

There are nevertheless still concerns that the de facto asset threshold for the mandatory offering of a DPA (effectively £23,250 in the first instance, as described above) and the apparent likelihood that only people with slightly more than that would be offered one on a discretionary basis effectively prevent the scheme from being universal, although the asset threshold could change. The Impact Assessment asserts that 'self-funders would not be eligible for a deferred payment if they had more than £23,500 [*sic*] in savings',[55] although it is presumably referring to eligibility for a *mandatory* DPA. While it justifies this situation on the basis that '[a]nyone above this threshold could typically afford to pay for a year of residential care out of their savings, without having to draw on their housing wealth',[56] it is a significant limitation that might risk greater use of unsuitable equity release products,[57] albeit that (as discussed in Section II) it could facilitate the protection of the home for the benefit of a co-resident inter alia.

The Impact Assessment also makes clear that 'local authorities will be required to seek adequate security for a deferred payment agreement',[58] which is borne out by the Care and Support (Deferred Payment) Regulations,[59] and such an authority can refuse to enter an agreement with someone who meets the general mandatory criteria if it is unable to obtain a first charge by way of legal mortgage over the person's property.[60] It also has a discretion to accept another form of security in line with a policy.[61] With regard to the sort of charge considered acceptable 'the majority [of consultation respondents] were opposed to local authorities being required to accept any legal charge, and in favour of authorities only being required to accept a first charge'.[62] The government noted that 'this response was not limited to local authorities, and included providers, the professional services sector, and representative

[52] See, eg, Spencer-Lane (n 38) [1-047]–[1-048].

[53] Department of Health, *Response to the Consultation on Draft Regulations and Guidance* (n 47) 28.

[54] ibid 28.

[55] Department of Health, *Impact Assessment: The Care Act 2014* (n 14) [8.11].

[56] ibid [8.11].

[57] See generally L Fox O'Mahony, *Home Equity and Older Owners: Between Risk and Regulation* (Oxford, Hart Publishing, 2012); *cf* Hopkins and Laurie (n 3) 137–138.

[58] Department of Health, *Impact Assessment: The Care Act 2014* (n 14) [8.46]; *cf* Hopkins and Laurie (n 3) 134.

[59] Care and Support (Deferred Payment) Regulations 2014, r 4(1).

[60] Care and Support (Deferred Payment) Regulations 2014, r 4; Department of Health, 'Care and Support Statutory Guidance' (n 9) [9.12]; see also Department of Health, *Response to the Consultation on Draft Regulations and Guidance* (n 47) 29; but *cf* Department of Health, 'Care and Support Statutory Guidance' (n 9) [9.62]–[9.63].

[61] Department of Health, 'Care and Support Statutory Guidance' (n 9) [9.62]–[9.63].

[62] Department of Health, *Response to the Consultation on Draft Regulations and Guidance* (n 47) 29.

groups and voluntary organisations', and that 'indeed more of the latter category were opposed than were in favour'.[63] An assumption is clearly being made that any acquisition or other mortgage that already burdened the property will generally have been discharged before a person requires care.

The final guidance makes clear that (as seen above) there will in some circumstances be an obligation to make DPAs available throughout England under the Care and Support (Deferred Payment) Regulations 2014. An adult must be offered a DPA if her needs are to be met in a care home, she has no more than £23,250 in assets excluding the home and the home is not disregarded.[64] A local authority may nevertheless offer an agreement to someone who does not meet these criteria, and is advised to take into account various matters, including the extent of the adult's accessible assets left after meeting care costs, whether the adult wants to use the home to purchase top-ups to secure more expensive care and whether she misses the mandatory criteria only narrowly.[65]

The guidance states that a local authority may refuse to enter a DPA to someone meeting the above criteria where it is unable to obtain a first charge, the person is seeking a top-up (in which case an appropriate agreement can still be offered) or the adult does not agree to the arrangement's terms and conditions,[66] although anecdotal evidence suggests that some local authorities are refusing to comply on other grounds.[67] Where mandatory criteria are unsatisfied, the local authority may and should consider exercising its discretion to offer a DPA.

A local authority may refuse to defer further costs under an existing agreement (as the amount actually spent on care increases) where the person's assets fall below the threshold or become disregarded such that the person becomes eligible for mean-tested help, the person no longer needs care in a care home or the person has committed a non-resolved breach of the agreement and the agreement permits a refusal to defer further.[68] Oddly, the situation where the person no longer needs support in a care home appears in both the discretionary and mandatory refusal categories.[69]

The guidance also states that a local authority should not exercise its discretion to refuse further deferrals where the person would be unable to pay any liability that became due as a result from their non-housing assets,[70] but it must refuse further deferrals where a person has reached their 'equity limit', with such refusal presumably prompting immediate sale (prejudicial to former co-residents) in some cases. This limit on the amount that can be deferred is effectively determined by the amount of equity the person has in the chosen security (usually the home), the amount that the person is contributing towards care costs from non-housing sources, and the

[63] ibid 29.

[64] Department of Health, 'Care and Support Statutory Guidance' (n 9) [9.7].

[65] ibid [9.8].

[66] ibid [9.12].

[67] See, eg, O Rudgard, 'Councils "Needlessly" Forcing Elderly to Sell Homes to Pay for Care', *Daily Telegraph*, 16 February 2016, available at www.telegraph.co.uk/finance/personalfinance/insurance/longtermcare/12140072/Councils-needlessly-forcing-elderly-to-sell-homes-to-pay-for-care.html.

[68] Department of Health, 'Care and Support Statutory Guidance' (n 9) [9.16].

[69] ibid [9.18].

[70] ibid [9.17].

total care costs that will be faced (including top-up payments made to secure more expensive accommodation).[71] The 'equity limit' will also leave some equity available to cover subsequent interest and variations in the value of the security.[72] It is set at the value of the property minus 10 per cent, minus the lower capital limit for means-tested assistance (currently £14,250) and minus the amount by which the property is already encumbered through security interests ranking in priority to the local authority's charge.[73]

When calculating the amount that a person is able to contribute from other sources, the local authority must enable her to keep (at that person's option) up to £144 per week as a 'disposable income allowance'.[74] A person should in principle be able to defer all care costs (including top-ups), but the agreement must be sustainable in an overall sense.[75]

Very significantly for present purposes, the statutory guidance provides that the local authority must also seek consent from anyone with a legal or beneficial interest in the property when proposing to enter a DPA,[76] which could, of course, include many of the former co-residents with which this chapter is concerned. This alleged obligation is not necessarily consistent with the regulations themselves, however, which state that consent should be obtained from a person 'who the authority considers has an interest in the land or other asset in respect of which a charge will be obtained' and 'whose interest the authority considers may prevent it from exercising a power of sale of the land or asset or recovering the deferred amount',[77] but only if 'the authority considers it is necessary to do so'.[78] This leaves much discretion in the hands of the local authority, although it will be in the local authority's interest to obtain consent.

The relevant consent is defined in the regulations as consent that 'in the opinion of the local authority is genuine and informed consent given in writing'[79] to 'the creation of a charge'; and 'the charge taking priority to and ranking before any interest the person [consenting] has in the land or other asset which will be the subject of the charge'.[80] The notion of 'priority' is extremely controversial in a context where the co-resident is in principle not intended to be liable for the care recipient's care in the first place. If the 'priority' is to have any substantive meaning beyond the ability to exercise a power of sale without resorting to the Trusts of Land and Appointment of Trustees Act 1996 (to be discussed in due course),[81] it presumably means that the co-resident's share can in principle be used to satisfy the debt where the originally

[71] ibid [9.35].

[72] Care and Support (Deferred Payment) Regulations 2014, r 5(5); Department of Health, 'Care and Support Statutory Guidance' (n 9) [9.36].

[73] Care and Support (Deferred Payment) Regulations 2014, r 5(5); Department of Health, 'Care and Support Statutory Guidance' (n 9) [9.38].

[74] Department of Health, 'Care and Support Statutory Guidance' (n 9) [9.44].

[75] ibid [9.50].

[76] ibid [9.58]–[9.61].

[77] Care and Support (Deferred Payment) Regulations 2014, r 4(4).

[78] ibid r 4(1)(b).

[79] ibid r 4(4).

[80] ibid r 4(5).

[81] Trusts of Land and Appointment of Trustees Act 1996, ss 14–15; *cf* Law of Property Act 1925, s 103.

assessed amount of the liability is greater than the amount raised by the care recipient's share on sale. The difficulties of valuing and including a care recipient's share where a co-owner also has a beneficial interest must, however, be taken into account.

If a local authority fails to gain consent from a former co-resident, it is presumably at risk of its charge ranking below any beneficial interest of that co-resident (provided that the interest is overriding[82] and has not been overreached),[83] and being subject to proceedings under the Trusts of Land and Appointment of Trustees Act 1996 if it wishes to sell the property. This legislation enables a court to consider a wide range of factors when deciding whether to order a sale (including the interests of equitable owners),[84] albeit that 'the courts tend towards ordering a sale on the general ground that a secured creditor should not be kept out of its money' in such cases (generally involving private creditors).[85] Since, by definition, the loan advanced under a DPA is not made by virtue of an acquisition mortgage, the principle in *Paddington Building Society v Mendelsohn* on the implied consent of an equitable co-owner in such circumstances cannot be directly applied.[86] It may be possible to argue by analogy, however, that the co-resident knew that care was required, that it prima facie had to be paid for and that a charge on the home as part of a DPA was the only means by which this could be achieved without selling the home.

The undue influence doctrine is presumably another means through which a local authority can lose priority to a former co-resident with a beneficial interest, specifically one who has purported to consent to a DPA in the face of pressure from a would-be care recipient who emphasises the lack of realistic alternatives.[87] The local authority is likely to be put on inquiry in respect of such influence being exerted by a care recipient, since it is unlikely that a care recipient and a co-resident would be considered to be receiving the loan for their joint benefit.[88] It may be arguable, however, that the co-resident is receiving indirect benefit for the loan, particularly if he is being relieved of informal caring responsibilities through the provision of formal social care. In any event, a would-be care recipient may be more readily considered a potential victim of undue influence rather than a potential perpetrator.[89]

The statutory guidance on the Care Act was amended inter alia to ensure that local authorities 'signpost' people to independent financial advice (including regulated financial advice) where appropriate before taking out a DPA.[90] The facilitation of access to independent financial advice is included within a local authority's

[82] Land Registration Act 2002, s 29; sch 3.

[83] Law of Property Act 1925, s 2.

[84] Trusts of Land and Appointment of Trustees Act 1996, s 15; *cf* Law of Property Act 1925, s 103, discussed below.

[85] M Dixon, 'To Sell or not to Sell: That is the Question—The Irony of the Trusts of Land and Appointment of Trustees Act 1996' (2011) 70 *Cambridge Law Journal* 579, 605. See, eg, *Bank of Ireland Home Mortgages Ltd v Bell* [2001] 2 All ER (Comm) 920 (CA).

[86] (1985) 50 P & CR 244 (CA).

[87] See, eg, *Royal Bank of Scotland Plc v Etridge (No 2)* [2001] UKHL 44, [2002] 2 AC 773.

[88] *CIBC Mortgages Plc v Pitt* [1994] 1 AC 200 (HL).

[89] See, eg, Sloan, *Informal Carers and Private Law* (n 7), Ch 7.

[90] Department of Health, *Response to the Consultation on Draft Regulations and Guidance* (n 47) 28; see also Spencer-Lane (n 38) [1-047]–[1-048], but *cf* Care and Support (Deferred Payment) Regulations 2014, r 4.

information and advice-related obligations under section 4 of the Act, though there are concerns that the advice-related duty is a general duty that does not seek to ensure that advice is received and understood,[91] and the focus is likely to be on the care recipient rather than any co-resident.

The regulations set out fairly restrictive provisions about the terms that a DPA must contain. It is not clear what effect a failure to comply with these obligations might have on the validity of the relevant charge, particularly in light of the basic conclusiveness of the land register.[92] The mandatory terms are described (somewhat generally) as 'any terms, conditions and information, without which the adult is unable to ascertain his or her rights and obligations under the agreement'.[93] They are expressed to include terms: 'to make clear that the local authority will make advances of [the] loan to the adult in instalments and when those instalments will be made';[94] 'to explain that the local authority must cease to defer amounts due … or advance instalments … if the adult is no longer receiving care and support in a care home or [similar] or if the local authority no longer considers that the adult's needs should be met by the provision of such accommodation';[95] 'to explain any other circumstances in which the local authority will or may' cease so to defer or advance;[96] requiring the local authority every six months (or when requested) to provide a written statement of the amount necessary to terminate the agreement and the accrued administration and interest charges[97] (in addition to information on the costs that may be charged);[98] requiring the local authority to give 30 days' notice of the date that the equity limit (which itself must be explained)[99] or agreed deferral limit will be reached;[100] to explain how the interest will compound;[101] to make clear that where there is genuine loan its purpose 'is to pay the costs of care and support in a care home or supported living accommodation … and that the adult must pay those costs as and when they fall due';[102] describing 'the adequate security accepted by the local authority';[103] 'requiring the adult to obtain the consent of the local authority for any person to occupy the property'[104] (which might prejudice the former co-resident, since it does not appear to exclude those who are already occupying the property); and 'to explain how the adult may exercise his or her right to terminate the agreement'.[105] This suggests that DPAs are heavily regulated, although,

[91] Spencer-Lane (n 38) [1-046].
[92] Land Registration Act 2002, s 58. The 'creation of a protected first legal mortgage' would trigger compulsory first registration of a previously unregistered freehold estate: Land Registration Act 2002, s 4(1)(g).
[93] Care and Support (Deferred Payment) Regulations 2014, r 11(1).
[94] ibid r 11(1)(a).
[95] ibid r 11(1)(b).
[96] ibid r 11(1)(c).
[97] ibid r 11(1)(d).
[98] ibid r 11(1)(g).
[99] ibid r 11(1)(i).
[100] ibid r 11(1)(e).
[101] ibid r 11(1)(f).
[102] ibid r 11(1)(h).
[103] ibid r 11(1)(j).
[104] ibid r 11(1)(k).
[105] ibid r 11(1)(l).

again, the focus of protection will inevitably be on the care recipient rather than any co-resident.

In addition, the DPA may 'include such other terms and conditions as the local authority considers appropriate'.[106] It is interesting that a power of sale is not expressly included amongst the mandatory terms, but in the case of a mortgage created by deed one will presumably be implied under the Law of Property Act 1925,[107] unless 'a contrary intention is ... expressed in the mortgage deed'.[108] It is clear that such a power is contemplated, moreover, by the explicit reference to one in the description of a person whose consent should be obtained.[109]

The statutory guidance acknowledges that a DPA may be 'regulated credit agreements to which the Consumer Credit Act 1974 ... and Financial Services and Markets Act 2000 (FSMA) apply',[110] while claiming that '[i]t is likely that most DPAs will fall within ... an exemption'.[111] It is certainly true that local authorities benefit from a wide range of exemptions relating to 'regulated mortgage contracts' for the purposes of the FSMA.[112] This reduces the relevance of the Mortgage Conduct of Business Rules (MCOB) themselves to charges possessed by local authorities,[113] although that should be seen in the context of the regulations governing the content of a DPA, the general statutory provisions applicable, the statutory guidance concerning them and the 'public law' principles relevant to local authorities.[114] Even second charges taken by local authorities were exempt from the provisions of the Consumer Credit Act 1974.[115]

The local authority's right to possession is not expressly mentioned in the DPA Regulations, but (similarly to the power of sale) in the case of legal mortgages such a right would presumably be conferred by the Law of Property Act 1925.[116] One local authority does indeed warn parties to DPAs that '[i]f you do not make payment when it falls due, legal proceedings may be issued against you for a judgment for the amount you owe and/or for possession of the Property'.[117] A purported exercise of the right to possession would trigger the Pre-Action Protocol for Possession Claims based on Mortgage or Home Purchase Plan Arrears in Respect of Residential Property (the Protocol)[118] because it applies even to 'unregulated residential

[106] ibid r 11(2).
[107] Law of Property Act 1925, s 101(1)(i).
[108] ibid s 101(4).
[109] Care and Support (Deferred Payment) Regulations 2014, r 4(4).
[110] Department of Health, 'Care and Support Statutory Guidance' (n 9) [9.81].
[111] ibid [9.83].
[112] Financial Services and Markets Act 2000 (Regulated Activities) Order SI 2001/544, rr 63A, 72G.
[113] Financial Conduct Authority, 'MCOB Mortgages and Home Finance: Conduct of Business Sourcebook', available at www.handbook.fca.org.uk/handbook/MCOB/ (accessed on 29 November 2016).
[114] See, eg, Department of Health, 'Care and Support Statutory Guidance' (n 9) Annex D [8].
[115] Consumer Credit Act 1974, s 16(1).
[116] Law of Property Act 1925, ss 85, 87.
[117] Gloucester County Council, 'Deferred Payments Agreement Policy' (2015), available at www.gloucestershire.gov.uk/extra/CHttpHandler.ashx?id=35219&p=0, 27 (accessed on 29 November 2016).
[118] Ministry of Justice, 'Pre-Action Protocol for Possession Claims based on Mortgage or Home Purchase Plan Arrears in Respect of Residential Property' (2015), available at www.justice.gov.uk/courts/procedure-rules/civil/protocol/prot_mha (accessed on 29 November 2016).

mortgages'.[119] McFarlane, Hopkins and Nield assert that the Protocol 'reflects MCOB 13',[120] which is significant in light of MCOB's lack of direct applicability to local authority mortgages. For example, the Protocol specifies a general expectation that the lender will not 'consider starting a possession claim for mortgage arrears' where the borrower has, inter alia, 'a reasonable expectation, providing evidence where possible, of an improvement in their financial circumstances in the foreseeable future (for example a new job or increased income from a lodger)'.[121] That said, Whitehouse has asserted that 'the potential for the … Protocol to impact significantly upon the behaviour of lenders prior to court action and, thereby, to assist borrowers in avoiding repossession, is minimal',[122] and once again the focus appears to be on the borrower herself rather than any co-resident. The process of enforcing the relevant debt and selling the home is considered in more depth in the next section.

IV. ENFORCING DEBTS AND SELLING HOMES

This section considers the actual recovery of debts under the 2014 Act, addressed by section 69, inter alia, and how this might impact upon the sale of the home still occupied by a former co-resident, whether or not a charge has previously been created as outlined in the previous section. The statutory guidance emphasises that debt recovery is a 'sensitive issue', albeit with particular reference to such recovery from care recipients rather than other people, including former co-residents.[123] It also states that '[c]ourt action should only be considered after all other reasonable avenues have been exhausted',[124] and contemplates circumstances where it would be inappropriate to recover a debt at all.[125]

One of the generally applicable statutory principles is the new well-being principle.[126] This provides that '[t]he general duty of a local authority, in exercising a function under [Part 1 of the Act] in the case of an individual, is to promote that individual's well-being',[127] with 'well-being' defined as encompassing several elements[128] and a number of matters being specified as mandatory relevant considerations.[129] While the principle is laudable and is not limited in scope to the direct recipients of social care (such that it may include some co-residents),[130] the government has admitted that it is 'designed to set out the overarching purpose

[119] ibid [4.1].

[120] B McFarlane, N Hopkins and S Nield, *Land Law: Text, Cases and Materials*, 3rd edn (Oxford, Oxford University Press, 2015) 1137.

[121] Ministry of Justice (n 118) [6.1].

[122] L Whitehouse, 'The Mortgage Arrears Pre-Action Protocol: An Opportunity Lost' (2009) 72 *Modern Law Review* 793, 794.

[123] Department of Health, 'Care and Support Statutory Guidance' (n 9) Annex D [6].

[124] ibid [6].

[125] ibid [9].

[126] ibid [8].

[127] Care Act 2014, s 1(1).

[128] ibid s 1(2).

[129] ibid s 1(3).

[130] Explanatory Notes to the Care Act 2014 [56].

of care and support into which specific duties … fit, rather than require a local authority to undertake any particular action in … itself'.[131]

In the documentation relating to the Draft Care and Support Bill pre-dating the 2014 Act, it was said that the provisions in what is now section 69 'consolidate various powers, including section 45 of the National Assistance Act 1948, and sections 22–24 of the Health and Social Services and Social Security Adjudications Act 1983',[132] with section 23 applying to Scotland only. Section 45 covered a person who, 'whether fraudulently or otherwise … misrepresents or fails to disclose any material fact',[133] causing the local authority to incur expenditure under Part III of that Act[134] or not to recover a relevant sum,[135] and allowed the local authority to recover the amount from the relevant person. Section 22 of the 1983 Act applied only to residential care, and (as we have seen) allowed the local authority to create a charge over land in which a person who 'fails to pay any sum assessed as due to be paid by him for the accommodation'[136] has a beneficial interest. In registered land, that charge was deemed by statute to 'be a registrable charge taking effect as a charge by way of legal mortgage'.[137] Section 24 allowed interest to be applied to the secured sum, but only from the date of the accommodated person's death.

The new debt recovery provisions were reported to be a 'significant area of concern' during the government consultation exercise, because the draft guidance was seen to be too 'light touch'.[138] Whereas the powers under the Health and Social Services and Social Security Adjudications Act 1983 were 'unilateral' because the opportunity for the local authority to create a charge did not provide the debtor with an alternative means of payment, the guidance goes as far as to claim that section 69 of the 2014 Act 'provides equal protection to both the local authority and the person',[139] and the Impact Assessment claims that it 'brings current practice up to the legal minimum expected in all other fields of debt recovery'.[140]

Section 69 expressly provides that '[a]ny sum due to a local authority under [Part 1 of the Act] is recoverable by the authority as a debt due to it',[141] and the cost of (at least attempting) to recover the debt can be added to it.[142] This is set out without regard to whether the care provided is residential. The local authority is required to offer a DPA where possible[143] under the relevant DPA regulations,[144] and can

131 Department of Health, *Response to the Consultation on Draft Regulations and Guidance for Implementation of Part 1 of the Care Act 2014* (n 47) 11.

132 HM Government, *Draft Care and Support Bill* (Cm 8386, 2012) 74.

133 National Assistance Act 1948, s 45(1).

134 ibid s 45(1)(a).

135 ibid s 45(1)(b).

136 Health and Social Services and Social Security Adjudications Act 1983, s 22(1)(a).

137 ibid s 22(8).

138 Department of Health, *Response to the Consultation on Draft Regulations and Guidance* (n 47) 25.

139 Department of Health, 'Care and Support Statutory Guidance' (n 9) Annex D [2].

140 Department of Health, *Impact Assessment: The Care Act 2014* (n 14) [1.129].

141 Care Act 2014, s 69(1).

142 ibid s 69(5).

143 ibid s 69(2).

144 Care and Support (Deferred Payment) Regulations 2014.

apply to court to enforce a debt only where a DPA is not possible or is refused by the person who owes the debt. This statutory obligation is unlikely to be relevant to the core situation addressed in this chapter, however, since this chapter is primarily concerned with cases where the amount advanced under any DPA has become due for payment (often because the care recipient has died) in any event.

The Care Act has apparently doubled the length of time (from three to six years) in which a debt can be recovered.[145] Provided that proceedings have been issued within six years, the debt can still be recovered, but otherwise it must be written off.[146] While there is a specific power for the Secretary of State to make regulations regarding the time a sum is due, when it is not recoverable and the charging of interest,[147] *Halsbury's Annotations* claim that no regulations have been made under section 69.[148]

The statutory guidance simply states that if, after the 90-day period following death of a care recipient where a DPA is in place,

> a local authority concludes active steps to repay the debt are not being taken, for example if the sale is not progressing and a local authority has actively sought to resolve the situation (or the local authority concludes the executor is wilfully obstructing sale of the property), the local authority may enter into legal proceedings to reclaim the amount due to it

in accordance with the general debt recovery provisions in section 69 of the Act and Annex D of the guidance.[149]

The preference given to a charge by way of legal mortgage presumably means that the statutory provisions usually governing such mortgages will potentially apply to many DPAs. This would include, for example, the restrictions on the exercise of a power of sale if the care recipient were still alive under the Law of Property Act 1925,[150] meaning that some interest under the mortgage must be in arrears and have been unpaid for two months after becoming due, three months must have elapsed since notice requiring payment of the mortgage money was served on at least one mortgagor (which may not be relevant where the care recipient has died) or there must have been some breach of a non-payment covenant by the mortgagor or someone who agreed to the mortgage.

If the care recipient has died (as many will have done by the time a DPA comes to be enforced) and the former co-resident lacked a pre-existing beneficial interest in the property, the home would fairly routinely be sold in the context of the personal representatives' duty to pay the debts of the estate.[151] This would be true even if the

[145] Care Act 2014, s 69(3). *cf* J Auburn, 'Care Act Conundrum: Recovering Care Home Fees', *Local Government Lawyer*, 10 February 2016, available at www.localgovernmentlawyer.co.uk/index.php?option=com_content&view=article&id=25929%3Acare-act-conundrum-recovering-care-home-fees&catid=52&Itemid=20 (accessed on 29 November 2016).

[146] Department of Health, 'Care and Support Statutory Guidance' (n 9) Annex D [11].

[147] Care Act 2014, s 69(6).

[148] 'Care Act 2014, s 69', *Halsbury's Annotations* (London, LexisNexis, 2016).

[149] Department of Health, 'Care and Support Statutory Guidance' (n 9) [9-104].

[150] Law of Property Act 1925, s 103. See, eg, Bury Council, 'Deferred Payments Scheme: Care Act 2014 (Residential Care Funding)' (2015) https://councildecisions.bury.gov.uk/documents/s9222/Deferred%20Payments%20Scheme%20Policy%20June%202015.pdf (accessed on 29 November 2016) [11.10].

[151] See generally R Kerridge, *Parry and Kerridge: The Law of Succession*, 13th edn (London, Sweet & Maxwell, 2016) ch 21.

former co-resident is prima facie entitled to inherit the relevant home under a will or the intestacy rules, particularly since it is thought that he would possess only a chose in action to compel due administration of the estate until that administration is complete.[152] Section 35 of the Administration of Estates Act 1925 imposes a presumption that secured debts should be paid out of the asset over which the security exists where it has been bequeathed by will. The section expressly provides that the rights of the chargee will be unaffected by the presumption,[153] which means that the local authority would retain a power of sale contained in a DPA.[154]

Such a sale also seems inevitable on death of the care recipient where the former co-resident did have a pre-existing proprietary interest but was bound by the local authority's charge, unless the former co-resident is able to discharge the relevant debt himself and the local authority consents to his doing so. Where the former co-resident has a pre-existing proprietary interest that is not bound by the charge (for the reasons considered in Section III), he could presumably use the Trusts of Land and Appointment of Trustees Act in an attempt to resist the sale.[155] While the outcome of any such application would probably reflect the trend towards sale, it is worth noting that *Mortgage Corporation v Shaire* was a case where a litigant successfully remained in the home notwithstanding an application for sale by her deceased's partner's creditor, subject to her ability to pay interest on a loan fashioned out of the creditor's equity.[156]

Section 36 of the Administration of Justice Act 1970 may apply where a local authority seeks an order for possession of the relevant home. The section allows a court to exercise its discretion to adjourn possession proceedings or suspend the execution of judgment for possession when the mortgagor is apparently 'likely to be able within a reasonable period to pay any sums due under the mortgage or to remedy a default'.[157] The 'mortgagor' is defined to include 'any person deriving title under the original mortgagor or mortgagee',[158] which, in turn, is likely to include a person with a beneficial interest in the property who was not a party to the original mortgage,[159] including a spouse or civil partner with relevant home rights.[160] There may be difficulties over whether it includes a person who lacked an interest before the care recipient died but was the intended inheritor of the property (inevitably subject to the rights of the now-deceased care recipient's creditors), whom we have seen in all likelihood possesses only a chose in action to compel due administration of the estate.[161] Hopkins and Nield have cogently criticised the lack of protection against creditors available under section 36 for those who lack a proprietary interest in the home,[162] which may well include some former co-residents as understood

[152] *Re Leigh's Will Trusts* [1970] Ch 277.
[153] Administration of Estates Act 1925, s 35(3).
[154] *Parry and Kerridge* (n 151) [21-49].
[155] See, eg, *Grindal v Hooper* [1999] EG 150 (CS).
[156] *Mortgage Corporation v Shaire* [2001] Ch 743.
[157] Administration of Justice Act 1970, s 36(1).
[158] ibid s 39(1).
[159] *Cheval Bridging Finance Ltd v Bhasin* [2008] EWCA Civ 1613.
[160] Family Law Act 1996, s 55(2).
[161] *Re Leigh's Will Trusts* (n 152).
[162] S Nield and N Hopkins, 'Human Rights and Mortgage Repossession: Beyond Property Law Using Article 8' (2013) 33 *Legal Studies* 431.

in this chapter. That said, on the facts surrounding *R v Somerset County Council, ex p Harcombe*,[163] a local authority decided that it would not be reasonable to enforce the charge it possessed under the 1983 Act while the care recipient's son used it as his main residence. Pertinent considerations were said to be the fact that the son had provided care for his mother at home, that he claimed to have an emotional attachment to the relevant house and that he was not in employment. It took the view, however, that further considerations would come into play on the death of the care recipient, not least the entitlement of the care recipient's daughter to a share in her estate.

Whatever the unfortunate circumstances that might arise for former co-residents where a local authority seeks to enforce a debt through the sale of the care recipient's home, the general law means that such a co-resident is unlikely to be in any worse position than in cases involving another form of secured creditor. Moreover, a local authority is in principle likely to be subject to human rights obligations that have been rejected by the High Court in the context of purely private mortgage arrangements.[164] The Care Act's impact assessment admitted that the previous power unilaterally to create a charge under the 1983 Act (now removed) 'could lead to successful challenges under Human Rights legislation'.[165] It must be noted, however, that even where a public body is the proprietor of a charge over a home and seeks to enforce it, it may be difficult for a former co-resident to argue that the interference with his Article 8 right to respect for his home is disproportionate.[166] Even so, while it may be legally permissible as a matter of general mortgage law for a mortgagee to exercise its power of sale without first obtaining a court order for possession,[167] this may not be an appropriate action for a local authority to take where it is opposed by a former co-resident.

Where there is no DPA or pre-existing charge on the care recipient's former home, a charging order (governed by the Charging Orders Act 1979)[168] is likely to be possible in order to enforce the debt owed to a local authority.[169] In proceedings concerning a charging order, a former co-resident may benefit from the fact that a local authority did not initially have a security interest in the care recipient's home. As Dixon notes, however, even in this context 'there remains a steady preference in favour of a sale against the wishes of the innocent co-owner'.[170]

[163] *R v Somerset County Council, ex p Harcombe* (n 7).

[164] *Horsham Properties Group Ltd v Clark* [2008] EWHC 2327 (Ch), [2009] 1 WLR 1255.

[165] Department of Health, *Impact Assessment: The Care Act 2014* (n 14) [1.128].

[166] See, eg, *Hounslow LBC v Powell; Birmingham City Council v Frisby* [2011] UKSC 8, [2011] 2 AC 186. *cf*, eg, Nield and Hopkins (n 162).

[167] *Horsham Properties Group Ltd v Clark* (n 164).

[168] See generally D Capper, H Conway and L Glennon, 'From Obligations to Proprietary Interests: A Critique of the Charging Orders System in England and Wales' in S Bright (ed), *Modern Studies in Property Law, Volume 6* (Oxford, Hart Publishing, 2011).

[169] Department of Health, 'Care and Support Statutory Guidance' (n 9) Annex D [43].

[170] Dixon (n 85) 599. See, eg, *Pritchard Englefield (A Firm) v Steinberg* [2004] EWHC 1908 (Ch), [2005] 1 P & CR DG2.

V. CONCLUSION

The law considered in this chapter is a relatively complex mixture of specific social care provisions, general public law principles and the general law of mortgages. In all likelihood, 'former co-residents' of a social care recipient will generally be in a stronger position than former co-residents of other types of debtors when it comes to the sale of the care recipient's former home, even if some of them have made contributions (in principle voluntarily) to the care recipient's care costs to increase the available standard of care. They will often benefit from protection before the loan arrangement is even entered through the 'disregard' system (even if they lack an entitlement relating to the home altogether), and the system is designed (subject to issues of 'priority' under a DPA) to ensure that they are not personally liable to pay for the care recipient's care. This is a highly distinctive feature of the regulation of security interests in the social care context, since it means that the former co-resident can be heavily protected while the would-be mortgagor is often able to obtain substantially the same benefit (ie the care) regardless of whether the charge is created.

Moreover, deferred payment agreements are relatively heavily regulated, and the status of the local authority as a public body in principle produces additional and justifiable safeguards, even if a former co-resident may find himself reliant on the benevolent exercise of discretion by a local authority. The removal of the local authority's power unilaterally to create a charge over the home (effectively meaning that only a charging order is likely to produce a security interest where there is no deferred payment agreement) is also welcome.

It may appear unfortunate for former co-residents still to be able to lose their homes, and care recipients relatively routinely to be deprived of their full testamentary freedom, in the manner facilitated even by the reformed social care system. This is particularly true if the cap on care costs is never implemented and the misfortune is ultimately caused by the policy choice to apply a means test for social care. It is noteworthy, moreover, that in an empirical study on public opinion surrounding the intestacy rules, 'participants felt strongly that the family home should always, initially at least, go to the surviving spouse or cohabiting partner or any relative, friend or companion who might be made homeless by any other arrangement'.[171] As I have argued elsewhere, however, any reduction in the resources going into the care system may prejudice its ability to cater for those who are genuinely unable to make a contribution towards their own care costs.[172]

[171] G Morrell, M Barnard and R Legard, 'The Law of Intestate Succession: Exploring Attitudes among Non-traditional Families' (London, NatCen, 2009) 26.

[172] Sloan, 'Adult Social Care and Property Rights' (n 25) 457.

10

Egoism and the Return of Charitable Gifts

JOHN PICTON*

I. INTRODUCTION

THE LAW ASSUMES that all donors to charity are altruistic, when they are not. It assumes that all donors care about the charitable ends to which they give their money, when they do not. In consequence of the law's misconception, judges sometimes proceed to return gifts without a sound legal rationale for doing so. It is argued that where gifts fail, the legal basis of return is that, in analogy with frustrated consumers who have paid for unobtainable goods, donors should get their money back. With reference to altruism and egoism as the concepts are understood in economic donative theory,[1] it will be seen that this legal logic is only pertinent in relation to individuals who genuinely care about the delivery of charitable outcomes.

The law has a blind spot in relation to egoistic intent. Such individuals donate for a personal satisfaction which is entirely removed from the achievement of any other-regarding charitable outcome.[2] If they are purely egoistic, these donors cannot be frustrated where gifts fail. End goals are unimportant to them. They had their satisfaction at the point of donation when they consumed a joy-of-giving.[3] They are not frustrated, so they are outside the rationale of return.

It is in difficult cases—failure cases—that judicial understandings of donor motivation come to the fore. In the normal course, when donors part with their money,

* University of Liverpool.

[1] See generally J Elster, 'The Valmont Effect: The Warm-Glow Theory of Philanthropy' in P Illingworth et al (eds), *Giving Well: The Ethics of Philanthropy* (Oxford, Oxford University Press, 2011) 67; A Kotzebue, *On Collective Goods, Voluntary Contributions and Fundraising* (Karlsruher, Springer Gabler, 2013) 4–13; AK Sen, 'Rational Fools: A Critique of the Behavioural Foundations of Economic Theory' (1977) 6 *Philosophy and Public Affairs* 317.

[2] See J Andreoni, 'Impure Altruism and Donations to Public Goods: A Theory of Warm-Glow Giving' (1990) 100 *The Economic Journal* 464; W Harbaugh, 'The Prestige Motive for Making Charitable Transfers' (1998) 88 *The American Economic Review* 227; see generally A Rutherford, 'Get By with a Little Help from My Friends: A Recent History of Charitable Organisations in Economic Theory' (2010) 17 *European Journal of Economic Thought* 1031.

[3] Joy-of-giving is itself understood a consumable good: D Ribar and M Wilhelm, 'Altruistic and Joy-of-Giving Motivations in Charitable Behavior' (2002) 110 *Journal of Political Economy* 424; Kotzebue (n 1) 10.

their gifts flow up a legal pipeline and into the lives of others without any cause for an analysis of the donor's wishes. In ordinary cases, the law channels, but does not query too deeply, the motivation behind the gift. But where the pipeline fractures because the donor's instructions prove impossible to effect, the law is put to much heavier work. It is at this pressure point of failure, where, for example, a donor has left insufficient funds,[4] a trustee disclaims[5] or a nominated charity has closed down,[6] that the law, which attempts to effect what the donor would have subjectively wished,[7] leaks its assumptions about the nature of the donor's motivation.

Critical economic analysis of the law's understanding of donor motivation marks a fresh line of enquiry. While economics and charity law have in recent times formed a fruitful critical pairing,[8] contemporary economic enquiry turns mostly upon issues of broad political economy: that is, charity's role within the so-called third sector between state and market.[9] Individual-level economic understandings of donor motivation have been left more or less untouched in legal scholarship. On the very rare occasions where micro-level economic concepts are applied to law, the focus has been on the impact of the law upon overall distributions of charitable wealth.[10]

This chapter departs from previous 'public' economic approaches, using micro-level concepts (economic altruism and economic egoism) to critique the courts' understanding of individual minds. This enables a fresh conceptual claim: that the rationale for return is based in frustrated economic altruism.[11] Building on that claim, it is further argued that where gifts are driven by unalloyed egoism, judges—unable to recognise the fact—sometimes return gifts without cause. The application of donative economic theory will therefore both reveal the altruistic basis of the law of return and also problematise the law's treatment of egoistic gifts outside that altruistic rationale. Most broadly, it will throw up deep-seated and hitherto unexamined legal assumptions about donative intent.

On an original view within economic donative theory, donors are modelled as altruistic.[12] Altruism in this context has a meaning more focused than the ordinary

[4] *Re Wilson* [1913] 1 Ch 314 (Ch); *Re Good Will Trusts* [1950] 2 All ER 653 (Ch); *Re Woodhams* [1981] 1 WLR 493 (Ch).

[5] *Re Robinson* [1923] 2 Ch 332 (Ch); *Re Lysaght* [1966] 1 Ch 191 (Ch).

[6] *Re Rymer* [1895] 1 Ch 10 (CA); *Kings v Bultitude* [2010] EWHC 1795 (Ch), [2010] WTLR 1571; *Phillips v Royal Society for Birds* [2012] EWHC 618 (Ch), [2012] WTLR 891.

[7] See, eg, *Re Broadbent* [2001] EWCA Civ 714, [2001] WTLR 967, [44]; *Executor Trustee and Agency Co of South Australia Ltd v Warbey* (No 2) (1973) SASR 336, 345.

[8] See, eg, J Garton, *Regulation of Organised Civil Society* (Oxford, Hart Publishing, 2009); J Garton, *Public Benefit in Charity Law* (Oxford, Oxford University Press, 2013).

[9] J Philips et al, *Between State and Market* (Montreal, McGill-Queen's University Press, 2001); L Salamon, *The State of Non-profit America*, 2nd edn (Washington, Brookings Institution Press, 2012); H Anheier, *Non-profit Organisations: Theory, Management, Policy*, 2nd edn (London, Routledge, 2014).

[10] M Bac, 'Restricted Charitable Donations and the "Cy Près" Doctrine' (2002) 14 *European Journal of Law and Economics* 15, 17; J Garton, 'Justifying the Cy-Près Doctrine' (2007) 21 *Trust Law International* 134, 145–49.

[11] See M Harding, *Charity Law and the Liberal State* (Cambridge, Cambridge University Press, 2014) 89–92 for analysis of a connection between altruism, charity law and political liberalism.

[12] P Warr, 'The Private Provision of a Public Good is Independent of the Distribution of Income' (1983) 13 *Economic Letters* 207; R Roberts, 'A Positive Model of Private Charity and Public Transfers' (1984) 92 *Journal of Political Economy* 136.

use of the word. Altruistic donors, in the economic sense, are minded to give because they derive satisfaction from the consumption of others.[13] They care about the charitable ends to which their gifts are applied. In *Strangers Drowning*,[14] MacFarquhar describes the lived experience of individuals she calls 'do-gooders'.[15] One of these, Julia Wise, matches altruism in the economic sense. Described as both rational and ardent,[16] she gives as much of her income away to charity as she can, leaving the minimum possible for her own restricted life. However, it is her motivation rather than her resulting penury which is important. She gives out of a concern to materially better the lives of others. She funds cost-effective medical interventions in low-income countries. Crucially, she is motivated only by material outcomes; economic results that benefit others. She gets no egoistic glow; only the ends matter.

Alongside altruism, in more recent times, donative economic theory has developed a complementary type of motivation—egoism, or the consumption of joy-of-giving.[17] It is central to the concept that an entirely egoistic donor is unconcerned with charitable outcomes. That is, she might happen to give to charity, but she will not care whether other people consume the charitable goods she incidentally provides. Her motivation does not lie in the material advantage of other people. Beveridge, in *Voluntary Action*,[18] a post-war report on the charitable sector, detailed the case of George Jarvis, who had been a man of substantial property in Herefordshire and who almost perfectly represents pure charitable egoism in this economic sense.[19] George Jarvis's neighbours reported that no intention to make a gift to charity had ever entered his mind until he became displeased with his daughter's choice of husband. Beveridge writes that 'he lived to see her become a mother and grandmother, but nursed his resentment to the end'.[20] Out of apparent spite to his daughter, upon his death, he established a charity for the relief of the poor, so as to disinherit her. George Jarvis can be described as an egoistic donor in the economic sense. In contrast to Julia Wise, the charitable outcome of his gift was unimportant. He was entirely indifferent whether poverty was in fact alleviated, he just wanted to spite his daughter. He was motivated by a joy-of-giving, albeit of a malign type.

The altruistic motivation of Julia Wise comes to us more readily than the purely egoistic intent of George Jarvis. We more naturally associate outcome-driven altruism with charitable giving. However, economic egoism, where the charitable goods supplied by the donor are incidental to the motivation behind the gift, does occur in a familiar modern context; it is often deliberately induced in circumstances of professionally organised fund-raising drives.[21] So, for example, in *Serpentine Trust*

[13] See, eg, Kotzebue (n 1) 5–10.

[14] L MacFarquhar, *Strangers Drowning: Voyages to the Brink of Moral Extremity* (St Ives, Penguin, 2016).

[15] ibid 3.

[16] ibid 71.

[17] See, eg, Andreoni (n 2); Harbaugh (n 2). Landry et al, 'Towards an Understanding of the Economics of Charity' (2006) 121 *The Quarterly Journal of Economics* 747; Buraschi and Cornelli, 'Donations', CEPR Discussion Paper 3488 (2002).

[18] W Beveridge, *Voluntary Action* (Oxford, Routledge, 2015).

[19] ibid 374.

[20] ibid.

[21] See, eg, M Worth, *Fundraising: Principles and Practice* (Thousand Oaks, SAGE, 2016) 309–314.

Limited v HMRC,[22] a set of inducements made by an art gallery, including inter alia opportunities for private hire, priority booking and free invitations to events, were held to be so vital in attracting donations as to be classed as transfers for consideration.[23] For any donors induced by these financial benefits alone, the charitable ends to which their money would be applied will have been entirely incidental to their motivation to give. They will have been egoistic consumers, unconcerned with the cultural cause.

First, I begin by acknowledging both the contribution and the limitations of this micro-level economic framework. Secondly, the altruistic basis of the law is uncovered. This builds into a claim that the rationale for return is found in frustrated altruism. Thirdly, I assess return in the context of purely egoistic giving. It is argued that, at the level of legal principle, egoistic gifts should always be kept in charity. Fourthly, moving to an applied precedential analysis of the theory, I then argue that the courts return egoistic gifts without any coherent doctrinal reason for doing so. Finally, equipped with a theoretical vantage point, I argue that attempted statutory reform in the context of public appeals suffers for want of clear theory.

II. THE LIMITS AND CONTRIBUTION OF A BINARY FRAMEWORK

Economic donative theory lends the analysis a particular view of donor motivation. In turn, it becomes possible to match that view with the existing law of return and so criticise the courts for their egoistic blind spot. It is important to note that donative theory builds on the voluntary nature of charity, emphasising that donors make choices according to their motivational preferences.[24] Yet it supplies only a binary framework of egoism and altruism. Every charitable impulse is slotted within two poles.

It is necessary to acknowledge the limits of the binary and to explain why, despite those limits, the framework is relevant to legal argument. In consequence of its double-edged nature, economic donative theory cannot provide us with a full-fleshed understanding of charity in complex society. It can tell us that donors might derive egoism-based or altruism-based satisfaction, but it cannot tell us why. Notably, the binary cannot explain why some of us might be compelled to take great risks for others, or why we might care so much that we have the capacity to take those risks. Monroe claims, with reference to risk-takers, 'that altruists simply have a different way of seeing things. Where the rest of us see a stranger, altruists see a human being'.[25] By its nature, the altruistic/egoistic binary is too formalistic to fully explain why some of us are Good Samaritans.[26]

[22] *Serpentine Trust Limited v HMRC* [2014] UKFTT 876 (TC).

[23] ibid [43].

[24] Based in neoclassical economics, both altruism and joy-of-giving depend on rational choice. See, eg, K Boulding, 'Notes on a Theory of Philanthropy' in Dickinson (ed), *Philanthropy and Public Policy* (Cambridge, Cambridge University Press, 1962) 57, 60–63.

[25] K Monroe, *The Heart of Altruism: Perceptions of a Common Humanity* (Princeton, Princeton University Press, 1996) 3.

[26] See, eg, R Wuthnow, *Acts of Compassion: Caring for Others and Helping Ourselves* (Princeton, Princeton University Press, 1991) 167–191.

But economic donative theory can make an important critical contribution to legal analysis, not least because the altruistic side of the binary so closely matches judges' own views of donors. In this chapter, the binary will be put to an analytical use: as a heuristic, it will help to unlock and then critique the courts' framework of return. Weaved throughout this chapter, it will be seen from the luxuriously detailed individual analyses of gifts made by judges that courts see charitable motivation as altruistically outcome-driven in the economic sense. And, most importantly, the concept of self-interested, ego-driven donation provides a new tool with which we can assess the law's basic assumptions. The economic framework is a methodological trowel for digging up and then critiquing the courts' own concepts.

III. THE LAW OF RETURN AND FRUSTRATED ALTRUISM

It is argued that the rationale for return flows from a judicial view of donors as altruist consumers. First, it is seen that donors are treated in law as being motivated by the achievement of altruistic outcomes, or, put another way, the delivery of charitable goods. Secondly, it is argued that judges divide between types of altruist. The law only returns to irredeemably frustrated altruists, termed as having a 'particular charitable intention'[27] at law.

A. Donors are Assumed to be Economic Altruists

Roberts defines altruism in charity as 'the case where the level of consumption of one individual enters the utility function of the other'.[28] Economic altruism is therefore the motivation to expend on the consumption of other people. This is a commonplace in our lives. We routinely give towards the material advantage of others. Crucially, such altruistic material impulse is outcome-orientated: we want to see something consumed by another person when we give. Culyer states, in the context of healthcare provision, that 'It is possible to model altruism in utilitarian terms ... in a health context, one is, perhaps, pleased to see another person healthier or with greater access to health care than would otherwise be the case'.[29]

An altruistic donor in a health context genuinely wants to see better health care delivered as a charitable good that others might consume.[30] Rutherford describes the theory as 'charity as caring about the ends'.[31] The key point is the focus on

[27] See, eg, *Woodhams* (n 4) 501; *Lysaght* (n 5) 202; *Re Ulverston and District New Hospital Building Trusts* [1956] Ch 622 (CA), 640.

[28] Roberts (n 12) 95.

[29] A Culyer, *The Dictionary of Health Economics*, 3rd edn (Cheltenham, Edward Elgar, 2014) 637.

[30] If the donor wishes the consume the good herself, then she is at least partly egoistic according to the definition here, as she will give in to an enjoyable anticipation of personal reward. For example, an individual might donate to public radio simply because she wants to wake up to it in the morning. Compare H Hansmann, *The Ownership of Enterprise* (Cambridge, MA, Harvard University Press, 1996) 230–31.

[31] Rutherford (n 2) 1038.

outcomes. So one way of understanding economic altruism is simply to say that the donor genuinely cares about her stated charitable objectives. For example, it is well known that Andrew Carnegie put much of his great industrial wealth towards the provision of public libraries.[32] For him to be classifiable as an economic altruist, it is sufficient that he was genuinely concerned to provide that charitable good for the consumption of others, and equally, that his true motivation was not a purely egoistic legacy. In that case, he would have been motivated only by the joy-of-giving.

Genuine concern with outcomes is the key to economic altruism. The mesh with legal charity is clear, as the law provides a catalogue of contexts in which expenditure on outcomes benefiting others is recognised. This is an ancient function of the law. The Preamble to the 1601 Statute of Charitable Uses, from which the modern law developed,[33] contains a brochure of broad material ends to which charitable funds might be validly applied. Of the lengthy list, many items remain familiar, such as the relief of aged, impotent and poor people, and the supportation, aid and help of young tradesmen. A more modern list is found in sub-section 3(1) of the Charities Act 2011, encompassing, in updated language, much of the historic law[34] and adding contemporary concerns such as the advancement of amateur sport[35] and the welfare of animals.[36]

The courts make the intuitive assumption that when donors give towards one of these charitable outcomes, they do so because they genuinely care about the consumption of others. The charitable pipeline is seen as altruistic plumbing to deliver an intended economic advantage to other people. The best evidence for this is the framework of frustrated outcomes and consequent return detailed in the next section. However, there is another clue: common law judicial deference to the donor's planned outcomes.

At common law, judges have proclaimed themselves bound to carry through the donor's most precise schemes, and equally bound to refrain from subverting them. This is most apparent in circumstances where donors have made workable but low-utility gifts and the courts have been called upon to reshape them into something more socially worthwhile. At common law,[37] the courts have refused to do so. Or, in the words of Sir John Romilly in *Philpott v Saint George's Hospital*, 'instances of charities of the most useless description have come before the Court, but which it has considered itself bound to carry into effect'.[38]

The judge does not pass comment; she simply effects the donor's wishes. It is therefore a matter of logic that the donor is thought to care about outcomes. So, in *Philpott*, Romilly MR continued to say that he would not speculate upon whether

[32] See, eg, A Van Slyck, *Free to all: Carnegie Libraries and American Culture* 1890–1920 (Chicago, University of Chicago Press, 1995) 8–19.

[33] See, eg, Beveridge (n 18) 193.

[34] ibid.

[35] Charities Act 2011, s 3(1)(g).

[36] Charities Act 2011, s 3(1)(k).

[37] This is no longer true in statute. See, eg, Charities Act 2011, s 67(3)(c).

[38] *Philpott v Saint George's Hospital* (1859) 27 Beav 107, 112, 54 ER.

'a different mode of application of the funds in charity should have occurred to the mind of the testator'.[39] The same sentiment can be found in *Re University of London Medical Sciences Fund*, Williams LJ saying that 'the Courts [have never] thought it right to be benevolent with a testator's money contrary to the plain intention of the will'.[40] Again, in *Attorney General for Northern Ireland v Forde*, Wilson J clearly articulated his respect for original donative intention, stating that he had 'always understood that the law was that a testator could leave his property by will to whomsoever he liked ... the duty of the court was simply to read the will'.[41]

Donors are assumed to be motivated by their stated plans. This is expressed by judicial deference to the donor's chosen charitable goal, even where it is low utility. This flows as a matter of logic from an assumption that the judge is genuinely committed to its delivery. Courts envisage a limited role for themselves: they effect and protect the donor's wishes, and they proclaim themselves resistant to any temptation to subvert her plans. An assumption of economic altruism is central to this judicial attitude; there would be no need to show such deference to a charitable end goal if it was thought that the donor did not truly care about its effectuation.

B. Return is for Irredeemably Frustrated Altruists

The clearest evidence of a judicial assumption of economic altruism is found in the relationship between frustration and return. Donors are considered genuinely motivated by the provision of charitable goods—material outcomes—for others. This leads to a micro-level economic understanding of the judicial rationale for return: where a gift fails, a donor will get it back because her outcomes are found to be frustrated.

The relationship between frustrated altruism and return is a complex one. Return is not automatic for every frustrated donor. The courts have attempted to classify their altruists into types: those who are irredeemably frustrated by failure and those whose frustration can be relieved by a judicial tonic. Upon a failure, only the truly frustrated will get a return. This is because, over a long period,[42] judges have taken the view that some donors who have made failed gifts would, in fact, prefer for them to be modified and kept in charity on new terms.[43] These donors, for whom frustration is thought redeemable, are described as having a general charitable intention.

Re Royce provides an example of the courts' approach to redeemable frustration and general intention. In the case, a gift was left to the vicar and churchwardens of Oakham Church for the benefit of the choir. The amount left was far in excess of anything that the choir needed, so the surplus sum was held to have failed. In order to prevent a return, Simonds J found a very general intention for the advancement of

[39] ibid.
[40] *Re University of London Medical Sciences Fund* [1909] 2 Ch 1 (Ch), 8.
[41] *Attorney General for Northern Ireland v Forde* [1932] NI 1, 12.
[42] See generally R Mulheron, *The Modern Cy-près Doctrine: Applications and Implications* (London, Routledge, 2006) 106–20.
[43] The concept of modification is well explained in *Woodhams* (n 4), 503.

religion behind the gift. He stated that 'The charitable intention (and I use the word "charitable" in its legal sense) in giving money for the purpose of musical services in a church is for the advancement of religion'.[44]

The donor was thought to have a type of intention which would license the courts to fix the failure, apply it to general religion and so keep the gift in charity. This precedential creation is an economically altruistic state of mind. A generally minded donor, such as found in *Royce*, is thought to be flexible, but still genuinely committed to the delivery of charitable goods for the consumption of others. The logic of the courts is, in essence, that her altruistic intention was so broad—in *Royce*, as broad as general religious consumption by humankind—that modification to keep the gift in charity would not frustrate her wishes.

A second class of donors, those with a so-called particular charitable intention,[45] comprises donors thought so irredeemably frustrated by the failure that nothing can be done for them. They are deemed to have been motivated only by a more specialised and unfixable charitable goal, causing the gift to be returned. To this end, Buckley J stated in *Re Lysaght* that 'a particular charitable intention exists where the donor means his charitable disposition to take effect if, but only if, it can be carried into effect in a particular specified way'.[46]

The best-known example of this narrow and return-causing intention is *Re Wilson*,[47] where restrictions and conditions attached to a gift were so detailed as to present a picture of a donor wedded to specifics and details. The testator, a vicar from Cumberland, had sought to establish a school. His will outlined a personal charitable vision; the school and a schoolmaster's house were to be paid for by the voluntary subscription of landowners and proprietors in specified parishes. The schoolmaster was to teach Latin, Greek and the elementary parts of mathematics to a timetable; scholars were to go free, but the cost for other pupils was to be 2s 6d at Midsummer and a quarter penny at Christmas. Faced with evidence of tightly particular outcomes, the court thought the failure irredeemable and so effected a return.

Crucially, the particular charitable intention—as developed by judges—is altruistic in the economic sense. It is perhaps true that the milk of material human kindness runs a little less fully in a donor with only a narrow and inflexible goal in mind, but this conception of intention still marks a gift motivated by the economic benefit of other people, so it is materially altruistic. The donor is thought to be driven by the delivery of charitable outcomes, albeit outcomes so inflexible and precise as to be irredeemable by the court through a process of judicial modification.

So, in an intention case, the court merely selects between two types of economic altruism, effecting a return where irredeemable frustration is found. The claim that the rationale for return rests in frustrated economic altruism is a layered one. Return is not automatic. Only the irredeemably frustrated get their money back. However, there is a clear conceptual point in play. The linked ideas of irredeemable frustration and return depend upon an assumption of economic altruism. It is only possible for donors who genuinely care about the delivery of charitable goods to others to

[44] *Re Royce* [1940] Ch 514 (Ch), 521.
[45] See n 27 above.
[46] *Lysaght* (n 5) 202.
[47] *Wilson* (n 4).

suffer frustration. An egoistic donor, who gives without thought or concern for the material benefit of others, will not be frustrated if such others do not receive it.

IV. THE EGOISTIC MOTIVATION

English judges have not taken a course in economic altruism. Nevertheless, an apparently intuitive understanding of economic altruism has been seen to underpin the law of return. The rationale for return is that where a donor's assumedly altruistic charitable outcome is irredeemably frustrated, she should get her money back.

An analysis in donative economics has led the argument to this point, but the methodological trowel can dig further still. Since the 1980s, donative economists have developed in egoistic consumption a complementary model of motivation based in self-interest. It posits that some donors give out of a desire for a self-interested joy-of-giving. The altruistic rationale for return, uncovered in the preceding section, cannot apply to them. Such donors give without concern for charitable outcomes. They give in consumption of a joy-in-giving and are indifferent to other-regarding charitable goods. In consequence, they are indifferent whether or not other people materially benefit from their gift, and so its failure does not frustrate them. First, the theoretical challenge posed by economic egoism to altruism will be analysed, then it will be argued that egoistic gifts are outside the legal rationale of return.

A. Economic Egoism and Charitable Gifts

Economic egoism is the 1980s child of its altruistic parent.[48] Within the literature,[49] egoistic motivation has been developed to provide an alternative aspect to the donor drive. Importantly, a purely egoistic donor will not be frustrated if certain charitable ends are not delivered. Her motivation is not charitable. The charitable end is incidental to her intent. She gives only because it is enjoyable to do so and without concern that any charitable plan is realised.

A theory of egoistic motivation developed from a testable empirical flaw in altruistic models, so causing the emergence of an alter ego to altruism.[50] It arose because goal-regarding motivation suffers from a free-rider problem. That is, if donors are modelled as deriving satisfaction from the delivery of charitable goods, they will have no motivation to give in circumstances where other hearts are willing to provide.[51] All they care about is that the goals are met by someone, not necessarily themselves.

That testable hypothesis has been found wanting.[52] There is no large-scale free riding; individuals give to charity even in the presence of contributions from

[48] For the chronological development of economic donative theory see J Andreoni, *The Economics of Philanthropy and Fundraising, Volume 1. Theory and Policy Toward Giving* (Cheltenham, Edgar Elgar, 2015).

[49] Andreoni (n 2); Harbaugh (n 2).

[50] See generally Kotzebue (n 1) 10–13; see especially Andreoni (n 2).

[51] Warr (n 12); Roberts (n 12).

[52] See especially Andreoni (n 2).

other donors. Egoism emerged as a theoretical response to that donation behaviour. In place of caring altruistically about charitable outcomes, it theorises that some donors give because they enjoy it. A new consumable good—often termed 'glow'[53]—is brought into the donor's thought processes. Kotzebue describes the donor's motivation as 'driven by the (essentially egoistic) wish to consume a purely private good'.[54] Thus egoistic motivation adds a new element to donative theory, located in the familiar economic terrain of self-interest. Boulding graphically illustrates the point: 'If we drop a dime in the blind man's cup, it is because the blind man gives us something. We feel a certain glow of emotional virtue, and it is this that we receive for our dime.'[55]

The mechanisms inducing joy-of-giving may, however, be less socially desirable than emotional virtue. A striving for social recognition is a key psychological driver of public consumption,[56] and research by Andreoni and Petri suggests that where donors are identifiable, the size of their in-study donation will increase. They find that 'by unmasking subjects, we allow for various social effects, like pride, shame, social comparison and prestige, to work'.[57] A second, and directly intuitive, mechanism to induce a joy-of-giving is found in circumstances where donors are enticed by the supply of, or the chance of winning, private material inducements. Landry et al show that lottery fund-raising increases the sum of voluntary contributions.[58] Similarly, in an analysis of records at the English National Opera, Buraschi and Cornelli find a class of donors induced to give by special events and gala dinners.[59] Where there is inducement through the supply of social benefit or material reward, the potential for egoistic joy-of-giving is clear.

In economic donative theory, it is consumption of the joy-of-giving which provides the satisfaction, not material inducements or intangible social rewards per se.[60] They operate only to indicate circumstances of egoistic consumption of charitable goods. Such egoistic pleasure is not kryptonite to altruism. There is nothing in theory to prevent a donor from holding both egoistic and altruistic intentions at the same time. In economic donative theory it is common to understand donors as existing on a spectrum with 'pure altruism' at one end and 'pure egoism' at the other. Thus, it is possible, in between both ends of the spectrum, to both care about charitable ends and simultaneously derive an egoistic joy-of-giving.[61] For example, a donor to a charitable lottery might both get a thrill from entry to the draw and

[53] Popularised by Andreoni (ibid).

[54] Kotzebue (n 1) 1035.

[55] Boulding (n 24) 58.

[56] Harbaugh (n 2); Dellavigna et al, 'Testing for Altruism and Social Pressure in Charitable Giving' (2012) 127 *The Quarterly Journal of Economics* 1.

[57] J Andreoni and R Petrie, 'Public Goods Experiments without Confidentiality: A Glimpse into Fund-Raising' (2004) 88 *Journal of Public Economics* 1605, 1620.

[58] Landry (n 17).

[59] Buraschi (n 17).

[60] See, eg, Harbaugh (n 2).

[61] J Andreoni, 'Philanthropy' in S Kolm and J Ythier (eds), *Handbook of the Economics of Giving, Altruism and Reciprocity* (Amsterdam, Elsevier, 2006) 1126; P Glimcher et al, *Neuroeconomics: Decision-Making and the Brain* (Amsterdam, Academic Press, 2009) 317; B Kingma, 'Public Good Theories of the Non-profit Sector: Weisbrod Revisited' (1997) 8 *Voluntas* 135, 139.

genuinely hope her money will go to good causes. Or a relative disinheriting mainly from spite might also care about the cat's home.

However, it is those economic models of donation where individuals are driven by nothing other than economic egoism—deriving no utility from charity itself—which challenge the law, and, in turn, provide the focus of the following section.[62] This is because, as will be seen, an entirely egoistic donor will sit outside of the law's rationale for return. A donor motivated only by egoism will have no concern at all for the provision of charitable goods. In turn, her charitable intention cannot be frustrated on failure, and there is no need, at law, to give the money back.

B. Why Purely Egoistic Gifts Should Be Kept in Charity

It has been argued that the law of return is based in frustrated altruism, so its rationale does not apply to an egoistic motivation that has not been at all frustrated. Later sections will discover instances of unacknowledged egoism in the precedents to pinpoint examples of return without any doctrinal basis. Here, however, the appropriate legal response to egoistic gift making is plotted. It is argued that purely egoistic transfers should continue to be treated as charitable gifts, but that they are outside the altruistic and end-driven rationale for return. They should be kept in charity.

The law is only seriously challenged by purely egoistic donors. Where an individual simultaneously derives a joy-of-giving and also genuinely wishes to materially advance the lives of others, she can still be scooped up within the legal net of altruism. She can, without distorting the truth, be said to be at risk of frustration if the altruistic side of her motivational binary cannot be effected. In such circumstances, the judicial blind spot to egoism is of conceptual interest, but of no legal consequence. It is only where the donor is a pure egoist[63] that the doctrine of return is truly challenged. In that circumstance, where a donor is not motivated by altruistic outcomes at all, charitable failure cannot frustrate her self-interested intent.

It is now possible to go where judges cannot, and map the purely egoistic motivation on to the law. Lost in a colder world of self-interest, it is initially tempting to leave behind charitable precedents and instead take recourse in the law of private express trusts. If egoistically motivated gifts were considered non-charitable, this would cause their return as a matter of precedent. As is well known, Megarry J suggested in *Re Vandervell's Trusts (No 2)*[64] that upon failure of a non-charitable gift, a resulting trust will occur automatically without any regard at all for intention. A later approach is more circumspect, but has similar effect. In *Air Jamaica Ltd v Charlton*, Lord Millett said of the resulting trust that it 'responds to the absence of any intention on his part to pass a beneficial interest to the recipient'.[65] Thus there

[62] See especially Harbaugh (n 2); Buraschi (n 17); A Glazer and K Konrad, 'A Signalling Explanation for Charity' (1996) 86 *American Economic Review* 1019.

[63] Harbaugh (ibid).

[64] *Re Vandervell's Trusts (No 2)* [1973] 3 WLR 744 (Ch), 764.

[65] *Air Jamaica Ltd v Charlton* [1999] 1 WLR 1399, 1412.

is a strong, but not irrefutable,[66] precedential presumption of return in most failed private express trust cases.[67]

Yet taking cold comfort in the law of private trusts does not quite wash. Even though entirely ego-driven donations are non-altruistic, such gifts cannot without strain be classed as legally 'non-charitable'. Ego-motivated donors will be aware that their gifts were, before failure, destined for a legally recognised charitable end. They will expect their gift to go to charity, even if they are unmoved by the prospect. The distinction between an ego-driven and an altruistic, outcome-driven donor goes to the nature of charitable motivation as it is understood at law, but it does not relate to any wider legal taxonomy. It is therefore necessary to look for a way to fit egoistic donors within the law of charitable return.

There is no doubt that the altruistic, outcome-driven logic of return does not apply in egoistic cases. The legal problem is that while an egoistic donor will be unconcerned with altruistic charitable ends, the law of return assumes their central importance. We have seen that courts treat donors as altruists, and that they return gifts in consequence of irredeemably frustrated altruistic goals. In consequence, the first reason not to return in cases of egoistic donation is simply that such donors are outside this rationale of the law. An egoistic donor has suffered no frustration of her altruistic plans. Despite the failure of her gift, she remains content because she derived egoistic satisfaction from the process of giving. For example, in *New Forest Agricultural Show Society v The Commissioners of Customs and Excise*, Nicol J described, in relation to fundraising, such a joy-driven enterprise as 'a function held in a vicarage or possibly manor garden (in the church hall if wet)', including enjoyably social, yet profitable, competition, such as 'guessing the length of a phenomenally large runner bean or the weight of a huge fruit cake, with a fee payable for each guess'.[68] Donors sampling such bucolic and personally profitable pleasures will have been satisfied at the point of giving. It would be wrong to call them frustrated altruists in any sense.

Alongside the negative reason not to return, there is also a second positive legal reason to keep egoistic gifts in charity. While an egoistic donor is evidently not motivated in the altruistic sense that she desires to see charitable outcomes, her gift is still a product of rational choice. She will expect it to go to charity, regardless of being unmoved by the prospect. She has therefore a type of legal expectation for the law to grasp a hold of. It must be conceded, however, that the grip is weak. Merely effecting what the donor can be said to have expected lacks the same legal normative force as carrying through what the donor positively wished, but in circumstances where there is no frustration at all, keeping the gift in charity remains a legal effectuation of her decision to give. While a tombola player, motivated by the chance of winning a prize, will not in truth be concerned about the state of the church roof, she will in a weak sense expect the gift to be applied to legal charity. Although that is not the motivation, it is the incidental expectation.

[66] See W Barr and R Stevens, *Pearce & Stevens' Trusts and Equitable Obligations* (Oxford, Oxford University Press, 2015) 212.

[67] See also *Westdeutsche Landesbank Girozentrale v Islington Borough Council* [1966] AC 669, 708.

[68] *New Forest Agricultural Show Society v The Commissioners of Customs and Excise* [2002] STI 1361, 2002 WL 1310956 (V&DT), [45].

Such a legal outcome—keeping purely egoistic gifts in charity—is, at root, intuitive. The altruistic donor's gift, if she was concerned with charitable outcomes, has truly failed. Her altruism is frustrated, and she is in a parallel position to a purchaser of unobtainable goods. By contrast, an egoistic donor will have been self-interestedly satisfied regardless of the failure. Following from her successful and contented consumption of joy-of-giving, she cannot also expect her money back.

V. RETURN WITHOUT A RATIONALE IN CONTEXTS OF PURE EGOISM

It has been argued that the rationale for return rests on a legal understanding of donors as irredeemably frustrated economic altruists. It has also been argued that when purely egoistic gifts are found, the courts should not return them. It will now be argued that, in the context of failed testamentary gifts and failed public appeals, the blind spot to egoism causes fundamental doctrinal problems.

A. Return without a Rationale: Purely Egoistic Motivation in the Testamentary Context

Egoism is present but not prevalent in testamentary giving, so while the existing framework of return falls into conceptual difficulty in egoistic cases, such instances of egoistic donation are infrequent enough to leave the system of testamentary construction as a whole unscathed. This section criticises the courts' approach to egoistic motivation where it arises, but concludes with an acknowledgment of the broadly altruistic nature of testamentary charity.

A first instance of purely egoistic donation in testamentary cases—gifts motivated by spite—graphically illustrates problems with existing rules which assume altruism. This is a most unfortunate joy-of-giving. Testamentary gifts to charity may disappoint survivors, and exclusion of hopeful recipients through a gift to charity, might induce a utilitarian joy akin to Bentham's 'pleasures resulting from the view of any pain supposed to be suffered by the beings who may become the objects of malevolence'.[69] Spiteful testamentary donors will give without concern for charitable ends, directing funds to charity in a far more malign frame of mind. The will in *Mills v Farmer* shows a striking but rare example of open hostility. In the case, a testamentary donor partly disinherited his kin. He stated in his will that he would later name charitable objects, but he did not do so, leaving the court confronted with the vaguest of intentions. His testamentary papers included the telling direction: 'It is needless to have any of my relations attend my funeral, as it is apt to breed ill will amongst them; and their grief on such occasions, is generally attended with hypocrisy.'[70]

[69] J Bentham, *An Introduction to the Principles of Morals and Legislation* (Oxford, Clarendon Press, 1970) 44.

[70] *Mills v Farmer* (1815) 19 Ves JR 483, 484, 35 ER 595, 595.

In *Mills v Farmer*, the donor's motivational enmity was presumably confined to his family. Yet in one remarkable instance, *Re Satterthwaite's Will Trusts*,[71] a donor was apparently motivated by her dislike of all humanity. Telling a bank official that she hated all human beings, the donor declared that she would leave everything to animals. She presented the bank official with a will written on brown paper but, after being advised to create a formal will, the donor then requested he compile a list of animal charities. With further insouciance to charitable outcomes, the gift was made by reference to the London classified telephone directory.

The altruistic framework of return cannot be coherently applied in such cases. They are outside its rationale and, as it has been argued, such gifts are best kept in charity. A court of construction searching for irredeemably frustrated altruism, prepared to return the gift where such altruism is found, misfires its precedents. Where donors are exclusively consuming joy-of-giving, charitable ends do not matter to them at all, and so the test for a general or a particular charitable intention has no traction. The law's inability to recognise purely egoistic giving causes it a conceptual problem: it forces the courts to look for an altruistic motivation which might not be there, and possibly to effect return without any reason for doing so. There is no frustrated altruism in these cases. The donors—being dead at the point of failure—have already consumed an egoistic joy-of-giving in life. However, the law is unable to recognise that state of mind. Without a theory of egoistic donation in its tool kit, it is not open for the courts to find that any altruistic charitable end was incidental to the gift. Instead, in each case, following the standard approach, the court looks incoherently for irredeemably frustrated altruism.

A second instance of purely egoistic donation in testamentary cases—a desire to create a personal memorial[72]—provides a direct example of return without a legal rationale. In the Victorian case *Re Gwilym*, a donor hoped for the 'Gwilym Art Gallery and Museum' to be opened in her own house after death. However, she did not leave enough money for the plan, causing the gift to fail. Smith J noted her motivation directly, stating, 'as appears from the direction that her name is to be attached to the museum and art gallery, she desired to establish a permanent memorial to herself'.[73] On the application of ordinary principles, Smith J apparently found a particular charitable intention, returning the gift to her testamentary estate. Such an outcome is incoherent, but inevitable, in a system of construction that does not recognise egoistic giving. Smith J was forced to discover, despite clear facts, an irredeemably frustrated concern for the benefit of others. This is a failure of the law, rather than a failure of the judge. It was simply not possible, within the existing legal framework, to find that the donor had before death successfully consumed joy-of-giving in contemplation of her self-interested goals.

This conceptual legal problem is a limited one because it impacts on only a relatively small number of cases. Although pure egoism in the form of spite and vanity can be inferred in the case reports, such instances are striking because they

[71] *Re Satterthwaite's Will Trusts* [1966] 1 WLR 277 (CA).

[72] See *Re Pinion* [1965] Ch 85 (CA); *M'Caig v University of Glasgow (No 2)* 1907 SC 231.

[73] *Re Gwilym* [1952] VLR 282, 285.

are unusual. While testamentary donors, giving in contemplation of death,[74] might be motivated by 'legacy', it is a generally altruistic inheritance that they have in mind. In an interview-based investigation into the meaning of 'legacy' in the context of aging, Hunter and Rowles identify three types: 'material', 'biological' and 'of values'.[75] For those authors, the ends to which property is devoted appears important; participants in their study suggested that it is the third element—the transmission of values—which holds the most salience. They state in later work that 'a primary task in creating a legacy is determining the values we cherish most in life and conveying these values to our descendants and to our communities'.[76] In another parallel to our legal understanding of end-driven altruism, Wade-Benzoni et al suggest that legacies allow donors to 'form a psychological bond with others in the future, thereby symbolically extending themselves into the future and helping to fulfil their desires to establish a positive legacy'.[77] While the personality of testamentary donors is undoubtedly wrapped up in their legacy, an end-driven and altruistic drive is likely to be present.

Altruism is also more commonly inferred in the case reports than spite and vanity. For example, gifts are often directed at social change and, where this is the case, it must be likely that altruistic contemplation of the future will motivate the gift. Historically there have been gifts to reform prisons[78] or to abolish slavery,[79] and more recently gifts for animal welfare have appeared in the reports,[80] alongside gifts for the promotion of peace.[81] Gifts are also often marked by a local flavour, suggesting a desire to confer genuine benefit upon a particular community. Gifts to local churches are relatively common,[82] such as in *Re Broadbent*,[83] where a bequest was left to a closed iron-framed mission church in Stalybridge. Community links can also be seen, such as in *Re Sanders' Will Trusts*, where a gift was left to the working classes, preferably dockers working in the Pembroke Docks,[84] and also in *Re Bagshaw*,[85] where a testamentary donor left a gift to the Bakewell and District War Memorial Cottage Hospital, which treated patients within a radius of five miles from the Bakewell Memorial Cross. Localised gifts suggest a genuine community end.

[74] See E Jonas et al, 'The Scrooge Effect: Evidence that Mortality Salience Increases Prosocial Attitudes and Behaviour' (2002) 28 *Personality and Social Psychology Bulletin* 1342.

[75] E Hunter and M Rowles, 'Leaving a Legacy: Toward a Typology' (2005) 19 *Journal of Aging Studies* 327.

[76] E Hunter and M Rowles, 'Beyond Death: Inheriting the Past and Giving to the Future, Transmitting the Legacy of One's Self' (2008) 56 *OMEGA* 313, 322.

[77] Wade-Benzoni et al, 'It's Only a Matter of Time: Death Legacies, and Intergenerational Decisions' (2012) 23 *Psychological Science* 704, 704.

[78] *Re Prison Charities* (1873) LR 16 Eq 129 (Ch).

[79] *Attorney General v The Iron Mongers' Company* (1834) 2 Mylne & Keen 57, 639 ER 1064; *Attorney General v Gibson* (1835) 2 Beav 317n.

[80] *National Anti-Vivisection Society v IRC* [1948] AC 31 (HL).

[81] *Re Harwood* [1936] Ch 285 (Ch); *Re Collier* (Deceased) [1998] 1 NZLR 81; *Re Koeppler Will Trusts* [1986] Ch 423 (CA).

[82] *Royce* (n 44); *Re Lepton's Charity* [1972] Ch 276 (Ch).

[83] *Broadbent* (n 7); For the legal/conceptual overlap between religion and community see M Turnour, 'Modernising Charity Law: Steps to an Alternative Architecture for Common Law Charity Jurisprudence' in M McGregor-Lowndes and K O'Halloran (eds), *Modernising Charity Law* (Cheltenham, Edward Elgar, 2010) 228.

[84] *Re Sanders' Will Trusts* [1954] Ch 265 (Ch).

[85] *Re Bagshaw* [1954] 1 WLR 238 (Ch).

In testamentary cases, the altruistic framework for return falters on occasion, but it is tested only rarely. It is true that where egoistic motivation is obviously present, such as in cases of spite or vanity, the law of return falls into a conceptual incoherence. There is no frustration of altruistic intention, and it is argued that such gifts, being successful instances of egoistic consumption outside the rationale of return, should be kept in charity. Yet being beyond the paradigm case of testamentary altruism, they rarely trouble the courts.

B. Return without a Rationale: Purely Egoistic Motivation in the Public Appeals Context

Failed appeals are a relatively new legal problem in the precedents. The law of return developed over a long period of time in the context of wills,[86] yet failed appeals emerged as a persistent legal issue only in the twentieth century.[87] Their emergence followed both a wider diffusion of surplus wealth throughout society and the establishment of professional fund-raising practices.[88] A shift to the mass funding of charity was heralded by Beveridge in *Voluntary Action* by his optimistic statement that 'the democracy can and should learn to do what used to be done for the public good by the wealthy'.[89]

Appeals often combine Beveridge's democratic virtue with self-interest.[90] Instances of purely egoistic donation will be identified from the case law. These are gifts made in return for a personal material reward and gifts made in pursuit of a social benefit, such as public prestige. While the law has developed a coherent response to material benefit, it flounders with regard to gifts made in socially advantageous contexts.

A first instance of public appeal donation—gifts motivated by a desire to receive a personal material benefit—is purely egoistic. Where donors are induced to pay into charity by the prospect of a personal reward, there is clear-cut joy-of-giving. There is also no incoherence to be found in the case law. There is no question of return. For example, if a contributor to a charitable campaign is motivated to receive concert tickets, publications or the chance to enter for prizes, she will be treated as having parted entirely with her money and so denied a right to return. In *Re West Sussex Constabulary's Widows, Children and Benevolent Fund*, a case concerning contributions to a non-charitable pension and dependent relative fund, Goff J stated, after detailed consideration of the charitable case law, that the motivation was contractual: 'The purchaser of a ticket may have the motive of aiding the cause or he may not; he may purchase a ticket merely because he wishes to attend the particular entertainment or to try for the prize.'[91]

[86] See, eg, Mulheron (n 42) 100–35.

[87] ibid 185–209.

[88] See, eg, J Hughes, 'Beyond the Rattling Tin' in C Hanvey and T Philpot (eds), *Sweet Charity: The Role and Workings of Voluntary Organizations* (London, Routledge, 1996) 173.

[89] Beveridge (n 18) 307.

[90] See, eg, W Lindahl, *Principles of Fundraising: Theory and Practice* (Boston, Jones and Bartlett Publishers, 2010) 98.

[91] *Re West Sussex Constabulary's Widows, Children and Benevolent Fund* [1971] Ch 1 (Ch), 11.

Although the courts are not equipped with a theory of egoistic donation, Goff J's statement comes startlingly close. It parallels the logic of economic analysis. The judge, who makes a distinction between outcome-driven gifts and those flowing from a joy-of-giving, shares its rationale. That is, if a donor is entirely motivated by such non-altruistic enjoyment as concert tickets, sweepstakes and lotteries, it is incoherent to look for irredeemable frustration of an intended altruistic outcome. In the case, Goff J stated: 'it appears to me to be impossible to apply the doctrine of resulting trust'.[92] Similarly, in *Re British School of Egyptian Archaeology*,[93] subscribers to an educational archaeological society were held to be motivated by the receipt of handsomely produced academic research publications. Finding a contractual relationship with the charity, Harman J prevented a return. So in this instance of pure egoism, the law is both settled and clear: such gifts are kept in charity.

By contrast, a second instance of purely egoistic donation—gifts prompted by a social reward—is met without such clarity. Where gifts are made out of a drive for social benefit or prestige, they are analogous to an egoistic exchange for material reward. Yet this is not recognised by the law. By way of example, a paradigm circumstance of gifts made for social benefit is found at charity auctions, where donors are prompted to bid excessively in order to gain social recognition.[94] Circumstances of social reward are not always so cut-throat or dramatic. A donor might derive a social benefit from smaller-scale social interactions,[95] such as a collection amongst colleagues in a work place. Where the gift is motivated exclusively by a self-interested goal, the charitable end will be incidental to the decision to give. The motivation will be egoistic and not altruistic.

The issue of egoistic social benefit has surfaced—albeit obliquely—in three cases involving community fund-raising for hospitals: *Re Welsh Hospital (Netley) Fund*,[96] *Re Hillier's Trusts*[97] and *Re Ulverston and District New Hospital Building Trusts*.[98] Unfortunately, no clear legal principle has emerged from repeated litigation. Taking the three cases together, it can be seen that certain judges have held that gifts made in contexts of social benefit should uniformly be kept in charity,[99] but others have expressed a preference for return. So in *Welsh Hospital*, PO Lawrence J expressed, with reference to social fund-raising, a very strong view that return would be 'absurd on the face of it'.[100] In that case, funds had been raised, inter alia, 'from collections in streets and at churches ... in most of the towns and villages of Wales'.[101] Lord Denning picked up the mantle in *Hillier's*, stressing the loss of a right to return for appeals in social contexts. The judge held that gifts raised

[92] ibid.

[93] *Re British School of Egyptian Archaeology* [1954] 1 WLR 546 (Ch).

[94] See, eg, Harbaugh (n 2); Andreoni and Petrie (n 57).

[95] G Becker, 'A Theory of Social Interactions' (1974) 82 *Journal of Political Economy* 1063, 1083.

[96] *Re Welsh Hospital (Netley) Fund* [1921] 1 Ch 655 (Ch).

[97] *Re Hillier's Trusts* [1954] 1 WLR 700 (CA).

[98] *Ulverston* (n 27).

[99] It has also been argued that return can be displaced by an 'out and out' intention to transfer absolutely. See D Wilson, 'Section 14 of the Charities Act 1960: A Dead Letter?' [1983] *The Conveyancer and Property Lawyer* 40; Mulheron (n 42) 109–11.

[100] *Welsh Hospital* (n 96), 661.

[101] ibid 655.

at 'a church collection, a flag day, a whist drive, a dance, or some such activity' are given 'beyond recall'.[102]

Yet at least two judges have countenanced the possibility of return with regard to funds raised in contexts of social benefit. So in *Ulverston*, Jenkins LJ stated *obiter* that if a person had, in the context of solicitation, put money into a collection box and could satisfy the court that he had done so, then he 'should ... be entitled to have his money back in the event of the failure'.[103] And in *Hillier's*, Romer J stated, in a dissenting judgment, that any donor, 'whether large or small',[104] should be entitled to a return in principle. This approach leaves the door wide open for the return of egoistic gifts, but supplies no rationale for doing so.

In contrast to testamentary donation, egoism is much closer to the paradigm in the context of appeals. In the context of gifts for material benefit (eg lotteries and prizes), the courts have come very close to recognising that fact. However, where there is a purely egoistic social benefit derived from a public appeal, return is just as inappropriate. But the courts, without a fully articulated theory of egoistic motivation, have been unable to clearly express this view.

VI. A CONCEPTUAL STICKING-PLASTER: REFORM OF PUBLIC APPEALS

In the preceding section it was argued that judges erroneously return purely egoistic gifts without a legal rationale for doing so in both testamentary and appeals contexts. In an ironic twist, targeted legislative reform prevents return, but without a satisfactory rationale for the change. Bereft of a theoretical underpinning, statute—directed at public appeals—turns the problem on its head. That is, return is prevented as a result of the statute, but the legal basis for doing so is theoretically flawed.

The key reform concerns gifts made by unidentifiable[105] and unknown[106] donors. Under section 64 of the Charities Act 2011, these donors are defined, inter alia, as those giving through a collection box, lottery, competition or sale.[107] They are automatically and conclusively presumed to have a general charitable intention,[108] with the effect that return is precluded.[109]

The micro-level economic perspective uncovers a conceptual problem: the statutory provisions sweep egoists under an altruistic carpet. It will be remembered that the general charitable intention is a form of broad and permissive altruism; it is the flexible and altruistic state of mind that permits judges to keep gifts in charity. It is also clear that collection box, lottery, sale and competition donors are likely to be deriving either a social or material benefit from giving. They are most likely egoistic.

[102] *Hillier's* (n 97), 714.
[103] *Ulverston* (n 27), 633.
[104] *Hilliers* (n 97), 721.
[105] Charities Act 2011, s 63(1)(a).
[106] Charities Act 2011, s 64 (1).
[107] Charities Act 2011, s 64(1)(a) brings such donors under s 63(1).
[108] 'Given for general purposes', Charities Act 2011, s 63(1).
[109] ibid.

While keeping their gifts in charity accords with the argument in this chapter—that egoistic gifts should not be returned—fixing such egoistic donors with a statutorily presumed general altruism is conceptually flawed.

The legislative reform to the law of public appeals was administratively, and not theoretically, driven. So at the House of Lords Committee stage in relation to precursor legislation,[110] Lord Silkin straightforwardly presented the view that the cases on appeals, insofar as they contradict or turn upon hair-splitting,[111] should be rationalised. Only Lord Denning, sitting in a legislative capacity, hinted at deeper theoretical issues, stating that 'in a public appeal of this kind I would submit to your Lordships that a person gives his money and that that is the end of it, he does not expect to have it back'.[112]

The sensible administrative reform impulse behind the legislation can be forgiven. Return of gifts to unidentifiable donors is an impossibility, and so conclusively fixing them with a general charitable intention permits the courts to take the prudent step of definitively ruling out such implausible action. However, without a clear grasp of the relationship between donor motivation and the precedents, the law can be seen to have tied itself in a conceptual knot. It applies a model of outcome-driven altruistic intention—the general charitable intention—to a category of donors very likely to be egoistically consuming the joy-of-giving.

The conceptual problem manifests itself in real-world legal artificiality. So, on occasion, intuitively egoistic donors have been conclusively presumed to have an altruistic general charitable intention. For example, in 'South Scarborough Swimming Pool Association',[113] the Charity Commission for England and Wales deployed the statutory power in relation to an underfunded swimming bath appeal,[114] noting that part of the fund was raised by 'dances, social evenings, sponsored events'.[115] Deploying the statute, a general charitable intention was found, permitting the gift to be used for the benefit of the local area. Yet in the context of dances and social evenings, it seems far more likely that the donors were entirely motivated by joy-of-giving.[116] The statute fixed the donors with a type of altruistic intention that they did not hold.

The statute, as it relates to unidentifiable donors, is a sticking plaster over a theoretical sore. From the economic perspective worked through in this chapter, it can be seen that the reason that egoistic donors should receive no return is that they have suffered no frustration; they have contentedly and successfully consumed a joy-of-giving. Instead, the legislation treats them as general altruists. The statute pushes the court to the right conclusion—keeping the gifts in charity—but by the wrong route. Without recognition of egoistic donation, and acknowledgement that such intention is outside the rationale of return, the conceptual sore is left to fester.

110 Charities Act 1960, s 14(2).
111 HL Deb 22 March 1960 vol 222, col 135.
112 ibid col 137.
113 Report of the Charity Commission for England and Wales (1980) 38.
114 At that time: Charities Act 1993, s 14.
115 Charity Commission for England and Wales (n 113) 38.
116 See also *Re Henry Wood National Memorial Trust v Moiseiwitsch* [1966] 1 WLR 1601 (Ch).

VII. CONCLUSION

Application of economic donative theory has uncovered the judicial rationale for return. The core point of the analysis is that the law treats donors as altruistic in the economic sense. Judges assume that donors care, and care deeply, about the delivery of material outcomes to others. In turn, this leads to the legal rationale for return. It is because the donor is thought to be giving in pursuit of genuinely desired charitable outcomes that, where those outcomes cannot be delivered, courts will return gifts with an apology note. Economic donative theory has shown that the rationale for return lies in an assumption of frustrated economic altruism.

Economic donative theory is a critical as well as an explanatory tool. It shows, as a legal conceptual problem, that the courts have no understanding of egoism. Judges, at the level of principle, are only able to proceed on the basis that the gift before them has been made in the spirit of economic altruism. This leads to a fundamental strain. Where a donor is motivated by a purely egoistic joy-of-giving, it makes no sense to ask whether or not her goals have been frustrated. She is happy regardless. If her true motivation was spite to family, entry into a lottery or the accrual of social esteem, then she will not care what the judge does with her gift upon its incidental failure.

These theoretical problems run deep, unsettling the doctrine once they are analysed. It is unsurprising that the sole attempt at legislative reform—in the context of public appeals—has been shown to founder. Without legal recognition of egoistic giving, both case law and statute will inevitably tie themselves in knots. To iron them out, the courts should start by acknowledging the existence of egoistic gifts and, in consequence, keep those gifts in charity on the basis that such self-interested motivation is outside the legal rationale of the doctrine.

Part C

Fraud and Title

11

Points of Tension: Fraud and Challenges under Guarantee of Titles Regimes

ROD THOMAS*

> Things fall apart; the centre cannot hold;
> ...
> The ceremony of innocence is drowned;
> The best lack all conviction, while the worst
> Are full of passionate intensity.[1]

I. INTRODUCTION

THE AUSTRALASIAN TORRENS regimes[2] and the Land Registration Act 2002 (LRA 2002) have been described as 'indefeasibility' of title regimes.[3] However, the use of this language is problematic. It conjures up associations and similarities which are more apparent than real. For New Zealand (if not Australasia), the indefeasibility concept has been understood as 'immunity from attack by adverse claim to the land or interest in respect of which [a party] is registered'.[4] However, this conceptualisation remains enigmatic. The Torrens concept has always had 'an element of legend about it simply because the idea was imprecise'.[5] *Megarry & Wade* adopts similar usage, with the expression 'qualified indefeasibility' being used as a descriptor of the underpinning schema of the LRA 2002. This is explained as identifying when the

* The genesis of this chapter arose from conversations with Martin Dixon and Emma Lees at Cambridge. Powerful insight was provided by Michael Bryan, University of Melbourne over a cup of coffee. I wish to acknowledge the insights and assistance given by Lynden Griggs, University of Tasmania; Rouhshi Low of QUT, Queensland; Janine Lay, Allan Beever, Mike French and Sally Al-joubory of AUT University; and Shananne Joyce of Auckland University. Useful comments were made on an earlier version by the 'blind' reviewer. The usual disclaimers apply. Email: rod.thomas@aut.ac.nz.

1 WB Yeats (1865–1939), 'The Second Coming' in *Michael Robartes and the Dancer* (Churchtown, The Chuala Press, 1920).

2 Each Australian jurisdiction (states and territories) has its own Torrens statute. They often are different in terms of style and perhaps on some issues of policy. New Zealand has the Land Transfer Act 1952.

3 The term is identified by Lord Wilberforce in *Frazer v Walker* [1967] 1 AC 569 (PC), 580–81, [1967] NZLR 1069, 1075–76 and is commonly used in describing foundational principles of the Torrens system.

4 [1967] 1 AC 569 (PC), 580, [1967] NZLR 1069, 1078–79.

5 A Mason, 'Indefeasibility—Logic or Legend' in D Grinlinton (ed), *Torrens in the Twenty-First Century* (Wellington, LexisNexis, 2003) 19.

'register can be rectified against limited classes of registered proprietor', and when it cannot be, the circumstances which give rise to an indemnity claim.[6] The association with the Torrens terminology appears intentional, but is not explained.[7] However, each regime comes from different places in terms of its underpinning rationale. Correspondingly, the concept of 'guarantee of title' equally bears different associations.

A useful point of comparison is the statutory powers given for alteration of titles. For the LRA 2002, these are found in schedule 4, and are set out in some detail. Australasian Torrens regimes are similar to each other in terms of alteration powers. If we avoid issues of internal registration error, the Torrens conceptualisation is brutally simple: registration is good, except in the case of a 'fraud' finding.[8] Yet this apparently simple concept has been applied differently on each side of the Tasman Sea.

An appreciation of what constitutes a fraud finding under the LRA 2002 and under the Australasian regimes is considered in this chapter. Under both regimes fraud is explained as a statutory, *sui generis* concept, relying on judicial interpretation as to its meaning. Where the regime is inflexible in terms of its application, as under the Australasian concept of indefeasibility, this is shown to invite judicial manipulation. This then leads to a discussion of an associated issue—the right to receive compensation.

Where a title can be challenged on a non-fault basis, such as under the LRA 2002, should a registered title holder receive 'out-of-pocket expenses' where he or she successfully defends his or her registered status? This, again, requires us to reflect on what we understand is meant by the indefeasibility label.

Through this analysis, the author argues that the alteration powers contained in schedule 4 of the LRA 2002 provide a better avenue for the development of a reasoned, workable scheme than the Australasian concept of immediate indefeasibility. However, the rectification powers as presently expressed under the LRA 2002 are argued (at least through the eyes of a Torrens lawyer) to be clumsy and underdeveloped in terms of achieving satisfactory outcomes.

II. STRUCTURE OF THE FRAUD EXCEPTION UNDER AUSTRALASIAN TORRENS STATUTES

The aim of Torrens systems is to provide for certainty of the registration result, except where a fraud finding is made. The fraud exception is usually referred to in a number of disparate provisions in a Torrens statute which are unclear in meaning. The following example uses the New Zealand Land Transfer Act 1952 (NZ) (LTA 1952) as illustrative of this point.

[6] C Harpum, S Bridge and M Dixon (eds), *Megarry & Wade: The Law of Real Property*, 8th edn (London, Sweet & Maxwell, 2012) [7-131].

[7] The expression 'qualified indefeasibility' is used by Harpum et al (ibid) at [7-131] to describe the workings of the LRA 2002, but without further attribution.

[8] This discussion does not extend to the many statutory exceptions to indefeasibility protection, inevitably including issues such as public works legislation or town planning regimes. See discussion by J Greenwood and T Jones, 'Automation of the Register: Issues Impacting on the Integrity of Title' in Grinlinton (n 5) 345.

First, section 62, often called the 'primacy provision'. Its emphatic language suggests a clear understanding of the indefeasibility concept. Registration is recognised as being final, except where a fraud finding is made out:

> **Estate of registered proprietor paramount**
>
> Notwithstanding the existence in any other person of any estate or interest ... the registered proprietor of land or of any estate or interest in land under the provisions of this Act shall, *except in case of fraud*, hold the same subject to such encumbrances, liens, estates, or interests as may be notified on the folium of the register. (Emphasis added)

Section 63 follows. It is known as the 'ejectment' section. Note the reference in section 63 to 'transferee bona fide for value'. This will be returned to later.

> **Registered proprietor protected against ejectment**
>
> (1) No action for possession, or other action for the recovery of any land, shall lie or be sustained against the registered proprietor ... except in any of the following cases, that is to say:
>
> ...
>
> (c) *the case of a person deprived of any land by* fraud, as against the person registered as proprietor of that land through fraud, or as against a person deriving *otherwise than as a transferee bona fide for value from or through a person so registered through* fraud. (Emphasis added)

Then section 182. This is the 'notice' provision. The language is exceptionally blunt. No 'notice' or 'knowledge', 'direct or constructive', is binding—no matter when it is received.

> **Purchaser from registered proprietor not affected by notice**
>
> *Except in the case of fraud*, no person contracting or dealing with or taking or proposing to take a transfer from the registered proprietor of any registered estate or interest shall be required or in any manner concerned to inquire into or ascertain the circumstances in or the consideration for which that registered owner or any previous registered owner of the estate or interest in question is or was registered, or ... shall be affected by notice, direct or constructive, of any trust or unregistered interest, *any rule of law or equity* to the contrary notwithstanding, *and the knowledge that any such trust or unregistered interest is in existence shall not of itself be imputed as fraud*. (Emphasis added)

Finally, section 183. This is the bona fide purchaser provision. This is the second reiteration of this equitable concept. Its wording suggests that a volunteer is not entitled to the benefits of 'indefeasibility' protection.[9]

> **No liability on bona fide purchaser or mortgagee**
>
> (1) Nothing in this Act ... shall be so interpreted as to render subject to action for recovery of damages, or for possession ... any purchaser or mortgagee *bona fide for valuable consideration* ... on the ground that his vendor or mortgagor *may have been registered as proprietor through fraud or error*, or under any void or voidable instrument, or may have

[9] This issue still remains uncertain some 146 years following the enactment of the Land Transfer Act 1870, New Zealand's first Torren statute. See the discussion by Tipping J in *Regal Hastings Ltd v Lightbody* [2009] NZLR 433 (SC), [135].

> derived from or through a person registered as proprietor through fraud or error, or under any void or voidable instrument … (Emphasis added)

When read against each other, the preceding provisions are not clear. Sections 62 and 182 are unequivocal: registration is king—except in the case of fraud. Notice or knowledge of an unregistered interest received prior to the registration event occurring is irrelevant. We then muddy otherwise clear waters, by introducing the concept of a transferee bona fide for value in sections 63 and 183. Arguably, mention of these concepts, derived as they are from equity, have no place in this registration statute. However, such confusions aside, we can readily agree that fraud (whatever it may be) is expressly made an exception to indefeasibility protection. We then consider how the alteration powers provided in schedule 4 of the LRA 2002 operate.

III. LRA 2002, SCHEDULE 4 POWERS

Fraud does not play such a key role in the LRA 2002. Instead, there is a more nuanced approach as to when the register can be altered.[10]

To an Australasian Torrens lawyer, the schedule 4 provisions, as they are presently drafted, appear unduly complicated, if not confused. Uncertainty as to their effect appears to be shared.[11] The analysis that follows is hopefully in alignment with what has been termed an 'orthodox' view of the schedule 4 powers.[12]

A. Schema of Schedule 4 Powers

By schedule 4, the register can be altered, inter alia, either to correct a 'mistake', or for the purpose of 'bringing the register up to date'.[13] Unlike the remorseless drive under the LTA 1952 to achieve certainty of registration, under the LRA 2002, a court must order rectification of the register 'unless there are exceptional circumstances which justify its not doing so'.[14] The fraud 'exception' is limited to circumstances where the register is to be altered to correct a 'mistake', where a proprietor is in possession.

B. The Need for a Proprietor to be in Possession

Where a registered proprietor is in possession, alterations can only take place without the consent of that party if one of two possible grounds apply:[15] first, where

[10] The following discussion does not focus on administrative powers of alteration arising from mere registration error.

[11] E Cooke, 'Chickens Coming Home to Roost: *Swift 1st Ltd v Chief Land Registrar*' [2014] *The Conveyancer and Property Lawyer* 444; A Goymour, 'Mistaken Registration of Land; Exploding the Myth of 'Title by Registration' (2013) 72 *CLJ* 617, 628–29, fns 61–63.

[12] Goymour (ibid), 631.

[13] LRA 2002, sch 4, para 2.

[14] ibid, sch 4, para 3(3).

[15] ibid, sch 4, para 3(2).

the proprietor has by 'fraud or lack of proper care caused or substantially contributed to the mistake'; and secondly, where 'it would for any other reason be unjust for the alteration not to be made'.

The relevant provision to this effect is set out below:[16]

(i) the proprietor has *by fraud* or lack of proper care caused or substantially contributed to *the mistake*; or
(ii) it would for any other reason be *unjust* for the alteration not to be made. (Emphasis added)

Whilst it is often suggested that this measure provides only a narrow exception to registration certainty,[17] this optimism is not shared.

C. Mistake

What is a 'mistake'? This term appears to be understood as having a broad application. The expression is not confined to any particular kind of mistake.[18] It has been suggested that there will be a 'mistake' 'whenever the registrar would have done something different had he known of the true facts at the time at which he made or deleted the relevant entry in the register'.[19] This debated, if not confusing area, is not explored further.

D. Fault-Finding Alteration

While fraud is within the category of 'mistake', so is 'lack of proper care'. This latter concept patently involves a less onerous finding than the occurrence of 'fraud'.

There is uncertainty as to the suitable yardstick courts may impose to determine 'the care to be expected of the claimant'[20] in order to justify a fault finding being made. Does this provision require a level of audit of any registration proposition to be undertaken, including the existence of 'off-register' third-party dealings? It appears so.[21] In this regard, *Megarry & Wade* discusses the issue of contributory negligence in terms of its effect on any entitlement to an indemnification payment, following an alteration having been made.[22] The authors suggest that 'the relevant conduct will normally be that of the claimant's conveyancer, and the care to be

[16] ibid, sch 4, para 3(2) for the court powers. The registrar powers stated by para 5 are similar.

[17] See, eg, M Dixon, *Modern Land Law*, 9th edn (London, Routledge, 2014) [2.10].

[18] Goymour (n 11), 631–35. See generally S Cooper, 'Regulating Fallibility in Registered Land Dealings' (2013) 72(2) *CLJ* 341.

[19] See Harpum et al (n 6), [7-133]. See also Cooper (ibid) 358–59; E Lees 'Title by Registration: Rectification, Indemnity and Mistake and the Land Registration Act 2002' (2013) 76 *MLR* 62, 70–3.

[20] *Prestige Properties Ltd v Scottish Provident Institution* [2002] EWHC 330 (Ch), [2003] Ch 1, Headnote (1). See also *Balevents Ltd v Sartori* [2014] EWHC 1163, where the registrant made relevant statements to the registry without proper care and which were incorrect, leading to his registration.

[21] In *Walker v Burton* [2013] EWCA Civ 1228, [77], [96–99], the Court discussed the issue in terms of 'the appropriate standard of care'.

[22] Harpum et al (n 6) [7-143].

expected of the claimant may be judged by reference to the ordinary duty of care owed by a conveyancer in the conveyancing transaction in question'.[23]

Surely such perceptions introduce some form of modified constructive notice principles, as part of the legislative scheme?[24] Does (for example) the level of culpability differ where the party taking a title interest undertook his or her own conveyancing, as opposed to employing a professional?[25] This is not clear. Nor should it be forgotten that constructive notice principles are, at heart, an objective standard of professional conduct imposed by a court of equity in terms of proficiency required of trained conveyancers.[26] One hopes, of course, that the level of liability should not be as extensive as under the informal deed conveyancing system.[27]

E. Non-fault Finding

The ability to alter the register where it is 'unjust for the alteration not to be made' does not appear to have been ascertained to date.[28] Further, there is no guidance provided in schedule 4 as to how this ground operates. Taken at face value, a fault finding is not required, as this measure is intended to operate as an alternative to where fraud or lack of proper care can be made out.

The fact finder's attention is presumably focused on the individual position of the dispossessed owner or third parties, rather than the fact that registration has been achieved and is intended to be final in its effect.[29] Again, it is important to reflect that the rectification must occur 'unless there are exceptional circumstances which justify [the fact finder] … not doing so'.[30]

Lack of any detail in terms of what may (or may not) be grounds for an 'unjust' finding to be made creates a sense of unease for a Torrens lawyer. The following questions emerge. Surely such a finding will invariably be fact dependent? Property cases are habitually recognised as 'fact heavy disputes'.[31] One is reminded of the words of Deane J of the Australian High Court, admittedly in a different context, that fairness

[23] Harpum et al (n 6) [7-143]. Reference is made to *Prestige Properties Ltd v Scottish Provident Institution* [2002] EWHC 330 (Ch), [36], [2003] Ch 1, 16.

[24] *Rees v Peters* [1011] EWCA Civ 836. See Dixon (n 17), [2.10.2]; NP Gravells, *Land Law*, 4th edn, (London, Sweet & Maxwell, 2010) [8.1.3.3] offers an extensive treatment of this subject, arguing that the provision should be conservatively interpreted.

[25] Dixon (n 17) [2.10.2]. In *Baxter v Mannion* [2010] EWHC (Ch), an adverse possessor obtained title but it subsequently transpired that the required period of adverse possession had not run.

[26] AH Chaytor and WJ Whitaker (eds), *Equity A Course of Lectures by FW Maitland* (revised by J Brunyate, Cambridge, Cambridge University Press, 1936). At 119 reference is made to a 'highly trained adviser'. On the same page the Conveyancing Act 1882, s 3 is stated to have been an attempted codification of the ingredients of constructive notice.

[27] Dixon too argues for a restricted interpretation. See Dixon (n 17) 89.

[28] *Baxter v Manning* [2010] EWHC 573 (Ch), [2010] 1 WLR 1965; and on appeal, [2011] EWCA Civ 120, [2011] 1 WLR 1994. The findings here appear an odd use of this ground as they rely on a fault finding for overturning the registration. See criticism by Goymour (n 11) 639–40.

[29] *Walker v Burton* [2013] EWCA Civ 1228, [100]–[106].

[30] LRA 2002, sch 4, para 3(3).

[31] This expression was used by conference attendees and keynote speakers at the Modern Studies in Property Law Conference, Queen's University, Belfast, 5 April 2016.

looks to the 'formless void of individual moral opinion'.[32] The author struggles with any suggestion that, over time, it may become clearer in such a fact-dependent area, when it will (or will not) be 'unjust' for the alteration to be made without a hearing first taking place.[33] Such a lack of clarity has already been recognised.[34]

Nor, surely, can it be a given that it would be 'unjust' for an existing title holder to be dispossessed. After all, an alternative to rectification taking place is the award of an indemnification payment. The response to even that issue may prove to be highly fact specific.

As with the Australasian experience, the 'fraud' exception is not defined.

IV. WHAT DOES FRAUD MEAN?

Is there any justification for the fraud exception under the LRA 2002 and the LTA 1952 to have the same or similar meaning? Perhaps not.

A. Fraud under Australasian Torrens Regimes

The Torrens system was introduced into Australasia from the mid-nineteenth century, as a straightforward and transparent system of land registration.[35] As is well known, it was designed to overcome the perceived deficiencies of what, in Australasian terms, is known as the deeds conveyancing system.[36] By this term, we are referring to private conveyancing, with standard *nemo dat* principles[37] in operation. Thus, under such principles, title is no better than that of the predecessor's title, subject to issues such as the application of Limitation Act principles, and other known defences.

What does not appear to have been discussed in depth before is the juridical basis of the fraud concept as an exception to the proffered indefeasibility protection. The concept appears to have been uncritically embraced from early English registry experiments in the nineteenth century.[38] However, such a ready adoption requires further thought. Only legal interests can exist under a Torrens construct, and those are achieved by obtaining registered status. Other dealings, being informal, may have a construct in equity, but have no place in terms of Torrens registration.[39] It therefore follows that incorporation of this concept into a Torrens regime may not carry the same meaning, originating as it did from a non-Torrens background.

[32] See *Muschinski v Dodds* [1985] 63 ALR 429 (HCA), [9].

[33] S Cooper, 'Resolving Title Conflicts in Registered Land' (2015) 131 *LQR* 108, 118.

[34] Harpum et al (n 6) [7-135], fn 912. *James Hay Pension Trustees Ltd v Cooper Estates Ltd* [2005] EWHC 36 (Ch) is given as authority for this proposition.

[35] T Bennion et al, *New Zealand Land Law*, 3rd edn (Wellington, Thomson Reuters, 2009) [2.1.03].

[36] ibid [2.1.03].

[37] *Nemo dat quod non habet*, literally meaning 'no one gives what he does not have'.

[38] WMC Gummow, 'Equity and the Torrens System Register' in Grinlinton (n 5). At p 64, Gummow J (as he then was) discusses this in terms of the Yorkshire Registries Act 1884.

[39] Sir Garfield Barwick famously stated that the Torrens system is 'not a system of registration of title but a system of title by registration'. See *Breskvar v Wall* (1971) 126 CLR 376, 381.

B. A *Sui Generis* Concept

It is sometimes thought that Torrens fraud may be compared to 'common law' fraud.[40] However, this cannot be so. By operation of Torrens principles, loss is caused by the act of registration being conclusive. This is a point of contrast with general law principles for fixing liability, where reliance on a representation is invariably the causative event leading to a damages claim. An illustration may be the tort of deceit, or even what is sometimes referred to as 'fraudulent misrepresentation'.[41] By way of contrast, under Torrens regimes whether any representation occurred is incidental. The loss is caused by the registration event being decisive in terms of rights.[42]

What, then, are the ingredients required for a 'fraud' finding to be made under a Torrens statute?

V. INGREDIENTS OF THE TORRENS FRAUD CONCEPT

Our understanding of the fraud concept emanates from two Privy Council appeals from New Zealand. Although the opinions were delivered at the start of the twentieth century, they remain definitive for Australasian understandings of the 'fraud' construct.[43] On close examination, they show that the fraud ingredient is developed as a stand-alone, statutory construct.

A. Privy Council Dicta

First, *Assets Co Ltd v Mere Roihi*.[44] Here the Board stated as follows:[45]

> [The key provisions of the Land Transfer 1870 Act] appear to their Lordships to shew that by fraud in these Acts is meant *actual fraud, ie, dishonesty of some sort, not what is called constructive or equitable fraud*—an unfortunate expression and one very apt to mislead, but often used, for want of a better term, to denote transactions having consequences in equity similar to those which flow from fraud. Further, it appears to their Lordships that the fraud which must be proved in order to invalidate the title of a registered purchaser for value … must be brought home to the person whose registered title is impeached or to his agents … The mere fact that he might have found out fraud if he had been more vigilant, and had made further inquiries which he omitted to make, does not of itself prove fraud on his part. But if it be shewn that his suspicions were aroused, and that he abstained from making inquiries for fear of learning the truth, the case is very different, and fraud may

[40] Bennion et al (n 35) [2.5].

[41] In terms of New Zealand law, the issue is whether there was a misrepresentation of not. Innocence as to belief of the truth of the representation, or proof of an intent to mislead is irrelevant in terms of a liability finding. See Contractual Remedies Act 1979, s 6 (NZ).

[42] The issue of deceit may be applicable where fraud is pleaded by the holder of an unregistered third party interest, who may have received an assurance that their interest would be honoured, and therefore relied on that representation. However, the loss is still reliant on the occurrence of the registration event.

[43] Bennion et al (n 35) [2.5].

[44] [1905] AC 176 (PC).

[45] ibid 210 (Lord Lindley).

> be properly ascribed to him. *A person who presents for registration a document which is forged or has been fraudulently or improperly obtained is not guilty of fraud if he honestly believes it to be a genuine document which can be properly acted upon.* (Emphasis added)

This is a high degree of culpability. A fraud finding cannot be made if there is an honest belief that the presented document is genuine.

Then *Waimiha Sawmilling Co Ltd v Waione Timber Co Ltd*. Here the Board stated as follows:[46]

> If the designed object of a transfer be to cheat a man of a known existing right, that is fraudulent, and so also fraud may be established by a deliberate and dishonest trick causing an interest not to be registered and thus fraudulently keeping the register clear. It is not, however, necessary or wise to give abstract illustrations of what may constitute fraud in hypothetical conditions, for each case must depend upon its own circumstances. The act must be dishonest, and dishonesty must not be assumed solely by reason of knowledge of an unregistered interest. (Emphasis added)

Thus a fraud finding is not conditional on any finding of reliance. Liability is expressed in terms of a 'deliberate and dishonest trick'. This suggests not only proof of actual intent, but also a high level of culpability.

The standard of culpability evident in these statements appears to be in line with the *mens rea* ingredients required to establish fraud under criminal codes. In New Zealand, we have the offence of 'obtaining by deception or causing loss by deception', provided by the Crimes Act 1961, section 240. The key ingredients of the offence in sub-section (2) of this provision are given as:

> In this section **deception** means—
>
> (a) *a false representation* ... where the person making the representation *intends to deceive* any other person and—
>   (i) knows that it is false in a material particular; or
>   (ii) is reckless as to whether it is false in a material particular; or
>
> (b) an omission to disclose a material particular, *with intent to deceive any person*, in circumstances where there is a duty to disclose it; or
>
> (c) *a fraudulent device, trick, or stratagem used with intent to deceive any person.* (Emphasis added)

B. Comparison with the Fraud Act 2006

In the England and Wales (and Northern Ireland) context, the Fraud Act 2006 may be an interesting counterpart. The useful parts of 'Fraud by false representation' are defined in section 2 as follows:[47]

> A representation is false if—
>
> (a) it is untrue or misleading, and
>
> (b) *the person making it knows that it is*, or might be, *untrue or misleading*. (Emphasis added)

[46] [1926] AC 101, 106–07, NZPCC 267, 273 (PC).

[47] Fraud Act 2006, s 2 (England and Wales).

By this comparison, it is hard to see a distinction between the *mens rea* ingredients of such criminal offences and the Torrens fraud test articulated by the Privy Council.

C. Proposed New Zealand Definition of Fraud

The New Zealand Law Commission has recommended the enactment of a statutory fraud test be incorporated as part of a new Torrens statute. The amended proposed definition was introduced into Parliament 2016, and still awaits enactment[48] is as follows:[49]

> **6. Meaning of fraud**
>
> (1) For the purpose of this Act, other than **subpart 3 of Part 2**, **fraud** means *forgery or other dishonest conduct* by the registered owner or the registered owner's agent in acquiring a registered estate or interest in land.
>
> (2) For the purposes of **sub-section (1)**, the fraud must be against—
>
> (a) the registered owner of an estate or interest in land; or
>
> (b) the owner of an unregistered interest, if the registered owner or registered owner's agent,—
>
> (i) in acquiring the estate or interest had *actual knowledge of, or was wilfully blind* to, the existence of the unregistered interest; and
>
> (ii) *intended at the time of registration of the estate or interest that the registration would defeat the unregistered interest.*
>
> …
>
> (4) The equitable doctrine of constructive notice does not apply for the purposes of deciding whether conduct is fraudulent. (Emphasis added)

Again, this definition is similar to the mental ingredient required for the criminal offence in that it requires evidence of a dishonest intent.[50]

VI. LRA 2002 FRAUD INGREDIENTS

To the author's knowledge, the ingredients of fraud under schedule 4 of the LRA 2002 has not been the subject of any judicial discussion to date. *Megarry & Wade* certainly does not discuss the fraud concept in terms of schedule 4 powers.[51] Indeed,

[48] See www.parliament.nz/en-nz/pb/legislation/bills/00DBHOH_BILL68258_1/land-transfer-bill (accessed 22 November 2016).

[49] See www.legislation.govt.nz/bill/government/2016/0118/latest/whole.html?search=ts_act%40bill%40regulation%40deemedreg_Land+Transfer+Bill_resel_25_a&p=1#DLM6731032 (accessed 22 November 2016).

[50] An earlier iteration of this statutory definition has been criticised by the author as not clarifying or advancing what is argued by the author to be a confused understanding of the New Zealand Torrens fraud test. See R Thomas, 'Reduced Torrens Protection: New Zealand Law Commission Proposal for a New Land Transfer Act' [2011] *New Zealand Law Review* 715, IV.

[51] Fraud has been discussed in the context of mortgage execution, undue influence and misrepresentation. See Harpum et al (n 6) [7-134]–[7-139], [25-120].

only limited material touching on this issue has been found.[52] It may be surmised that 'fraud' is probably to be conservatively understood as an intention to deceive, although even this is not clear.[53] As with the Australasian fraud and (for the same reasons) the tort of deceit, misrepresentation (fraudulent or negligent) or other common law grounds for fixing liability cannot apply. This is because the event causing the loss is the registration event. However, unlike the Torrens test for registration, it is not clear that equitable principles can so easily be dismissed from the operation of the LRA 2002. Thus, it is tenable that the fraud test (whatever it may be) may include elements of equitable notice or knowledge.

VII. PRESSURE ON THE POWERS OF ALTERATION

The purpose of Torrens registration is to provide for certainty of outcome.[54] Thus, under such a construct, the contest may well be between two innocent parties, one of whom is dispossessed by a third party fraudster. Fairness of individual outcomes does not feature in terms of which of those contestants will be preferred as the registered owner.

Proponents of Torrens, such as the author, argue in favour of such outcomes as leading to predictability of the registration result. Under such a construct, the outcome may not be judged 'unfair' if the loser in terms of the registration contest is entitled to be indemnified for that loss—hopefully on a full and proper indemnification basis.[55] However, despite aspirational desires for such conceptual purity, the candid reality is that Torrens regimes are inevitably placed under significant pressure. If the outcome arising through application of such principles is seen as too harsh, the result has sometimes been manipulated by the appropriate decision maker to achieve fair results in 'hard' cases. This is illustrated next, in light of the Australasian (and other) Torrens experiences.

The discussion that follows focuses on two issues: first, an extension of the fraud exception well beyond its original Torrens conception; and secondly, development of what has become known in Australasian terms, as the *in personam* exception to indefeasibility, again arguably well beyond its original conception.

[52] M Conaglen and A Goymour, 'Knowing Receipt and Registered Land' in C Mitchell (ed), *Constructive and Resulting Trusts* (Oxford, Hart Publishing, 2010) 179–80 suggest that the fraud test may have a similarity to the Torrens fraud test. Under *Norwich & Peterborough Building Society v Steed* [1992] Ch 116, 134 the court held that the fraud had to be against the registry, and not against the prior registered proprietor. This was a decision under the 1925 Act. There is a suggestion that this judgment may apply to the LRA 2002. See MP Thompson, *Modern Land Law*, 5th edn (Oxford, Oxford University Press, 2012) 174.

[53] To date there seem to have been factual findings that certain actions are fraudulent without considering the necessary ingredients. See *Barclays Bank Plc v Guy* [2008] EWCA Civ 452. In *Lyus v Prowsa Developments Ltd* [1982] 1 WLR 1044, 1044, a constructive trust was raised to counter unconscionable conduct or fraud. *Peffer v Rigg* (1976) 242 EG 123, [1978] 3 All ER 745, [1977] 1 WLR 285, [1976] EWHC Ch 1 and *HSBC v Dyche* [2009] EWHC 2954 (Ch) more generously applied the fraud concept.

[54] Bennion et al (n 35) [2.1.03].

[55] This is often the fly in the proverbial ointment. See *Registrar-General of Land v Burmeister* [2012] NZCA 340 and the lower court reports in *Burmeister v Registrar-General of Land* [2011] 2 NZLR 678, (2011) 12 NZCPR 704 (HC). Here the payment made was significantly less than on an indemnification basis.

VIII. NEW ZEALAND APPLICATION OF TORRENS FRAUD

In New Zealand, at lower court level, the fraud test has been developed in an expansive manner, giving a greater expectation that the registration event may be overturned in 'hard' cases.[56] Indeed, it is a matter of some fascination that this has occurred, notwithstanding the two definitive (and binding) Privy Council authorities already discussed, which still (theoretically at least) define for New Zealand the required fraud ingredients.

This development is highlighted by what has proved to be the highly influential *dicta* of Salmond J[57] in *Waimiha Sawmilling*.[58] In his Court of Appeal judgment, Salmond J developed the liability finding as follows:[59] 'The authorities show, I think ... that *fraud is not limited to cases of actual and certain knowledge*.'

So far, no issue can be taken. However, the judge then continued as follows:

> *The true test of fraud is* not whether the purchaser actually knew for a certainty of the existence of the adverse right, but *whether he knew enough to make it his duty as an honest man to hold his hand, and either to make further inquiries before purchasing, or to abstain from the purchase, or to purchase subject to the claimant's rights rather than in defiance of them*. If, knowing as much as this, he proceeds without further inquiry or delay to purchase an unencumbered title with intent to disregard the claimant's rights, if they exist, he is guilty of that wilful blindness or voluntary ignorance which, according to the authorities, is equivalent to actual knowledge, and therefore amounts to fraud. (Emphasis added)

Such an analysis removes us from the need to make a finding of actual fraud. We instead move into the arena of when an 'honest man' will withhold his hand. What is an 'honest man'? Unsurprisingly, this may invite individual judges to impose what may amount to subjective criteria as to what an 'honest man' may think, and how such a man may act.

We also need to be aware of the persuasive *dicta* of Turner P in *Sutton v O'Kane*.[60] A portion of his judgment is set out below, giving, as it does, an acknowledgment (not often found) that the fraud test is *sui generis*.

The President stated as follows:[61]

> It is plain from the authorities that fraud under the Land Transfer Act is *sui generis*; as the word is used in that Act it means dishonesty, no more and no less. If it is dishonest, in the circumstances of the particular case for the registered proprietor with a clear title to refuse to recognise an unregistered interest, it will be fraud to do so.

What, then, is 'dishonesty'? In this regard, the President went on to state as follows:

> To discover, then, whether conduct amounts to fraud, it is necessary to inquire whether it is dishonest. This inquiry includes the question, what conduct is it, that must be called

[56] Mason (n 5) 4, 10.

[57] This is Sir John Salmond, author of the standard texts, *Salmond on Jurisprudence* and *Salmond on Torts*.

[58] See Bennion et al (n 35) [2.5], n 259. See in particular RP Thomas, 'Land Transfer Fraud and Unregistered Interests' [1994] *New Zealand Recent Law Review* 218, 226–27.

[59] [1923] NZLR 1137 (CA), 1175–77.

[60] [1973] 2 NZLR 304 (CA).

[61] ibid 321.

> dishonest? I must confess that though I had supposed that most men, and certainly lawyers of experience, would be able easily enough to define the essentials of dishonesty with some measure of agreement, I have found the notion of dishonesty more difficult to define with precision than I had expected ...

This line of thinking then enabled the President to re-word the fraud issue as an issue of 'honour':

> Here is clearly the idea of conduct forbidden by honour, not conduct discountenanced by the law; and I think that moralists may agree that while it must be regarded as dishonest dishonourably to deprive another of that which in honour is his, such dishonest conduct is sometimes for reasons of expediency deemed legitimate by the law, and is therefore countenanced by the civil law and left without penal consequences by the criminal code. (Emphasis added)

Thus, on a careful reading, fraud becomes 'conduct forbidden by honour, not conduct discountenanced by the law'. Indeed, it may be conduct 'for reasons of expediency deemed legitimate by the law'. The President continued in this vein:

> When an inquiry, then, is made, as to whether, for the purposes of the Land Transfer Act, the conduct of a registered proprietor is to be regarded as fraud, this is to be tested by the answer to the question whether that conduct is dishonest; whether it is dishonest does not always depend upon whether it is made legitimate by the law.

One must pause at this point and reflect. Is 'conduct forbidden by honour' a more certain test of culpability than the application of constructive notice principles operating under informal deeds conveyancing, intended to be overthrown by the Torrens system's introduction?[62]

This New Zealand development has not, however, been the Australian experience. That jurisdiction applies a more conservative application of the test,[63] despite earlier pressures to impose liability based on equitable constructs of fair dealing.[64] However, this has not necessarily led to a registered title being more secure against attack. Instead, this development has been accompanied by an expansive and uncertain development of the *in personam* 'exception' to indefeasibility. This is discussed next.

[62] See further Thomas (n 58) 230–31.

[63] See generally P Butt, *Land Law*, 6th edn (Sydney, Thomson Lawbook Co, 2010), [2 18] and fn 114. *Cassegrain v Gerard Cassegrain & Co Pty Ltd* [2015] HCA 2; *Bank of South Australia Limited v Ferguson* [1998] HCA 12, 192 CLR 248, 72 ALJR 551, 151 ALR 729. In *Ferguson* (as with *Frazer v Walker*), the competition was between a bank and a defrauded owner. In both, the bank's title to the land was recognised over the prior owner's by the application of Torrens principles. See also *Vassos v State Bank of South Australia* [1993] 2 VR 316.

[64] Gummow (n 38) 65 refers to the views of Dixon J in *Clements v Ellis* (1934) 51 CLR 217 that fraud had a more general meaning. In *Latac Investments Pty Ltd v Hotel Terrigal Pty Ltd* (1965) 113 CLR 265, 273–74, Kitto J considered that a species of equitable fraud involved dishonesty or moral turpitude could apply. In *Bahr v Nicolay (No 2)* (1988) 164 CLR 604, the High Court embraced the concept of 'moral turpitude'. See 614 (Mason CJ and Dawson J). At 645, Brennan J preferred to rely on the concept of equitable fraud. An analysis of these judgments is carried out in JG Tooher, 'Muddying the Torrens Waters with the Chancellors Foot?; *Bahr v Nicolay*' [1993] *Australian Property Law Journal* 1, 4.

IX. *IN PERSONAM* 'EXCEPTION' UNDER TORRENS REGIMES

First, what then do we understand by *in personam* exceptions to indefeasibility? This is probably best explained by returning to *Frazer v Walker*, where Lord Wilberforce opined as follows:[65]

> First ... [the principle of indefeasibility] in no way denies the right of a plaintiff to bring against a registered proprietor a claim *in personam*, founded in law or in equity, for such relief as a Court acting *in personam* may grant. That this is so has frequently, and rightly, been recognised in the Courts of New Zealand and of Australia ...

This explanation is unremarkable.[66] It cannot seriously be argued that the registration of a title enables the registrant to avoid personal obligations he or she may be exposed to in terms of contractual, tort or general law obligations.[67] There are, however, limits to this, as his Lordship recognised:

> Their Lordships refer to these cases by way of illustration only without intending to limit or define the various situations in which actions of a personal character against registered proprietors may be admitted. *The principle must always remain paramount that those actions which fall within the prohibition of ss 62 and 63 [of the Land Transfer Act 1952] may not be maintained.* (Emphasis added)

The last sentence is of paramount importance. It provides a litmus test by recognising that personal rights of action will not be acceptable if they offend the schema of the legislation. However, despite this Delphic warning, courts in Torrens regimes have extended the *in personam* grounds to what are argued to be impermissible lengths.[68] There has been some academic support for such a response.[69]

This discussion breaks down into two issues: first, patent confusion about when the *in personam* exception will apply, and indeed what it is; and secondly, where recovery is allowed based on a judicial finding that a continued pre-existing proprietary rights continues, unaffected by the registration event.

A. Cause of Action Issue

Australian courts, in particular, have not consistently applied the *in personam* exception, suggesting a lack of common understanding of what constitutes its core principles.[70] In *Mercantile Mutual Life Insurance v Gosper*,[71] the court considered that a 'personal equity' against a registered mortgagee could provide a basis for

[65] *Frazer v Walker* [1967] 1 AC 569 (PC), 585, [1967] NZLR 1069 (PC), 1078–79.
[66] See also Barwick CJ in *Breskvar v Wall* (1971) 126 CLR 376, 384–85.
[67] Mason (n 5) 16.
[68] Mason (ibid) 11 suggests that the *in personam* exception has been stretched, given the blunt reality of the fraud exception. See also Butt (n 63) [20 106].
[69] R Chambers, 'Indefeasible Title as a Bar to a Claim for Restitution' [1998] *Restitution Law Review* 126.
[70] A useful recent summation of present confusions is found in LB Moses and B Edgeworth, 'Taking it Personally: Ebb and Flow in the Torrens System's *In Personam* Exception to Indefeasibility' (2013) 35(1) *Sydney Law Review* 107.
[71] (1991) 25 NSWLR 32 (CA).

deriving a party of its registered status.[72] In *Tutt v Doyle*, in addition to a proven cause of action, Meagher JA opined that it was necessary to also show presence of unconscionability before a remedy could be granted.[73] Then in *White v Tomasel*,[74] a title was overturned based on a restitutionary basis, notwithstanding that, under Torrens registration principles, good title can be given if the registered dealing is void or voidable.[75]

The need for what has been described as a 'superadded requirement of unconscionability' affecting the mind of the registrant is particularly worrying.[76] Such a requirement appears unduly restrictive,[77] adding an additional complexity that is surely unnecessary, and has no statutory foundation. Ultimately one must surely return to the words of Lord Wilberforce in *Frazer v Walker*, that *in personam* remedies will, of necessity, operate as an exception to indefeasibility, but they cannot do so in a way that undermines principles of certainty of the registration result.[78]

How this may play out on a case-by-case basis may cause some uncertainty, but the need for recognised causes of action operating at general law is surely the necessary key foundational principle.[79]

B. The Continued Recognition of a Beneficial Property Interest Continuing after the Registration Event

Such a result will be unexceptional where the registered proprietor expressly takes title subject to beneficial interests. An example may be a change of trustee under an express trust or proof of breach of a fiduciary relationship, or where an estoppel against the freshly registered proprietor can be pleaded.[80] However, there is a more alarming tendency.

Some causes of action require findings that a beneficial interest in land survives the registration event, due to the operation of general unconscionability principles

[72] Here a mortgagee acquired its registered status under a forged mortgage. The worrying aspects of such an approach are commented on by D Sonter in his case note 'Mercantile Mutual Life Assurance Co Ltd v Gosper' 15 *UNSW Law Review* 546.

[73] *Tutt v Doyle* (1997) 42 NSWLR 10 (CA), 12.

[74] [2004] 2 Qd R 438 (CA).

[75] The issue before the court was the effect of a successful appeal which found in favour of the displaced prior owner, that determination being made after the registration event. See, however, a similar fact scenario in *Waimiha Sawmilling Co Ltd v Waione Timber Co Ltd* [1926] AC 101, NZPCC 267, where the Board found that, in the circumstances, the registration event was definitive, in the absence of a fraud finding.

[76] Butt (n 63) [20 104.1], fn 738.

[77] Butt (n 63) [20.104.1]. See also K Sanders, 'Land Law in the New Zealand Supreme Court', paper presented at Conference on the New Zealand Supreme Court: The First Ten Years, 2014, hosted by the Law Faculty, University of Auckland, available at https://cdn.auckland.ac.nz/.../Supreme%20Court%20 Conference/K%20S (accessed on 22 November 2016); TH Wu, 'Beyond the Torrens Mirror: A Framework of the In Personam Exception to Indefeasibility' (2008) 3 *Melbourne University Law Review* 672. See also M Bryan, 'Recipient Liability under the Torrens System: Some Categorical Errors' (2007) 26 *University of Queensland Law Journal* 83.

[78] Wu (ibid), 680.

[79] ibid 686, 689.

[80] ibid 686; other examples are also given.

affecting the mind of the owner of the newly minted title. However, such principles are explainable only in terms of non-Torrens concepts.[81] To reconfigure the point being made, such a finding is that an equitable, *in rem* entitlement survives the registration event. A ready example may be following property into the hands of third parties (who have achieved registered status) based on an *in rem* claim.[82] In essence, this is a remedies-based claim, justified on the basis of the continuation of a beneficial property right to the land, notwithstanding the registration event.[83]

An example concerning a Torrens regime is available outside of Australasia. In *Arthur v The Attorney General of the Turks & Caicos Islands*,[84] the Privy Council imposed liability on constructive notice principles,[85] imposed on grounds of unconscionability. In the words of the Board,[86] 'the recipient state of knowledge must be such as to make it unconscionable to him to retain the benefit of the receipt'.[87] In delivering the Board's advice, Sir Terence Etherton even described the necessary conduct as requiring a finding of 'equitable fraud'.[88]

The application of such principles (and the use of such language) surely stands in stark contrast to Torrens principles of registration certainty.[89] The result of such reasoning is indeed somewhat circular. We have a Torrens regime which (under the Board's understanding in *Arthur*) operates as a state guarantee of title regime, but subject to constructive notice principles![90]

Tracing arguments along similar lines have been recognised as untenable in terms of the Australian Torrens concept by the High Court of Australia.[91] The position in New Zealand is not clear. In *Equiticorp Industries Group Ltd v The Crown*,[92] receiver liability for Torrens titles was argued in terms of the five *Baden, Delvaux*[93]

[81] Thus a trustee will be bound by the terms of an express trust, notwithstanding a registration event.

[82] See generally J Palmer, 'Attempting Clarification of Constructive Trusts' (2010) 24 *New Zealand Universities Law Review* 113.

[83] See Wu (n 77) 680.

[84] *Arthur v The Attorney General of the Turks & Caicos Islands* [2012] UKPC 30, 2012.

[85] ibid. This was a strike-out application. For the purpose of the hearing, it was assumed as proven that the defendant knew that the property he had held was trust property.

[86] ibid. On the facts before the Board, the applicant appears to have acquired the property as a party to a fraud. Before taking title, he on-sold the freehold at a vastly inflated price. The pleadings allege the transfer was fraudulent and/or corrupt and/or a breach of trust.

[87] *Bank of Credit and Commerce International (Overseas) Ltd v Akindele* [2001] 1 Ch 437 (CA), 445 is given as authority for this.

[88] *Arthur* (n 84) [36].

[89] R Thomas, 'Knowing Receipt Reasoning Imposed for a Torrens Title Regime' [2013] *Restitution Law Review* 93. The point is teased out here in more detail. For a Torrens lawyer it is an anathema to interpret Torrens principles of certainty of the registration result in a way that makes those principles subject to equitable notice principles. The article argues that on the given facts, it was open to the Board to achieve the same result by a finding of actual fraud.

[90] Discussed at 96.

[91] See *Farah Constructions Pty Ltd v Say-Dee Pty Ltd* (2007) 230 CLR 89, [193]–[196]; discussed by Butt (n 63) [20 105], fn 747. This distinction has not proved to be easy for trial judges to apply: see *Super 1000 v Pacific General Securities* [2008] NSWSC 1222. See a discussion of subsequent inconsistent authorities by E Bant, 'Registration as a Defence to Claims in Unjust Enrichment: Australia and England Compared' [2011] *The Conveyancer and Property Lawyer* 309.

[92] [1996] 3 NZLR 586 (HC), 605–6.

[93] *Baden v Société Generalé pour Favoriser le Développement du Commerce et de l'Industrie en France* [1983] BCLC 325, [1993] 1 WLR 509.

criteria. There was no discussion of how such reasoning may have affected Torrens title principles.[94]

X. WHAT RELEVANCE DOES THIS HAVE TO THE SCHEDULE 4 POWERS OF ALTERATION?

As with Robert Southey's 1837 *Tale of Goldilocks and the Three Bears*,[95] we need alteration powers that are 'neither too hot, nor too cold, but just right'.[96] We need to strike a balance between flexibility in terms of achieving fair results, but in a way that does not cause confusion or uncertainty as to registration result. As discussed, under the schedule 4 powers, we have the ability to overturn registration where the result is 'unjust'. What does this mean? Argument has been given that this test is too open ended,[97] especially for an area of law where the disputes have been described as 'fact heavy'. There is surely a point at which too great an uncertainty as to outcome makes a mockery of any assertion that the LRA 2002 implements something like an 'indefeasibility' regime.

A. When Should a Party be Entitled to an Indemnification Payment?

Although not clearly expressed in the legislation, the LRA 2002 appears to provide for an indemnification payment to be made only as a consequence of registration being overturned or where a registered interest is lost.[98] Yet a registrant will have to incur litigation risk and 'out of pocket' expenses in successfully defending his or her registration result where a claim is made that the result is 'unjust' in terms of the schedule 4 grounds. Although it may be argued that a successful plaintiff may be entitled to court costs, this may not be awarded on an indemnity basis, and begs the question why the successful title holder should have to bear such a risk.

Surely, where a registrant survives a legal challenge launched on a non-fault basis but still incurs cost the result is at odds with any meaningful concept of guarantee of the registration result? The newly minted registered proprietor may even be unaware of the circumstances leading to an assertion that an 'unjust' result has occurred. In the words of Sir Anthony Mason, 'title to property is an area par excellence where a high degree of certainty is expected', where 'we need to be sure that any [future] remedy will generate not only better results [than an existing system], but also confidence in the system'.[99]

[94] Recently, in *Burmeister & Anor v O'Brien & Ors* (2009) 19 TCLR 539, [2010] 2 NZLR 395 (2009) 12 NZCPR 9 (extract), the recipient of the trust property was found to be fraudulent, and therefore receiver liability was determined on that basis. See [176]–[179] of the judgment.

[95] I Opie and P Opie, *The Classic Fairy Tales* (Oxford, Oxford University Press, 1974) 199.

[96] ibid 201.

[97] See also Goymour (n 11).

[98] LRA 2002, sch 8, paras 1, 3. This applies to rectification of the register, and the existence of a 'mistake'. LRA 2002, sch 4, para 9 enables the registrar to pay 'such amounts as he thinks fit' in non-rectification cases, but only where 'the registrar is altered'.

[99] Mason (n 5) 18.

B. New Zealand—the 'Manifest Injustice' Test

In 2010 the New Zealand Law Commission proposed that title registration be able to be overturned where a fraud finding could not be made.[100] This was on the basis that the registration created a 'manifest injustice'.[101] This development occurred, apparently, out of an inherent feeling that Torrens principles of certainty were too blunt.[102] In contrast to schedule 4 powers, this proposal includes guidelines. This is discussed next.

A Land Transfer Act incorporating this concept was introduced to the New Zealand Parliament in early 2016. By the bill, where the transaction is found to be either 'void' or 'voidable' at law, 11 grounds may apply for overturning a title which, on examination, favours return of the land to the dispossessed owner. This legislative proposal was subjected to academic criticisms which are not rehearsed here,[103] but which led to the key aspects of the proposal being altered, both at its second reading stage and in September 2016, following the bill being reported back to Parliament.[104] The draft legislation on this point, as it is presently proposed, is given in the appendix to this chapter.

In terms of a Torrens bias favouring certainty of registration result, three points of concern were raised in academic commentary. First, the bias in favour of overturning titles was argued to be inconsistent with the Torrens construct of finality of the registration event. In this regard, it was argued that conveyancers should be able to advise their clients with some confidence as to whether their title could be impeached. Where a clear answer to such a core question could not be answered with confidence, a client may determine to settle, rather than face litigation risk. This concern still remains under the wording of the bill, as reported back. However, the issue has been somewhat ameliorated by insertion of a new clause 57(3), which provides that an order for return of the land should only be made if a compensation payment will not provide adequate recompense. This appears to be an attempt to exclude claims from holders of registered securities who, arguably, have only a financial interest in the land.

Secondly, where a newly registered proprietor successfully defends his or her title, that party has to absorb his or her own, unrecoverable, out-of-pocket expenses.[105] This point has already been raised in terms of the 'unjust' ground operating under the LRA 2002. Rehearsing the same argument, it appears inherently wrong that a

[100] New Zealand Law Commission, *A New Land Transfer Act* (Law Com No R116, 2010) [R2].

[101] There is a difference between the two, but it is subtle. Indefeasibility does not apply where fraud can be shown. By way of contrast, the manifest injustice ground applies where there is no fraud and indefeasibility protection otherwise exists.

[102] Law Commission (n 100) [2.12].

[103] Thomas (n 50).

[104] See www.legislation.govt.nz/bill/government/2016/0118/latest/whole.html?search=ts_act%40bill%40regulation%40deemedreg_Land+Transfer+Bill_resel_25_a&p=1#DLM6731109 (accessed on 22 November 2016). See the commentary in the report on cl 57, which is now extended out to be cll 56–57B of the redrafted bill.

[105] The bill only allows compensation claims to be made as a result of a loss of land arising through the registration process, or actions of the registrar. See part 2, subpart 3 of the bill.

registrant not be fully indemnified where he or she is facing a challenge which is not based on that party's wrongdoing. As stated, the challenged party may not even be aware of the circumstances leading to the claim being advanced. Again, this concern still remains under the draft bill.

Finally, under the original drafting, the grounds for overturning the registration result were so broadly worded as to potentially make the fraud test otiose. This led to speculation that an easier path to litigation success would be for the dissatisfied party to assert that the registration result was 'unjust', rather than face the higher evidential burden inherent in any fraud allegation. To overcome this, clause 57(2) has now been inserted into the draft bill to make it clear that the existence of 'forgery or other dishonest conduct' disentitles an applicant from making an assertion that a 'manifest injustice' application can be advanced.

XI. CONCLUSION

Uniform to both the LRA 2002 and the Australasian Torrens regimes is the concept of state guarantee of title. However, what is the reality behind this 'imprecise' idea?

This chapter suggests that the simplicity of the Australasian Torrens construct is under increasing pressure to allow for hard cases. This is not to say that the Torrens system has not been phenomenally successful. However, it is incapable of incorporating nuanced approaches in terms of providing individual 'just' results.

By way of comparison, the LRA 2002 provides for a more even realised response to the issue of alteration of the register. However, those provisions lack clarity as to how the alteration principles should operate.[106] As with Goldilocks, we need a recipe that is 'just right'. Too little attention to detail may lead to too much uncertainty. The New Zealand Law Commission's 'manifest injustice' proposal may provide a useful launching pad for further dialogue in this regard. Further, if it is accepted that 'fraud' under the LRA 2002 is *sui generis*, the expression needs context. How are 'fraud' and an 'unjust' result meaningfully differentiated, one from the other? There needs to be a point of distinction or demarcation between the two concepts in terms of consequences. This could occur by an indemnity payment being available for out-of-pocket expenses where the 'unjust' allegation (as opposed to a fraud allegation) is argued and successfully refuted.

We return to the wonderfully rich prose of WB Yeats, introduced at the beginning of the chapter. Too inflexible an understanding of the registration result does not provide for a sustainable, long-term result. Too wide a discretion endangers registration certainty. Given Yeats's conclusions, do the views expressed here represents a sensible lack of conviction in terms of the present registration regimes or do they express a 'passionate intensity' giving rise to Yeats's corresponding conclusion?

[106] See also Goymour (n 11) [VI].

The Amended New Zealand Proposed Land Transfer Act Test of 'Manifest Injustice' as Presently Set Out in Clauses 57 and 57A

57 Court may make order only in cases of manifest injustice

(1) The court may make an order cancelling the registration of person B only if it is satisfied that it would be manifestly unjust for person B to remain the registered owner of the estate or interest.
(2) For the purpose of sub-section (1), the existence of forgery or other dishonest conduct does not, of itself, constitute manifest injustice.
(3) An order under this section may be made only if the court is satisfied that in the circumstances the injustice could not properly be addressed by compensation or damages, whether under subpart 3 or otherwise.
(4) In determining whether to make an order, the court may take into account—

  (a) the circumstances of the acquisition by person B of the estate or interest; and
  (b) failure by person B to comply with any statutory power or authority in acquiring the estate or interest; and
  (c) if the estate or interest is in Māori freehold land, failure by a person to comply with Te Ture Whenua Maori Act 1993; and
  (d) the identity of the person in actual occupation of the land; and
  (e) the nature of the estate or interest, for example, whether it is an estate in fee simple or a mortgage; and
  (f) the length of time person A and person B have owned or occupied the land; and
  (g) the nature of any improvements made to the land by either person A or person B; and
  (h) the use to which the land has been put by either person A or person B; and
  (i) any special characteristics of the land and their significance for either person A or person B; and
  (j) the conduct of person A and person B in relation to the acquisition of the estate or interest; and
  (k) any other circumstances that the court thinks relevant.

(5) The court may make an order under this section on any conditions that the court thinks fit (for example, an order relating to possession of the land).

57A Court must not make order if estate or interest transferred to third person

The court must not make an order under section 57 if person B has transferred the estate or interest to a third person, that third person acting in good faith.

12

How Should a System of Registered Title to Property Respond to Fraud and Sharp Practice?

GRAHAM FERRIS*

I. INTRODUCTION

WE NEED A better account of registration of title to land in England and Wales. The register plays a central role in a broader system of property law that includes background law of property, institutional elements such as conveyancing professionals, lenders and the Financial Conduct Authority, and insolvency law. The narrative generally accepted is that unregistered conveyancing was needlessly complex and expensive, and led to uncertainty in title, and registration was a technocratic reform that simplified, reduced costs and ensured certainty in title or—if that was not possible—then compensation for failure of registered title.

The ideal was commercial land markets that approached the transaction costs of government stock, as described by Anderson: 'Comparison of land transfer with the transfer of public stock—consols—began in the 1840s and became a staple.'[1] This rhetorical emphasis on low transaction costs, speed of transaction and security in reliance upon the register was continued in the Law Commission Report that led to the Land Registration Act 2002.[2]

Obviously this emphasis on the marketability of land, that is, land as exchange value, creates a tension with conceptions of land as specific property, valued for its use and expressive value.[3] Registration deals with this tension by the linking of

* Nottingham Trent University.

[1] S Anderson, 'Property' in W Cornish, S Anderson, R Cocks, M Lobban, P Polden and K Smith, *Oxford History of the Laws of England, vol XII. 1820–1914: Private Law* (Oxford, Oxford University Press, 2010) 190.

[2] Law Commission, *Land Registration for the Twenty-First Century* (Law Com No 271, 2001) para 1.5. See WR Cornish and G de N Clark, *Law and Society in England 1750–1950* (London, Sweet & Maxwell, 1989) 176.

[3] Historically, class conflict between aristocratic and middle class ideas about property provided a frame for the politics of reform: Anderson (n 1) 193; Cornish and Clark (n 2) 166–72; TE Scrutton, *Land in Fetters, or, the History and Policy of the Laws Restraining the Alienation and Settlement of Land in England* (Cambridge, Cambridge University Press, 1886). Currently the tension is more between home

simple tradeable ownership interests with complex beneficial interests via the trust as the mediating institution. This enables much complexity to be dealt with outside of the market, treating the specific property as a fund of value to be distributed behind trusts.[4] Interests behind trusts can be detached from the land and realised as money.[5] Law thereby enhances marketability and favours dynamic security at the price of putting at risk static security interests.[6]

Therefore, registration must deal with the opportunities for sharp practice and fraud in the land market it creates, and a narrative limited to reduced transaction costs is inadequate in this context. Furthermore, at a systemic level, failure to set out a clear position of principle on the issue is inadequate. Thus, we need a registered land analogue of the bona fide purchaser doctrine, because that doctrine managed to combine a principled narrative with prophylactic systemic effects.

The argument will begin with a short account of how the bona fide purchaser doctrine operated. Then two types of systemic issues will be addressed, one establishing the complementary nature of fraud and sharp practice to market systems, and the second seeking to identify system design features that counteract this predictable mischief. Only after this will the evidence for problems in the operation of the current narrative be reviewed, specifically that the lack of a principled account puts pressure on the judiciary to undermine the articulated aims of the registration system. Finally, brief proposals for reform will be introduced.

II. WHY IS THE INEFFICIENT BONA FIDE DOCTRINE IN UNREGISTERED CONVEYANCING IN CERTAIN RESPECTS SUPERIOR TO THE MORE EFFICIENT REGISTERED SYSTEM OF LAND TRANSFER AND OWNERSHIP?

Efficiency in land transfer was always a central aim of registration, and lies behind the desire for electronic conveyancing. Efficiency here does not mean the optimal distribution of resources, but the lowest possible transaction costs.[7] Transaction costs include time and fees expended on finding a suitable property; registration fees; legal fees; fees for surveys; and time spent visiting the property to view it and make inquiries of occupiers. Obviously not all of these costs can be reduced by title registration, or be quantified. Some costs, such as those imposed in finding a property or buyer, are independent of title investigation. However, land registration is almost certainly more efficient, in the sense of imposing lower total costs than the older

owners and mortgagees: L Fox, 'The Meaning of Home: A Chimerical Concept or a Legal Challenge?' [2002] *Journal of Law & Society* 580; L Fox O'Mahony, *Conceptualising Home: Theory, Laws and Policies* (Oxford, Hart Publishing, 2007).

[4] B Rudden, *The New River* (Oxford, Oxford University Press, 1985) 214; B Rudden, 'Things as Thing and Things as Wealth' (1994) 14 *OJLS* 81.

[5] *City of London Building Society v Flegg* [1988] AC 54 (HL).

[6] E Cooke and P O'Connor, 'Purchaser Liability to Third Parties in the English Land Registration System: A Comparative Perspective' (2004) 120 *LQR* 640.

[7] Efficiency as optimal distribution of resources is the evaluative criterion of much law and economics scholarship: R Posner, 'The Economic Approach to Law' (1975) 53 *Texas Law Review* 757.

system of unregistered conveyancing, which involved the investigation of title deeds and included the bona fide purchaser doctrine.[8]

Land registration has some element of state guarantee of title which provides certainty, and the law limits the potential impact of notice or its registered analogue,[9] thus simplifying and cheapening the process of title investigation. Official searches provide quick and very reliable information, with compensation for Registry error. Of course, overriding interests impair the reliability of the Register, and inaccurate entries which fail to warn of overriding interests do not generally result in the payment of compensation.[10] However, for purchasers, whether seeking to obtain an estate in the land for occupation or other use or as security over land, the Register offers a relatively cheap and secure means to ascertain whether the vendor or mortgagor owns the land. Finally, as noted above, registration is part of a larger system; most importantly, for dynamic security, all purchasers can rely upon the operation of overreaching, and mortgagees can rely upon the special priority accorded to acquisition mortgages.[11]

Thus, it will be assumed that registration is, at least whilst Land Registry fees are at relatively low levels, more efficient in transaction cost terms than unregistered conveyancing. It therefore seems perverse to argue that any aspect of unregistered conveyancing was superior. However, efficiency is not the sole relevant criterion for evaluation of property law. Two further criteria must be considered. First, whether the law offers a satisfying account of the justice of the system: does it offer a principled narrative of justification for its results? Secondly, does the law discourage fraud and sharp practice? This is not to dispute the value of efficiency, but to argue for the necessity of a richer evaluative frame.

The doctrine of the bona fide purchaser has at its foundation an ethical approach to the land market. Unregistered conveyancing protected legal interests through a strong principle of *nemo dat quod non habet*, which was robust against such frauds as forgery or identity theft. However, *nemo dat* could be a blunt instrument that left good-faith purchasers vulnerable to undiscoverable fraud or error. The bona fide purchaser doctrine was inherently concerned with a fair balance between equitable owner and purchaser:

> Such a purchaser, when he has once put in that plea, may be interrogated and tested to any extent as to the valuable consideration which he has given in order to shew the bona fides or mala fides of his purchase, and also the presence or the absence of notice; but when once he has gone through that ordeal, and has satisfied the terms of the plea of purchase for valuable consideration without notice … [i]n such a case a purchaser is entitled to hold that which, without breach of duty, he has had conveyed to him.[12]

[8] TJ Miceli, HJ Munneke, CF Sirmans and GK Turnbull, 'Title Systems and Land Values' (2002) 45 *Journal of Law and Economics* 565.

[9] The registered analogue to notice is occupation, as explained by *William & Glyn's Bank v Boland* [1981] AC 487 (HL) and entries in the Register; there is an analogue of the purchaser for value element of the bona fide purchaser in the Land Registration Act 2002, ss 29 and 30.

[10] *Re Chowood's Registered Land* [1933] 1 Ch 574 (Ch).

[11] *Flegg* (n 5); *Abbey National Building Society v Cann* [1991] 1 AC 56 (HL).

[12] *Pilcher v Rawlins* (1872) 7 Ch App 259 (CA) 268–69.

The ethical case is clear: equitable ownership will be protected as property rights are worthy of protection; however, if a purchaser has in good faith done all that it is reasonable to expect, then it takes free of the equitable right. An innocent property holder should not be deprived of its property, but neither should a good-faith market participant be forced to risk the loss of the purchase money. The purchaser's ethical claim is based on a good-faith purchase for value, and care in seeking out any hidden interest.

For current purposes, it is not necessary to distinguish the prudential 'duty of care' placed upon a purchaser and their good faith. Traditionally, the 'duty of care' was found in the doctrine of constructive notice, and the requirement of good faith was divided between the express requirement of good faith and aspects of imputed and constructive notice. Hence, instructing an agent not to report back on the existence of a defeasible equitable interest would be bad faith, and was made impossible by the doctrine of imputed notice. Similarly, constructive notice was capable of extending the necessary inquiries when circumstances raised suspicions—a Nelsonian denial was not safe, and this also has the effect of requiring good faith from the inquirer. Registration of title totally disrupted the details by which this division of labour and sharing of function between the concepts was made concrete in the law. For current purposes, it is argued that the presence of circumstances that suggest fraud or sharp practice may be taken either to engage the requirement of good faith or to extend the prudential duty of care.

Under this doctrine, static security is protected, even without active efforts to bring it to the notice of potential purchasers. However, in support of dynamic security, if a purchaser for value investigates title in an appropriate and rigorous fashion, and does not uncover the interest, then it takes free of the interest. Thus, it was always about the balancing of two legitimate interests. The distinction between legal and equitable interests was an arbitrary aspect of the doctrine; however, subject to this aspect, the courts tried to decide on the basis of principles of justice.

The same approach also generates a prophylactic incentive for equitable owners and purchasers. Equitable owners can protect their interests through acts that publicise their interest. Purchasers are driven by prudential self-interest to investigate title thoroughly and actively seek to discover any undisclosed interests—as failure to be assiduous risks taking subject to the undiscovered interest. The doctrine harnesses self-interest to the system aim of honest dealing; it gives all the relevant parties an incentive to take steps to avoid fraud and sharp practice.[13]

The monitoring role is assigned to the purchaser, as it is in the best position to carry out the function; it knows a transaction is envisioned, and the structure of our law enables the purchaser to take well-known steps to discover information about the property. The owner should be protected by right of ownership; nevertheless, it makes sense to encourage the owner to take reasonable actions that make its interest more secure. Providing mechanisms for owners to so protect themselves is an aspect

[13] In this, it resembles the approach taken to undue influence in *Barclays Bank plc v O'Brien* [1994] 1 AC 180 (HL); *CIBC Mortgages plc v Pitt* [1994] 1 AC 200 (HL); *Royal Bank of Scotland v Etridge (No 2)* [2001] UKHL 44, [2002] 2 AC 77. See G Ferris, 'Why is the Law of Undue Influence so Hard to Understand and Apply?' in E Cooke (ed), *Modern Studies in Property Law* (Oxford, Hart Publishing, 2007) 49.

of registration; the systemic challenge is to provide the incentives to all actors in the market to promote the honesty and reliability of the system.

III. WHY SHOULD WE EXPECT FRAUD AND SHARP PRACTICE TO APPEAR IN PRACTICE?

It has long been recognised that fraud is a field of human creativity, and we should expect new forms of fraud and sharp practice to develop in response to changes in the law and institutional environment:

> Fraud is infinite, and were a Court of Equity once to lay down rules, how far they would go, and no farther, in extending their relief against it, or to define strictly the species of evidence of it, the jurisdiction would be cramped, and perpetually evaded by new schemes which the fertility of man's invention would contrive.[14]

Legal thought recognises the always provisional and reactive nature of legal attempts to eradicate fraud as 'Fraud is infinite in variety'.[15]

More recently, economists have reflected upon the ubiquity and chameleon nature of fraud and sharp practice.[16] George Akerlof and Robert Shiller have argued that competitive markets produce fraud and sharp practice, or what they term 'phishing for phools', through normal market mechanisms: 'competitive markets by their very nature spawn deception and trickery, as a result of the same profit motives that give us our prosperity'.[17] Akerlof and Shiller do not produce any significant new empirical data or theoretical model, but they do argue that the dominant economics paradigm obscures the important issues of how markets generate harm:

> We believe it is wrong—as in the textbooks, and the standard mental frame of almost every economist—only to picture the healthy (ie efficient) working of markets, with economic pathologies depicted as due only to externalities and income distributions ... because it means that modern economics fails to grapple with deception and trickery. People's naiveté and susceptibility to deception have been swept under the rug.[18]

Their argument is that systemic and predictable 'phishing' should be seen as a normal product of free markets.

Akerlof and Shiller apply the central concept of economic theory—equilibrium—to phishing. Where people are weak-willed and susceptible to irrational forms of persuasion, are unable to judge their own best interests or are lacking in self-knowledge, businesses will see an opportunity for profit. Unfortunately, people are weak-willed, lacking in self-knowledge, unable to calculate their own best interests and susceptible to persuasion. Therefore, businesses exploit these profit opportunities and phish for phools, and are successful businesses as a result.[19]

[14] Lord Hardwicke as cited in PJ Baker and P St J Langan, *Snell's Principles of Equity*, 28th edn (London, Sweet & Maxwell, 1982) 538.

[15] *Reddaway v Banham* [1896] AC 199 (HL) 221.

[16] GA Akerlof and RJ Shiller, *Phishing for Phools: The Economics of Manipulation and Deception* (Princeton, Princeton University Press, 2015). Reviewed by G Ferris in (2016) 25 *Nottingham Law Journal* 162.

[17] Akerlof and Shiller (ibid) 165.

[18] ibid 164. Here 'efficiency' means optimal allocation of resources.

[19] ibid 1–9.

The narrative in *Phishing for Phools* places the cause of fraud and sharp practices on those engaging in fraud and sharp practices. The system will generate exploitative equilibria as naturally as it will generate beneficial equilibria. As Akerlof and Shiller emphasise, the beneficial equilibria have brought unparalleled benefits, but that does not negate the detrimental effects of the exploitative equilibria. The characteristics of individual agents, consumers or businesspeople have only a small intrinsic role to play in such an equilibrium analysis. However, as Akerlof and Shiller emphasise, our narratives are very important. Economists have a narrative of cause, and they place their emphasis on the phools, consumers who fail to live up to (or down to) the requirements of economic man—hence the emphasis on advice, education and improving decision making in regulatory discourse.[20]

What the standard economic accounts and the regulatory responses to identified risk miss is the central point, that the problems are systemic and not individual. Markets naturally produce exploitative equilibria. Thus, both legal and economic thought support an approach to fraud and sharp practice that is responsive and assumes that there is no a priori solution. Human ingenuity seeking to find the highest profits will always devise means to exploit the features of any fixed definition or institutional response to fraud and sharp practice. Therefore, the response has to be based on principle rather than on rules, and will be more effective the more it can align the incentives of parties with honest practice.

IV. WHAT INSTITUTIONAL FEATURES PRODUCE COOPERATIVE ACTION?

Douglass North makes a distinction between the institutional structure of social action and the organisations that act within and in response to that structure.[21] The distinction is not one of essence (for some purposes the Land Registry may be institutional, while for others it may be an organisation), but the distinction is essential for clarity of analysis.

The level of analysis will often determine whether the Land Registry is to be treated as organisation or institution. From the point of view of a lender seeking to ensure recovery of its debts through the use of a mortgage, the Land Registry is an institution. From the point of view of the legislature when framing the powers and duties of the Land Registrar, it is an organisation.[22] The key to classification is

[20] H McVea, 'Financial Services Regulation Under the Financial Services Authority: A Reassertion of the Market Failure Thesis?' (2005) 64 *CLJ* 413; L Fox O'Mahony and L Overton, 'Financial Advice, Differentiated Consumers, and the Regulation of Equity-Release Transactions' (2014) 41 *Journal of Law and Society* 446; Office of Fair Trading, 'Sale and Rent Back: An OFT Market Study', OFT1018 (2008), available at http://oft.gov.uk/OFTwork/publications/publication-categories/reports/consumer-protection/oft1018 (accessed on 7 October 2015).

[21] DC North, *Institutions, Institutional Change and Economic Performance* (Cambridge, Cambridge University Press, 1990) 4–5. See also E Ostrom, *Understanding Institutional Diversity* (Princeton, Princeton University Press, 2005) 3766.

[22] In this context, the lobby activities of Fortescue-Brickdale can be understood. See Cornish and Clark (n 2) 176; Anderson (n 1) 202, 219; A Offer, *Property and Politics 1870–1914: Landownership, Law, Ideology and Urban Development in England* (Cambridge, Cambridge University Press, 1981) 71–87. For levels of analysis see also E Ostrom, *Governing the Commons: The Evolution of Institutions for Collective Action* (Cambridge, Cambridge University Press, 1990); Ostrom (n 21).

asking, for present purposes of analysis, whether the Land Registry is part of the rules of the game being played or is a player in a game.

Organisations will invest in developing knowledge, understanding and expertise in response to the institutional structure they face.[23] The market will not naturally distinguish between socially beneficial investment and economic activity, and socially detrimental investment and economic activity. There will be an equilibrium responding to the possibilities of phishing for phools:

> The institutional matrix defines the opportunity set, be it one that makes the highest pay-offs in an economy income redistribution or one that provides the highest pay-offs to productive activity. While every economy provides a mixed set of incentives for both types of activity, the relative weights are crucial factors in its performance. The organizations that come into existence will reflect the pay-off structure. More than that, the direction of their investment in skills and knowledge will equally reflect the underlying incentive structure. If the highest rate of return in an economy is to piracy we can expect that the organizations will invest in skills and knowledge that will make them better pirates.[24]

Thus, if fraud and sharp practice will arise whenever it can produce higher than normal profits, then systems need to be designed to minimise profitable opportunities for such conduct.

We tend to think of the Land Registry as an institution. However, it is important to also think about it as an organisation—and what incentives it has to act in various ways. If it merely seeks to minimise costs, it may under-produce public goods. A simple example is the power under paragraph 10(1)(a) of schedule 8 of the Land Registration Act 2002 to pursue at law the person ultimately responsible for payment of an indemnity through their fraud. Viewed as an asset of the Land Registry or an income opportunity, only easy cases would be pursued, as investigation and litigation are expensive and hazardous. Viewed as a duty to police fraudulent conduct in the land market through civil sanction, all cases should be investigated with a view to enforcement whenever possible, on a test similar to that used by the Crown Prosecution Service. If this view is taken, the power will almost certainly be a drain on Land Registry resources, though it promises to deliver a public good.

North tells us what questions needs to be answered, but his analysis is more abstract than the level of analysis at which lawyers work.[25] We need an approach that can ask more detailed questions that are better suited to our purposes.[26]

Elinor Ostrom studied problems around cooperative action in the context of common pool resources (CPRs).[27] As common pool resources share characteristics with public goods, and the provision of an institutional frame that supports land

[23] DC North, *Understanding the Process of Economic Change* (Princeton, Princeton University Press, 2005) 59–64.

[24] ibid 61. See also G Ferris, 'The Path-Dependent Problem of Exporting the Rule of Law' (2012) 101 *The Round Table* 363.

[25] However, see B Chimpango, *The Development of African Capital Markets: A Legal and Institutional Approach* (London, Routledge, 2017).

[26] For one attempt to formulate a model for the land market see G Brennan, *The Impact of eConveyancing on Title Registration: A Risk Assessment* (Cham, Springer, 2015).

[27] A Clarke, 'The Life and Work of Elinor Ostrom' (2014) 22 *Nottingham Law Journal* 141.

transactions is a public good, some of this research can be directly applied to land law. Also, Ostrom was working towards a set of universally applicable concepts and methods, so we can consider common resources as her starting point rather than the limit of her theoretical ambition.[28] Ostrom found that a vital feature of successful common pool resource schemes was effective monitoring, sometimes through appointed officials, but always with a strong element of mutual monitoring.[29] Effective monitoring requires both opportunity and motivation. Investigation of title serves the function of tying self-interest to monitoring of other actors in the land market, hence the prophylactic effect of the bona fide purchaser doctrine discussed above. Good institutional design will preserve, so far as possible, this monitoring effect under land registration.

The Land Register makes public information about the land title, thereby facilitating discovery of false claims to title. The Land Registry has robust systems to avoid the entry of false information on the Register. Guaranteed title limits the need to investigate how an entry was obtained on the Register. This is a vital advantage of registration that lowers transaction costs. There is no need to investigate prior transactions, which is expensive and not optimal, as monitoring should focus on current practice.

Prima facie guarantee of title, subject to possible rectification, which in turn substitutes compensation for title guarantee in appropriate circumstances, is a paradigmatic feature of the English and Welsh system of land registration. The prima facie guarantee suffices for the vast majority of transactions, and is a central element in the efficiency of the system. Rectification, it will be argued below, could be made more comprehensible in practice, but the current legal position broadly reflects a good compromise between efficiency, justice, and the control of fraud and sharp practice. Provisions that deny legal effect to the registration of forged documentation would strengthen the position of a registered owner, but at the expense of imposing a potentially arbitrary cost upon good-faith purchasers. A system of prima facie effective title, subject to possible rectification, is in principle a better system, just as the bona fide doctrine was a better response to threats to static security than the *nemo dat* doctrine, as argued above.

The guarantee of title leaves some room for self-interested monitoring to play a beneficial role. Due to rectification, entries obtained through the use of forged documentation or identity theft can be altered.[30] Indemnity will not be paid to those who suffer loss from a rectification that was necessary due to their own fraud or lack of care.[31] Therefore, a person taking as purchaser has incentives to be on their guard against fraud.[32]

Therefore, many of the features of the current system of land registration are in line with institutional design features identified by Ostrom that are associated with

[28] Ostrom (n 21). Ostrom referred to this as the Institutional Analysis and Development framework.

[29] Ostrom (n 22) Ch 3.

[30] Land Registration Act 2002, sch 4.

[31] Land Registration Act 2002, sch 8, para 5.

[32] Not only fraud, of course, but discoverable overriding interests. The Land Registration Act 2002, sch 3, para 2 is obviously drafted to encourage self-interested monitoring and to protect a purchaser from undiscoverable interests.

successful long-term collaborative action.[33] Despite a lack of a clear justice narrative in land registration, there are important elements of land registration that can protect static security rights and counteract fraud and sharp practice, thereby providing materials for constructing a robust narrative about fairness in land registration.

V. NORTH EAST PROPERTY BUYERS LITIGATION

There was, in the recent past, a form of phishing known as the sale and rent back market.[34] People who were desperate to retain occupation of their homes, but whose occupation was threatened by debts secured upon the land by mortgages that had fallen into arrears, were offered a lifeline by businesses. The businesses offered to purchase their homes (at a significant discount), pay off any secured debts and rent the property back to the vendor for a guaranteed long period of time. The businesses advertised upon television and in national newspapers, and had professional-looking websites—and were seen by the vendors as legitimate businesses. However, this was a phishing market, and very many of the businesses were telling lies to obtain money which they could keep in exchange for promises they could break.

Central to the phish was the availability of cash, from loans made by lenders who would lend on the security of the acquisition mortgages taken out by the purchasers. In almost all cases, these loans could only be obtained if the purchaser agreed that no longer or more secure tenancy than an assured shorthold tenancy for six months would be granted. Therefore, central to the whole phish was the telling by the phisher of two inconsistent stories to the other two parties: the vendor was promised a secure long-term tenancy arrangement[35] and the lender was promised that the land would only be let on short-term insecure tenancies. When the payments under the mortgages were not made by the purchasers, the lenders enforced against the property and sought possession against the vendors. At this point, the vendors became aware that they had been phished, as they had lost the equity in their homes and had not received any security of occupation in return. The courts had to decide which of the two deceived parties—the vendors or the mortgagees—had priority.[36]

The law, specifically the equity jurisdiction, has a long tradition of protecting people who are vulnerable to being phished out of their property:

> On the other hand, to protect people from being forced, tricked or misled in any way by others into parting with their property is one of the most legitimate objects of all laws; and the equitable doctrine of undue influence has grown out of and been developed by the

[33] Some feature she identifies are limited in application to CPRs and there is insufficient space here to explore all of the relevant features: Ostrom (n 22) table 3.1, 90.

[34] For this and the next two paragraphs see Office of Fair Trading (n 20) Annexes A, B, K and L; the facts set out in *Redstone Mortgages plc v Welch* [2009] 3 EGLR 71 (CC); and the facts set out in *Southern Pacific Mortgages Ltd v Scott* [2014] UKSC 52, [2015] AC 385. The sector is now regulated by the FCA, but seems to evidence no activity: in a regulated form the market does not function.

[35] Sometimes only an assured shorthold for a short term was promised to vendors, though combined with an assurance of subsequent grants, with or without terms limiting rent increases for the subsequent grants.

[36] As noted by Behrens J in *Various Mortgagors v Various Mortgagees* [2010] EWHC 2991 (Ch) [24].

> necessity of grappling with insidious forms of spiritual tyranny and with the infinite varieties of fraud.[37]

In *Redstone Mortgages plc v Welch*,[38] an early case dealing with sale and rent back, the court ruled in accordance with this tradition, and held that the vendors were protected, due to the promises made to them by the purchasers. It was held that these promises, and the detrimental reliance upon them by the vendors, affected the estate in the purchaser's hands, and created an interest that had priority over the mortgages of the lenders. After all, the vendors had been in occupation throughout the transactions and remained in occupation until the lender sought possession under the mortgage. There was an obvious argument that the case concerned an overriding interest.[39]

One obstacle in the path of this conclusion was *Abbey National Building Society v Cann*.[40] *Cann* held that acquisition mortgagees had priority over any competing interest that arose upon acquisition of land. The law was derived from cases dealing with priority upon insolvency,[41] and gave a principled priority to purchase money interests—security interests that operate upon the very asset the secured credit made it possible for the insolvent entity to acquire.[42] *Cann* extended this purchase money security logic to competing interests other than other charges, overruling a line of cases concerned with priority disputes between tenants and mortgagees in the process.[43] Since *Cann*, the ratio has been extended in two ways:[44] it was extended to the contract, so that contract, transfer and mortgage were all treated as a single indivisible transaction in *Nationwide Anglia Building Society v Ahmed*;[45] and it was extended to an interest other than an acquisition mortgage in *Whale v Viasystems Technograph Ltd*.[46]

In *Whale*, the purchase money security principle was applied. The premium for the interest given priority (an underlease) provided the finance to obtain the asset (the headlease). Once the possibility of an interest other than an acquisition mortgage gaining *Cann* priority existed, the possibility of a clash of purchase money type interests arose in theory. The judge in *Redstone* in effect analysed the sale and rent back transaction as a clash of two purchase money interests: the vendor's interest and the interest of the acquisition mortgagee.[47]

[37] *Allcard v Skinner* (1887) 36 ChD 145 (CA) 183.

[38] [2009] 3 EG LR 71 (CC).

[39] Under Land Registration Act 2002, sch 3, para 2 and developed in R Crozier, 'A Question of Priorities: Mortgages, Sell-to-Rent-Back Tenancies and Overriding Interests' [2012] *Landlord & Tenant Review* 220.

[40] [1991] 1 AC 56 (HL).

[41] *In Re Connolly Brothers, Limited (No. 2)* [1912] 2 Ch 25 (CA); *Security Trust Co Appellant v Royal Bank of Canada Respondent* [1976] AC 503 (PC).

[42] Law Com CP164, paras 4.155–4.156.

[43] *Church of England Building Society v Piskor* [1954] Ch 553 (CA).

[44] In *Stroud Architectural Systems Ltd v John Laing Construction Ltd* [1994] British Company Law Cases 18 (HC) the ratio of *Cann* was assumed to apply to goods.

[45] *Nationwide Anglia Building Society v Ahmed* (1995) 70 P&CR 381 (CA). The point did not have to be decided because the ratio of the Supreme Court in *Southern Pacific Mortgages v Scott*, Collins and Sumption [85] thought *Ahmed* was correct and should be extended, generally treating the three legal events as indivisible. The majority rejected the extension of *Cann* to contracts in the normal run of events [121] and [123].

[46] *Whale v Viasystems Technograph Ltd* [2002] EWCA Civ 480.

[47] [1994] BCC 18 (HC) [63].

Redstone threatened the interests of acquisition mortgagees in sale and rent back cases, and the number of these cases starting to appear in the courts on possession hearings was increasing. A test case was litigated, involving numerous vendors and mortgagees to nominees for an entity known as North East Property Buyers.[48]

The North East Property Buyers litigation provides a clear example of phishing, fraud or sharp practice in the market. The technical resolution of the dispute was made through an analysis of the interest held by a purchaser under the contract to buy land. Due to specific performance, the purchaser obtains an equitable property interest of some type.[49] The Supreme Court held that this interest was not sufficient to support a grant to another of an equitable interest in the legal estate.[50] Therefore, there was no proprietary interest capable of being made overriding by occupation of the vendor upon completion under paragraph 2 of schedule 3 of the Land Registration Act 2002. Therefore, the vendors had to give up possession to the mortgagees.

Both Lord Collins and Baroness Hale expressed sympathy with the vendor, Mrs Scott, and other vendors who faced repossession after selling to nominees of North East Property Buyers.[51] Nevertheless, the law and, for Lord Collins at least, the policy behind the law, meant that the mortgagees must prevail.[52] However, neither substantive judgment argued that this was so because it advanced the principled aims of the registration system. The defence of registration was made in terms of efficiency through low transaction cost and certainty. Etherton LJ in the Court of Appeal had tried to defend the law in terms of principles, but ended up blaming the vendor victims in the process.[53]

Not only was no narrative of the principles behind registration given in justice terms, it was also asserted implicitly by Baroness Hale that registration has no such justificatory principles. She claimed that: 'It is important to bear in mind that the system of land registration is merely conveyancing machinery.'[54] She proceeded to identify three potentially conflicting and potentially aligned 'policies' at play: (i) the importance of protecting dynamic security; (ii) the protection of overriding interests without registration; and (iii) the accuracy of the Register (by which she seems to have intended its correspondence to the legal position prior to registration).[55] Baroness Hale described the first and third of these as 'public policies'.

Thus, *Southern Pacific Mortgages v Scott*, as the North East Property Buyers litigation was known in the Supreme Court, with its emphasis on public policy, provides strong evidence of a lack of a justice narrative in connection with registration.

[48] *Various Mortgagors v Various Mortgagees* [2010] EWHC 2991 (Ch); *Mortgage Business plc v O'Shaughnessy* [2012] EWCA Civ 17, [2012] 1 WLR 1521; *Southern Pacific Mortgages v Scott* (n 34).

[49] *Raynor v Preston* (1881) 18 Ch D 1 (CA).

[50] *Southern Pacific Mortgages v Scott* (n 34) [60]–[79] per Lord Collins and [104]–[112] per Baroness Hale.

[51] ibid [24] and [94] per Lord Collins and [95] and [122] per Baroness Hale.

[52] ibid [25] and [35]–[37] per Lord Collins and [97] and [122] per Baroness Hale.

[53] *Mortgage Business plc v O'Shaughnessy* [2012] EWCA Civ 17, [2012] 1 WLR 1521, [55]–[56].

[54] *Southern Pacific Mortgages v Scott* (n 34) [96].

[55] ibid [97].

It also provides evidence of a judicial reluctance to abandon the victims of fraud and sharp practice to the mechanics of the conveyancing machinery:

> I confess to some uneasiness ... Should there not come a point when a vendor who has been tricked out of her property can assert her rights even against a subsequent purchaser or mortgagee? ... Should there not come a point when the claims of lenders who failed to heed the obvious warning signs that would have told them that this borrower was not a good risk are postponed to those of vendors who have been made promises that the borrowers cannot keep?[56]

In this passage, the arguments seem to be directed to issues of fairness rather than efficiency. However, Baroness Hale's judgment offers no solutions for the problems felt to lie in a technocratic system which is unable to moderate its response to fraud or sharp practice in order to fulfil 'one of the most legitimate objects of all laws' by protecting the victims of trickery, cajolery or bullying.[57]

VI. *MACLEOD v GOLD HARP PROPERTIES LTD*

Priorities and fraud or sharp practice came up again in the case of *MacLeod v Gold Harp Properties Ltd*.[58] Once again, a businessman, Mr Ralph Snr, sought to phish for phools and acquire valuable property without having to reach an agreement with the owners nor pay them a market price:

> On the judge's findings—which indeed reflect his [Mr Ralph Snr's] own candid admissions in evidence—he orchestrated a sequence of events which he hoped would enable him to acquire the roof space without having to make any payment to the claimants. The judge found that Mr Ralph was aware that 'the claimants ... and their agents were somewhat unworldly folk, not well attuned to defeating attempts to take their property'.[59]

The property desired was the third floor of a house in London, and subject to two long leases which divided the floor into two halves.[60] The tenants spent a lot of time in Africa, and relied upon their local agents and attorneys, Mr Gibbons and Mr MacLeod, to manage their interests in the UK. The landlord, Mr Ralph Snr, was a property developer who had previously acquired both the freehold and the leasehold interests in the ground and first floors of the property. He planned to forfeit the leases for non-payment of ground rent and then to grant a new lease to a nominee, who would pass it on to another nominee, who would pass it on to Gold Harp—a company owned and controlled by Mr Ralph Snr. The first stage was to transfer the freehold to Mr Ralph Jnr, who became entitled to the ground rent and whose address was unknown to the leaseholders; it was found by the judge that Mr Ralph Jnr would act upon the direction of Mr Ralph Snr.

Ground rent was not paid on time, and bailiffs were instructed to make a formal re-entry. However, this move was premature. The ground rent was delivered to the

56 ibid [122] per Hale.
57 *Allcard v Skinner* (1887) 36 ChD145 (CA) 183.
58 *MacLeod v Gold Harp Properties Ltd* [2014] EWCA Civ 1084, [2015] 1 WLR 1249.
59 ibid [5].
60 This and the next three paragraphs are a summary of *Gold Harp* (ibid) [1]–[12].

address of Mr Ralph Snr before the leases became liable to forfeiture, but was not accepted in payment or passed on to Mr Ralph Jnr. The judge found this tender to be effective, therefore there had been no forfeiture of the leases.

Mr Ralph Jnr made a statutory declaration declaring re-entry by bailiffs on a date that would have justified forfeiture for non-payment of ground rent. Three days later he sent the declaration, and a letter in support, to the Land Registry, together with an application to close the two leasehold titles. The Land Registry accepted these documents as valid. Therefore, the Registry closed the substantive title entries for the leasehold titles and removed the notice of the leases from the freehold title. As a result, the Register showed a third floor unencumbered by any leases at this point. Mr Ralph Jnr then granted a long lease to a nominee of Mr Ralph Snr, which nominee assigned to a second nominee, which assigned to Gold Harp. Although the original grant and each assignment recorded purchase monies, the judge found that no money had changed hands. The grant and subsequent assignments were recorded on the Register, a new substantive title for the long lease granted was created and the lease was noted on the freehold title.

The judge found that Mr Ralph Snr was guilty of sharp practice but not fraud. However, the closures of the titles of the tenants were mistakes, as was the removal of the entries on the leases schedule to the freehold. There had been no forfeiture. Therefore, he ordered the Register to be rectified, under the powers given to the court by schedule 4 of the Land Registration Act 2002.[61] This raised the issue of the priority between the restored leases and the newly granted lease. At the time of the grant there had been no adverse entry, so if the purchaser could rely upon the Register then the new lease should be given priority. However, if the new lease was given priority over the older leases, then the act of rectification was futile, as the new lease would effectively retain all the value. The judge ordered that the restored leases should be given priority over the new lease, in effect rendering the new lease valueless.[62]

Both the judge and the Court of Appeal ignored the impact of the finding that no valuable consideration had been paid for the new lease upon grant or upon assignment. Therefore, section 29 of the Land Registration Act 2002 did not apply, and it was section 28 that governed priorities.[63] The point was noticed late and not argued, and the case was resolved through the interpretation of paragraph 8 of schedule 4 of the Land Registration Act 2002, which reads:

> **Rectification and Derivative Interests**
>
> The powers under this schedule to alter the register, so far as relating to rectification, extend to changing for the future the priority of any interest affecting the registered estate or charge concerned.

[61] ibid [26].

[62] The problem is closely analogous to one analysed in A Goymour, 'Mistaken Registrations of Land: Exploding the Myth of "Title by Registration"' (2013) 72 *CLJ* 617. See also A Goymour, 'Resolving the Tension between the Land Registration Act 2002's "Priority" and "Alternation" Provisions' [2015] *The Conveyancer and Property Lawyer* 253.

[63] *Gold Harp* (n 58) [10], [15], [18], and [34].

The argument revolved around what was intended by 'changing for the future the priority'.

If the words prohibited affecting priority obtained prior to rectification, then the new lease would keep its priority obtained at a date when the old leases were not protected by any entry on the Register. 'For the future' would mean that nothing of value was gained through rectification, merely that subsequent encumbrances would take subject to the old leases. This construction would uphold the interests of anyone who relied upon the Register—even a person who deliberately engineered the situation in order to rely upon the Register through sharp practice.[64] In *Gold Harp*, the Court of Appeal, in line with legal developments in the decisions of the deputy adjudicators of the Land Registry, construed the words narrowly,[65] and upheld the judge's order that gave priority to the old leases over the new lease.

Gold Harp thus extended the *ratio* of the earlier case law, and in order to do so imposed a somewhat strained interpretation of the statutory words. To make the alteration of the Register effective, it was necessary to have the power to alter priorities between derivative interests—the old leases and the new lease.[66] The words 'for the future' were read as merely preventing the retrospective arising of any cause of action from actions taken by the derivative interest holder during the period of time the Register was incorrect.[67]

Underhill LJ justified the substance of the decision in three points. First, consistency of treatment within the registration scheme: that priority between derivative interests that arise upon alteration of the register should be treated in the same way as priority issues are resolved when an owner of a registered title and a derivative interest holder are in conflict, as in *Argyle Building Society v Hammond*.[68] Secondly, that registered title is not absolutely indefeasible as rectification is possible. Thirdly, that schedule 4 allows a fair balance between competing interests to be struck, and the right to an indemnity can compensate an interest holder who loses.[69]

As Goymour notes, this account of the reasons behind the law is lacking; registration requires a principled narrative:

> From a presentational perspective, it is schizophrenic and misleading for the LRA 2002 to make promises of title security and priority in the main body of the Act, but for those promises to be nullified via its alteration provisions (as expansively interpreted by the courts), which are sparse on detail and less visibly positioned within the Acts schedules.[70]

However, the difficulty is less in the drafting of the Act than the failure to articulate the disparate aims of the system. The law rightly safeguards static security as well as dynamic security, and the judiciary is rightly unwilling to allow practitioners of sharp practice and fraud to exploit title security that is provided as a public good to those involved in the land market.

[64] Compare *Midland Bank Trust Co Ltd v Green* [1981] AC 513 (HL).

[65] *Ajibade v Bank of Scotland plc* (Ref 2006/0163/0174) *Stewart v Lancashire Mortgage Corpn Ltd* (Ref 2009/86) *Knights Construction (March) Ltd v Roberto Mac Ltd* [2011] 2 EGLR 123.

[66] *Gold Harp* (n 58) [92]–[96].

[67] ibid [96].

[68] ibid [97]; *Argyle Building Society v Hammond* (1985) 49 P & CR 148 (CA).

[69] Although presumably not in *Gold Harp*.

[70] Goymour, 'Resolving the Tension' (n 62) 265.

Both Goymour and Baroness Hale present this tension as one between general property law and registration.[71] In the context of alteration and rectification of the Register, it might be argued that judicial developments mean that it is the general law that is dominant. But as Goymour suggests, we will be better served by an integration of two aspects of one system.[72] However, this cannot be done whilst registration rhetoric adheres to an exclusive focus on dynamic security justified by appeals to efficiency. Judges are unwilling to permit phishers and fraudsters to prevail, and this judicial instinct is correct. In short, lack of an articulated justice principle in justifications of registration combined with judicial hostility to fraud and sharp practice are putting pressure on such concepts as statutory title. The pressure on statutory title and the reliability of the Register suggests that an exclusive focus upon efficiency is not only inadequate as a narrative, but is also untenable. The demands of static security and the justice of protecting people from fraud and sharp practice are proving too strong.

There is no inherent reason why registration should pretend it can ignore the ethical quality of the users of the registration system, and such a posture has not been adopted universally:

> As far as the powers of rectification are concerned ... rectification should be available whenever the register does not accurately reflect the title to the land according to the otherwise established rules of land law ... and rectification would be just in all the circumstance (in particular if it is shown that there has been fraud in the obtaining of an entry in the register, or if the transferee or grantee lacked good faith or did not give value).[73]

Property law has to deal with situations in which both parties may be innocent of any wrong. Registration seems to offer a technocratic neutral arbiter between the innocent, but, because it imposes priority without taking into account circumstances and conduct, only at the cost of being an arbitrary arbiter. Therefore, there is need to recognise a central role for rectification. As Simon Cooper argues: 'The inability of the vesting rule to distinguish the meritorious from unmeritorious indicates the desirability of a liberal regime for correction which possesses the sophistication to undertake a more sensitive assessment of competing priority claims.'[74] Where there is misconduct, the protection of victims and pursuit of malefactors are ends that justify higher transaction costs if necessary.

VII. *SWIFT 1ST LTD v THE CHIEF LAND REGISTRAR*

Swift 1st Ltd v The Chief Land Registrar concerned the aftermath of fraudulent charges registered over property belonging to Mrs Rani, who was the registered proprietor in occupation throughout the relevant events.[75]

[71] Goymour, 'Mistaken Registrations of Land' (n 62) 649–50; Goymour, 'Resolving the Tension' (n 62) 265–66; *Southern Pacific Mortgages v Scott* (n 34) [96].

[72] Goymour, 'Mistaken Registrations of Land' (n 62) 650.

[73] Law Commission, *Third Report on Land Registration* (Law Com No 158, 1987) para 3.6.

[74] S Cooper, 'Regulating Fallibility in Registered Land Titles' (2013) *CLJ* 341, 367.

[75] *Swift 1st Ltd v The Chief Land Registrar* [2015] EWCA Civ 330. The facts summarised in the following two paragraphs are taken from the report of the first instance judgment, [2014] EWHC 4866 (Ch) [45]–[63].

The fraudsters obtained personal information about and personal documents of Mrs Rani, and applied through a broker for a mortgage. Using the same means, they did the same with Swift, a second lender, who redeemed the first mortgage. This phish earned some £60,000. Although the report does not give details of the methods used on the first occasion, we can assume they were similar on both occasions. The fraudsters almost certainly knew what would be required from them by the lender, and prepared accordingly. No one visited the property and no one met with Mrs Rani, which greatly simplified the fraud.

Several telephone numbers were provided, one of which was a landline, but not to the property. Swift telephoned the landline number. The telephone was answered by a young woman (apparently, over the telephone, younger than Mrs Rani), who had the required personal details, and enough knowledge of the transaction to pass the standard interrogation. A copy of a debit card with a signature had been provided, but the signature on the card bore no resemblance to the one on the mortgage deed. She was not asked about the discrepancy in the signatures, presumably as it did not form part of the standard script. Neither the lender not the mortgage broker employed a conveyancer, presumably to save the cost. The judge held that the precautions taken by Swift met the industry standard at the time of the fraud, and that those standard were not careless.[76]

Swift accepted that there had been a fraud and that their charge was based on a forged document, and therefore the Register should be rectified by the removal of the charge. Therefore, they sought an indemnity for their loss, under schedule 8 of the Land Registration Act 2002, and the Land Registrar opposed them. The Registry argued that Swift had suffered no loss when their charge had been removed from the Register. This was on the basis that Mrs Rani always had an overriding interest in the property free of the charge, or an overriding interest to rectification. Therefore, following *Re Chowood's Registered Land*,[77] the alteration of the Register did not change the situation, as Swift never had a valid claim under the charge.[78] As both parties accepted this logic, that Mrs Rani had an overriding interest through her occupation and right to rectification,[79] the case turned upon the construction of paragraph 1 of schedule 8, in particular paragraph 1(2)(b), which reads:

> The proprietor of a registered charge claiming in good faith under a forged disposition is, where the register is rectified, to be regarded as having suffered loss by reason of such rectification as if the disposition had not been forged.

The point of construction was tortuous, and involved the Court of Appeal wrestling with the difference between alteration and rectification, and when the *Re Chowood*

[76] [2014] EWHC 4866 (Ch) [55] and [61].

[77] See n 10 above.

[78] *Swift* (n 75) [20].

[79] ibid [37]. However, if the right to rectification founds the overriding interest, then it seems to arrive too late to be effective and there is nothing to rectify until the charge is entered on the register: see M Dixon, 'A Not So Conclusive Title Register?' (2013) 129 *LQR* 320, 323; E Lees, '*Richall Holdings v Fitzwilliam: Malory v Cheshire Homes* and the LRA 2002' (2013) 76 *MLR* 924, 932; E Cooke, 'Chickens Come Home to Roost' (2014) 78 *The Conveyancer and Property Lawyer* 444, 447, fn 21; E Lees, 'Indemnity and the Land Registration Act 2002' (2014) 73 *CLJ* 250, 252; P Milne, 'Guarantee of Title and Void Dispositions: Work in Progress' (2015) 79 *The Conveyancer and Property Lawyer* 356, 362–63.

principle should apply;[80] whether loss and prejudice are synonyms or overlapping terms; the statutory intention behind the provision, and specifically whether it was exclusively directed at reversing the effects of *A-G v Odell*;[81] and whether the decision that a person taking under a forged disposition took only a bare legal title upon registration of the disposition in *Malory Enterprises Ltd v Cheshire Homes (UK) Ltd* was *per incuriam*.[82] Eventually paragraph 1(2)(b) was given a reading that entitled Swift to an indemnity by deeming it had suffered a loss by reason of the rectification.

If the courts are willing to overturn guarantees of statutory title or priority to counteract the effects of fraud, then it is important that indemnity be available to compensate for the consequences of such alterations of the register.[83] Therefore, *Swift* is to be welcomed in principle, although resting the decision on the deeming provisions of paragraph 1(2)(b) leaves other potential casualties of rectification vulnerable.[84] It would be preferable for a broader and less arbitrary rule to be established.

However, the approach to industry standards, and the acceptable standards of inquiry by lenders, falls short of what is systemically desirable for monitoring by lenders of other participants in the land market. An industry standard, given the existence of phishing industries as a natural feature of markets, must be subject to critical scrutiny. If an industry decides to enjoy lower operating costs by not employing conveyancers, thereby accepting increased risk of fraud, then that industry should bear the costs of the fraud it risked. If the Land Registry fee is an insurance premium, then it is universal, compulsory and not adjusted for risk profile.[85] Therefore, it is susceptible to free-rider problems.

As has been argued above, the land market depends upon self-protective monitoring by participants in the market. Lenders, as organisations, will invest strategically. If monitoring—or, as we usually term it, investigation of title—is thought to be necessary, then they will invest in people and systems to reduce fraud. If all lenders are investing in such activity, then no competitive disadvantage is incurred. If some lenders reduce their anti-fraud efforts and rely instead upon a compulsory insurance system, they gain a competitive advantage by free riding. As more lenders realise the competitive advantage of free riding, the burden on those not free riding rises and the pressure to free ride increases. A phishing equilibrium will be reached, and the public good of an honest land market will be undersupplied. Which returns us

[80] See n 10 above; if the principle applied before it was determined whether rectification had taken place, which requires the alteration to affect a registered proprietor's title prejudicially, it might mean there was no prejudice and therefore no rectification, merely an alteration, and therefore no right to indemnity could arise: see Land Registration Act 2002, sch 4, para 1(b) and sch 8, paras 11(2) and 1(1)(a).

[81] *A-G v Odell* [1906] 2 Ch 47 (CA).

[82] *Malory Enterprises Ltd v Cheshire Homes (UK) Ltd* [2002] EWCA Civ 151, [2002] Ch 216.

[83] M Dixon, 'Land Registration and Time Travel' [2014] *The Conveyancer and Property Lawyer* 189, 191; M Dixon, 'Rectification and Priority: Further Skirmishes in the Land Registration War' (2013) *CLJ* 207, 213; Lees, 'Indemnity' (n 79) 253.

[84] Milne (n 79) 364; Cooke (n 79) 447.

[85] As forcefully put by Lees, 'Indemnity' (n 79) 253, 'confidence in the register is ... the entire point of the new registration system. By paying your fee, and placing your faith in the Land Registry, they pay when you lose out ... The Land Registry fee can be considered, in effect, an insurance premium'.

to the concerns expressed by Baroness Hale: 'Should there not come a point when the claims of lenders who have failed to heed the obvious warning signs that would have told them that this borrower was not a good risk are postponed?'[86] *Swift* represents a damaged compromise. The court should have and did find rectification and loss that justified indemnity. However, the approach taken to care may have been overly influenced by assumptions that industry standards reflect some public interest, because markets naturally incline towards efficiency. This neglects the need to actively maintain honest markets and dangers posed by the phishing equilibrium.

VIII. CONCLUSIONS

Land registration cannot be reduced to the single objective of lowering transaction costs at the cost of static security and principles of justice. The system has a fundamental interest in the protection of static security, and the judiciary has a strong impulse towards opposing egregious misconduct. The problems the case law is grappling with are generated by the presence of fraud and sharp practice, and these activities are never going to go away because markets produce phishing equilibria as effectively as they produce social benefits. Our institutional designs—the law including the law of land registration, the Land Registry, professional conveyancers, the tribunal and court system—are the foundations of our land market and all elements need to be responsive to threats from phishing to good-faith participants in the market.

The cases reviewed demonstrate that there is a tension within our system. Land registration is seen as unprincipled and technocratic. It is not obvious how it embodies principles of protection for static security and institutional guards against fraud and sharp practice. The lack of a principled narrative for registered land is productive of hard cases, as solutions for injustice are sought outside the land registration scheme.[87]

At the same time, at a deeper level of analysis, we neglect real systemic problems, partly because our law is mediated through very complex and somewhat opaque statutory provisions, and partly as a residual effect of rhetorical attacks on unregistered conveyancing. Those attacks led to the establishment of a system of land registration that is almost certainly better than the old system. However, they also obscured the systemic importance of the doctrine of the bona fide purchaser: by harnessing self-interest to monitoring and organisational investment in fraud prevention, it helped maintain a public good, an honest land market.

A narrative is a way to understand something. It provides a frame for interpretation and action. In property law, both a positive and a negative principle are needed. Land registration lacks a convincing narrative, and to remedy this inadequacy we should start by declaring a principle that land registration exists to protect the interests of good-faith purchasers for valuable consideration, and invite the courts to give substantive content to good faith and valuable consideration. Articulation of this

[86] *Southern Pacific Mortgages v Scott* (n 34) [122].

[87] As exemplified by *Malory Enterprises* (n 82).

positive principle might also help to draw attention to features of land registration that already serve this end. This narrative is not merely rhetorical, but offers a means to develop the law in a principled manner. This is our positive principle.

We should declare that fraud and sharp practice will be met by disfavour, that the law is biased against dishonestly and oppression. Therefore, attempts to use the system for dishonest or oppressive purposes will be opposed and sanctioned. At first, the content of dishonesty and oppression will be informed by our existing law: forgery is dishonest, but so are knowing misrepresentations; duress and undue influence of protected categories of people are oppressive, but sometimes the very terms of an agreement may be so one-sided they should lead to protection being extended to people who would not normally be protected.[88] In time, specific mischiefs in the land market may lead to novel legal response—as fraud is protean, a power of novel response is necessary. As part of the enactment of our negative principle, the Land Registry should be subjected to a duty to pursue fraudsters whose schemes lead to rectification and indemnity, not merely to recover money paid out, but as part of the sanctioning system.

The incentive of lenders to rigorously seek out fraud and sharp practice should be reviewed with an eye to the need the land market has for lenders to be vigilant. Title guarantee and indemnity are good principles for land registration. There is sense in awarding purchase money lenders a higher priority than other lenders, including those whose interests and security may pre-date that of the purchase money lender. Overreaching is a necessary mediator between specific property and property as wealth. However, we may have neglected to consider the cumulative effects of all of these individually defensible legal protections. If lenders are overly secure from the hazards of fraud, then they will be unwilling to bear the necessary costs of maintaining an honest land market.

[88] See, eg *Credit Lyonnais Bank Nederland v Birch* [1997] 1 All ER 144 (CA).

13

Sham Trusts

SIMON DOUGLAS* AND BEN MCFARLANE**

I. INTRODUCTION

THE CLASSIC DESCRIPTION of the 'sham' doctrine is found in the following passage from Lord Diplock's judgment in *Snook v London and West Riding Investments Ltd*:

> But one thing, I think, is clear in legal principle, morality and the authorities ... that for acts or documents to be a 'sham', with whatever legal consequences follow from this, all the parties thereto must have a common intention that the acts or documents are not to create the legal rights and obligations which they give the appearance of creating.[1]

Although a contract law case, the *Snook* doctrine has long been applied to the law of trusts. The allegation that a trust is a sham is typically made when a settlor, desirous of avoiding the effects of an insolvency, a large tax bill or a division of assets on divorce, purports to divest himself of his assets by settling them upon trust. The trust declared is often a discretionary one where the settlor is named as a beneficiary and, in practice, he retains a great deal of control over the trust fund. Interested parties (usually creditors, the revenue authorities or the settlor's spouse) may then allege that the declaration of trust is no more than a 'sham', and that in truth the settlor never divested himself of the assets.

To give an example, take the Australian case of *Raftland Pty Ltd v Federal Commission of Taxation*,[2] where three brothers controlled the 'Raftland' unit trust and had turned a substantial (and taxable) profit. They took steps to acquire another unit trust, the 'E & M trust', which had substantial tax losses. They resolved to make the E & M trust a beneficiary of the Raftland unit trust. It was found, however, that the brothers had no intention ever to distribute assets to the E & M trust. Their 'real' or 'true' intention was not to make E & M a beneficiary of the trust, but to

* Jesus College, Oxford.

** University College London. The authors are grateful for support provided by a British Academy/Leverhulme Trust Small Research Grant.

[1] [1967] 2 QB 786, 802, citing *Yorkshire Railway Wagon Co v Maclure* (1882) 21 ChD 309 and *Stoneleigh Finance Ltd v Phillips* [1965] 2 QB 537.

[2] [2008] HCA 21. Discussed by Hon Just T Pagone, 'Sham Trusts Revisited' (2014) 20 *Trusts & Trustees* 1081.

offset the tax liabilities of E & M against the taxable profits of the Raftland trust. This was held to amount to a sham, with Kirby J stating:

> The key to a finding of a sham is the demonstration, by evidence or available inference, of a disparity between the transaction evidenced in the documentation (and related conduct of the parties) and the reality disclosed elsewhere in the evidence. Where, for example, the evidence shows a discordance between the parties' legal rights or obligations as described in the documents and the actual intentions which those parties are shown to have had as to their legal rights and obligations, a conclusion of sham will be warranted.[3]

The *Raftland* case illustrates the difficulties in conceptualising this area of law: in what sense did the brothers 'not intend' to make E & M a beneficiary of the trust? Is it the inner 'subjective' mental state that is important, or the intention expressed in communications? Is the court effectively making the settlor's motives justiciable? These questions go to the very heart of the 'certainty of intention' requirement in trusts.

II. TWO VIEWS ON SHAM TRUSTS

How are we to make sense of the decision in *Raftland*? Despite expressing a clear intention in declaring a trust in favour of the E & M unit trust, the court, applying the sham doctrine, held that there was no validly declared trust. Broadly speaking, there are two views on the operation of the sham doctrine.

First, some argue that sham is not, in itself, a distinct doctrine in the law of trusts. It is trite law that express trusts have a 'certainty of intention' requirement, meaning that a settlor must intend the creation of a trust over specific rights. In proving a sham, the argument goes, a litigant is doing no more than establishing that the certainty of intention requirement has not been met. Jessica Palmer, an advocate of this approach, argues:

> [S]hams are arrangements whose appearances do not reflect the underlying actual intention or purpose of the relevant parties. In the trusts context, a trust will be a sham where the settlor did not actually intend to create a trust. The doctrine of sham trusts is hence an aspect of the law relating to certainty of intention required for a valid trust. Where the settlor did not intend to create a trust, no trust exists because the required certainty of intention is absent.[4]

To apply this argument to *Raftland*, the court, in concluding that the trust was a sham, was simply reaching the conclusion that there was no intention to declare a trust. In this sense, whilst sham may describe the motivation of the defendants in the case, it adds little to the legal analysis.

[3] ibid [145].

[4] J Palmer, 'Dealing with the Emerging Popularity of Sham Trusts' [2007] *New Zealand Law Reports* 81, 92. One of the authors of the present piece made a similar argument in the context of sham licenses granted by landlords wishing to avoid the protection afforded to the tenant by the grant of a lease: see B McFarlane and E Simpson, 'Tackling Avoidance' in J Getzler (ed), *Rationalising Equity and Trusts* (London, Lloyd's of London Press, 2003). See too the suggestion of Hon D Bowman, 'Sham' (2016) 22 *Trusts & Trustees* 490, 493: 'It is, in my view, high time that lawyers and judges eliminated the word sham from their legal lexicon.'

The alternative view holds that sham is a distinct doctrine, separate from the certainty of intention requirement. This was most clearly articulated in the New Zealand case of *Official Assignee v Wilson*.[5] In rejecting Palmer's argument, Robertson and O'Reagan JJ stated:

> The two situations (valid trust and sham trust) do not fall into combination. The finding that a purported trust is void as a sham does not amount to an invalidation of a trust. It is not the trust as such which is the sham. There is no trust to be a sham. It is the documentation that is the sham.[6]

The notion that the sham doctrine is distinct from the standard 'certainty of intention' requirement has been forcefully advocated by Matthew Conaglen. Conaglen has argued that the sham doctrine requires a litigant to establish different facts from those that are relevant to the standard 'certainty of intention' requirement. Specifically, when a sham is pleaded, the court looks to material outside of the trust deed in order to ascertain the subjective intention of the settlor. This is distinct, the argument goes, from the normal 'certainty of intention' inquiry, where the court looks to the terms of the trust deed in order to ascertain the objective intention of the settlor. As Conaglen states:

> [N]either the subsequent conduct of the parties, nor their subjective intentions, are considered when ascertaining what rights and obligations the parties intended to create by the trust documents which they signed. The importance of this in the context of the sham doctrine is that it is precisely these sorts of factors that *can* be considered in order to determine whether an arrangement is a sham.[7]

There are perhaps two ways in which the sham doctrine, so far as it exists, is distinct from the normal 'certainty of intention' requirement. The first, according to Conaglen, is that it is a subjective inquiry. The certainty of intention inquiry is normally considered an objective one, where a court attempts to ascertain what the settlor's words meant, not what he meant by them. If, by pleading sham, a litigant must establish the settlor's subjective state of mind—what he 'actually' meant—then the inquiry becomes a very different one. Secondly, the sham doctrine may be distinct at an evidential level, in the sense that it permits the court to consider a wider range of material in ascertaining the settlor's intention. Conaglen alludes to this idea in the above quote when he refers to the subsequent conduct of the parties, evidence which is often excluded by the parol evidence rule in a normal 'certainty of intention' inquiry.

If Conaglen is correct, and sham is a distinct doctrine, separate from the certainty of intention requirement, then this may have important consequences for how it is pleaded by litigants. For one, it may have a bearing on the burden of proof. A party alleging the existence of a trust bears the burden of establishing the settlor's intention. However, if sham is a separate doctrine which requires a litigant to establish a separate fact (namely the negative fact that no trust was intended), then

[5] [2008] 3 NZLR 45.

[6] ibid 55.

[7] M Conaglen, 'Sham Trusts' [2008] *CLJ* 176, 182 (original emphasis). See also M Conaglen, 'Trusts and Intention' in E Simpson and M Stewart (eds), *Sham Transaction* (Oxford, Oxford University Press, 2013).

it would appear that the burden should shift to the party denying the existence of a trust. Secondly, it may have implications for the remedies available. If sham is no more than a failure to establish certainty of intention, then no trust ever comes into existence, and proprietary rights under a trust are never created. If sham is separate, however, then the position may be more complicated. It may be that a trust does come into existence, but the sham makes it void or voidable. What then happens to rights purportedly created under the trust? Finally, and most importantly, the status of sham determines what a litigant must prove in order to establish his case. If sham is a separate doctrine, then it follows that a litigant must establish a different set of facts to those which are relevant to the 'certainty of intention' requirement (otherwise sham and 'certainty of intention' become conceptually indistinguishable). If sham is a separate doctrine, then what are these separate facts?

This chapter will ask whether Conaglen is correct to argue that sham is a distinct doctrine, separate from the 'certainty of intention' requirement. We will consider the two purported features of the doctrine—that it is a subjective inquiry and that it permits the admission of parol evidence—in turn. We will also consider a final conceptualisation of the doctrine, which is that it is a specialised form of 'rectification'.

In conducting this analysis, we will argue that Conaglen is wrong to suggest that sham is separate from the normal 'certainty of intention' doctrine. We accept that the normal 'certainty of intention' inquiry is an objective one that depends on the communicated mental state of the settlor. However, we will argue that when a sham has been pleaded in the decided cases, the courts have not, as Conaglen suggests, switched to a subjective inquiry. Rather, we will show that the courts' attitude in sham cases continues to be an objective one.

III. SHAM AS A SUBJECTIVE INQUIRY

The principal claim made by Conaglen is that sham is distinct from the 'certainty of intention' requirement because the former, unlike the latter, involves a subjective inquiry. As he argues:

> the certainty of intention principle generally focuses on the negative fact that the court has been unable to identify a clear objective intention to create a trust, whereas sham doctrine focuses on the positive finding that the parties involved subjectively *did not* intend to create a trust such as that recorded in the sham documents.[8]

This argument has found support in the case law. In *Raftland*, for instance, we find several references to a search for the 'real' or 'actual' intention of the settlor, and Kirby J, when describing the sham doctrine, states: 'The test as to the parties' intentions is subjective. In essence, the parties must have intended to create rights and obligations different from those described in their documents.'[9]

[8] Conaglen, 'Sham Trusts' (ibid) 184 (original emphasis). The requirement of common subjective intention for a sham is assumed by, for example, S Gadhia, K Rodgers and J Ho, 'Sham Trusts' (2016) 22 *Trusts & Trustees* 464, 468: 'Asserting sham is always a grave accusation of dishonesty.'

[9] See n 2 above, [146].

In *Official Assignee v Wilson*, Glazebrook J expressly endorsed Conaglen's views:

> In my view, where a sham is alleged, the search is for the subjective intent that the transaction is a sham. After all, the whole point of a sham is that it is intended to have an effect other than the effect it would have if looked at objectively.[10]

In order to test this conceptualisation of the sham doctrine, two things must be established. The first is that the normal 'certainty of intention' requirement, as asserted in these quotes, involves an *objective* inquiry into the settlor's mental state. Secondly, that when a sham is pleaded, the court switches to a *subjective* inquiry.

A. Do Courts Construe Declarations Objectively?

The first question that must be asked is whether Conaglen is correct to say that the normal approach to ascertaining a settlor's intention is an objective one. Before answering the question, it is first necessary to explain what 'objectivity' means in the trusts context. Most attempts to define objectivity draw some distinction between the meaning attached to a statement by the speaker and the meaning conveyed to the addressee, or a reasonable person in the addressee's position.[11] The facts of *Byrnes v Kendle*[12] provide an illustration. The defendant in the case, using both his own and his then wife's savings, had acquired freehold title to a house. He then executed a trust deed, which stated, amongst other things, that he held the title 'on trust' for the benefit of himself and his then wife. Following his separation from his wife, and her assigning her interest to her son (the claimant), a dispute arose as to the payment of rent, as the defendant had permitted his own son to live at the premises rent free. If there was a trust of the freehold, with the claimant holding a beneficial interest, then it was clear that he was entitled to the receipt of rent. The defendant attempted to introduce evidence that he believed, in executing the deed, that he was merely undertaking to share the sale value of the land should he ever sell it in the future, and hence no trust was ever created. The dispute in the case, therefore, was whether the 'certainty of intention' requirement for the establishment of a trust had been satisfied. The case illustrates how objective and subjective inquiries can point in different directions. A subjective approach—what did Mr Kendle mean by his words 'on trust'?—would result in there being no trust, as Mr Kendle meant no more than a promise to split the proceeds of sale in the future. An objective approach—what would the reasonable addressee understand the words 'on trust' to mean?—would result in a trust, those words clearly conveying an intention to settle the title in this way.

[10] See n 5 above, 64.

[11] J Spencer, 'Signature, Consent and the Rule in *L'Estrange v Graucob*' [1973] *CLJ* 103, 106. For a discussion of the objective theory in contract law, and whether there is any room for a subjective inquiry, see D McLauchlan, 'Objectivity in Contract' (2005) 24 *University of Queensland Law Journal* 479, 484; D McLauchlan, 'The Contract the Neither Party Intends' (2012) 29 *Journal of Contract Law* 26.

[12] [2011] HCA 26, [114].

The High Court of Australia decided that the latter inquiry, the objective one, was appropriate in the trusts context, Heydon and Crennan JJ stating:

> the 'intention' referred to is an intention to be extracted from the words used, not a subjective intention which may have existed but which cannot be extracted from those words. This is as true of unilateral declarations of alleged trust as it is of bilateral covenants to create an alleged trust.[13]

Whilst this appears to make the position in Australian law clear, the issue is a controverted one. The High Court was strongly influenced by the position in contract law, where it is well established that a court should objectively construe the terms of a contract.[14] Yet some may be reluctant to push the analogy with contract too far. Trusts, it must be noted, are often unilateral, in the sense that their creation depends entirely on the settlor's exercise of his power to create a trust. The resulting focus on the settlor's intention, to the exclusion of any other party such as the trustee or beneficiary, may lead some to favour a subjective approach. This tendency may be particularly strong where the settlor is acting gratuitously: if Mr Kendle, for instance, was under no obligation to divest himself of the value of his title, then why should he be bound by a construction that he never intended? There is an obvious temptation to favour a subjective approach in the context of trusts law. This is perhaps encouraged, as Heydon and Crennan JJ note, by the 'constant repetition of the need to search for an "intention to create a trust"'.[15] Indeed, the conclusions of the High Court are undermined somewhat by the suggestion that Mr Kendle should be able to plead 'rectification' so as to bring the declaration of trust into line with his subjective state of mind.[16] This potential contradiction is considered further in the final part of this chapter.

There is some evidence of a subjective approach to interpretation in trusts law. The best example is the problematic Australian case of *Commissioner of Stamp Duties (QD) v Jollife*.[17] Under a statute, it was illegal for an account holder to hold a second account at a bank, except where the second account is held on trust for another. The defendant, already holding an account, deposited money in a second account and made a declaration to the bank that he held it on trust for his sisters. The defendant subsequently denied the existence of a trust. His argument succeeded as the court permitted him to introduce evidence that, notwithstanding his declaration of trust, his real intention was to retain title to the fund and earn interest on it. As this intention was never disclosed (until the legal proceedings), it could only be ascertained by conducting a subjective inquiry into the defendant's mental state; an objective inquiry—what meaning did the defendant convey to a reasonable person in the position of the bank?—would yield nothing other than an intention to create a trust, as that is all that was communicated.

It is sometimes asked whether *Joliffe*, which has now been overruled in Australia by *Byrnes v Kendle*, ever represented the legal position in England. *Lewin on Trusts*,[18]

[13] ibid [114].
[14] See generally D McLauchlan, 'Objectivity in Contract' (n 11).
[15] *Byrnes v Kendle* (n 11) [114].
[16] ibid [115].
[17] (1920) 28 CLR 178.
[18] *Jollife* is cited in the 11th to 16th editions of *Lewin on Trusts*.

in citing the case in successive editions, appeared to support the view that *Joliffe* is correct in English law, and one can certainly find some support for it in the old case law. In the nineteenth-century case of *Field v Lonsdale*,[19] which involved facts almost identical to those found in *Joliffe*, the Master of the Rolls, Lord Langdale, refused to give effect to the obvious (objective) meaning of the defendant's declaration of trust over the second bank account: 'the only intention was to evade the provisions of the Act of Parliament [prohibiting a second account], and not to create a trust. The declaration is, therefore, ineffectual, and the claim must be dismissed.'[20]

Yet *Joliffe*, and similar cases like *Field v Lonsdale*, despite never being expressly rejected in the English courts, are clearly inconsistent with principles developed in relation to the certainty of intention requirement. Specifically, the cases do not square with the traditional exclusion of evidence of an undisclosed or secret intention. It is not mental states per se which constitute trusts, but the communication of them. Indeed, this was pointed out in *Joliffe* in the strong dissenting judgment of Isaacs J:

> It is just as improper morally to permit a man who has openly undertaken such a trust to escape his conscientious obligation by reason merely of a secret mental reservation not to fulfil what he has openly undertaken. An open declaration of trust is therefore an expression of intention that is final and beyond recall.[21]

Trusts may be unilateral, in the sense of depending solely on the settlor's decision to exercise his power to create a trust, but they also impose duties on some and create rights for others. The consequences of the creation of a trust for persons other than the settlor make it entirely reasonable for the law to insist on some act of communication. This is evident from the need for a 'declaration' in order to establish an express trust.[22] To 'declare' a trust a settlor must 'manifest',[23] or communicate, his intention to another. This was emphasised by French CJ in *Byrnes v Kendle*, where he said: 'the relevant intention in such a case is that manifested by a declaration of trust'.[24] Secret intentions do not pass this threshold and, hence, are irrelevant to the question of whether or not a trust has been constituted. As Megarry J said in *Re Vandervell*, 'To yearn is not to transfer'.[25]

What we have established so far is that a basic requirement for the creation of an express trust is the communication of intention by the settlor. We may now ask how these acts of communication are interpreted by the courts: do courts attempt to ascertain what the settlor meant by his words, or do they ask what a reasonable person would understand those words to mean? Whilst the law of trusts does not

[19] (1850) 13 Beavan 78, 51 ER 30.

[20] (1850) 13 Beavan 78, 81, 51 ER 30, 31.

[21] See n 17 above, 187.

[22] The classic statement of the need for a declaration is found in Lord Nottingham's judgment in *Cook v Fountain*, where he said: '[E]xpress trusts are declared either by word or writing; and these declarations appear either by direct or manifest proof, or violent and necessary presumption': (1676) 3 Swan 585, 591, 36 ER 984, 987.

[23] J. Mowbray et al (eds), *Lewin on Trusts*, 18th edn (London, Sweet & Maxwell, 2008) 4-01. The need for a 'declaration' does not require the settlor to use, orally or in writing, the specific words 'I declare …'. For instance, in *Paul v Constance* [1977] 1 WLR 527, the settlor was held to have constituted a trust over a sum of money merely by saying that the money 'is as much yours as mine'.

[24] (2011) 243 CLR 253, 263.

[25] *Re Vandervell (No 2)* [1974] 1 Ch 269, 294.

have the same body of case law on this issue as that found in contract law, there is more than enough evidence to show that the courts ask the latter question, ie the inquiry is an objective one.

Perhaps the leading case on this issue is the House of Lords' decision in *Commissioners of Inland Revenue v Raphael*.[26] A testator had left money to his son on the condition that the son settle it on a trust with specific terms. The son attempted to follow his father's instructions. However, the wording he used when settling the trust was clearly incompatible with the conditions set out in the will and, consequently, the gift failed. The son attempted to save the gift by arguing that the terms of the trust that he had settled should be interpreted subjectively, so that the words carried the meaning he had hoped for, namely a meaning consistent with the conditions set out in the will. Rejecting the argument, Lord Wright said: 'It must be remembered at the outset that the court, while it seeks to give effect to the intention of the parties, must give effect to that as expressed, that is, it must ascertain the meaning of the words actually used.'[27] What the son desired the words to mean, therefore, was wholly irrelevant.

B. Who is the Reasonable Addressee?

Although these cases may make the objective approach secure in English law, we must still consider the specific form of objectivity that is applied. We have seen that an objective approach inquires into what meaning was reasonably conveyed by the settlor's words. The difficulty in asking this question, however, is that a settlor's words can reasonably convey different meanings to different persons. Take the nineteenth-century charitable trust case of *Shore v Wilson*,[28] where a testatrix left a sum of money on trust for 'poor and Godly preachers of Christ's holy gospel'. To a detached observer, who shares the testatrix's language but little else, the words can reasonably be understood to mean that any person of the Christian faith is a potential beneficiary. However, to the persons to whom the will was addressed (the trustees), who were aware that the testatrix was a strict Calvinist, the words could reasonably be understood to refer to a much narrower group of people, namely those belonging to the non-conformist group. Tindal CJ, in a much cited speech, said that evidence could be introduced to show that 'besides their general common meaning, [the words] have acquired, by custom or otherwise, a well-known peculiar idiomatic meaning … in the particular society of which [the testatrix was] former[ly] a member'.[29] For Tindal CJ, the important question is what meaning was conveyed to a reasonable person in the position of the trustees.

Declarations of trust are acts of communication that, if successful in creating a trust, must instantiate a legal relationship between the settlor, trustee (if a different person) and beneficiary. Let us say that a purported settlor, alone in his living

[26] [1935] AC 96. See also *Twinsectra Ltd v Yardley* [2002] 2 AC 164, [71].
[27] *Raphael* (ibid) 142.
[28] (1842) 9 Cl & Finn 355, 8 ER 450.
[29] (1842) 9 Cl & Finn 355, 567, 8 ER 450, 533.

room, says 'I declare myself trustee'. Aside from the difficulties of proving this, it is unlikely, as a matter of law, that this can constitute a trust. The settlor's intention must, at some point, be communicated to the relevant parties, namely the trustee and beneficiary. As declarations of trust are acts of communication addressed to specific persons, then it logically follows that the court, when interpreting the declaration, should ask what meaning is conveyed to the addressee (ie the trustee or beneficiary). This is sometimes referred to as 'promisee objectivity', or 'addressee objectivity'.[30] The difficulty that can arise is that a settlor may have different addressees in mind when he makes a declaration. His words could be directed towards to the putative trustee or beneficiary; or he may have some third party, such as the court, his creditors or the revenue authorities, at the front of his mind when he makes a declaration of trust. Given that a settlor's words can convey different meanings to different persons, which perspective does the court adopt for the purposes of construction?

It is not clear if this question has been explicitly addressed in the trusts context.[31] Some guidance may be found in the doctrine of secret trusts. Such trusts arise where a testator is desirous of settling some of his estate on trust for a particular beneficiary on his death, but does not wish to disclose this in his will.[32] Instead, the testator purports to make a gift in his will to a donee, but privately communicates to the donee that he is to take it upon trust for the beneficiary. To a detached observer, who sees nothing but the will, the transaction has the desired effect of looking like an outright gift to the donee; but to the donee, who is privy to other private communications, a very different meaning is communicated. Secret trusts are similar to sham trusts, in the sense that the settlor deliberately conveys different messages to different persons. What courts have long held in the context of secret trusts is that it is the testator's intention as conveyed to the donee that counts, not the impression given to the detached observer who just sees the will. Sham trusts, as we will see, follow this pattern. When a sham is pleaded, courts consider what meaning is conveyed by the settlor to the putative trustee or beneficiary, not a detached observer.

C. Are Sham Trusts Construed Subjectively?

The first premise of Conaglen's argument, that courts adopt an objective approach when construing a declaration of trust, is correct. We must now ask whether the sham doctrine operates differently by conducting a subjective inquiry. The evidence for this, as we will see, is rather thin.

Let us begin by considering cases where the sham allegation has succeeded, leading to the conclusion that there is no trust. In *Raftland Pty Ltd v Federal Commission*

[30] W Howarth, 'The Meaning of Objectivity in Contract' (1984) 100 *LQR* 265, 267.

[31] In contract law it is clear that the court asks what meaning was reasonably conveyed to the other party to the contract, rather than some third party. An example is *Hartog v Colin Shields* [1939] 3 All ER 566, where the defendant was aware that the claimant had made a mistake in offering the defendant a number of hare skins at a certain price 'per lb', when all of the preceding negotiation had been conducted in terms of price 'per skin'. To a reasonable person in the position of the purchaser, who is aware of previous communications and the market practice, it would be obvious what the vendor intended.

[32] eg *McCormick v Grogan* (1869) LR 4 HL 82.

of Taxation, a case discussed at the beginning of this chapter, three brothers who owned the Raftland unit trust executed a trust deed which declared that another unit trust, the E & M trust, was a beneficiary under the Raftland trust. However, the owners of the E & M trust, who were paid some $250k by the three brothers, were led to the clear understanding that they would receive no further payments as beneficiaries once the trust had been declared. The parties had a clear agreement, therefore, that, notwithstanding the declaration of trust, the E & M trust was not entitled to a beneficial interest in the Raftland trust. In holding the declaration of trust to be a sham, the court was of the view that it was giving effect to the subjective intention of the parties. This view seems to be based on the idea that the 'objective intention' was encoded in the written declaration of trust and, in looking at the 'reality' behind the declaration, the court's approach had become a subjective one. As Kirby J said: 'In other words, where it is legally warranted, sham analysis affords the court a ground for ignoring, instead of merely construing, the primary documentary material in determining the rights and obligations of the parties.'[33]

In ignoring the written declaration of trust, was the court giving effect to the subjective intention of the parties? We would suggest that it was not. It is important to recall that when it conducts an objective inquiry the court does not adopt a detached perspective and ask what the settlor's words mean to a distant observer. Rather, it puts itself in the position of the person to whom the words were addressed, which, in the case of *Raftland*, would be the purported beneficiary, the E & M unit trust. The crucial point is that the owners of the E & M unit trust were privy to two separate communications: first, the written declaration of trust, which conveys a clear intention to make the E & M unit trust a beneficiary; and secondly, private oral statements that conveyed precisely the opposite intention, that the 'declaration' was to have no legal effect and they would not be beneficiaries. A person in the position of the E & M unit trust would reasonably understand that three brothers had no intention of making the E & M unit trust a beneficiary under the Raftland trust. The outcome in the case is perfectly explicable under normal principles of objective construction.

A similar case where the sham allegation succeeded is that of *Midland Bank v Wyatt*,[34] where the defendant, worried about his business failing, purported to declare title to his land upon trust for his wife and his daughter. His wife signed the declaration, after which the defendant put the document in his safe and continued to deal with the freehold title. The court held that the declaration was a sham. Crucial to this finding was the wife's evidence that when she signed the declaration she had no idea what she was putting her name to, and was not aware of the 'import or effect' of the document.[35] Whilst an intent to declare a trust may be readily inferred by a third party who merely reads the trust deed, the defendant had deliberately ensured that no such intention was communicated to his wife, the purported beneficiary.

[33] See n 2 above, [143]. Pagone (n 2) also assumes that the court in *Raftland* was concerned with subjective intentions. He notes, however, at 1084–85 that the 'objective facts' were critical in the court's assessment of intention; this is consistent with our suggestion below that the result in the case is consistent with the application of a standard objective test.

[34] [1997] 1 BCLC 242. See also *A v A* [2007] EWHC 99; *Minwalla v Minwalla* [2004] EWHC 2823; *Painter v Hutchison* [2007] EWHC 758.

[35] *Wyatt* (ibid) 252.

As the court stated, the wife knew 'nothing about' the trust.[36] An objective approach, which asks what meaning was conveyed to the defendant's wife, yields nothing, as there was no communication of the intention to create a trust. It was this lack of communication, not the defendant's subjective mental state, that led the court to conclude that there was a sham.

The strongest evidence that courts do not switch to a subjective approach when sham is pleaded can be found in cases where the allegation has not been proved. The leading English case is *Shalson v Russo*,[37] where the defendant, who was the sole beneficiary of a trust worth approximately £39m, instructed the trust company to resettle the trust fund on a discretionary trust for the defendant and his family. The claimant argued that this was a sham, as the defendant was implicated in a number of fraudulent schemes and had resettled the trust so as to protect himself from potential claims. Rimer J held that even though the defendant may not have had the intention to divest himself of his equitable interest, he never disclosed this to the trustee and, hence, it was something that the law could not take cognisance of. Rimer J said:

> The settlor may have an unspoken intention that the assets are in fact to be treated as his own and that the trustee will accede to his every request on demand. But unless that intention is from the outset shared by the trustee (or later becomes shared), I fail to see how the settlement can be regarded as a sham.[38]

So far as the defendant in the case had an intention to retain his assets under the trust, this was never communicated to the trustee or any other party and, hence, could only be disclosed by a subjective inquiry. Consequently, the allegation that the trust was a sham failed.

The irrelevance of uncommunicated mental states is further supported by the case of *In re Esteem's Settlement*.[39] The defendant, a former director of the claimant company, had defrauded the company of several million dollars and had settled part of this sum on a trust. As in *Shalson v Russo*, it was strongly suspected that the defendant had no intention of parting with his ownership of the money, but this was not communicated to the trustee, who had been instructed to hold the trust funds in the normal way. Again, the court held that an uncommunicated intention, which can only be disclosed by a subjective inquiry, could have no legal effect. Birt DB gave the following example of the absurd results that would follow if secret mental states could determine the rights created:

> Let us suppose a case in which A executes a formal deed of gift of his car to B but, unknown to B, secretly intends that he should really only lend the car to B so that he retains the beneficial interest in the car. The car is delivered to B who then treats it as his own for many years. A continues to say nothing of his secret intention.[40]

Just as it would be wrong for A to insist that the car remained his in this example, the defendant's secret intention in *re Esteem* to retain his assets could not prevent the creation of a trust. Most would agree with this as a statement of principle, and

[36] ibid 252.
[37] [2005] Ch 281.
[38] ibid 342.
[39] [2003] JLR 188.
[40] ibid 216.

the example illustrates why courts should not start to conduct subjective inquiries merely because a litigant has pleaded sham in a particular case.

Critics of this approach may attempt to explain the outcome in these cases on different grounds. Palmer, for instance, tries to explain the inability of a settlor to lead evidence of an uncommunicated intention to retain assets on the basis of an estoppel:

> the trustee may rely on estoppel principles to prevent the settlor from acting unconscionably because he or she has led the trustee to believe that the trust was valid and genuine and cannot therefore rely on its invalidity against the trustee.[41]

Palmer's point is that the settlor, having deliberately given the impression of an intention to create a trust, cannot then lead evidence of an entirely different mental state. However, whilst estoppel may explain why the settlor is precluded from pleading evidence of an uncommunicated intention to sham, it would not explain why a third party, such as the creditors in *Shalson v Russo* and *In re Esteem's Settlement*, were prevented from doing so. The only explanation for this is that uncommunicated mental states are fundamentally irrelevant, given that the intention is assessed objectively.

A second explanation for the outcome in these cases, advocated by Conaglen, is that allegations of sham require a litigant to show that the 'shamming intention' was common to both the settlor and trustee. The requirement for a common intention is mentioned in the classic *Snook* definition, where, it will be recalled, Lord Diplock said that 'all the parties thereto must have a *common intention* that the acts or documents are not to create the legal rights and obligations which they give the appearance of creating'.[42] For Conaglen, the outcomes in *Shalson v Russo* and *In re Esteem's Settlement* make sense as the requirement that '*all parties* to the sham must have … an intention to mislead'[43] was not met in either case.

The view that there must be a 'common intention' to sham has support in the case law. In *A v A*, for instance, Munby J said:

> a trust will not be a sham—in my judgment cannot as a matter of law be a sham—if *either* (i) the original trustee(s), *or* (ii) the current trustee(s), were not, because they lacked the relevant knowledge and intention, party to the sham at the time of their appointment.[44]

Conaglen, we would suggest, is correct to say that an allegation of sham will not be upheld unless it can be shown that the settlor and trustee have a 'common intention' to sham. Yet, it is our view that this does not support Conaglen's overall thesis that the sham inquiry is a subjective one. Rather, the need to show a common intention supports precisely the opposite view, namely that the court is conducting an objective inquiry. The reason for this is that a 'shamming intent' can only be common to both the settlor and trustee if the former has communicated it to the latter. In the absence of a common intention, where the settlor has not disclosed his wish to retain his assets to the trustee, an allegation of sham will fail because it would hang entirely upon the settlor's subjective state of mind.

[41] Palmer (n 4) 104.
[42] *Snook* (n 1) (emphasis added).
[43] Conaglen, 'Sham Trusts' (n 7) 188 (emphasis added).
[44] See n 34 above, [49].

To conclude this section, just because a court is looking behind the written declaration of trust does not mean that it is adopting a subjective approach. As we have seen, the objective approach employed in trusts law requires the court to ask what the settlor's words meant *to a reasonable person in the position of the addressee*. Such a person in sham cases (usually the trustee, but sometimes a beneficiary) is privy not just to the 'declaration of trust', but also to other communications which inform the trustee of the settlor's desire to keep hold of his assets. To ask what a reasonable person in the position of the trustee would have understood the settlor to mean, therefore, naturally forces the court to 'look behind' the declaration of trust as the trustee was privy to other communications.

IV. SHAM AS A RULE OF EVIDENCE

So far, we have seen that the sham doctrine is indistinguishable from the standard 'certainty of intention' requirement in the sense that both involve an objective inquiry into the settlor's mental state. We will now ask whether sham is distinctive in a different sense, namely as an evidential rule. Specifically, we will ask whether the sham doctrine consists of an exception to the rule that parol evidence is normally excluded when a settlor has executed a declaration of trust.

In the *Raftland* case there are several statements that suggest that this is what the 'sham doctrine' permits a court to do. Kirby J noted that, under the ordinary 'certainty of intention' requirement, 'courts will ordinarily give legal effect to documents according to their language, [but] sham analysis is an exception to that conventional approach'.[45] The suggestion here is that when sham is pleaded the court is permitted to look behind the written declaration, something which it is not normally able to do, when ascertaining the intention of the parties. So, whilst the inquiry may remain, fundamentally, an objective one, sham permits the court to consider a wider range of material when ascertaining the intention of the settlor.

The strongest suggestion that this is the role of the 'sham doctrine' comes from the Canadian case of *Antle v R*.[46] The husband in the case, in an attempt to avoid capital gains tax, purported to transfer his shares in a company to a trustee on trust for his wife; his wife then purported to sell the shares and make a loan of the proceeds back to her husband. Whilst written documents were executed recording each stage of the 'transaction', in fact the shares were never transferred to a trustee, and no money was ever paid to the husband. The husband, citing the parol evidence rule, attempted to argue that the court was only able to consider the written documentation, and was not permitted to look at other factors, when construing his intention. In rejecting the argument, the court was in effect rejecting the application of the parol evidence rule to the case, with Noel JA stating:

> It would be a surprising result if courts were bound by the formal expression of the parties and could not look to the surrounding circumstances, including the conduct of the parties, in ascertaining whether the intent to settle a trust is present.[47]

[45] See n 2 above, [144].
[46] [2010] FCA 280.
[47] ibid [11].

In looking behind the declaration of trust at other factors, the court came to the view that there was a clear sham and no trust had been validly declared. What this suggests is that the 'sham doctrine' may be understood as an exception to the rule that courts are usually prohibited from looking at parol evidence where parties have committed their declaration of trust to a written document.

In order to test this version of the 'sham doctrine', we must first say something about the parol evidence rule and the significance of a settlor committing his intention to declare a trust to writing.[48] Whilst there is no legal requirement for a settlor to do this, should he decide to, then the normal inference to be drawn is that the settlor has intended the trust to be constituted according to the terms expressed in the writing. This is best illustrated by the leading case on parol evidence in the context of trusts, *Rabin v Gerson*,[49] where the claimants, after seeking an opinion from counsel, expressed the wish to advance money to a Jewish educational association upon a charitable trust. However, the trust deed subsequently drafted by the counsel and executed by the claimant did not properly reflect this, and the words used in the deed were held to mean that there was an absolute transfer to the association. The claimants wished to introduce into court the opinion that they had received from counsel in order to demonstrate that their intention had been to transfer the money upon trust. Rejecting the argument, Fox LJ said: 'Such evidence, I think, is simply parol evidence of the intention of the grantor ... The result, in my view, is that the opinions cannot be referred to generally for the assistance that their contents may give.'[50] It is worth pausing to consider this. Given that the claimant, prior to the execution of the deed, may well have expressed an intention to transfer funds on trust rather than absolutely, and given that the counsel's opinion may be evidence of this, why would the court exclude it when it conducts the certainty of intention inquiry? The trust deed was not a formal requirement, in that there was no need to execute it in order to constitute the trust. Why, then, in searching for the settlor's intention, are we not permitted to consider, in addition to the trust deed, prior communications or statements that shed light on the settlor's intention? The answer to this is that the claimant, in executing the trust deed, clearly intended the transfer to take effect on the terms contained in the deed. This is what Fox LJ alluded to when he described the opinion as 'parol evidence'.

Although a trust deed may not be a formal requirement in most cases, when a settlor executes one, the normal inference is that the settlor intends to be bound by the terms of the deed and, consequently, previous expressions of intention are substituted by the written terms. We would not be giving effect to the settlor's intention, therefore, if we were to look behind the trust deed to other communications.[51] By contrast, where a settlor has not intended the trust to take effect on the terms contained in the trust deed, then there is logically no reason why extrinsic evidence of other communications cannot be admitted in order to ascertain his intention.[52]

[48] R Stevens, 'Objectivity, Mistake and the Parol Evidence Rule' in E Peel and A Burrows (eds), *Contract Terms* (Oxford, Oxford University Press, 2007).

[49] [1986] 1 WLR 526.

[50] ibid 531.

[51] Stevens (n 48) 107.

[52] *Walker Property Investments v Walker* (1947) 177 LT 204.

This was made clear in *Hawke v Edwards*,[53] where Jordan J, discussing the parol evidence rule in the context of contract law, made clear that it has no application to cases outside of its logic:

> When two persons enter a contract, they may constitute it in writing ... or they may, in the course of entering into the contract which is not constituted by writing, bring into existence writing which relates to it but is not intended by them to constitute it. In the latter type of case, although the writing, if relevant, may be given in evidence, its existence does not preclude the reception of oral evidence of the terms of the contract ... To make [the parol evidence] rule of exclusion operative, it is necessary that it should be intended by the parties that the written document should be a complete record of their bargain.[54]

Under this conception of the parol evidence rule, the rule is not a technical one of evidence, but is just a way of giving effect to the intention of the parties. As such, there is a logically prior question of whether the document is genuinely intended to be the sole source of obligations. Where parties have intended their transaction to take effect according to the written terms, then a court would be ignoring their intention if it were to look behind the document at other facts. However, where the parties have not so intended, there is no reason why the court is not permitted, in attempting to ascertain the relevant intention, to look at evidence other than the document.

This conceptualisation of the 'parol evidence' rule explains why it can have no application in cases where a sham is alleged. The essence of the sham allegation is precisely that the settlor did not intend to be bound by the terms of the trust deed that he executed. In *Antle v R*,[55] although the settlor wished to give the impression of settling a trust, his intention, objectively assessed, clearly showed that he did not wish to arrange his affairs according to the written declaration. The parol evidence rule can have no application to the facts of the case because it is outside of the logic of the rule. Sham is not, therefore, an exception to the parol evidence rule, but simply a case where the rule can have no application.

V. SHAM AS A FORM OF RECTIFICATION

The final question we will ask is whether sham can be explained on the same basis as the doctrine of rectification. Just as 'sham trusts' are said to be an exception to the basic principles for ascertaining the settlor's intention to create a trust, so too is the doctrine of rectification. An interesting question, that may shed some light on both doctrines, is whether the facts of a sham case could be pleaded as a claim for rectification.

In *Allnutt v Wilding*, Mummery LJ explained that the process of rectifying a trust deed 'involves bringing the trust document into line with the true intentions of the settlor as held by him at the date when he executed the document'.[56] The remedy is

[53] *Hawke v Edwards* (1947) 48 SR (NSW) 21.
[54] ibid 22.
[55] See n 46 above.
[56] [2007] EWCA Civ 412, [11].

available, he continued, when, 'owing to a mistake in the drafting of the document, it fails to record the settlor's true intentions'. To give an example, take the case of *Re Farepak Food and Gifts Ltd*,[57] where a company, about to go bankrupt, told its solicitor that it desired to protect customers paying funds into their customer account by declaring a trust over the account. However, when the trust deed was drafted by the solicitor, the wrong account number, which referred to an empty account, was recorded. This mistake in the recording of the settlor's intention needed to be remedied by rectifying the document so as to make it reflect the settlor's prior communication.

The conceptual similarity between rectification and sham becomes clear when one sees that rectification is commonly thought of as a subjective process. The objective approach to interpretation of a settlor's mental state can lead to results that are sometimes seen as unfair. Take *Byrnes v Kendle*, where the defendant, in declaring his freehold title on trust, argued that he meant no more than a promise to share the proceeds of the sale of the land should he ever sell it. Given that the transaction was purely voluntary, it may seem unfair to hold him to the effect of his words if that effect was never desired by him. Perhaps to mitigate the asperity of this objective approach, it was suggested that a rectification claim could be brought, so as to bring the deed into line with Mr Kendle's subjective intentions.[58] The clearest endorsement of this view of rectification comes from the recent case of *Day v Day*.[59] A mother, who had a freehold title to land, instructed a solicitor to draft a deed which would make her son, the defendant, a joint tenant of the legal estate. The solicitor, probably acting under the influence of the defendant, went beyond these instructions and also included a declaration of trust in the deed, with the son as a beneficiary. The court rectified the deed, with the reference to the trust in favour of the son being expunged, and being replaced with a trust for the benefit of the mother. Etherton LJ said: 'What is relevant in such a case is the subjective intention of the settlor. It is not a legal requirement for rectification of a voluntary settlement that there be an outward expression or objective communication of the settlor's intention.'[60] This view has also found favour amongst some academics. Paul Davies, for instance, writes: 'It is entirely appropriate that rectification should operate as a *subjective* "safety-valve" from the objectivity of the common law rules of interpretation. This is how equity can *complement* the common law.'[61]

This 'subjective' view of rectification shares an obvious similarity with the 'sham trust' cases: in both cases the settlor has said one thing but has meant another. Take the case of *Joliffe*, where, it will be recalled, the settlor declared a trust over a second bank account in favour of his sister. He successfully argued that his real (uncommunicated) intention was to retain his rights in the account absolutely, and the declaration was no more than a ploy to avoid a rule against holding more than one account at the bank. The facts in the case are an example of a divergence between what was said and what was meant. If rectification has the purpose of bringing written

[57] [2006] EWHC 3272, [2008] BCC 22.
[58] *Byrnes v Kendle* (n 11).
[59] [2014] Ch 114.
[60] ibid 122.
[61] P Davies, 'Rectifying the Course of Rectification' (2012) 75 *MLR* 412, 421 (original emphasis).

documents into line with the settlor's subjective state of mind, could Mr Joliffe have structured his claim as one for rectification?

One objection to such a move would be to focus on Mr Joliffe's motive in misstating his intention. In the normal rectification case the difference between the expressed meaning and the subjective state of mind of the settlor is the result of a mistake, as the settlor chooses the wrong words to encode his thoughts. By contrast, in *Joliffe* the difference between what was said and what was meant was entirely deliberate, as Mr Joliffe's purpose was to deceive third parties. Should this make a difference? This depends on who brings the claim for rectification. If it was Mr Joliffe who argued that his written declaration should be brought into line with his secret 'real' intention, then a bar to rectification may come into play. Mr Joliffe, in attempting to give the impression to third parties of a trust, but promising himself that he retained the fund, was trying to have his cake and eat it, and the courts would rightly be reluctant to assist him in so doing. However, if it is a third party who brings the rectification claim, should it make a difference that it is a case of deception rather than a mistake? We would suggest that it should not. Let us say that it is a taxation authority, for instance, that is arguing that Mr Joliffe's trust deed should be rectified (and hence that he should be taxed on the basis that he owns the account absolutely). Could Mr Joliffe object to this claim for rectification by saying, 'Aha, the misleading impression I gave in the trust deed was not the result of mistake, but was deliberate'? Such an objection would make little sense. Indeed, a deliberate misstating of intention should ground a stronger case for rectification than a mistaken one.

This discussion of *Joliffe* is entirely hypothetical as the claim was not pleaded as one for rectification. However, if the purpose of rectification is to bring the written declaration into line with the settlor's 'real' intention, then we can see no reason why a rectification claim would not succeed on the facts of *Joliffe*. This is a rather startling conclusion, and it highlights a fundamental problem with the subjective view of rectification. It may be recalled that earlier in this chapter it was argued that the decision in *Joliffe* does not represent English law. The English law of trusts is clear in stating that an uncommunicated mental state, which can only be disclosed by conducting a subjective inquiry, is legally irrelevant. As such, were *Joliffe* decided today in an English court, the court would give effect to Mr Joliffe's communicated intention and ignore his secret one. However, if the court could easily reach the opposite conclusion, and give effect to Mr Joliffe's secret intention to retain the bank account, merely by treating it as a claim for rectification, then the jurisdiction to rectify would seriously undermine the law's objective approach to interpretation. It is to be questioned whether the law can tolerate such a contradiction in its doctrines.

This chapter is not the place to develop arguments concerning rectification. Nevertheless, it is worth noting that there is another conception of the doctrine that would not lead to the strange results discussed in the last paragraph. Professor Stevens has recently argued that rectification does not involve a subjective inquiry, but is better understood as an exception to the parol evidence rule. To explain this, let us say that a settlor orally states to a trustee that he wishes to create a trust on terms *xyz*, and then executes a trust deed which contains terms *abc*. If the settlor has intended the trust to take effect on the terms communicated in the trust deed, then we are prohibited, by the parol evidence rule, from considering his earlier communication when ascertaining his intention. What rectification does, as Stevens explains, is to rescind the settlor's intention to be bound by the terms contained in the document; the error in the recording of the settlor's intention in the document allows the court to ignore the settlor's wish that the trust take effect subject to those written terms only.[62] The consequence of this is that, in the example, when attempting to ascertain the settlor's intention, the court is not confined to examining the words contained in the deed (which point to terms *abc*), but can also examine the earlier oral communication (which points to terms *xyz*). The important point is that it does not follow, from this description of rectification, that the court must switch from an objective inquiry to a subjective one. If rectification merely permits the court, when conducting the 'certainty of intention' inquiry, to look at communications of intention prior to those contained in the trust deed, then there is no reason why it should not construe those earlier communications in the normal objective way. This conception of rectification would have been of no assistance to Mr Joliffe as there were no earlier communications in the case: Mr Joliffe's 'shamming' intention was never disclosed.

This objective view of rectification is conceptually similar to the type of allegation made when a sham is pleaded. The crucial feature of rectification under Stevens's account is that it is an exception to the parol evidence rule, and hence it permits a court to consider the settlor's earlier oral communications. When a sham is pleaded, the essence of the allegation is that the parol evidence rule should not apply in the first place as the settlor does not intend to be bound by any words contained in the trust deed. To put it a little differently, there is no room for the doctrine of rectification to apply in sham cases as the court is already permitted to consider parol communications.

VI. CONCLUSION

The principal conclusion in this chapter is that sham is not a separate doctrine within the law of trusts. If we begin with a clear understanding of the operation of the parol evidence rule, and how it interacts with the rules for ascertaining a settlor's intention, then we see there is no need to explain 'sham trusts' under a separate principle. The main allegation made when sham is pleaded is that the settlor did not intend the trust to take effect on the terms set out in the trust deed. As we have seen, if this is established, then it simply means that a court is not confined to looking at the written document when ascertaining the settlor's intention, but can look to other oral communications (which may disclose the 'shamming intention'). Its attitude towards those oral communications continues to be an objective one in that the court asks what meaning is reasonably conveyed to the addressee. If a settlor has privately communicated to a trustee that, notwithstanding the 'declaration', no trust is in fact intended, then the normal objective inquiry can give effect to this.

[62] Stevens (n 48) 119.

Part D

Property, Place, and Development

14

Planning Law Reform and Reconceptualising the Regulation of Land Use

CHRIS WILLMORE*

I. INTRODUCTION

APPROACHES TO LAND use regulation differ between jurisdictions, reflecting the differing geopolitical pressures in play at the time of their gestation. In seeking to analyse these differences, three key matrices are whether power in the regulatory process is locally or nationally focused, the relationship between professional expertise and lay participation, and the extent to which the process is positioned as a regulator or facilitator of the mapping of public policy imperatives onto individual decisions.

An analysis of planning law can also shed light upon whether a jurisdiction sees property as essentially fungible, so that consistency of answer and minimal transaction costs are key. If so, we may expect to see regulation focused upon national policy statements consistently applied, enabling market solutions to locational and regulatory questions. Or does planning law reflect a 'spheres of influence' approach to property that sees property as about place-specific relationships? In such a model, defining and managing the tensions that result from this intersection places local perceptions of appropriate uses of space in a particular relationship to development, and requires planning to adopt a different approach to other regulatory regimes. Such an approach places emphasis upon the specificities of place and space.

In England, through the vicissitudes of the past 70 years, planning law has been centred on local decision making by lay councillors as a regulator of the application of public policy in a particular geographical context. This model of local lay decision-making process, in which elected representatives triangulate national planning policy, community pressure and other geographical factors in a site-specific context, has become embedded in public perceptions of both local government and planning processes. This chapter looks at whether recent changes signal a move away from this rooted approach to a more fungible view of property.

* University of Bristol.

To explore the way in which changes in planning law can reflect changing perceptions of property, this chapter looks at changes in the planning system in England in recent years, and in particular in the period following the election of a Conservative government in 2015. It argues that, cumulatively, the changes reposition English planning law. Those changes have seen the transformation of the system to one that is a locally delivered system but in which the power and policy are now centralised. It thus retains the formal structures of local lay decision making, but around that a network of changes have left little residual local choice. As part of that, planning is now firmly seen as a facilitator of government policy rather than its regulator. However, public perceptions of planning as a local lay decision-making process are proving persistent. The public continue to expect the local lay decision-making process to have real power, and in particular the ability to reflect local views. That expectation, in the face of a different reality, is leading to public disillusionment. For many, it is their first direct encounter with democratic decision making (apart from voting), so can also have an impact upon their perception of democracy itself, for example in terms of whether they see 'government' as responsive.

Planning law in England is in a state of considerable flux, with proposals for radical reform at various stages of consultation and implementation.[1] No wonder the public is confused, with the *Daily Telegraph* unusually campaigning against Conservative government changes and positioning itself to oppose deregulation of the planning laws that it describes as having 'protected the countryside for almost 70 years'.[2] Few would disagree with the description of the current planning system as 'sclerotic';[3] but there is less agreement about the purpose of the system. Without that clarity of purpose, it is difficult to assess the suitability and effectiveness of reform proposals, or to reach agreement on them. Planning law and policy has always been subject to change to reflect changing governmental priorities, but this chapter argues that the current changes amount to a fundamental change in the role of planning law. Failure to make that change explicit is contributing to growing frustration with the ability of the planning system to deliver the outcomes communities expect, and reduces the effectiveness of the reforms.

Back in 1980, in his seminal book entitled *Ideologies of Planning Law*,[4] Patrick McAuslan identified three ideologies in play in planning: private property, public interest and public participation. As recently as 2014, Adshead was able to conclude that the balance between these remained much as they had been in 1980.[5] This chapter, however, argues that since then changes have altered this balance, reducing the

[1] The lengthy catalogue of legislative and policy consultations and changes considered in this chapter illustrates the complexity of these.

[2] 'Hands Off Our Land' campaign, promoted through the website www.telegraph.co.uk/news/earth/hands-off-our-land/ May 2015 (accessed September 2016), covering a series of articles, eg 'First They Came for Coniston Water', *Daily Telegraph*, 9 March 2015.

[3] Greg Clark, then Minister, Department for Communities and Local Government in the House of Commons, when announcing the publication of the National Planning Policy Framework and the government response to select committee criticism, HC Deb 27 March 2012, vol 542, col 1337.

[4] P McAuslan, *The Ideologies of Planning Law* (Oxford, Pergamon Press, 1980).

[5] J Adshead, 'Revisiting the Ideologies of Planning Law: Private Property, Public Interest and Public Participation in the Legal Framework of England and Wales' (2014) 6 *International Journal of Law in the Built Environment* 174.

power of the third aspect and enhancing the second, but reformulated as a national articulation of public interest.

At the core of these changes is a rethinking of the concepts of place and space. This is not about the death of specificity, the end of the importance of place and space, but rather its remaking. This chapter argues that we are witnessing a reformulation of both the concepts of and the role of place and space in planning processes, through a move to a nested suite of ideologies, involving:

- the repositioning of planning from regulation of the application of national public policy to a tool in its delivery, shifting power from local regulator to national policy formulators, reformulating the decision-making space and locale for 'public interest' to be determined;
- reducing the significance of place through marketisation; and
- reformulating public participation through selective deployment of the 'trust' discourse.

Whilst the precise formulation of land-use planning regulation varies by jurisdiction, the formulation can reveal something about the perception of the role of place and space within that jurisdiction, and the role of specificity of place. This chapter argues that the reduction in local decision-making space and the remaking of the remaining local space are indicative of a move towards a more fungible approach to property. As the scope for site-specific decision making is reduced, the focus is increasingly upon land as an economic commodity.

Ownership conceptualisations of property containing an internal/externality paradigm have at their core a binary of things over which I exercise property rights/obligations and things economists would consider externalities. Regulatory control is justified by reference to those externalities and, whilst the precise framing of which externalities will be recognised as such and which should be regulated will vary, the concept remains unchanged. The property in the form of an estate in land, or indeed the land itself, is seen as being in a vacuum. Planning law is predicated on a belief that it is legitimate for the state to regulate the externalities resulting from choices about the exercise of individual property rights. It is possible to stop there, and say that particular choices about the extent of that regulation are public policy matters and that, whilst regulatory theory and public engagement theory may shed light upon the particular exercises of that, regulatory power changes do not raise fundamental issues for property law.

The changes in planning law may be seen simply as reflections of a complex public policy landscape. They can be seen as differing ad hoc responses to policy challenges within a broader ideological context, or considered to shed light upon the changing theoretical nature of planning law—and in particular the extent to which it needs to be more aligned with other regulatory frameworks in terms of its construction of space and place. The changes can also be seen as reflections of different concepts of property, and in particular the importance of specificity. At this level of analysis, changes in the scope for place- and space-specific analysis is not merely a matter of changed regulatory loci, but one of a change in the underlying concept of property. In a fungible model, where land is solely a way of holding value, it can be treated as a non-unique commodity; however, when land is seen as being a unique part of a specific place and space, then changes of power loci can change perceptions of land.

Other conceptualisations start from seeing property as socially situated,[6] a product of place and space. When we look at the question of externalities not from the angle of what the state should regulate but from the angle of what we consider as our home, or place of belonging, it becomes more complex. Our sense of belonging to a place engages not just the space over which we may have some sort of property law right, but also a wider domain, with which we interact and which forms part of our place. At a slightly wider level, there is a sense of community, of belonging to a wider whole. Traditionally, planning law, with its focus upon local decision making, has operated in that space. It has never gone as far as Radin's conceptualisation of local space as 'personal property',[7] nor has it seen locality as not replaceable by money or other property, but as 'part of the way [people] constitute [them]selves as continuing personal entities in the world'.[8] In planning law, this has involved the provision of a strong local participatory voice in decision making, with decisions framed by a strong sense of place and space, identified by McAuslan in his core ideologies.

In the absence of any overarching statutory purpose to planning law,[9] save that of providing a vessel for the regulation of land use, justifications have varied from a social control model,[10] through self-determination,[11] environmental[12] and economic growth models,[13] to its current framing in terms of 'sustainable development'.[14] A continuing feature through all of these differing policy agendas has been the concept of planning regulatory decision making as uniquely grounded in place and space, in which ideas are grounded in specificity. This chapter argues that the current reforms effectively break that link in terms of the locus of power, whilst maintaining a formal structure that is grounded in local decision making.

II. WHAT RATIONALES ARE BEING ARTICULATED FOR THESE CHANGES?

Before looking at the impact of these reforms on concepts of planning law and its conceptualisation of property, some analysis of the articulated rationale of the reforms is needed.

[6] JW Singer, 'The Ownership Society and Taking of Property: Castles, Investments, and Just Obligations' (2006) 30 *Harvard Environmental Law Review* 309.

[7] M Radin, 'Property and Personhood' (1982) 34 *Stanford Law Review* 957, 959.

[8] ibid.

[9] The closest to a statement of purpose is the Planning Act 2004, s 39(2), which requires public bodies to exercise their functions in relation to local development documents 'with the objective of contributing to the achievement of sustainable development'. The National Planning Policy Framework 2012, para 6 states '[t]he purpose of the planning system is to contribute to the achievement of sustainable development', and it creates a presumption in favour of sustainable development in para 14.

[10] See, eg, M Clawson, 'Introduction: Social Controls over Private Land Use' (1977) 22 *South Dakota Law Review* 479; McAuslan (n 6); Adshead (n 7).

[11] McAuslan (n 6); Adshead (n 7); G Haughton and P Allmendinger, 'Moving on—from Spatial Planning to Localism and Beyond' (2011) 80(4) *Town and Country Planning* 184; Localism Act 2011.

[12] eg Adshead (n 7); JM Kozlowski, 'Sustainable Development in Professional Planning: A Potential Contribution of the EIA and UET Concepts' (1990) 19(4) *Landscape and Urban Planning* 307.

[13] eg R Stimson, R Stough and B Roberts, *Regional Economic Development*, 2nd edn (Berlin, Springer, 2006).

[14] National Planning Policy Framework 2012, paras 6, 18–219. See also the UK Sustainable Development Indicators (London, Department for Environment, Food and Rural Affairs, 2013), which include provision of sufficient housing as a headline sustainability objective of equal weight to climate change, the preservation of habitats and food security.

In recent years, several diverse discourses have been in play simultaneously—namely, deregulation, consistency and 'trust' localism as a brand of self-determination—leading to different strands of change, which are not always consistent in their application or consequences, creating an apparently confusing picture of the direction of change in planning. Some of this change is a product of a shifting balance of priority between national and local public policy imperatives (such as the housing shortage), and some a product of ideologies of marketisation (as opposed to more traditional discourses of deregulation). This chapter explores three particular trends: reforming the decision-making space; marketisation that reduces the role of specificity of place; and the role of concepts of 'trust' and localism in redefining the remaining role of specificity.

When the new National Policy Framework, including the presumption in favour of sustainable development, was announced in 2012, the minister at the Department for Communities and Local Government, Greg Clark, told the House of Commons that the reforms had three fundamental objectives:

— to put unprecedented power in the hands of communities to shape the places in which they live;
— to better support growth to give the next generation the chance that our generation has had to have a decent home, and to allow the jobs to be created on which our prosperity depends; and
— to ensure that the places we cherish—our countryside, towns and cities—are bequeathed to the next generation in a better condition than they are now.[15]

This reflects a strong rhetoric about the importance of place, and the extent to which influence over place is significant to quality of life, coupled with rhetoric of deregulation, clearing out 'sclerosis' in the planning system. At face value, it appears to reflect the continuation of McAuslan's three factors.

The 2015 Conservative Party Election Manifesto[16] reflected a slightly different balance. It included a commitment to 'let local people have more say on local planning',[17] but made strong commitments to deliver ambitious housing targets designed to address a continuing housing shortage. It was silent about the inconvenient truth of continuing local opposition to large-scale development. This change of focus from 2012 appears to presage a significant change of emphasis. Following the election, as this chapter explores below, a veritable tumult of consultations, policy statements and legislative measures have created turmoil in the planning world, with the emphasis moved to delivery of national policy objectives away from the rhetoric of place and a reformulated role for participation.

A key feature in that transformation has been the use of Treasury documents to announce changes in policy or legislation in relation to planning, with the Department for Communities and Local Government (DCLG) as the planning ministry dealing

[15] Clark (n 3).

[16] 'Strong Leadership, a Clear Economic Plan, a Brighter More Secure Future', The Conservative Party Manifesto 2015.

[17] Without any links to specific commitments except to giving local people a 'final say' on wind farm applications.

with more detailed aspects. Starting with the Barker Reports,[18] the Treasury seems to have exerted growing influence over the direction of planning policy. Since the 2015 election, the Treasury has been the source of major land-use planning announcements, rather than the DCLG. That, in itself, offers a crucial clue to one key facet of the change: the changed role of planning to an adjunct to national economic policy rather than a regulator of geographic specificities. That, in turn, has implications for the shape and scale of the local decision-making space and the scope for place and space in decision making.

Meta-policy priorities, such as housing targets, are reflected by proposals in the government's Productivity Plan,[19] published two months after the 2015 election, and the Rural Productivity Plan[20] that rapidly followed. Both included a suite of measures designed to facilitate planning consent for residential development. It is not insignificant that these Treasury documents are used as core references in much that has followed. The focus in these documents is economic, with reform of planning positioned as a core part of enabling productivity, and current planning law and practice perceived as 'hindering competition by raising barriers to entry, adaptation and expansion'.[21] This Treasury engagement is not confined to what may be seen as factors affecting macroeconomic issues; for example, the 2016 budget included proposals about deregulating loft extensions in London![22]

The second strand one might expect is the role of public participation, a concept strongly linked to perceptions of planning as being about place and space. But articulation of participation, even in David Cameron's language of 'trust', has been noticeable by its absence since the 2012 launch of the National Planning Policy Framework. The 'trust' debate stems from the remaking of modern Conservatism under Cameron's leadership prior to his resignation in June 2016. In his defining Demos speech, shortly after becoming leader in December 2005, he said 'We start with an instinctive desire to put more trust in civil society and in the individual, rather than in the bureaucratic apparatus of the state'.[23] In McAuslan's analysis, this is an ideology of public participation, but it is a distinctive one in that it is individualised rather than the collective democratic modes of participation previously articulated. It contributed to the changes introduced by the Localism Act 2011,[24] but has not been apparent more recently, except (as we will see later) as a means of justifying central government policy.

[18] K Barker, *Review of Housing Supply* (London, HM Treasury 2004); K Barker, *Review of Land-Use Planning* (London, HM Treasury 2006).

[19] *The Productivity Plan, Fixing the Foundations: Creating a more prosperous nation*, Cm 9098 (London, HM Treasury, 2015).

[20] *Towards a One Nation Economy: A 10-Point Plan for Boosting Productivity in Rural Areas* (London, Department for Environment, Food and Rural Affairs, 2016).

[21] Treasury (n 19) para 9.4.

[22] Budget 2016, HC Deb 16 March 2016, vol 607, col 901.

[23] D Cameron, 'Modern Conservatism', Demos speech, 30 January 2006, available at www.demos.co.uk/files/davidcameronmodernconservatism.pdf (accessed on 1 September 2016).

[24] See *A Plain English Guide to the Localism Act* (London, Department for Communities and Local Government, 2011) for a summary of the intentions of the Act to empower local authorities and encourage them to transfer power to local communities.

The perception of planning as a tool for the delivery of central government policy was encapsulated in the launch of the Housing and Planning Bill,[25] aimed at delivering the principles set out in the Treasury Autumn Statement 2015. The government referred to it as being the first step in a 'national crusade to get 1 million homes built by 2020'.[26] The launch focused discourses around the bill upon delivery of a particular policy imperative (housing), with a tacit problematising of local authorities as resisting a public demand for housing. This positioning of public perspectives in support of central policy is considered further in Section V of this chapter.

In summary, the language, particularly since May 2015, has become one of planning as an instrument in central policy delivery. The next step is to consider the way this change is being delivered and how the changing delivery mechanisms are affecting perceptions of place and space and property specificity.

III. REFRAMING THE DECISION-MAKING SPACE

Whilst there has been a change of rhetoric, to understand the impact of the changes, a series of threads need to be unpicked. The first change that can be discerned is a change in the space in which the public policy aspects of planning are being framed. The public policy facet of planning has always been a complex product of geographically specific, locally derived policies and responses to broader national or global policy imperatives. The core locus for decision making has been the local planning authority, based on a model of planning as a reconciling of these pressures in the context of specific place and space. This, in turn, is firmly rooted in perceptions of the distinctiveness of each parcel of land.

A number of changes are squeezing the space for this local decision making. At one end of the spectrum, the broadening of permitted development is taking growing amounts of activity out of the scope of development control regulation. At the other end of the scale, standardisation, marketisation and nationalisation of decision making are leaving limited scope for locally based decisions. This is reflected not only by changes in law and policy, but through government financial incentives to deliver more housing, national announcements of strategic housing sites and ultimately the announcement of a central government unit to take over delivery of Local Plans where local authorities fail to deliver them. Yet more changes have affected the flexibility within the local decision-making space for those matters apparently still to be determined in that space. Each of these needs to be considered in turn.

The first category of redefinition of the decision-making space derives from removing matters from that space altogether through extensions of permitted development. 'Permitted development' has always existed as a defined category of changes permitted without regulatory control.[27] Historically, this was limited to what were

[25] Housing and Planning Bill, HC Bill (2015–16) [75].

[26] Brandon Lewis MP, then Minister, Department for Communities and Local Government, press statement, 13 October 2015.

[27] Town and Country Planning (Use Class) Order 1987, SI 1987/764; Town and Country Planning (General Permitted Development) (England) Order 2015, SI 2015/596; L Smith, 'Planning: Change of Use', House of Commons Briefing Paper 01301 (2016); L Smith, 'Permitted Development Rights', House of Commons Briefing Paper 00485 (2016).

perceived as small-scale activities. In one sense, permitted development rights have always been subject to the vicissitudes of public policy in terms of what is significant enough to require regulatory oversight. However, since the 2015 election, some fundamental changes have been made to take development out of local regulatory control and into the category of permitted development. The most recent example of this is a government proposal[28] to extend permitted development rights to enable state-funded schools to be created and to expand without submitting a planning application.[29] The explicit purpose[30] is to facilitate the development of free schools and the expansion of schools to address the need for school places. This exemplifies two trends: the removal of scope for local participation in decision making and the subjugation of planning's regulatory function to a national public policy imperative. The consultation makes clear that this does not mean there will be no regulation; before changing the use of a building to school premises, approval will still be required from the relevant education minister.[31] So here we have functional ministerial approval continuing and only local planning approval being removed. Planning is harnessed and subjugated to a manifesto commitment to provide more school places and more free schools, through removing decisions from local regulation.

This is not the first or only example of changes to permitted development. The Conservative–Liberal Democrat Coalition government (2010–15) made a number of changes, a few giving local communities regulatory control,[32] but most of a deregulatory nature, for example, taking proposals to change use to housing from some other uses out of regulatory control.[33] The widening of permitted development extends beyond housing,[34] showing the same process as the schools example. The most controversial change was the creation of new permitted development rights in relation to fracking.[35] These are all examples of an approach in which, when regulation within local decision-making space represents an obstacle to speedy implementation of national public policy priorities, it is being reworked. It is difficult to articulate this as a general process of deregulation, as the deregulation is targeted, removing regulation only where it is inconvenient to national policies. Its selectivity suggests that it is about reframing the regulatory space to ensure more effective delivery of national government policy. More changes are in the pipeline, but all are associated with public policy imperatives to deliver specific outcomes.[36]

[28] *Technical Consultation on Implementation of Planning Changes* (London, Department for Communities and Local Government, 2016) Ch 11.

[29] To allow extensions of up to 25% of the floor space of schools or 250 m^2 if greater; extend the duration of temporary right to use property within the same use class as a state funded school; and allow temporary buildings for up to three years on brownfield sites.

[30] DCLG (n 28).

[31] ibid para 11.7.

[32] Making it a change of use to convert a public house to other uses, if the public house had been listed as an asset of community value locally.

[33] Through changes to the Use Class Order (n 27).

[34] eg enabling more renewables—Town and Country Planning (General Permitted Development) (England) Order 2015, SI 2015/596.

[35] Town and Country Planning (General Permitted Development) (England) (Amendment) Order 2016, SI 2016/332.

[36] eg mobile phone masts. Written statement, Brandon Lewis, HC Deb 17 March 2016, vol 607, col WS631.

At the same time as this selective deregulation, other decisions have been moved from local to central government, or to bodies that are centrally appointed.[37] Not all of these originate entirely from the 2015 government, but cumulatively their existence and exercise restructures decision-making space.

As an example of centralisation, projects deemed to be 'nationally significant infrastructure projects' are now handled nationally[38] within a policy framework set by the Secretary of State for the relevant policy area. Applications are handled by the National Infrastructure Planning Unit, but with the final decisions taken by the Secretary of State for the relevant infrastructure service (transport, waste, water, energy). Although geographical specificity is considered, the extent to which the schemes are delivering national policy aspirations determined by that ministry alters the shape of the decision-making space to a central decision where the person responsible for the infrastructure policy agenda determines the application.[39] There is a manifest risk that decisions will reflect the service agenda rather than a regulatory one, and that the geographical specificities of particular sites will carry less weight than might be the case in a local decision-making space. Indeed, this is part of the aim of the process.

Building upon that subjugation of planning's regulatory function to specific functional aims, the Treasury has now established a National Infrastructure Commission.[40] The choice of subject by the Treasury,[41] and the source of the announcements, gives a flavour of the positioning of the Commission's work. The work will cut across strategic land use planning processes, and is likely to provide a long-term flow of public policy imperatives to follow those on housing, fracking and schools.

Whilst these examples of centralisation have reflected a complete transfer of decision making in key areas, there is a second layer of reshaping of decision-making space in which the powers of intervention are wide, but are only exercised where central government considers there is a risk of the normal processes not delivering the desired outcome. This approach preserves apparent local decision-making space, but planning authorities feel constrained within that space because of the risk of central government intervention. These constraints operate directly through actual exercise and indirectly through anticipatory reshaping in the local decision-making space. As with deregulation, the changes look neutral, but through selective application they reshape the decision-making space to implement specific policy agendas. The Secretary of State for Communities and Local Government (Secretary

[37] eg Development Corporations take over the planning function for the area covered, Urban Development Corporations in England (Planning Functions) Order 1998, SI 1998/84.

[38] Using 'Development Consent Orders', Planning Act 2008, as amended by the Infrastructure Act 2015; L Smith, 'Planning for Nationally Significant Infrastructure Projects', House of Commons Briefing Paper 06881 (2015).

[39] The only counter indicator is that onshore wind generation of 50 megawatts and above has been returned to local authority decision making, subject to a strong 'trust' discourse: Housing and Planning Act 2016.

[40] Set up on an interim basis under Lord Adonis, pursuant to the Treasury's 2015 Spending Review and Statement.

[41] Letter Chancellor to Lord Adonis, 16 March 2016, available at www.gov.uk/government/uploads/system/uploads/attachment_data/file/508109/DOC150316-15032016124609.pdf (accessed on 1 September 2016).

of State (DCLG)) can intervene before any decision is taken locally by 'calling in' an application.[42] Anyone can apply to have an application called in. When this occurs, the Secretary of State (DCLG) takes the decision. Whilst the local planning authority and community can comment, they are no longer the decision makers. The Caborn principles[43] suggest that the use of these call-in powers should be confined to issues of more than local importance, issues which conflict with national policies or issues that may have 'significant' long-term impacts. The determination of planning applications which may have an impact upon economic growth and attainment of government policy objectives in relation to such things as housing, schools, fracking, transport or retailing qualify under this approach, the only question being when something is sufficiently significant. The power is extensive and, whilst used selectively, the desire to avoid call in can have a significant impact on the local authority decision-making space.

If a case is not called in, the Secretary of State (DCLG) has a later opportunity to intervene, through use of 'recovered appeal' powers.[44] Decisions about specific development proposals are primarily taken by local planning authorities. Appeals by a developer against local planning authority decisions are in most cases determined by an independent inspectorate. However, the Secretary of State has the power to 'resume' jurisdiction over the appeal. This covers a wide range of proposals, including those of 'major importance having more than local significance', regionally controversial proposals, proposals raising novel concerns, town centre developments, residential schemes over 150 dwellings, significant green belt development or proposals to which a government department objects. Relatively few appeals are 'recovered', but the jurisdiction is wide and enables central government to intervene, or threaten to intervene, to ensure that central government policy is implemented. It offers an interventionist government a wide power to intervene.

Since the 2015 election, new provisions have added to these restrictions on local decision-making space through a process of empowering the Secretary of State (DCLG) to grant 'consent in principle'. This is a stark provision in terms of power transfer. Unlike the previous examples given in this chapter, this centralisation of decision making is not constrained by the language of 'strategic significance'. The Housing and Planning Act 2016 introduced a new system for the Secretary of State to grant 'consent in principle', leaving local authorities to deal with the subsequent 'technical details'.[45] In February 2016, the government explained what would trigger this new 'consent in principle' process[46]—local plans, neighbourhood plans and brownfield registers. Local and neighbourhood plans have been through a local participatory decision-making process, but inclusion of brownfield sites (that is, land that has had a previous non-agricultural use) is different. The 2016 Act imposes a duty on local authorities to keep a register of brownfield land,[47] but does

[42] Town and Country Planning Act 1990, s 77; L Smith, 'Calling-In Planning Applications', House of Commons Briefing Paper No 00930 (2016).

[43] First articulated by Richard Caborn in a ministerial answer, HC138 W 16 June 1999, revised 2012 in a written ministerial statement (HC29 WS 9 September 2012).

[44] Planning Act 1980.

[45] Housing and Planning Act 2016, s 150.

[46] DCLG (n 28).

[47] Housing and Planning Act 2016, s 15; see also Treasury (n 19).

not make the process of compiling the register a transparent participatory one akin to local and neighbourhood plans. It is a factual process, and one that is not based on whether sites have had a previous use. It does not involve a judgment about suitability for development. 'Consent in principle' applications are determined by the Secretary of State. Local decision making is located at the point of including a site on the brownfield register, itself not a product of public consultation or planning judgment. Subsequent local participation is confined to technical matters.

The third approach to the reshaping of the decision-making space involves decision making remaining in its current location but with constraints on the choices of the decision maker. This can be harder to evidence because of its indirect nature. It has always been the case that when a local planning authority determines an application for development, it has to have regard to a range of factors. In its current formulation, the authority must determine it in accordance with any statutory development plan in place unless 'material considerations' indicate otherwise.[48] A crucial material consideration is the suite of national planning policy documents. The most recent incarnation of these is the National Planning Policy Framework (NPPF).[49] This document 'sets out the Government's planning policies for England and how these are expected to be applied'.[50] However, the documents are not merely an expression of governmental policy aspirations; rather, they have a specific legal role in both the formulation of statutory strategic plans and in the determination of individual applications. Local strategic plans drafted by local authorities have to comply with the policies set out in the NPPF to achieve statutory status. When individual proposals for development are considered, the local planning authority must have regard to the NPPF (and the local strategic plans, which themselves must be compliant to be valid). Whilst other material considerations are also part of the decision-making process, the NPPF has a particularly strong status, and the NPPF and local strategic plans both play a central role in any appeal.

As a result, changes in the NPPF have an immediate and strong influence on the local decision-making space. The 2012 rewrite of planning policy reduced 1000 pages of guidance across many documents to a 52-page National Planning Policy Framework. At first, this may appear to represent a radical slimming down of central policy constraints, with a resulting increase in local decision-making space, contrary to the arguments in this chapter; in practice, though, this is to fail to understand the significance of the requirement for authorities to facilitate development unless one of the (reduced) number of specific policies points in a different direction.[51] The slimming down does not operate as a reduction of central intervention, but rather as a reduction in the number of situations in which a local authority has a basis for refusing consent. Although in the previous formulation there was more detailed central government policy on more topics, a local planning authority could always grant consent notwithstanding those detailed provisions, so the provisions served to provide reasons for local authority refusal. Reducing those provisions reduces

[48] Planning and Compulsory Purchase Act 2004, s 38(6).

[49] National Planning Policy Framework (London, Department for Communities and Local Government, 2012).

[50] ibid para 1.

[51] ibid para 15.

the opportunity for refusal. Thus, a reduction in the complexity of the framework, coupled with the stronger articulation of a presumption in favour of development, creates less scope for local refusals and more pressure to grant consent.

The way in which the latest NPPF reshapes the decision-making space can be seen in its impact upon affordable housing. Local authorities had hitherto been able to set appropriate housing mix policies through conversations in a local participatory decision-making space. However, the emphasis has now moved to 'objectively assessed' housing need studies using a single national methodology, the Strategic Housing Market Assessment.[52] In one sense, this is simply providing an evidence basis for decisions, but the wording of the NPPF is such that authorities have no scope to depart from the centrally approved methodology, and that is an entirely market-based methodology in which local perceptions of place and space are juxtaposed to the objective, expert methodology. The space in which local people can contribute to shaping their own community has been constrained by this professionalisation.

A different approach, but with the same consequence for decision-making space, can be seen in relation to 'windfall' sites. In identifying development sites to meet nationally set housing targets, authorities may make allowance for 'windfall' sites—that is, sites that were not anticipated at the local plan-making stage as becoming available for development, but which subsequently became available.[53] Historically, it has not been for the local authority, whilst drafting its strategic planning documents, to decide how much land may come forward unexpectedly as windfall sites during the planning period. This was a nuanced, locally highly contextualised judgment taken by elected lay members on the basis of professional advice. The NPPF reduces the scope for these judgments by imposing strong historic evidence requirements that there must be 'compelling evidence' that such sites have consistently become available in the past,[54] rather than enabling authorities to also consider factors that might point to a different future trend. Here there is no single methodology, but nonetheless the scope for local influence is reduced.

A particularly topical example of the pervasiveness of the NPPF 'policies' is the concept of the five-year supply of land set out in the NPPF. This requires an authority to have a deliverable set of sites capable of providing five years' worth of housing towards its overall housing requirement.[55] Failure to have such a supply available is a strong factor when determining appeals against refusal of consent to develop. The decision at one level remains in the local decision-making space, but the developer will be very likely to secure consent on appeal from an inspector or minister.[56] This development is on top of the development allocated in the strategic plan and provides a free for all, with the first developers who get their site to appeal likely to secure consent.

[52] ibid para 47.

[53] ibid para 48. For example, a site which is an industrial property at the time of the local plan, but which subsequently becomes available for redevelopment.

[54] The extensive body of precedent around the interpretation of this is beyond the scope of this chapter.

[55] NPPF, para 47. The five-year figure requires five years' worth of development at the rate set in the strategic plan, plus a 5% buffer, increased to a 20% buffer where authorities or developers consistently underdeliver against their housing requirement.

[56] The Planner, 19 June 2015.

Because the local decision-making space still exists (albeit heavily, though largely invisibly, structured in these cases), it can feel as if there is still an element of local participation in decision making. However, planning appeal decisions indicate otherwise. Independent inspectors, who are required to use the NPPF and national methodologies for determining applications, determine appeals. So, for example, they use DCLG housing projection figures to decide the level of new housing development to be granted consent in an area, rather than accepting alternative methodologies that may be proposed by local authorities or third parties (such as carrying capacity methods).[57] This means that decisions on how many houses to build in an area are driven by central government through the NPPF. Until the local authority has enough active developments taking place to meet the government's nationally set housing figures, developers will be able to secure consent on almost any site they take through the appeals process.

The next set of changes to consider are those that derive from performance standards set by central government. The Secretary of State has power[58] to put local planning authorities into special measures if they are designated as underperforming.[59] The consequences are such that authorities strive to avoid designation; for example, where a local authority is designated, a developer can apply directly to the Secretary of State for planning consent, bypassing the local decision-making space altogether.[60] The power afforded to the Secretary of State to define what merits designation means that authorities can become anxious to comply not only with central requirements, but also with central exhortations.

The proposed changes to the NPPF in December 2015[61] mark a further move towards supporting the development of housing, placing emphasis upon rapid development, including, for example, revising national policy 'to be explicit that substantial weight' should be given to the benefit of using brownfield land,[62] to allowing neighbourhood plans to allocate 'appropriate small scale sites' in the Green Belt for starter homes, and to strengthening pressure to grant consent on small sites by requiring local plans to contain a positive policy in support of development on small sites. For existing plans, which will not have such a policy, the NPPF revisions override the plan statement. Whilst these proposals were the subject of an inquiry by the House of Commons Communities and Local Government Committee,[63] the focus of the inquiry was upon detail, rather than the extent to which these changes affect the shape and size of local decision-making space.

[57] eg a 2012 appeal APP/X1165/A/11/2165846.

[58] Growth and Infrastructure Act 2013, s 1.

[59] Which means they have failed to determine 30% or more of their major applications within 13 weeks (a major application is 10+ homes or equivalent commercial floorspace), or that more than 20% of decisions are overturned on appeal. If the local authority is in 'special measures', it is also penalised financially by losing a proportion of the planning application fee, with proposals for extending this in the 2016 Technical Consultation (n 28).

[60] Growth and Infrastructure Act 2013, s 1.

[61] *Consultation on Proposed Changes to National Planning Policy* (London, Department for Communities and Local Government, 2015).

[62] ibid, para 22.

[63] ibid.

At times, this central government emphasis upon national policy delivery has exceeded its legal powers, and been successfully challenged in the courts.[64] What is crucial to the argument in this chapter is the cumulative effect of the diverse ways in which the decision-making space is being reshaped.

IV. REFORMULATING THE ROLE OF PLACE THROUGH MARKETISATION

One issue running through the changes is the impact of this centralisation of decision making upon the role of place in those decisions. Separate from the centralisation strand considered in the previous section, a further strand in the current changes is marketisation. The impact of marketisation on the scope for site-specific decision making can be seen most clearly in the changes to the system for ensuring developers contribute to infrastructure costs. Here we see a break with the concept of each piece of land being unique, with distinctive infrastructure opportunities and costs. The changes have been articulated as an efficiency measure, but their impact is to reduce the role of site specificity in infrastructure funding and commodify contributions. Under section 106 of the Town and Country Planning Act 1990, planning authorities were empowered to enter agreements with developers about the funding and provision of infrastructure required as a result of development. These were site-specific contextualised agreements, providing flexibility for the planning authority and developer, reflecting the particular needs derived from the development contextualised to the locality. Whilst case law developed some outer parameters for the exercise of these powers,[65] the key was the specific context of the development and the needs it generated.

The Planning Act 2008[66] introduced a new way of securing financial contributions from developers: the Community Infrastructure Levy (CIL). Through this, the scope for site-specific negotiation has been scaled back dramatically to cover a residual range of issues.[67] For our purposes, the key to the new CIL approach is that it is a predetermined authority-wide tariff, not tied to the specific needs of the community affected by development or the impact of the specific development. The global figure is based upon the strategic planning commitment to development and linked infrastructure needs in the context of economic viability. It does not, and cannot, reflect the actual cost of infrastructure provision, as that depends on where exactly development takes place.[68] It is an overall figure for the whole local authority, not a site-by-site calculation. It does not reflect the actual cost to the community of any specific development, but reflects an estimate of the overall impact. Each developer then pays an appropriate figure. However, whilst the resulting income must be spent on new infrastructure provision within the local authority area to address needs arising from development, it is not tied to funding the infrastructure needs arising from the site from which the contribution arose.

[64] See *R (on the application of West Berkshire District Council and another) v Secretary of State for Communities and Local Government* [2016] EWCA Civ 441, [2016] 1 WLR 3923 (CA).

[65] See, eg, *Tesco v Secretary of State for the Environment* [1995] 1 WLR 759; *R (on the application of Lichfield Securities Ltd) Lichfield District Council* [2001] EWCA Civ 304, [2001] All ER 78 (CA).

[66] s 205; see also Community Infrastructure Levy Regulations 2010, SI 2010/948.

[67] 2010 Regulations (ibid) reg 122, replacing Circular 1/97.

[68] ibid reg 123, although it can have some subdivisions.

The CIL represents a straight commodification of property relationships. The aim, as well as the result, has been to decontextualise a crucial part of the planning process. In the case of residential development, for example, irrespective of the location, one or at most two tariffs are set for the whole authority, based upon a flat fee per square metre of development.

Crucially for the issues in this chapter, the amount a developer contributes is not linked to the specifics of the locality or the measures needed to address the impact upon neighbours. Whilst neighbourhood factors are still material considerations in the granting of consent, and in the framing of the now less significant planning obligations and agreements, the scope for geographical specificity is reduced. This change is not accidental. The focus of the process leading to the introduction of the CIL and the government guidance on it gives priority to transactional efficiency—speed, transparency, fairness and certainty.[69] The CIL is 'intended to provide infrastructure to support the development of an area rather than to make individual planning applications acceptable'.[70] This is the language of marketisation, in which the uniqueness of sites is replaced by a purely financial approach to land use change impacts.

Developers are taking an active role in lobbying local authorities in the development of the levy tariff for an area. This moves the debate about developer contribution away from the site-specific stage to a more abstract stage, where there is less public engagement and less public awareness of its significance. This is similar to the way in which the development of brownfield registers is a key administrative process that will reshape consent decisions. The question is no longer what issues affect my place and space, which the developers could address, but how much should developers contribute to overall infrastructure expansion in the wider area? The scope for site-specific place and space decision making is reduced.

Whilst barely fully operative, in November 2015 the government announced a review[71] of the community infrastructure. It has been specifically instructed to consider the Conservative manifesto commitment to ensure 'communities know up front that necessary infrastructure such as schools and roads will be provided'.[72] This presents the concerns as being about information and efficiency, not about local place and space issues.

V. REFORMULATING PUBLIC PARTICIPATION: THE 'TRUST' DISCOURSE

The final factor identified at the start of this chapter as contributing to a significant reformulation of the role of place and space, and the changing role for specificity of site in planning, relates to a changing role for the public.

[69] *Community Infrastructure Levy, an Overview* (London, Department for Communities and Local Government, 2011) para 3.

[70] ibid para 59.

[71] 'Community Infrastructure Levy Review, The Peace Review 2015–16', available at www.gov.uk/government/consultations/community-infrastructure-levy-review-questionnaire (accessed on 1 September 2016).

[72] Conservative Party Manifesto 2015 (n 16); Peace Review terms of reference (ibid).

Reference has already been made to the significance of the concept of 'trust', particularly in David Cameron's articulation of modern Conservatism, as the Conservative Party's articulation of McAuslan's public participation ideology. However, since the 2015 election it has been used only selectively. In its first post-election use in the planning sphere, the Autumn Statement in November 2015,[73] the Treasury proposed empowering local communities to allocate land for development that had not been so allocated through the formal strategic planning processes—but did not empower them to delete allocations of land for development made through the strategic process. That autumn, the NPPF was revised to say that authorities should only grant consent for onshore wind generation facilities if, inter alia, 'following consultation, it can be demonstrated that the planning impacts identified by affected local communities have been fully addressed and therefore the proposal has their backing'.[74] This looks like an adoption of the concept of 'trust'—empowering residents as opposed to local government processes. However, in both cases, the government is using 'trust' as a means of seeking to circumvent what it anticipates to be obstacles to the implementation of its priorities within the local statutory decision-making space. In the case of housing, it is empowering residents to allocate more land for housing than the local decision-making space has permitted, and in the context of highly controversial wind generation schemes, the government must have been aware that this would operate as an obstacle to further wind power. The crucial point for the purposes of this chapter is that this is a very specific application of the trust concept, in that it is applied to an issue where the central government thinks local people will agree with it. It is a deployment of trust as a tool for delivering a specific agenda, and cannot be read as a commitment to trust in its own right, irrespective of outcome. As such, it continues to play to a centralism agenda, in which what McAuslan would see as ideologies of participation are subjugated to public policy articulated in a national policy space.

However, the Localism Act 2011[75] might be seen as pointing towards a different type of reformulation of public participation, changing the local decision-making space in a way that could increase site-specific consideration. The Act has been described as 'the most radical reform to planning law in 20 years'.[76] It introduced a new neighbourhood level to the planning process, with specific powers and opportunities, articulated through a 'Neighbourhood Development Plan'. The development of the plan is community led, through the voluntary sector rather than elected bodies, reflecting the 'trust' agenda. The resulting Neighbourhood Plan, unlike its Community Plan predecessor,[77] has a land use development focus, and is subject to examination in public and a neighbourhood referendum. At face value, this looks like a strong move in the opposite direction to the CIL process, and seems rooted in a different sense of the role of community, specificity, and possibly even a different view of property. It looks like a strong reassertion of the importance of place as a local, socially constructed concept.

[73] Treasury Autumn Statement (2015).
[74] HC Deb 18 June 2015, vol 597, col WS41.
[75] See also Neighbourhood Planning (General) Regulations 2012.
[76] S Ricketts and D Field, *Localism and Planning* (London, Bloomsbury, 2012).
[77] Local Government Act 2000, community strategy requirement.

Government guidance[78] on the new neighbourhood planning powers, issued in the same year as the CIL guidance, explains the problem that the reforms in the Localism Act are intended to solve—namely, that planning did not give 'members of the public enough influence over decisions that make a big difference to their lives'. The guidance posited that the centrally driven approach to housing numbers 'had the effect of making people feel put upon and less likely to welcome new development'.[79] 'Instead of local people being told what to do, the government thinks that local communities should have genuine opportunities to influence the future of the places where they live.'[80] The idea was for communities to come together to develop plans which would be used in the planning process following a neighbourhood referendum, as long as the proposals were consistent with national planning policy and strategic planning documents. Conceptually it fully articulates a concept of place and space as being important in development decisions. However, there is a crucial limitation to the process: it provides for community choice in the same way as the apocryphal Henry Ford choice ('any colour as long as it is black'). The neighbourhood plan must be compliant with the national planning policy and strategic plans, unless allocating more land for development. As such, the process offers a limited articulation of place and space.[81] A neighbourhood plan cannot prevent development allocated through the strategic planning process, though it can provide additional land for development—for example, small-scale development, brownfield redevelopment or community facilities. The rhetoric of trust is, on crucial issues, a trust in the community to deliver more development, not a trust in their judgment about less development.

Whilst the rhetoric of localism is pervasive, its delivery has been more limited. Hundreds of neighbourhood plans are in place, but in some parts of the country none have yet been approved. Given the complexity of the process for developing a neighbourhood plan, the requirement for it to be community (not council) led, the length of the process and its increasing juridification, it is not surprising that there is an emerging correlation between areas adopting such plans and the relative affluence of communities.[82]

A second approach to the question of local support for development has been tried through the New Homes Bonus Scheme (2011). Whilst ostensibly about public participation, it is rooted in a fungible approach to land and our relationship to it—everything has a price. At the time it was launched, it was positioned as part of a commitment to 'a radical reform of the planning system to give neighbourhoods far more ability to determine the shape of the places in which people live'.[83] The New Homes Bonus Scheme was at least rhetorically predicated upon a perception

[78] DCLG (n 24).

[79] ibid 11.

[80] ibid 12.

[81] Much has been written on the question of the impact and potential of the new localism. See, eg, G Haughton and P Allmendinger, 'Spatial Planning and the New Localism' (2013) 28(1) *Journal Planning Practice and Research* 1.

[82] Data calculated from table, *Planning Magazine*, update 26 February 2016.

[83] DCLG press release on launch, cited, eg, at www.remarkableengagement.co.uk/councils-to-be-given-localism-grant-as-part-of-new-homes-bonus-scheme (accessed on 1 September 2016).

that localism matters. It was designed as a financial incentive to encourage local support for housing growth, and was tied to the number of new homes in an area. Local government areas were given money from central government dependent upon the number of new homes built there. The assumption was that the money would make new development more acceptable, and therefore face less opposition. The underlying concept is one of fungibility—that the reasons people articulate for being opposed to (or less often supportive of) development proposals are fungible, capable of being traded for financial value.

In 2014, the Coalition government carried out an evaluation of the policy to see if it had affected attitudes and behaviours.[84] The policy, whilst providing a welcome injection of money into communities affected by new development, appears to have been unsuccessful in speeding up the granting of consent or reducing local objections to residential development. In December 2015, the DCLG issued a consultation on the reform of the New Homes Bonus 'in order to better reflect authorities' delivery of new housing', 'increasing the focus' of the payments and changing the duration of payments. The public, locality and neighbourhood are not mentioned in this consultation. The focus is now upon using the fund to influence planning authority behaviour, for example by making the payment dependent upon a valid local plan being in place. The rhetoric of that consultation is now of the New Homes Bonus as an economic tool designed to affect local planning authority conduct, not public behaviour. The failure of this overtly market-based tool perhaps indicates the strength of local commitments to changes of land use as being firmly rooted in their conceptualisation of place and space, and not merely a feature of economic transactions. As such, it illustrates why the process of commodifying land and land use changes will continue to run up against different understandings of the significance of land in constructing our sense of place and space.

VI. CONCLUSION

It is possible to go on and map other provisions in the wave of changes in a similar manner. One might comment that this is nothing new: planning policy has always been subject to these changes of emphasis. Indeed, the durability of its legal framework is precisely because of this capacity to act as a vehicle for current political priorities. The growing pace of change might be seen as simply ephemeral, part of the (as yet unsuccessful) drive[85] towards addressing a nationally identified housing shortage that has been around since at least the Barker Reviews in 2004.[86]

However, cumulatively, the provisions amount to the biggest shift in emphasis of the planning system in a generation, not just in the rhetoric of public policy statements,[87] reshaping the space in which planning decisions are taken.

[84] *Evaluation of the New Homes Bonus* (London, Department for Communities and Local Government, 2014).

[85] *Investing for Prosperity* (London, London School of Economics Growth Commission, 2013).

[86] Barker (n 18).

[87] Treasury (n 19) para 9.13 called it 'an urban planning revolution'.

The scope for people to articulate and realise conceptions of the importance of place, specificity and locality are severely diminished compared to any previous time. The thesis of this chapter is that this is not just a changed public policy position, but reflects also a changing perception of the importance of place in constructing perceptions of the relationship between the individual in his home and the state.

The current array of changes cannot be justified by a single conceptual rationale. Multiple influences and rationales are in play, with many of the changes justified by free market or individualist ideologies, but some key aspects of the approach lie outside of those. This chapter argues that planning is being repositioned as a tool for the delivery of central policy imperatives rather than a regulator of their implementation, and that the changes highlighted in the introduction add up to a significant change in the decision-making space. Cumulatively the move away from local decision making may be driven by desires to deliver particular policy agendas, but its effect is to alter the scope for consideration of, and therefore significance of, the specificities of place and space. Perhaps unwittingly, they point towards commodification of property.

This may be an ephemeral change, but it would seem as if a reshaping of the decision-making space for planning is occurring. There is sufficient evidence to conclude that there has been, possibly inadvertently and certainly not explicitly, a reshaping of the role of concepts of local place in planning processes. The ideologies of public participation and property ownership identified by McAuslan have been subjugated to a centrally determined public policy ideology; planning has been repositioned from a regulator of national public policy imperatives to an instrument in their delivery, concepts of 'trust' are displacing other ideologies of public participation, and marketisation of planning space is reducing the role of place and specificity. There is, however, evidence, for example from the New Homes Bonus failure, that the concept of property as distinctive and associated with place, space and identity is tenacious and is not easily going to be displaced by commodification of land.

The shifts in social perceptions of property and planning are being signalled through shifts in a complex regulatory structure, which is at best opaque. The public continue to engage with the local decision-making space, with increasingly unrealistic expectations of its scope to reflect their constructions of place and space. The piecemeal approach to the delivery of this change risks the public not being aware of the change or in a position to affect it. Planning guidance and procedures are still embedded in the local, with complex public consultation processes and local decision making in the formal sense. However, around that formal process, the policy and targets are now coming directly from the Treasury, and marketisation is reducing scope for place and space influence. The public still believe the language and procedures of formal planning—that this is about decisions by local elected representatives—and blame those representatives for decisions which are locally unpalatable. Are we doing anyone a service by continuing with the mythology of a 'local' planning system or would it be better to articulate a new deal, which is explicit about the shift in power in planning? At least then the public would find it easier to identify where the real decision-making power lies.

15

The Anti-wilderness Bias in the Common Law and Modern American Property Law

JILL FRALEY*

I. INTRODUCTION

IN 1996, PROFESSOR John Sprankling argued that, for the purposes of ensuring development, American property law cultivated a particular approach to land that disfavoured wilderness.[1] Drawing on Morton Horwitz's *Transformation of American Law*,[2] along with James Willard Hurst's influence more generally,[3] Sprankling articulated a theory of courts as major forces behind the destruction of wilderness land.[4] Sprankling argued that American property law developed a substantial bias towards development.[5] This bias, he argued, was not accidental,[6] but rather the specific result of courts working to 'further economic development'.[7] Scholars have interpreted Sprankling's causality argument widely. JB Ruhl, for

* Associate Professor and Director of the Center for Law and History at Washington and Lee University School of Law. I am grateful for the helpful comments of the conference attendees and the anonymous reviewers.

[1] JG Sprankling, 'The Antiwilderness Bias in American Property Law' (1996) 63 *University of Chicago Law Review* 519, 533 (1996). Sprankling's approach drew, to some degree, on the larger argument that American judges carefully explored the common law, adopting only those doctrines that suited the new ways of thinking that emerged in America. For a further discussion of this approach see A Brophy, 'Property and Progress: Antebellum Landscape Art and Property Law' (2009) 40 *McGeorge Law Review* 603, 606–07. Others have also suggested that the ostensible 'heroes of the nineteenth-century courts acted to tilt American common law toward the anti-wilderness bias'—MC Blumm and JB Ruhl, 'Background Principles, Takings, and Libertarian Property: A Reply to Professor Huffman' (2010) 37 *Ecology Law Quarterly* 805, 830.

[2] MJ Horwitz, *The Transformation of American Law 1780–1860* (Cambridge, Harvard University Press, 1977) 30.

[3] JW Hurst, *The Growth of American Law* (Boston, Little, Brown & Co, 1950); James Willard Hurst, *Law and the Conditions of Freedom in the Nineteenth-Century United States* (Madison, University of Wisconsin Press, 1956).

[4] Sprankling (n 1) 519.

[5] ibid 521. Sprankling argued a similar premise in an earlier article—JG Sprankling, 'An Environmental Critique of Adverse Possession' (1994) 79 *Cornell Law Review* 816 (arguing that adverse possession laws reflect a pro-development ideology that encourages exploitation of wilderness lands).

[6] Sprankling (n 1) 521.

[7] ibid 522.

example, describes Sprankling's argument as concluding that American courts 'systematically subverted incentives to conserve wilderness'.[8]

While Sprankling briefly considered other common law doctrines, such as adverse possession, he focused, in large part, on waste law. This focus is not accidental. Waste law has traditionally provided a point of debate about the development of American law and its relationship to the British common law. One of the most notable examples of this phenomenon is Morton Horwitz's deeply influential theory of transformations in American law. Horwitz, relying in large part on waste law as an example, set out to prove that '[b]y 1820 the legal landscape in America bore only the faintest resemblance to what had existed forty years before'.[9] Horwitz attributed those changes to the pressures of economic development. Even while Horwitz's theories of the transformation of law have been criticised in other contexts, his approach to waste law has remained the primary narrative on the topic. Other persuasive legal thinkers, including John Sprankling and Jed Purdy, have similarly employed the traditional story of the transformation of waste law to support larger assertions about the transformation of the common law from Britain to America.[10] More recent scholarship has questioned the validity of this narrative about the transformation of waste law.[11] For the moment, however, the primary point is that any historical story about the development of the common law in America naturally focuses on waste law due to its historical prominence in American scholarship. Sprankling's account is no different. He chooses waste law as a focus and even relies upon Horwitz's approach. For this reason, this chapter also focuses on waste law and includes surface water liability because of its similar position at the line between property law and tort.

The purpose of this chapter is not to protest Sprankling's conclusion that American courts acted to favour industrial development on many occasions. Nor does this chapter suggest that British courts never acted to preserve land or that American law never acts to preserve land now. Rather, the purpose of this chapter is to expose the false starting point and contrast of Sprankling's argument: the idea that the British common law acted consistently as a force for conservation and preservation and, therefore, that American courts acted uniquely when they favoured industrialisation. This chapter focuses on waste law, which is an excellent example of how the British common law already contained an anti-wilderness bias long before American industrialisation.

Waste law allows recovery against a tenant for changes to the estate that detrimentally impact the property that will return to the landlord or transfer to a future interest holder.[12] The strict common law rule forbade changes, even those changes that increased the property value.[13] A tenant could not tear down the

[8] JB Ruhl, 'The "Background Principles" of Natural Capital and Ecosystem Services—Did Lucas Open Pandora's Box?' (2007) 22 *Journal of Land Use & Environmental Law* 525, 526.

[9] Horwitz (n 2) 30.

[10] Sprankling (n 1); J Purdy, 'The American Transformation of Waste Doctrine: A Pluralist Interpretation' (2006) 91 *Cornell Law Review* 653 (2006).

[11] See J Fraley, 'A New History of Waste Law' (2017) 100 *Marquette Law Review* (forthcoming).

[12] 8 *Powell on Real Property* §56.02.

[13] RC Minor, *The Law of Real Property* (St Paul, West Publishing Co, 1910) 333.

old and non-functional manor house and build a new one, even though the landowner would acquire the much more valuable improvement. Later, American courts rejected the strict rule, choosing instead to evaluate waste via property value. Only a decrease in value constituted waste. Sprankling saw the change in waste law as 'the most obvious example of anti-wilderness retooling'.[14] American courts needed a new rule for waste because the common law 'was a poor tool for encouraging the exploitation of virgin land'.[15] The British system, according to Sprankling, 'focused on preserving the condition of land already in productive use in a mature agrarian economy'.[16]

As for American courts, Sprankling described the courts as refashioning waste to allow land clearing,[17] because the courts were '[d]riven by [an] instrumentalist vision' of land development in America.[18] The new American rule of waste law, Sprankling found, encouraged the destruction of the wilderness in pursuit of development. Courts created the rule deliberately and particularly to support the westward expansion of the country and the development of industries.

Sprankling's anti-wilderness bias approach to American property law has been persuasive.[19] Yet, ample evidence demonstrates that American property law did not need to retool the common law in pursuit of an anti-wilderness bias. Instead, American property law inherited such a bias from the common law, which, rather than being conservation oriented, as Sprankling imagined, itself contained a substantial bias against wilderness.

II. THE COMMON LAW PREFERENCE FOR ARABLE LANDS

Sprankling's thesis depends on the idea that the British common law was a force for conservation and preservation of land—a position that he can then contrast with the American common law's preference for development. In significant ways, however, the British common law, rather than favouring conservation, strongly favoured the productive use of lands and, indeed, contained an elaborate hierarchy that created common law measures to protect lands of better quality from damage and to encourage development.

Writing in 1584, in *Tyrringham's Case*, Lord Coke precisely described how the common law favoured lands that were planted.[20] Coke says, 'It is true that agriculture and tillage is greatly respected and favoured as well by the common law, as by the common assent of the king, lords spiritual and temporal, and all the commons, in many Parliaments'.[21] Coke more specifically declares that 'The common

[14] Sprankling (n 1) 533.
[15] ibid 523.
[16] ibid 524–25.
[17] ibid 534–35.
[18] ibid 534.
[19] See J Lovett, 'Doctrines of Waste in a Landscape of Waste' (2007) 72 *Missouri Law Review* 1209, 1228 (describing Sprankling's thesis as 'incontrovertible').
[20] Quoted in WA Bewes, *The Law of Waste* (London, Sweet & Maxwell, 1894) 30.
[21] E Coke, *The First Part of the Institutes of the Laws of England, or, A Commentary upon Littleton* (London, Luke Hansard & Sons, 1809) vol 1, §85b.

law prefers arable land before all other, and therefore for its dignity ought to be named in praecipe before meadow, pasture, wood, or any other soil'.[22] Lord Coke concludes that 'the common law gives arable land, the pre-eminency and precedency over meadows, pastures, woods, and mines, and all other ground whatsoever'.[23]

Courts emphasised arable land within the hierarchy for a variety of social reasons. As Coke explained, if arable land were converted into something else, meadow perhaps, then it led to 'deplorable consequences', namely 'the increase of idleness, the root and cause of all mischiefs'.[24] Converting arable land into other types of land tended to 'the subversion of the policy and good government of the land, and all this by decay of agriculture, which is there said to be one of the greatest commodities of this realm'.[25] The common law hierarchy, which preferred cultivated land to ploughed land demonstrated an understanding of the economics of providing for a hungry population. Cultivated land provided for the population directly. As a result, the common law emphasised cultivation, reasoning that 'Agriculture or tillage is of great account in law, as being very profitable for the common wealth, wherein the goodness of the habit is best known by the privation'.[26] Pasture lands were rated as worse than cultivated lands, and woodland were rated as worse than either, because neither pasture nor woodlands so effectively supported the population. As Coke explains, 'where in some town two hundred persons were occupied and lived by their lawful labours, by converting of tillage into pasture there have been maintained but two or three herdsmen'.[27] Supporting full employment and providing for a hungry population meant encouraging the use of land for cultivation above all other potential uses.[28] The ideal of the British landscape was that all lands were 'profitable and habitable'.[29]

These designations mattered because they represented the court's views on the quality and economic value of a particular piece of land. Practically speaking, this mattered in the context of waste law. If a tenant converted one type of land into another type that was less preferred, then logically the owner had a strong argument for waste—that his land had been made less valuable by the conversion. Economically speaking, the courts found that 'The garden is the highest state of cultivation; open fields and common pastures the lowest'.[30] Thus, determinations in waste law could rely on the hierarchy of land uses to quickly and accurately indicate whether there had been a change in value.[31]

Notably, there is also a line of waste cases that discusses the standard hierarchy of land values and then deviates from applying the normal hierarchy to determine whether the tenant committed waste. The reason for this deviation is found in the

[22] ibid.
[23] ibid.
[24] ibid.
[25] ibid.
[26] ibid.
[27] ibid.
[28] Quoted in Bewes (n 20) 31. The term messuage referred to what in American history was known sometimes as the homestead—the principal dwelling along with the adjacent land intended to support it.
[29] T Cox, *Magna Britannia et Hibernia*, vol 3 (London, Nutt, 1720–31) 470.
[30] W Marshall, *The Rural Economy of Yorkshire*, vol 1 (London, T Cadell, 1788) 50.
[31] For a more thorough discussion of the history of waste law see Fraley (n 11).

doctrine of waste, which extends to more than simple economic harm to land. The traditional prongs of waste law included not only harm, but also 'impairing of the evidence of title'.[32] Normally such designations as meadow or pasture referred to the 'quality of land' as well as its identity.[33] The hierarchy of land uses, which align with economic values, could not fully govern the question of waste because land uses marked property boundaries. As a result, even if a tenant ploughed up for planting land that had been used as pasture, he was guilty of waste despite the economic improvement in the value of the land.[34] This particular line of boundary-maintenance cases was, however, an exception to the overall perspective in British cases about the quality of land and the most desirable uses of land. This hierarchy of land uses expressed the anti-wilderness bias that existed in the common law at the time. It explicitly encouraged the fenced garden as the ideal land use, by assigning it the highest quality designation and economic value. This hierarchy of land uses encouraged the development and cultivation of land, specifically, the process of improvement, which would later be integrated into the common law of property as it existed in colonial America.

III. EMPHASISING IMPROVEMENT

The preference for cultivated lands pushed forward an agricultural movement in seventeenth- and eighteenth-century England, Wales and Scotland. During this time, landowners increasingly became obsessed with the idea of improvement. Improvement wedded optimism and perseverance with the concept that landowners might take land that was otherwise not arable, such as swamps, heaths or lowlands, and, by draining, ditching, fortifying and fertilising, might be able to coax them into bringing forth harvests.

Surveys began to not only describe the lands of any area, but also to consider whether such lands might be amenable to the process of improvement. The worst of land could be described as 'a most dreary tract of heath land', which was 'scarcely capable of any improvement'.[35] Even while little-used areas might have provided some fish or fowl, fodder or light grazing to some members of the local population, those who were keen to see 'new wealth and raw materials' embraced improvement as the way to create true productivity in all the lands, no matter how marginal such tracts initially appeared.[36] With a great amount of work, it was possible to take a 'vast tract of uncultivated wild place' and turn it 'into a profitable arable farm'.[37]

[32] CT Boone, *Law of Real Property*, vol 1 (San Francisco, Bancroft-Whitney, 1901) 300.

[33] *Simmons v Norton* (1831) All ER Rep 343, 345.

[34] For a full discussion of waste law, land quality and the use of waste law to maintain property boundaries see Fraley (n 11).

[35] W Stevens, *General View of the Agriculture of the County of Dorset* (London, Board of Agriculture, 1812).

[36] S Solnick, 'Ecocriticism from Shakespeare to James Lovelock' in L Bruckner and D Brayton (eds), *What Else Is Pastoral?* (Ithaca, Cornell University Press, 2011) 2.

[37] O Price, P Russell, W Adlard and J Browne, *England Displayed*, vol 1 (London, Adlard & Browne, 1769), 308.

The improvement obsession generated an extensive literature of land management,[38] which included instructions for improvement and drainage.[39] The ideal desire of the landowner was 'forming excellent pasture land out of the swamps and bogs, and even making them capable of producing large crops of corn'.[40] Only a strong cultural push towards cultivation, along with the pressures of population and the availability of labour, would have supported such optimistic and expensive endeavours. The leading minds of the time had concluded that 'the importance of agriculture to the public interest is such that the knowledge thereof cannot be too much cultivated, nor the means of its improvement too much regarded'.[41] At the heart of this improvement, movement was the one clear call to action: all land could be cultivated and all land, therefore, should be cultivated.

IV. LAND USE AND ENCLOSURE

The constant call to cultivation, embedded in the common law preference for agriculture, is most evident in the continuing pressures towards enclosure in Britain. This, in turn, was significant for the American common law's development in the colonial period because it set standards for ideal property maintenance that were incorporated into early American property law addressing everything from establishing land claims to building dams.

The process of enclosure in Britain began slowly, with initially much of the country's land continuing as open fields, commons and wastes. With each century, however, commonly held land decreased as parcels were distributed and enclosed, moving the lands from common to private ownership.[42] Strong social pressures forced this movement forward, branding the commons as 'wasted, desolate and chaotic'.[43] The commons represented the 'state of nature', unshaped by man, and thus doomed to minor productivity.[44] Wilderness or uncultivated land was 'absolutely useless'.[45] However enclosure meant the possibility of increased crop yields and support of a populous nation.[46] At the heart of it, '[t]he process of enclosure replaced

[38] Examples include A Blackwell, *A New Method of Improving Cold, Wet and Barren Lands* (London, J Walthoe, 1741); R Bradley, *A General Treatise of Agriculture, Both Philosophical and Practical* (London, W Johnston, 1757); J Mills, *A New and Complete System of Practical Husbandry* (London, R Baldwin, 1762–65); J Mortimer, *The Whole Art of Husbandry, or the Way of Managing and Improving of Land* (London, H Mortlock, 1708); G Markham, *Markham's Farewell to Husbandry* (London, W Wilson, 1653); J Smith, *England's Improvement Reviv'd* (London, Tho Newcomb, 1670). For a more thorough discussion of this literature see JM Fraley, 'Water, Water, Everywhere: Surface Water Liability' (2015) 5 *Michigan Journal of Environmental & Administrative Law* 73.

[39] J Mordant, *The Complete Steward* vol 1 (London, W. Sandby, 1761) 70–74.

[40] R Brookes, *Brookes' General Gazetter Abridged* (London, B Law & C Dilly, 1796) (unpaginated).

[41] Bradley (n 38) A2.

[42] GE Mingay, *Parliamentary Enclosure in England* (Oxon, Routledge 1997). Mingay reviews the earlier history of 'piecemeal' enclosure before continuing to the later parliamentary enclosures.

[43] L Brace, 'Husbanding the Earth and Hedging out the Poor' in AR Buck, J McLaren and NE Wright (eds), *Land and Freedom: Law, Property Rights and the British Diaspora* (Farnham, Ashgate, 2001) 5, 9.

[44] See Brace (n 43) 9.

[45] RF Nash, *Wilderness and the American Mind* (New Haven, Yale University Press, 2001) 32.

[46] DC Webb, *An Address to the Public, Setting forth the Benefit Accruing to the Community at Land, by Enclosing the Lands Now Laying Waste in Great Britain* (London, SN, 1795) 9.

the chaos of open fields and common lands with a neat patchwork of hedged fields securely held as private property by virtuous, improving individuals'.[47] Such gardens then provided the sustenance of a nation. According to Arthur Young, the way to prosperity was to 'bring the waste lands of the kingdom into culture, instead of ling, whins and fern', and then 'bread and beef will be plentiful'.[48]

The processes of improvement and enclosure went hand in hand. Enclosure was viewed as 'a thing that lays a foundation for industry and good husbandry'.[49] The process of enclosure and improvement also neatly aligned with the emphasis on labour in securing rightful property claims. Good citizens should go about the kingdom's business by labouring on the land to establish productive agriculture on any unused areas. Specifically, they should 'convert barren and heathie ground, left unhusbanded for many ages, into commodious arable land with pastures and meadows, as any bee in this kingdom [would]'.[50] Enclosure supported the investment of labour and allowed the improvement movement to flourish.

Some advocates for enclosure pushed the link between enclosure and improvement even further. Advocates of enclosure believed that its benefits for improvement began immediately, even before investments of labour and fertiliser. Such advocates went so far as to argue that the process of creating walls and hedgerows itself improved the arability of land. As Daniel Webb wrote in 1795, 'enclosing land will in a degree assist vegetation, by preventing the winds from carrying away those fertile juices, which are the chief support of plants'.[51] Webb's assertion, of course, arose from the agricultural knowledge of the time, which favoured the idea that the earth emitted some sort of natural elixirs.[52] The walls of enclosure mattered then because 'whatever rises from the earth by exhalation, proceeds till its own natural gravity, or some object detains it'.[53] Relying on this logic, the very process of enclosing land took the first step of improving the arability of the parcel.

During the period of the British settlement of North America, these ideas of commons and enclosure, land uncontrolled and land moulded by labour, formed a central foundation for British understandings of property.[54] Within the North American continent, these sentiments emerged regularly in the contrast of the enclosed garden with the wilderness.[55] The next section considers these points in further detail.

[47] See Brace (n 43).

[48] A Young, *Observations on the Present State of the Waste Lands of Great Britain* (London, W Nicoll, 1773) 38.

[49] J Mortimer, *The Whole Art of Husbandry* (London, SH, 1707) 1.

[50] S Hartlib, *A Discours of Husbandrie used in Brabant and Flanders* (London, Du Gard, 1652) 2.

[51] Webb (n 46) 6.

[52] In 1652, Samuel Hartlib explained the state of agricultural knowledge: 'It is a main deficiency in husbandry, that though we know by experience [some thing] do cause fertility; yet we are very ignorant of the true causes of fertility'. He explained that fertility might arise through 'something essential, or accidental; material or immaterial; corporal or spiritual; principal or instrumental; visible or invisible; whether saline, sulphureous or mercurial; or … whether all things are nourished by vapours, fumes, atoms, effluvia?'—Hartlib (n 50) 16.

[53] Webb (n 46) 6.

[54] See Brace (n 43) 16.

[55] See Nash (n 45) 26.

V. DEVELOPMENT BIASES IN THE PROCESS OF LAND CLAIMING IN NORTH AMERICA

The concepts of improvement and enclosure generally, along with the common law hierarchy of land uses, served as cornerstones of the British colonisation process, establishing the hierarchy of land uses within the early American common law of property. A key part of the process of establishing colonies was justifying the empire's territorial claims, both vis-à-vis Native Americans and vis-à-vis other Europeans who also sought territorial control. In both contexts, British colonisers repeatedly relied on cultivation and improvement to support their territorial claims.

The availability of land that could be improved suggested, at least to the British, that such lands might be acquired as new territory. Speaking of Pennsylvania, Nathaniel Crouch explained,

> It is the jus gentium, or law of nations, whatever waste or uncultured country is the discovery of any price, it is the right of that prince who was at the charge of that discovery … to preserve and improve.[56]

Lands wanted improvement and, therefore, also wanted labour. If the existing population could not or did not provide such labour, then there was a want of settlement of that land. The British employed precisely such an argument to support their colonisation of Ireland, reasoning that 'The fertile kingdom of Ireland, for want only of people to cultivate its rich and vast wastes and territories, maintaineth but a small trade in comparison of its neighbours'.[57] The solution was colonisation, which would then allow for 'an industrious tilling and improving of lands'.[58] Settlement provided a new labour force, which would set about bringing the land to its maximum economic use: fenced and planted fields.

Colonisation, therefore, focused on fostering a 'spirit of planting', which would 'spread[] wider and wider daily'.[59] The ultimate object was no less than 'the enclosure and improvement of all the open grounds and waste land of the whole country' of England.[60] Although colonists would begin with a 'waste of savage country', they would soon transform the landscape into orderly and fenced fields and gardens.[61] Following this thinking, British settlers and those who remained in Britain but spoke out in support of the colonial enterprise reasoned that 'in a new settled country, the chief strength and stock of the people ought to be employed in agriculture'.[62] People supplied the labour that both developed the land, creating exportable resources, and staked the national claim upon that land.

[56] N Crouch, *The English Empire in America* (London, Bettesworth, 1735) 100.

[57] J Worlidge, *Mr Worlidge's Two Treatises* (London, M Vvotton, 1694) viii.

[58] ibid.

[59] W Strahan and T Cadell, *Present State of Husbandry in Scotland*, vol 1 (Edinburgh, W Strahan & T Cadell, 1778) 184.

[60] D O'Pheilly, *The Ants, A Rhapsody* (London, L Davis & C Reymers, 1767) 41.

[61] R Dodsley, *The Annual Register, or a View of the History, Politicks, and Literature for the Year 1763* (London, T Burton, 1764) 18–19.

[62] A Grant, *A Dissertation on the Chief Obstacles to the Improvement of Land* (Aberdeen, 1755) 27.

British colonisers appealed to the concept of land improvement to justify their claims to land vis-à-vis other European powers.[63] This is evident in terms of how the British colonists argued the law of land claiming when European powers disagreed about territorial claims. The British approach to land claiming focused primarily on possession[64] and, more particularly, on improvement of the land.[65] More specifically, the British concept of arable land—straight rows and fenced gardens, which demonstrated labour on the landscape—was crucial to British territorial claims.[66] British settlers emphasised agricultural techniques that created visible changes to the landscape, and, more importantly, tangible evidence of occupation and investments of labour. The British approach to colonisation very much mapped the legal hierarchy of land in the common law. The degree of change from nature represented civilisation: 'The garden is the highest state of cultivation; open fields and common pastures the lowest'.[67] For this reason, early colonial laws in North America strongly encouraged fencing and cultivation, often requiring these things explicitly to either establish or maintain an individual claim to private property. The colonial governments enforced planting and fencing, meanwhile using the process of planting and fencing as their justification for their rightful possession.

Cultivation, therefore, as the highest state of land in the common law, served as the pinnacle of possession for British land claims.[68] This formed a central part of the arguments justifying Native American dispossession.[69] British arguments emphasised a hierarchy of land uses, favouring cultivation and describing native uses of land as unproductive, even when those lands may have been agriculturally productive before colonisation.[70] British land uses required more labour and produced more visible changes to the landscape. This narrative allowed British colonists to argue the superiority of labour, which they contrasted with simple occupation.

Locke's theories of labour and property underpinned much of this approach. By grounding claims to property in labour rather than occupation, Locke provided the theoretical backbone for a British view of colonisation that emphasised cultivation.[71] This approach then provides a justification for taking lands when the settled population 'does not use its soil but keeps it idle and waste'.[72] Locke began

[63] C Tomlins, 'In a Wilderness of Tigers: Violence, the Discourse of English Colonizing, and the Refusals of American History' (2003) 4 *Theoretical Inquiries in Law* 451, 481.

[64] For an excellent account of the British reliance on possession—and particularly cultivation and fencing—as justification against competing European territorial claims see P Seed, *Ceremonies of Possession in Europe's Conquest of the New World 1492–1640* (Cambridge, Cambridge University Press, 1995).

[65] Tomlins (n 63) 481.

[66] B Arneil, *John Locke and America: The Defence of English Colonialism* (Oxford, Clarendon Press, 1996) 18.

[67] Marshall (n 30) 50.

[68] See Seed (n 64).

[69] For an in-depth explanation of how agricultural arguments contributed to dispossession of native lands see Wilcomb E. Washburn, *Red Man's Land, White Man's Law* (Norman, Oklahoma University Press, 1995).

[70] A Sluyter, 'Colonialism and Landscape in the Americas: Material/Conceptual Transformations and Continuing Consequences' (2001) 91 *Annals of the Association of American Geographers* 410, 411.

[71] See Arneil (n 66) 18.

[72] ibid. 51.

with the premise that land was 'of so little value without labour',[73] and in placing all his emphasis on labour, attributed poverty to the failure to appropriately utilise land.[74] The whole idea of property then was conditional with proper ownership finding its justification within labour upon the land.[75] Locke's ideas, being strongly utilitarian,[76] supported a utilitarian approach to the maximisation of land use as measured by economics.

This strategy effectively argued against both rightful native possession[77] and the sparsely populated settlements of Europeans, such as the Spanish oversight of native colonies or the barely inhabited French lines of forts.[78] Rather than planning 'to plant and settle', the French instead 'erected military forts'.[79] In the British view, 'when any members of a civilised people leave their native land to settle in a waste, uncultivated country, the natural employment of these emigrants must be agriculture and a confined sort of a commerce'.[80]

The development-focused approach to colonisation also fitted the dominant religious approach to labour. Within many of the early colonies, a Calvinist approach meant that '[f]or the improvers, the notion of improvement was fundamental to God's intentions for the earth and for mankind'.[81] The greatest duty was to 'obliterate[]' as much as possible 'the broad lines of nature'.[82] Cultivation represented labour and marked God's favour.[83] That representation of labour provided evidence for the process of land claiming, while the favour of God blessed both the work ethic and the colonial endeavour more generally. The concepts of improvement and enclosure generally, along with the common law hierarchy of land uses, moved to America as a continuation of the traditional common law, adapted to the colonial context. The British common law's hierarchy of land uses became a key part of the early American common law of property because land use became the mechanism for perfecting title to land both in the local context and as the British argument in the international contests over territory. In both contexts, British colonisers repeatedly relied on cultivation and improvement, to support their claims to land.

[73] J Locke, *The Works of John Locke*, vol 2 (London, Bettesworth, 1727) 68.

[74] CC Geisler, 'Land and Poverty in the United States' [February 1995] *Land Economics* 16, 17.

[75] See Brace (n 43) 16.

[76] H Rashdall, 'The Philosophical Theory of Property' in *Property: Its Duties and Rights* (London, Macmillan, 1915) 39–40.

[77] The argument followed along these lines for native peoples: 'For they account it a very just cause of war, if any nation will hinder others to come and possess a part of their soil, of which they make no use, but let it lie idle and uncultivated; since every man has by the law of nature a right to such a waste portion of the earth as is necessary for his subsistence'—T More, *Utopia, or the Happy Republic* 61 (Edinburgh, Hamilton & Balfour, 1743).

[78] For further explanation of why the occupation/labour distinction was important, and for Locke's role in formulating these arguments for British colonists see Arneil (n 66) 18.

[79] JH Wynne, *A General History of the British Empire in America*, vol 2 (London, W Richardson, 1770) 11. In the British view, only 'barbarous nations … abolished improved agriculture', instead 'possessing, without labor or trouble, the vast deserts which their arms had made, and cultivated, very superficially, only a small spot near their habitations'—Mills (n 38) v.

[80] Wynne (ibid) 11.

[81] Brace (n 43) 6.

[82] W Marshall, *The Rural Economy of the West of England*, vol 2 (London, G Nicol, 1796) 2.

[83] J Flavel, *The Whole Works of the Reverend Mr John Flavel* (Glasgow, J Orr, 1754) 163.

VI. DRAINAGE AND LAND CLAIMING IN NORTH AMERICA

The British approach to improvement fostered drainage plans in North America as it had in the British Isles. These drainage plans also impacted the development of property law in colonial America. The British approach to wetlands meant that marshes, fens and swamps were 'utterly a waste',[84] and therefore should be ditched and drained to the ultimate end of cultivation. In their natural state, these lands were of no value—and, indeed, were merely 'a nuisance' for their owners.[85] In Daniel Defoe's words, marshy areas were 'dangerous places to man and beast' where 'many have been swallowed up in them'.[86]

During colonisation, the British embraced land drainage as a solution to the many marshy lowlands of eastern North America[87] and sought to cultivate all types of landscapes.[88] This philosophy was not just an abstract idea, but was explicitly built into British property law as it was being transplanted in North America. Patentees could settle their lands (thereby vesting their property rights) either by planting three of every 50 acres granted or by clearing and draining three acres of wetlands.[89]

Embracing drainage to this degree required a particular agricultural perspective—one very different from that of modern farmers. Agricultural science provided this perspective. In the eighteenth century, the best of agricultural science supported drainage as a method of creating new, arable lands. As of the mid-century, agricultural science failed to fully determine the source of nutrients for plants, which might be either 'juices' or 'furnished by the air, and put into action by the sun'.[90] Relatively undeveloped science permitted extensive belief in the arability of lands below water.[91] The problem was simply that the land was 'too wet to admit the plough' and so previous generations of farmers had simply 'passed by it'.[92] As a result, British colonial laws strongly supported drainage and specifically encouraged it by allowing some colonies to drain a small portion of lands as a substitute for the general requirements of cultivation and fencing of a larger part of granted lands. Such a preference for drainage naturally influenced the development of other laws—particularly those related to liability for draining water onto neighbouring lands. Such liability laws, often called surface water liability regimes, provide one example of how British attitudes to land during the colonial era continue to influence American property law today.

84 Mordant (n 39) 70.
85 ibid 70–71.
86 D Defoe, *A Tour Thro' the Whole Island of Great Britain* (London, D Browne, 1761) 248.
87 Fraley (n 38).
88 Young (n 48) 43.
89 ET Price, *Dividing the Land: Early American Beginnings of Our Private Property Mosaic* (Chicago, University of Chicago Press, 1995) 115.
90 Bradley (n 38) 13.
91 Fraley (n 38).
92 J Smith, *General View of the Agriculture of the County of Argyll* (Edinburgh, Mundell & Son, 1798) 171.

VII. THE MODERN ANTI-WILDERNESS BIAS

Despite the development of statutes providing environmental protections, a number of scholars have suggested that such an anti-wilderness bias continues in modern American law, particularly (i) during the judicial process which implements those statutes and (ii) within areas of law such as property and tort where doctrines such as nuisance and trespass impact the process of land development. Most commonly, scholars either cite Sprankling generally for the proposition that such a bias can exist or observe the phenomenon in some particular narrow circumstance. Peter Appel, for example, explores the degree to which such a bias may be observed when federal courts review agency decision making.[93] Joseph Feller suggested that such anti-wilderness biases exist within federal agencies and may be corrected during the process of federal court review.[94] Similarly, Josh Eagle suggests that easement subsidies may also perpetuate the anti-wilderness bias by relying on

> two faulty assumptions: that the right to use and enjoy property in these ways is valueless, and that the right to use and enjoy property for extensive use or development is objectively the most important kind of right to use and enjoy.[95]

There may, of course, be a variety of sources of anti-wilderness biases within American law. Additionally, such biases may have developed at a variety of points along the chronological spectrum from the colonial period to the present. This chapter does not suggest that the British common law is the only source of an anti-wilderness bias in the American common law. Rather, the intention here is to refute the argument that the problem of an anti-wilderness bias is a uniquely American problem that emerged as a product of American industrialisation, as Sprankling argued.

Having established that Sprankling began with a false premise of a common law that was wedded to preservation and conservation, this chapter is concerned with considering whether there are any continuing influences of the anti-wilderness bias that can be traced lineally from the British and colonial common law through to the modern doctrines, particularly within the context of the common law of property. The following pages focus specifically on two such instances, which demonstrate that such biases in the British common law were quite capable of continuing through to the modern period, where they remain influential, if not largely unchanged despite the intervening centuries. Such instances of doctrines passed forward from the common law are significant as a counterpoint to Sprankling's story of an anti-wilderness bias in American law that is entirely created by the American courts in support of industrialisation.

[93] P Appel, 'Wilderness, the Courts, and the Effect of Politics on Judicial Decision Making' (2011) 35 *Harvard Environmental Law Review* 275.

[94] J Feller, 'Have Judges Gone Wild? Plaintiffs' Choices and Success Rates in Litigation Against Federal Administrative Agencies' (2014) 44 *Environmental Law* 287.

[95] J Eagle, 'Notional Generosity: Explaining Charitable Donors' High Willingness to Part with Conservation Easements' (2011) 35 *Harvard Environmental Law Review* 47, 79.

VIII. THE MODERN ANTI-WILDERNESS BIAS: WASTE LAW

As I have demonstrated elsewhere, Sprankling incorrectly postulated that American courts changed the law of waste so as to promote development; there are other technological reasons for the shift.[96] That said, modern American waste law does contain an anti-wilderness bias—not one generated through an American desire for development, but rather one inherited from and strongly shaped by the common law influence.

Specifically, waste law offers support for development because it has incorporated an approach to measuring injury known as the good husbandry standard. The good husbandry standard determines what types of acts in managing land constitute waste. Those 'acts dictated by "good husbandry" are not in law waste'.[97]

The good husbandry standard is not a creation of American waste law.[98] Indeed, it reaches back to the earliest waste cases in the common law.[99] Historically, common law courts implied a rule that encompassed the idea of good husbandry. The tenant was 'bound to manage his agricultural land in a husband-like way according to the custom of the country'.[100] The good husbandry standard dated to the oldest cases on waste. *Maleverer v Spinke*[101] found that while the tenant could not 'convert land into wood or wood into arable land', he could 'root up bushes, furze, and thorns growing upon the land, for melioration, for that is good husbandry'.[102]

This standard of good husbandry is a central component of American waste law. It is also one that has substantially impacted land usage patterns, both historically and in modern cases. In an earlier period of American history, the largest implication of the good husbandry doctrine occurred in properties that were timbered. The good husbandry standard granted the 'right to open and clear for cultivation wild and uncultivated land'.[103] Cutting trees for 'mere profit' was waste, but for the purposes of cultivation it was acceptable.[104] Courts reasoned that

> This right only gives the privilege to sell timber cut from such land as is necessary to fit the land for agricultural purposes, and out of such sale there may be reimbursement for the reasonable expense of clearing, removing, and fitting the land for agriculture, according to the rule of good husbandry, under the circumstances of the particular case.[105]

[96] Fraley (n 11).

[97] *Threatt v Rushing* 361 So 2d 329, 331 (Miss. 1978).

[98] Sprankling saw the good husbandry doctrine as a part of the American approach. Jedediah Purdy summarises Sprankling's view as 'contend[ing] that an "instrumentalist" view of the natural world, coupled with a perceived imperative to bring the new continent under the ax and plow, led to the good husbandry standard, which allowed tenants to clear and develop land in the interests of advancing cultivation'—J Purdy, *The Meaning of Property* (New Haven, Yale University Press, 2010) 46.

[99] For a further discussion of the evolution of waste law and the continuities between the common law and the modern American rules see Fraley (n 11).

[100] Bewes (n 20) 32.

[101] *Maleverer v Spinke* (1538) 1 Dyer 35 b.

[102] Quoted in Bewes (n 20) 134.

[103] *Warren Cty v Gans* 80 Miss 76, 81, 31 So 539, 540 (1902).

[104] *Learned v Ogden* 80 Miss 769, 779, 32 So 278, 279 (1902).

[105] *Guest v Guest* 234 Ala 581, 585, 176 So 289, 292 (1937).

As the Indiana Supreme Court explained, 'a large portion of our territory consists of vast forests, requiring ... that these forests should be turned into cultivated fields ... [and this] makes the rule of the common law ... wholly inapplicable'.[106]

Modern cases concerning good husbandry demonstrate that the traditional doctrine continues to shape land use. In particular, the good husbandry standard now effectively ensures that cultivation continues even if the tenant or present interest holder would prefer to conserve the land. Good husbandry now requires continued planting. Traditionally, good husbandry required the 'seeding' and 'fertilizing [of] the fields'.[107] Recently, cases have emphasised not allowing the land to return to its natural state—ie not allowing weeds or overgrowth. The tenant has 'a duty to maintain the land in a good workmanlike manner, in keeping with principles of good husbandry'.[108] One can violate this standard, for example, by allowing the 'growth and expansion of a noxious weed'.[109] As one case explained, 'Every good farmer knows that average land can be extensively and continually cultivated without injury to it, if good judgment is used in the selection and rotation of crops; the keeping down of weeds, briers and underbrush'.[110]

Good husbandry requires that the tenant 'return the premises in the same general condition in which they were [let]'.[111] It would, then, be problematic for a tenant to have left land uncultivated, to simply fail to 'keep the weeds mowed'.[112] A basic assertion of waste became that the tenant had 'allowed the weeds to grow'.[113] A tenant could be damned by a trial court's conclusion that the land was 'unduly weedy'.[114] This emphasis is consistent with Blackstone's initial formulation of waste law—as being devoted to protecting the home and cultivation. Blackstone defined waste as 'spoil or destruction in houses, gardens, trees or other corporeal hereditaments'.[115]

For modern waste law, particularly as it is applied to leases of agricultural properties, the good husbandry approach implies consistent cultivation, the use of modern chemical fertilisers and avoiding allowing land to return to a more natural—more weedy—state. As a result, tenants are not able to prefer lighter land uses without potentially facing liability for those choices under the good husbandry standard of waste law. A liability rule that requires cultivation and penalises the option of returning a piece of land to a 'state of nature' is a rule that favours more developed land uses and penalises tenants for choosing less developed uses. Such a rule continues a common law anti-wilderness bias within the more modern context.

[106] *Dawson v Coffman* 28 Ind 220, 224 (1867).
[107] *Paul v Snyder* 66 Pa D & C2d 463, 470 (CP 1974).
[108] *Butler v Robbins* 2013 Del CP LEXIS 22, 2013 WL 3717730 (Del CP 2013).
[109] ibid.
[110] *Fisher's Ex'r v Haney* 180 Ky 257, 263, 202 SW 495, 498 (1918).
[111] *Moser v Thorp Sales Corp* 312 NW2d 881, 906–07 (Iowa 1981).
[112] *Cook v Frazier* 5 Ill App 3d 380 (1972).
[113] See, eg, *Gault v Gault* 158 Mich 303 (1909).
[114] *Tong v Borstad* 231 NW2d 795, 801 (1975).
[115] 2 Bl Comm 281.

IX. THE MODERN ANTI-WILDERNESS BIAS: SURFACE WATER

Surface water liability provides another area of common law property-based claims that continue to show an anti-wilderness bias in the modern context.[116] Surface water liability governs the rights of two neighbouring landowners when one landowner—often, but not always, the owner of the higher elevation parcel—increases the flow of water to a neighbouring parcel of land. Such increases tend to occur either when new construction projects inadvertently change elevations and thus impact the natural flow of water or when a neighbour intentionally diverts water in an effort to protect their own land from flooding. Recent increases in floodwaters, particularly in coastal urban areas, make this area of law a likely site of extensive future litigation.[117]

The earliest American rule for drainage emerges directly from the colonial emphasis on drainage and improvement. As a result, the rule virtually insulated the offending landowner from liability. This rule rarely continues in its pure form within American jurisdictions, but the influence of a pro-drainage, pro-improvement approach to land usage continues. Under the original rule, 'a landowner has an unqualified right to embark on any improvements of his or her land allowed by law'; in more modern iterations, the rule requires that the party 'limit the harm caused by changes in the flow of surface water to that which is reasonably necessary'.[118] The central feature of this rule was that it assumed that all land would undergo improvement. While the early rule, often known as the common enemy rule, rarely continues in full force in American jurisdictions, the reasonableness approach incorporates much of the original doctrine.[119]

Under modern rules, one of the primary approaches to determining surface water liability is the reasonableness approach. The reasonableness rule assumes that each landowner will improve the land through some type of development and that all improvements are likely to cause some increase in surface water flow to neighbouring properties. Thus, the reasonableness rule finds that an owner 'is legally privileged to make a reasonable use of his land, even though the flow of surface waters is altered thereby and causes some harm to others'.[120] The rule essentially provides an insulating privilege to landowners who want to develop—allowing them some freedom to throw water onto the land of others without incurring any liability. In essence, this rule is simply a slightly lightened form of the original common law rule that preferred development and fully insulated landowners who sought to drain their lands.[121] Modern courts that have adopted this rule often note that this

116 Liability for surface water is not an environmental law question under American law; it is a question of common law liability or it is addressed by statutes specific to surface water. Those state level statutes sound in property and tort rather than environmental law (which is, in contrast, largely a creature of federal law). American environmental statutes generally do not provide remedies to individual citizens. Instead, citizens must look to property and tort law.

117 Such flooding frequently results in nuisance claims. For a more extensive discussion of the implications of increased coastal flooding see Fraley (n 38).

118 *Currens v Sleek* 138 Wash 2d 858, 867, 983 P2d 626, 631 (1999).

119 For a full discussion of the history of the common enemy doctrine see Fraley (n 38).

120 *Farley v Wappapello Foods* 959 SW2d 888, 894 (1997).

121 For a full discussion of the original rule and the various modern methods of making the rule less strict see Fraley (n 38).

approach is 'the one most likely to promote the optimum development and enjoyment of land'.[122] The courts often explicitly endorse a pro-development ethic when applying this rule.[123]

The reasonableness rule, with its close relation to the earliest pro-drainage approach in the common law, is perhaps the most explicitly anti-wilderness of the multiple approaches to surface water liability. Additionally, this approach is one of the most common across modern jurisdictions. Just less than half (around 20) of the American states follow this approach.[124] Integrating the anti-wilderness bias explicitly, courts have reasoned that the reasonableness approach to surface water is the approach that will most promote development.[125] The reasonableness approach involves a factors-based analysis, which focuses in part on foreseeability and emphasises the ordinariness of the expectation of development of land. Courts also balance the harm and the benefit, emphasising the easily quantifiable goods that result from land development.[126] In summary, the reasonableness rule quite explicitly and unapologetically maintains the anti-wilderness bias of the original common law rule.

Other jurisdictions follow a rule that mirrors the good husbandry rule of waste law. In the context of surface water liability, the good husbandry approach means maximising the availability of land that can be farmed and therefore favours drainage.[127] The rule specifically responded to the need for 'the draining of marshy land',[128] and modern courts continue to recognise the project of draining wetlands as a primary force behind the rule.[129] Under the rule, the owner may accelerate the flow of surface water 'without liability for damages to the owner of the lower lands if the water is not diverted from its natural channels'.[130] The key question in these cases is whether drainage has 'improved the[] ability to farm the subject property'.[131] The justification for this rule is that to 'drain their land of surface water for agricultural purposes' is necessarily 'an act of good husbandry' and therefore should create no liability.[132]

Courts view drainage as 'the proper improvement of the surface of the ground'.[133] As a matter of law, '[g]ood husbandry is promoted by the reclamation of ... waste land and using it for tillage purposes. But for its wet character because of the

[122] *Heins Implement Co v Mo Highway & Transp Comm'n* 859 SW2d 681, 691 (Mo 1993).

[123] ibid ('It is, of course, true that society has a great interest that land shall be developed for the greater good. It is therefore properly a consideration in these cases whether the utility of the possessor's use of his land outweighs the gravity of the harm which results from his alteration of the flow of surface waters').

[124] *Currens v Sleek* 138 Wash 2d 858, 866, 983 P2d 626, 631 (1999). For a full discussion of the various approaches now used in the United States and the jurisdictions following these approaches see Fraley (n 39).

[125] *Heins Implement Co v Mo Highway & Transp Comm'n* 859 SW2d 681, 691 (Mo 1993).

[126] For a more extensive discussion of the reasonableness rule and its implications for development specifically and climate change more generally see Fraley (n 38).

[127] The landowner may 'make such drains, for agricultural purposes, on his own land, as may be required by good husbandry'—*Peck v Herrington* 109 Ill 611, 619 (1884).

[128] *Shulte v Flowers* No 4-12-0132, 2013 IL App (4th) 120132 at 27 (Ill Ct App 8 February 2013).

[129] *Shulte v Flowers* 983 NE2d 1124, 1129 (Ill 2013).

[130] *Garbarino v Van Cleave* 214 Or 554, 558–59, 330 P2d 28, 31 (1958).

[131] *Victor Twp Drainage Dist v Lundeen Family Farm P'ship* 19 NE3d 652, 661 (Ill 2014).

[132] *Dudley Special Rd Dist v Harrison* 517 SW2d 170, 180 (Mo 1974).

[133] *Gene B Glick Co v Marion Constr Corp* 165 Ind App 72, 78 (Ind Ct App 1975).

conformation of the surface, the land would be as useful and valuable as other farm lands'.[134] Thus, the landowner has a right to 'fill[] up the wet and marshy places to his own advantage', even though 'his neighbor's land is so situated as to be incommoded by it'.[135]

The impact of the good husbandry rule goes beyond agricultural contexts. Courts have held that 'although the good husbandry exception developed to promote agriculture, the general principle applies to urban and suburban settings'.[136] The exception applies 'regardless of whether it was caused by diversion from another watershed, the installation of septic tanks, the grading and paving of streets, or the construction of houses, basements and appurtenances'.[137] Indeed, some courts view the modern reasonableness approach as simply being the extension of the good husbandry rule to urban contexts.[138]

The social utility approach to managing surface water contains a similar bias. This approach allows the court to weigh the gravity of the harm caused to the plaintiff against the social utility of the defendant's conduct.[139] Within this context, the courts define social utility in terms of the utility of the defendant's conduct for society as a whole.[140] Social utility approaches inherently favour development, because courts conclude that 'society has an interest in developing land for general welfare'.[141] Thus, courts reason, for example, that 'today's mass home building projects … are assuredly in the social good'.[142]

Notably, in many circumstances, courts combine two of these doctrines in ways that further promote an anti-wilderness bias. Specifically, courts frequently combine the reasonableness approach, a light modification of the original common law rule that essentially gives a limited privilege to drain onto neighbouring land, and the social utility approach, which weighs the social benefits of the defendant's conduct. In such cases, courts apply the reasonableness approach while also looking to see the 'purpose for which the improvements were undertaken', which can, again, prevent liability.[143] Both approaches to surface water liability promote drainage and development, and they do so even more strongly when combined.

Despite modern jurisdictions disagreeing repeatedly on the appropriate way to deal with surface water liability, each of the primary approaches continues to explicitly favour development and cultivation. When it comes to surface water liability, courts demonstrate a strong anti-wilderness bias that supports drainage and the destruction of natural wetlands.[144] This occurs because courts reduce or eliminate

[134] *Todd v York Cty* 72 Neb 207, 211, 100 NW 299, 301 (1904).

[135] *Peck v Herrington* 109 Ill 611, 619–20 (1884).

[136] *Bollweg v Richard Marker Assocs* 353 Ill App3d 560, 574 (Ill Ct App 2004).

[137] *Templeton v Huss* 57 Ill 2d 134, 141 (1974).

[138] *Shulte v Flowers* 983 NE 2d 1124, 1130 (Ill 2013).

[139] Farley v Wappapello Foods (n 120) 891–92.

[140] The courts weigh the social utility against the harm. Thus, the question becomes whether 'the gravity of the harm may be found to be so significant that it requires compensation regardless of the utility of the conduct of the defendant'—*Pendergrast v Aiken* 293 NC 201, 218 (1977).

[141] *State v Deetz* 66 Wis 2d 1, 15 (1974).

[142] *Armstrong v Francis Corp* 20 NJ 320, 330 (1956).

[143] *Locklin v City of Lafayette* 7 Cal 4th 327, 337, 867 P2d 724, 729 (1994). Another case demonstrating this approach is *Farley v Wappapello Foods* (n 120) 891–92. For a more thorough discussion of the evolution of doctrines in this area see Fraley (n 38).

[144] The full version of this argument is found in Fraley (n 38).

potential liability for ditching, draining and diverting, perpetuating the same preferences for draining and improvement that were characteristic of the common law as imported into colonial America.

X. CONCLUSION

Sprankling is not wrong about the existence of an anti-wilderness bias in American property law, but that bias was not a new invention of the American courts in the nineteenth century that never existed in any of the same doctrines in the British common law. The bias did not originate through some attempt to throw off the yoke of a more conservation-orientated British common law. Instead, the British common law incorporated a number of anti-wilderness biases that continued on in the American courts. American courts have allowed these anti-wilderness biases to continue unchecked in a variety of areas of law, particularly within the law of waste and the law of surface water liability. In both cases, the anti-wilderness biases inherent in modern approaches can be traced lineally through the years to common law approaches to cultivation, to drainage and to improvement that specifically created the anti-wilderness biases.

16

The Four Dimensions of Public Property

JOHN PAGE* AND ANN BROWER**

I. INTRODUCTION

IN NOVEMBER 2014, the New South Wales government announced the latest addition to its conservation estate, the Everlasting Swamp National Park. Australia's most populous state created its 237th national park by consolidating an existing State Conservation Area with 1,700 hectares of newly acquired private wetlands. Some three months earlier, the New Zealand government disestablished its 60-year-old Te Urewera National Park, an 'ancient and enduring [land], a fortress of nature, alive with history; its scenery ... abundant with mystery, adventure, and remote beauty'.[1] The Crown ceded ownership of the former park, and Te Urewera now owns itself,[2] as an entity overseen by a statutory board tasked with divining what the land wants.

These two decisions, proximate in time and space, reflect the polarities of our understandings of the public ownership of public lands. Both concern the future of significant conservation areas. At the Everlasting Swamp, the state acquired private land and stepped into the shoes of the private owner. There, ownership vests in the Crown in the right of the state of New South Wales, with management and control exercised by the National Parks and Wildlife Service. By contrast, Te Urewera escaped Amnon Lehavi's 'Blackacre Paradigm',[3] occupying a 'revolutionary'[4] parallel reality where ownership itself is a contested, if not anachronistic, term.

Using these two antipodean parks as examples, this chapter proposes a novel way of seeing public property in land—as a multidimensional spectrum of diverse

* Senior Lecturer in Law, Southern Cross University, Australia.

** Senior Lecturer in Environmental Policy, Lincoln University, New Zealand.

[1] Te Urewera Act 2014 (NZ), s 3(1).

[2] ibid s 11(1).

[3] A Lehavi, *The Construction of Property; Norms, Institutions, Challenges* (Cambridge, Cambridge University Press, 2013).

[4] J Ruru, 'Tūhoe-Crown Settlement: The Te Urewera Act 2014' (2014) *Māori Law Review*, available at http://Māorilawreview.co.nz/2014/10/tuhoe-crown-settlement-te-urewera-act-2014/ (accessed on 2 December 2014).

ownerships. We canvass the extent of that 'sorely under-theorized'[5] spectrum—from the orthodox view that public ownership is essentially a variant of the private, to a model that accommodates a plurality of ownerships, a middle ground where ownership vests in a diffuse 'unorganized public', and ending where ownership itself seems redundant.

As well as descriptive, this spectrum also suggests that there is no 'totalizing and universalizing'[6] rule about the public ownership of public lands. Indeed, its ever-expanding scope underscores that orthodox ideas of ownership, exemplified by the Everlasting Swamp, are increasingly ill-suited to the modern world, rich in its multidimensional tapestry of colours, cultures, nooks and crannies. Instead, we adopt the plain logic that 'all property law is local, … the place where the land lies'.[7] In discerning that lie of the land, we use the legal-geographic dimensions of space and time to articulate new points on our spectrum that better reflect our complex propertied relations with public land. We argue that spatio-temporal contexts transform public property from the two dimensions of Plato's cave to the four dimensions of the modern world, to encompass human culture, the landed history of people and the peopled history of land.

Section II of this chapter frames the spectrum as a descriptive tool to depict the extent of public ownership of public lands. Section III then begins the spectral journey with the traditional view of the state as owner. Here, the public owner holds essentially private sticks in the bundle, albeit impressed with an alleged public trust. Section IV explores a more complex grounded reality, that of a plurality of public owners, a patchwork that is multi-layered, diverse and simultaneous. Section V leaves the discrete owner behind, and migrates to Carol Rose's 'unorganized public at large', a comedy of the commons where ownership by the more facilitates the merrier. Section V also explores the amorphous notion of property as belonging, an idea adept at explaining what happens on the ground despite its legal implausibility. Sections VI and VII end the spectral traverse at Te Urewera, and its seeming leap beyond ownership doctrine. Section VIII concludes by exploring the alternative potential of the emerging discipline of legal geography to reprise the conundrum that is public property in land.

While Everlasting Swamp and Te Urewera may be polar extremes in ownership form and in their propertied relation to context, they also share common ground, their enactment of a form of property beyond a private, land as commodity model.[8] Public property in land may be sorely under-theorised, but it is widely loved, used and enjoyed for its universal values of propriety, inclusion and egalitarianism.[9] Understanding the extent of what we claim to own helps to better understand the

[5] Alexander describes the social-obligation norm as a sorely under-theorised aspect of Anglo-American property law; we submit public property is equally under-theorised, GS Alexander, 'The Social-Obligation Norm in American Property Law' (2009) 94 *Cornell Law Review* 745.

[6] N Blomley, *Law, Space and the Geographies of Power* (New York, Guildford Press, 1994).

[7] JV Orth, *Reappraisals in the Law of Property* (Farnham, Ashgate, 2010).

[8] GS Alexander, *Commodity & Propriety Competing Visions of Property in American Legal Thought 1776–1970* (Chicago, University of Chicago Press, 1997).

[9] J Page, 'Towards an Understanding of Public Property' in N Hopkins (ed), *Modern Studies in Property Law*, vol 7 (Oxford, Hart Publishing, 2013); JL Sax, *Mountains without Handrails: Reflections on the National Parks* (Ann Arbor, University of Michigan Press, 1980) 42, 105, 106.

vast, frequently invisible, public estate that surrounds us. More deeply, it helps us to understand who we are.[10]

II. THE SPECTRUM OF PUBLIC OWNERSHIPS

The ownership spectrum is an organising principle around which currently threadbare ideas of public property in land take form and promise a measure of substance. The spectrum begins in Section III with the orthodox State as Owner model and ends with the 'hitherto unthinkable'[11] Land as Owner. In between, it describes a variety of contexts that have real-world resonance, if not legal plausibility. It is first and foremost a descriptive tool that depicts the vast diversity of the public estate.

As a descriptive tool, the spectrum is porous. There is no clear line where one form of public ownership ends and the next begins. Rather, each shades into the other, in a gradated continuum that is overlapping and incremental. While messy around the edges, the spectrum nonetheless identifies distinctive forms of public ownership along its axis. The State as Owner model is individualised and elegantly bare. By contrast, the Many Owners model is necessarily multi-layered and complex. Meanwhile, the dispersed 'unorganized public' eschews state intervention, and Te Urewera merges the once disparate notions of land and ownership into one. As it demonstrates, no single model accounts for the breadth of public ownership; many public lands exhibit the blurred indicia of several different models. Yet, despite its porosity, the spectrum seems a reasonably comprehensive account, a defensible place to start to describe the vast public estate.

The spectrum also exposes the paradox that is public property in land, a resource critical to our well-being and propriety, yet, as already observed, sorely under-theorised in the common law. Such unclear thinking about what is nominally ours is evident when we begin with the muddied State as Owner model, exemplified by the Everlasting Swamp National Park. Despite its venerable heritage,[12] this model offers few explanations and many imponderables. The novelty of the spectrum metaphor demonstrates the theoretical poverty of public property, an ill-defined topic into which few legal scholars wade.[13]

[10] L Roberts et al, *The Nature of Well-Being: Science for Conservation* (Wellington, Department of Conservation, 2015).

[11] C Stone, 'Should Trees Have Standing?—Toward Legal Rights for Natural Objects' (1072) 45 *Southern California Law Review* 450.

[12] National parks are an American invention. Yellowstone and Yosemite parks were quickly followed by 25 others in the period 1890 to 1916. In New Zealand, the model also caught on early, with Tongariro the first in 1894, followed by Egmont in 1900: DH Fischer, *Fairness and Freedom: A History of Two Open Societies, New Zealand and the United States* (Oxford, Oxford University Press, 2012) 319. In Australia, Sydney's Royal National Park, affectionately known as the 'Nasho' or simply the 'Royal', was established in 1879, and is claimed to be the world's second oldest national park: see www.nationalparks.nsw.gov.au/visit-a-park/parks/royal-national park?gclid=CIypv5GflMsCFU9xvAodFUgBrg (accessed on 10 February 2016).

[13] JA Souder and SK Fairfax, 'In Lands We Trusted: State Trust Lands as an Alternative Theory of Public Ownership' in C Geisler and G Daneker (eds), *Property and Values: Alternatives to Public and Private Ownership* (Washington DC, Island Press, 2000) 89. By contrast, public property literature in disciplines such as geography or sociology is rich and varied.

As it is framed in this chapter, our spectrum differs from most spectra in one fundamental respect. Normally, a spectrum is a two-dimensional structure that extends from one point in space to another. However, the trajectory of this spectrum escapes these two-dimensional limits as it evolves. Context progressively alters the dynamics, an ever-increasing accumulation of individual geographies and their temporal past and present. By the time we reach Te Urewera, the spectrum is in another, richer space, a multidimensional construct far removed from the linear abstract. In its journey, our spectrum starts with de-peopled lands and de-landed peoples, and ends in peopled lands and landed peoples.

III. THE STATE AS OWNER

The New South Wales government's purchase of environmentally sensitive private land to create the Everlasting Swamp National Park is a well-tested conservation strategy premised on substituting the private owner with a public one.[14] Upon acquisition, the lands are then dedicated as national park,[15] or reserved in some other form, such that they become in effect a quasi-public fee simple.[16] In this structure, the state or its agency[17] holds the key sticks in the ownership bundle, most notably, the gatekeeper right to exclude, private property's *sina qua non*.[18] This is seen in the most everyday of circumstances, when popular national parks charge admission fees for entry. A failure or refusal to pay invokes the state's power to exclude, a clear control over access to the resource.

In invoking the state as owner, what do we understand by the concept of the modern state? Patrick Dunleavy defines the state as a recognisably cohesive set of institutions that operate within a discrete space, whose existence serves to 'define and enforce collectively binding decisions'[19] on society and its members and, in so doing, delineates between the private and public spheres.[20] The state claims to advance the public will of the members, and is thus accepted as legitimate both by members and other states. It regulates the affairs of society by means of the law, and regulates its own affairs by means of a constitution, written or unwritten. Importantly for property, the state defines boundaries, membership, and rules of entry and exit.

While elegant in its simplicity, this descriptive view of the state yields a barren terrain for public property and public ownership. Theoretically, the public estate's common

[14] 9% of the US federal public domain was acquired from private owners. SK Fairfax et al, *Buying Nature; The Limits of Land Acquisition as a Conservation Strategy, 1780–2004* (Cambridge, MIT Press, 2005) 4.

[15] For example, lands reserved as national park become Crown Lands, National Parks and Wildlife Act 1974 (NSW), s 33(4).

[16] S Douglas, 'The Content of a Freehold: A 'Right to Use' Land' in Hopkins (n 9) 359–60.

[17] Freyfogle suggests that state agencies are more managers than owners, ET Freyfogle, *The Land We Share: Private Property and the Common Good* (Washington DC, Island Press, 2003) 177, 203.

[18] TW Merrill, 'Property and the Right to Exclude' (1998) 77 *Nebraska Law Review* 730.

[19] R Jessop, *State Theory: Putting Capitalist States in their Place* (Cambridge, Polity Press, 1990) 341.

[20] P Dunleavy, 'The State' in R Goodin and P Pettit (eds), *A Companion to Contemporary Political Philosophy* (Oxford, Blackwell Publishers, 1995).

law jurisprudence remains (surprisingly) thin.[21] From a normative perspective, individual state ownership is paradigmatically defined by inapt private values—exclusion, commodification and the primacy of the individual[22]—a closed loop that precludes public property generating its own 'specific normative meanings'.[23] And descriptively, the public estate's lack of definition and structure has real-world implications, most notably a myopic inability to see the vast public estate in our midst, a pauperised view[24] that leads to its diminution.

The State as Owner model conforms to an atomistic, essentially private concept of property in land, an abstraction where the emphasis is on relationships and rights between persons about things.[25] Perversely, this view is at odds with the interconnected nature of natural landscapes, the ecological reality that 'everything is connected to everything else'.[26] This tension manifests in false enclaves, where natural areas become adrift of the cultural and ecological forces that surround and sweep over them.

Eric Freyfogle sees this retreat into refuge as a consequence of the private tendency to 'fragment everything into pieces'.[27] When 'nature is fragmented into distinct parts—into parcels of land and discrete natural resources', the undesirable outcome is that it becomes 'hard to spot and appreciate the connections'.[28] As a consequence, little 'common vocabulary'[29] is generated; there is too much focus on arbitrary property lines, and little regard for the lands between and across those lines.[30] Freyfogle describes this as a 'tragedy of fragmentation'. Retreat into the enclave is not an escape from environmental woes, but a turbulent log-ride, 'climbing aboard a timber in a free-flowing river and getting carried by the many currents'.[31] When public lands end at the dividing fence, already pale public values tend to shrink to size, to fit their bounded dimensions.

The values of commodity likewise have unwelcome consequences. In the United States, disputes over the 'ownership' of iconic place names, such as Awahnee or

[21] 'There is little written about public property … except in contradistinction to private property': JW Hamilton and N Bankes, 'Different Views of the Cathedral: The Literature on Property Law Theory' in A McHarg et al (eds), *Property and the Law in Energy and Natural Resources* (Oxford, Oxford University Press, 2010) 19–20.

[22] Merrill (n 18); S Balganesh, 'Demystifying the Right to Exclude' (2008) 31 *Harvard Journal of Law and Public Policy* 593. Commodification ascribes market values to individual components of landscapes, while 'ardent individualism' engenders a 'rights-based reasoning that makes all talk of community suspect': ET Freyfogle, *Agrarianism and the Good Society: Land, Culture, Conflict and Hope* (Lexington, University Press of Kentucky, 2007) 14.

[23] R Barnes, *Property Rights and Natural Resources* (Oxford, Hart Publishing, 2009) 154.

[24] CM Rose, 'Seeing Property' in CM Rose (ed), *Property and Persuasion Essays on the History, Theory and Rhetoric of Ownership* (Boulder CO, Westview, 1994).

[25] W Hohfield, 'Some Fundamental Legal Conceptions as Applied in Legal Reasoning' (1913) 23 *Yale Law Journal* 16.

[26] M Metzger, 'Private Property and Environmental Sanity' (1975–1976) 5 *Ecology Law Quarterly* 793, 796.

[27] Freyfogle (n 22) 13.

[28] ibid 12–13.

[29] ibid 21.

[30] C Meine, *Correction Lines: Essays on Land, Leopold, and Conservation* (Washington DC, Island Press, 2004).

[31] Freyfogle (n 22) 11.

Badger Pass in Yosemite National Park,[32] pit the Park Service against major in-park commercial operators, and highlight private property's colonising impulses. More prosaically, Richard Brewer lists 'transactions costs, initial capital expenses, and costs of continuing stewardship'[33] as private factors that militate against the public estate's viability and capacity to expand, exacerbated in times of budgetary austerity when taxpayer dollars are scarce. There is widespread acknowledgement that 'palatable or not, acquisition is simply too expensive to be more than a minor player in land conservation'.[34]

The latter issues were evident in the immediate aftermath of the Everlasting Swamp's dedication as national park. While glowingly described as 'one of the largest intact coastal wetlands remaining in New South Wales', containing 'rare and globally significant ecosystems', the discourse of commodity and enclave retreat was ever-present. Critics noted 'if [conservation areas] are not connected and not large enough, they do struggle in the long term to afford … protection'.[35] The state environment minister admitted that the costs of acquiring small coastal tracts was 'very expensive' and that this rendered the NSW coast 'at the risk of being loved to death'.[36]

Aside from ascribing inapt private values to public property, public–private equivalence also leads to the public estate vanishing from both descriptive and literal view. Crawford Macpherson describes 'state property' as 'corporate private property', where a 'smaller body of persons authorized to command its citizens exercise a corporate right to exclude'.[37] Similarly, Margaret Davies observes that 'governments are … significant owners; they own resources such as office buildings essentially privately'.[38] Where there is no apparent differentiation between what is public and private, the former is marginalised to the point of near-invisibility, a unidirectional trend evident since the enclosures.[39] Yet, non-private property has not always been such an outlier. Past legal traditions had sophisticated public taxonomies;[40] and the

[32] K Alexander, 'Names of Yosemite's Sacred Sites Threatened by Trademark Spat', *San Francisco Chronicle*, 2 January 2015; Associated Press, 'Company Seeks Rights to Names of Iconic Grand Canyon Lodges', 26 January 2015; Associated Press, 'Dispute Could Lead to Name Changes at Yosemite', *New York Times*, 2 January 2015.

[33] R Brewer, *Conservancy The Land Trust Movement in America* (Lebanon NH, Dartmouth College Press, 2003) 133.

[34] Fairfax et al (n 14) 259.

[35] www.abc.net.au/news/2014-11-12/new-national-park/5885736. (accessed on 12 November 2014).

[36] www.abc.net.au/environment/articles/2014/11/12/4126866.htm. (accessed on 12 November 2014).

[37] CB Macpherson, 'The Meaning of Property' in CB Macpherson (ed), *Property: Mainstream and Critical Positions* (Toronto, University Toronto Press, 1999) 5–6; K Gray and S Gray, 'Private Property and Public Propriety' in J McLean (ed), *Property and the Constitution* (Oxford, Hart Publishing, 1999) 13.

[38] M Davies, *Property: Meanings, Histories, Theories* (Abingdon, Routledge, 2007) 63–64.

[39] N Graham, *Lawscape: Property, Environment, Law* (Abingdon, Routledge, 2010); Blomley (n 6).

[40] For example, Spanish-Mexican law in pre-1845 California, D Dyer, 'California Beach Access: The Mexican Law and the Public Trust' (1972) 2 *Ecology Law Quarterly* 571; Roman public property, DR Coquillette, 'Mosses from an Old Manse: Another Look at Some Historic Property Cases About the Environment' (1979) 64 *Cornell Law Review* 761; CM Rose, 'Romans, Roads and Romantic Creators: Traditions of Public Property in the Information Age' (2003) 66 *Law & Contemporary Problems* 89. In Scots law, Jill Robbie discerns a modern 'Division of Things', derived from Roman law and the institutional writings of the seventheenth-century Scots jurists Stair and Craig. This 'historical framework' forms a coherent albeit widely ignored basis for a contemporary hierarchy of public property rights in Scots law. J Robbie, *Private Water Rights, Studies in Scots Law* (Edinburgh, Edinburgh Legal Education Trust, 2015) 10–44.

common estate was once a vital everyday component in the property framework.[41] Our modern failure to describe and see public property is confirmed where property and private property are synonymous terms, used interchangeably.

Lastly, the simple State as Owner model is muddied by an intuitive assumption that the citizenry is the public estate's true beneficial owner. Yet, this little-scrutinised perception is at odds with the state's ostensible bare title.[42] The notion that the public estate is held on behalf of an amorphous public is typically invoked when well-loved parks are threatened by private encroachment, or conversely when public milestones are celebrated. In Sydney, private encroachment onto public harbour foreshore enraged the city's North Shore residents.[43] Contrarily, upon the 50th anniversary of the US National Park Service Act, founding director Stephen Mather was quoted as saying 'they [our national parks] belong to everyone—now and always'.[44] The landmark US Report of the Public Land Law Review Commission in 1970 repeated this common legacy view, '[t]hese lands are a natural heritage and national asset that belong to us all'.[45] Such rhetoric suggests 'an inclination for public property to vest in the collective sum of us'.[46] Indeed, this inference is reinforced when express trusts over public lands do arise, be they statutory trusts under Crown lands legislation[47] or entrenched common law doctrines like the US public trust.[48]

The individual State as Owner model is a thin account of the public ownership of public lands. While it may resonate with the bundle metaphor, it also carries bundle baggage. As Henry Smith says (when writing of the bundle), it is 'only as good as far as it goes'.[49] Indeed, as much of this chapter describes, it is only as good as far as it goes in portraying a small slice of the public estate. Section IV explores another way of seeing public ownership that goes further, a model of multi-layered public ownerships where many actors hold simultaneous, diverse interests in public lands.

IV. THE MANY OWNERS

That public lands may have more than one owner is a logical corollary of the disaggregated bundle of rights, where separate sticks are hived off and vested in different

[41] JM Neeson, *Commoners: Common Right, Enclosure and Social Change in England, 1700–1820* (Cambridge, Cambridge University Press, 1993) 180.

[42] In Canada, the Crown has 'an unencumbered right of ownership in the lands to be included in the park': Canada National Parks Act 2000, s 5(1)(a). Compare this to Scotland, where 'an awkward theory of the Crown's trusteeship of certain public [common law] rights' over public lands and resources persists. Robbie (n 40) 43.

[43] www.smh.com.au/nsw/tony-abbott-faces-liberal-revolt-over-middle-head-aged-care-home-20141107-11ism7.html (accessed on 28 December 2014).

[44] MB Grosvenor, 'Today and Tomorrow in Our National Parks' (1966) 130(1) *National Geographic* 2.

[45] *One Third of the Nation's Land: A Report to the President and to the Congress by the Public Land Law Review Commission* (1970) 20.

[46] Page (n 9).

[47] For example, Crown reserve trusts under Crown Lands Act 1989 (NSW), pts 4 and 5.

[48] JL Sax, 'The Public Trust Doctrine in Natural Resource Law: Effective Judicial Intervention' (1969–70) 68 *Michigan Law Review* 471.

[49] H Smith, 'Property as the Law of Things' (2012) 125 *Harvard Law Review* 1691, 1692.

owners. It is affirmed in those instances of express trust observed in the preceding paragraph. Yet, it remains a view of public ownership defined by essentially private parameters, where discrete owner(s) hold stick-rights in their respective ownership bundles.

This model's strength is that it often better reflects the truth on the ground.[50] There are many instances of public lands where multiple parties claim vested interests in the landscape. Local governments, state agencies, reserve trusts, historic trusts, and so on, frequently converge and overlay on individual tracts of public land, each holding different proprietorial rights of use and control. Rail trails illustrate this publicly owned, multi-layered model. In New Zealand, the pioneering Otago Central Rail Trail is a 150-kilometre-long ribbon of public land that cuts through an empty landscape of schist, tors and tussock.[51] Formerly owned by New Zealand Railways as a functioning rail line, the corridor was transferred to the Department of Conservation (DoC) in 1993, with the intention of developing the nation's first rail trail. Upon acquisition, the disused line was declared a recreation reserve under the Reserves Act 1977, inserting a statutory trust into the ownership hierarchy and mandating that the land be preserved for all New Zealanders for its recreational, scenic and environmental values.[52] The DoC also realised that community ownership of the proposal was vital to the trail's long-term viability.[53] In 1994, the Otago Central Rail Charitable Trust (the Trust) was formed, its stated purpose being to:

> Establish, develop and maintain the trail and any part of it for public recreation and enjoyment, and to assist and coordinate with the Department of Conservation, any local or regional authority or other group or person in that purpose. Walking, cycling and horse riding uses of the trail shall be paramount.[54]

The Trust became the 'face of the project … gathering support for the trail as a recreational facility, ensuring its sustainability, coordinating its promotion and fundraising'.[55] The Trust's community ownership added yet another layer to the title hierarchy, over and above the DoC's bare legal title and the Reserve Act's statutory trust.[56] Such multi-party arrangements reflect a landed reality, where multiple parties manage and control public lands through the prism of diverse ownerships.

[50] Blomley writes of property patterns matching the truth on the ground, N Blomley, *Unsettling the City: Urban Land and the Politics of Property* (New York, Routledge, 2004).

[51] Otago poet Brian Turner writes of the 'unsurpassed glory' of place, B Turner, *Elemental Central Otago Poems* (Auckland, Godwit, 2012).

[52] Under the Reserves Act 1977 (NZ), s 17(1), recreation reserves provide 'areas for the recreation and sporting activities and the physical welfare and enjoyment of the public, and for the protection of the natural environment and beauty of the countryside, with emphasis on the retention of open spaces and on outdoor recreational activities, including recreational tracks in the countryside'. The public has freedom of entry and access under s 17(2)(a), meaning that entry fees cannot be charged.

[53] *From Steam Trains to Pedal Power: The Story of the Otago Central Rail Trail* (Dunedin, Otago Central Rail Trail Trust, 2004) 12.

[54] ibid 64–5.

[55] ibid 12. 'With the Trust's support, DoC re-built the line from 1994 to 2000, re-surfacing the former tracks, re-decking bridges, and restoring historic infrastructure': ibid 13.

[56] The Malpai Borderlands in New Mexico and Arizona is another multi-owned landscape the subject of scholarly scrutiny; CM Rose, 'The Several Futures of Property: Of Cyberspace and Folk Tales, Emission Trades and Ecosystems' (1998) 83 *Minnesota Law Review* 129, 178; R Keiter, 'Public Lands and Law Reform: Putting Theory, Policy and Practice in Perspective' (2005) *Utah Law Review* 1127, 1175.

Conservation easements[57] likewise illustrate the reality of multiple public ownerships. They also add complexity, with their simultaneity with private rights. Conservation easements burden both public and, more typically, private lands with covenanted obligations to preserve in perpetuity natural landscapes, farmlands, views or watersheds. The rights are vested in state agencies or land trusts. Public ownerships in this guise are truly incorporeal, disconnected from the land's physicality, but appurtenant to it in their conservation of public goods.

Sally Fairfax and her colleagues call such patchworks of multiple ownerships 'mosaics', long-standing arrangements that date back, at least in the United States, to the eighteenth century. Their recent proliferation[58] is testament to an increasing awareness of the limits of 'buying nature'. The drawbacks identified in Section III are inherent in the outright purchase of conservation lands:

> Mosaics are a positive trend. At their best, they represent a ... collaborative and sophisticated approach that can approximate the elusive win–win model so frequently touted in conservation circles ... They are positive outcomes, compared with older models of top-down scientific management. They are also clearly preferable, in many instances, to waiting for adequate budgetary resources to ensure the protection of threatened sites.[59]

Multiple ownerships improve on the descriptively paler State as Owner version. Yet, as a category, it does not cover the field. What of those public places where ownership is diffuse, those inherently public properties where the idea of the individual owner(s), layered or otherwise, is at odds with the almost universal assumption of something else, where bonds of belonging to place seem proprietorial despite the lack of good title?

V. THE 'UNORGANIZED PUBLIC' AS OWNER

Here, the ownership of certain public lands is shorn of its thin veneer of state legal title, the pretense of trust. Likewise, this model starts to discard the bundle analogy, its relevance falling away. As we traverse further along the spectrum, we encounter an ownership form premised on the instinctive assumption that certain public lands do not require state intervention. These are everyone's lands, not someone's, whether it is a plural or singular someone. Carol Rose identifies such public lands as 'inherently public property', a distinct class outside private property and government-controlled property that is 'fully controlled by neither government nor

[57] Uniform Conservation Easement Act, §1(1). In NZ and Australia, the instrument is more commonly termed a conservation covenant, D Donohue, 'The Law and Practice of Open Space Covenants' (2003) 7 *New Zealand Journal Environmental Law* 119.

[58] 'By the beginning of the 21st century, conservation easements were the fastest-growing method for protecting land in the United States, preserving 1.2 million acres from development, at growth rates over the preceding decade of 377%': J Gustanski, 'Protecting the Land: Conservation Easements, Voluntary Actions, and Private Lands' in J Gustanski and R Squires (eds), *Protecting the Land: Conservation Easements Past, Present and Future* (Washington DC, Island Press, 2000) 14.

[59] Fairfax et al (n 14) 272.

private agents'[60] but owned and managed by an 'unorganized public at large'. Rose observes:

> Since the Middle Ages this category of 'inherently public property' has provided each member of some 'public' with a bundle of rights, neither entirely alienable by state or collective action, nor necessarily 'managed' in any explicitly organized manner ... [It is] property collectively 'owned' and 'managed' by society at large, with claims independent of and superior to the claims of any purported governmental manager.[61]

Beaches spring readily to mind in envisaging inherently public property. Here, ownership is 'dispersed',[62] vested in a citizenry that is 'indefinite and informal, yet nevertheless capable of self-management'.[63] While unorganised, this public is not disorganised; its use and regulation of the public commons is ordered by custom-like norms that are recognisable, persuasive and widely observed.[64] Offshore, surfer norms enforce proprietary-like entitlements to surfing waves,[65] while onshore, indicia of possession, such as the placement of towels, or the staking of beach umbrellas or sun shelters, assert temporary, seemingly exclusive use-claims over desirable stretches of sand.[66]

Central to the management of inherently public property is custom, historically an important source of law, yet in modern times seen as a quaint anomaly.[67] For its proponents, the custom of community is a critical and overlooked factor that fosters 'civilized behavior and eschews churlish practices',[68] as the above beach examples illustrate. Indeed, in the United States, custom has proven instrumental in protecting public access to wet sands, famously so in the state of Oregon.[69] Custom also speaks surprisingly forcefully.[70] What makes custom surprising is how often it prevails over formal law, a propensity Robert Ellickson calls 'order without law'.[71]

[60] CM Rose, 'The Comedy of the Commons: Custom, Commerce, and Inherently Public Property' (1986) 53 *University of Chicago Law Review* 711, 720.

[61] ibid. In Scotland, 'inherently public property' enjoys legislative mandate, where the incorporeal right to roam under s 28 of the Land Reform (Scotland) Act 2003 is held by the Scottish public directly, without the need for any Crown intermediary role, Robbie (n 40) 42.

[62] Davies (n 38) 64.

[63] Rose (n 60) 742.

[64] ibid 744–45.

[65] D Nazer, 'The Tragicomedy of the Surfers' Commons' (2004) 9 *Deakin Law Review* 655, 677. In Australia, no one is excused from compliance with the rules of 'inherently public property'. In March 2016, ex-prime minister Tony Abbott was widely criticised for his breach of surfing norms, 'dropping in' on a wave 'belonging' to an adjacent 17-year-old surfer, www.theguardian.com/australia-news/2016/mar/29/teenage-surfer-to-tony-abbott-thats-my-wave (accessed on 1 April 2016).

[66] An analogy is the ordering of campus food carts, GM Duhl, 'Property and Custom: Allocating Space in Public Spaces' (2006) 79 *Temple Law Review* 199.

[67] 'The common law tradition is not entirely friendly to group rights': CM Rose, 'Property and Language, or the Ghost of the Fifth Panel' (2006) 18 *Yale Journal of Law and Humanities* 1, 13.

[68] Rose (n 60) 745.

[69] D Bederman, 'The Curious Resurrection of Custom: Beach Access and Judicial Takings' (1996) 96 *Columbia Law Review* 1375.

[70] A Brower and J Page, 'When the Law is Silent, Trespassers W ...: Law and Power in Implied Property Rights' (2012) 42 *Environmental Law Reporter News & Analysis* 10 242.

[71] R Ellickson, *Order Without Law: How Neighbors Settle Disputes* (Cambridge, Harvard University Press, 1991).

For inherently public property to arise, its degree of use is critical. It is a resource vulnerable to 'under-investment',[72] yet capacious in its potential. Hence, the more *is* the merrier, in what Rose calls an exponential 'comedy of the commons'. Overuse does not descend into Hardin's familiar tragedy, but rather it increases the 'solidarity and fellow-feeling of the whole community'[73] such that the greater the use, the better for all. Indeed, the land's very publicness creates the rent that precludes its private capture,[74] yielding sociable 'returns to scale'[75] as its use expands. For Rose, inherently public property is critical for its socialising values, providing the physicalised places that 'allow us to get along with each other'.[76]

Another way of seeing inherently public property is through the nascent literature of Property as Belonging. Belonging is not premised on the plausibility of proof of title, but rather on vague notions of connection to 'proper or rightful place',[77] landed links imbued with personal or communitarian meaning. In the Māori language, this is called *whakapapa*.[78] Davina Cooper uses Summerhill School in southern England as a study in linking a school community's sense of belonging with its propertied place, 'a quite different understanding of property … one constitutive of community life'.[79] Cooper compares property's hallmark right to exclude, and its definition (by exclusion) of space, with converse norms of inclusion that make space formative of community. Cooper surmises that her case study only makes real-world sense if 'the black box of unofficial property interests' is opened up. For Cooper, looking at property relationships through the crude lens of ownership not only 'misses, but also misrecognises' what happens.[80] In 2013, Cooper returned to Summerhill to further explore property as belonging, recognising that belonging informs many expressions of ownership, from the orthodox 'subject–object belonging' to belonging as 'a relationship of proximity, attachment or connection'.[81] 'As a way of imagining [and unsettling] property, belonging emphasises the place of connection and relationship.' Indeed, belonging is not without property provenance. In the unenclosed lands of eighteenth-century agrarian England, the interest of commoners was said to be a 'form of ownership without possession … [a bond that] created a sense of self; it told commoners who they were, a part of a tribe'.[82]

Belonging is a legally implausible concept that nonetheless resonates with lived experience, particularly so in well-loved public landscapes. In seeking to rationalise inherently public property, Rose begins with 'strong' doctrines such as dedication, prescription or the public trust. In the end, though, she opts for the 'weaker' doctrine

[72] Rose (n 60) 768.
[73] ibid 767–68.
[74] ibid 774.
[75] ibid 776.
[76] ibid.
[77] D Cooper, *Everyday Utopias* (Durham, Duke University Press, 2013) 163.
[78] A Salwen, H Matunga, E Lewis, C Berneheim and A Brower, 'Māori Land Ethics and the Spirit of Leopold', paper presented at IUCN World Conservation Congress, Honolulu, HI, 1–10 September 2016.
[79] D Cooper, 'Opening up Ownership: Community Belonging, Belongings, and the Productive Life of Property' (2007) 32(3) *Law and Social Inquiry* 625.
[80] ibid 625.
[81] Cooper (n 77) 163.
[82] Neeson (n 41) 180.

of custom to best explain this dispersed form of public ownership. Belonging is no doubt weaker again, deeply contextual, intuitive and far removed from the objective bundle analysis. Its implausibility seems a bridge too far. Yet, as Sections VI and VII will show, the equally implausible idea that land could own itself is no longer as preposterous as it once appeared.

Indeed, Belonging captures the evolution of Te Urewera, where the people have long belonged to the land[83] but the inverse has been hotly contested for centuries. Te Urewera is a 'remote, rugged, immense' wilderness on the North Island's East Coast, 'famous for its lakes, forested beauty and stormy history'.[84] Its stormy history is one of conflict between the Crown and the local Māori *iwi*, the Tūhoe. This conflict left a legacy of 'large scale land confiscations, brutal military campaigns and unjust land purchases'.[85] Layered atop this history was, from 1954 to 2014, its status as Urewera National Park.

If one were to ignore the Tūhoe's history of belonging to the land, Crown ownership of a public park would seem inviolable, inalienable. National Park status further entrenches that perception.[86] Indeed, ignoring history, National Park status implies a contract in perpetuity, between the people of a nation and its precious nooks, crannies and misty forest gorges. The peopled past and present of that land is often innocently forgotten, or actively erased, in the land's elevation to National Park. A layperson ensconced in the present day could be forgiven for assuming that park status can never be rescinded, that the state cannot just cede public ownership and that park ownership is somehow different. Understanding the land's and people's history without romanticising or essentialising the relationship[87] allows us to understand that the land owning itself is not preposterous, but sometimes the only way out of an untenable situation.

VI. THE LANDED HISTORY OF A PEOPLE AND THE PEOPLED HISTORY OF A LAND: ONE EVOLUTION OF THE LAND AS OWNER

To understand Te Urewera is to understand its specialness of place and its temporal past and present. Te Urewera was a peopled land and the Tūhoe were a landed people long before the British Crown asserted ownership in 1840 by way of treaty, signed by only one of the parties. The story of the Te Urewera is often told through a song, a *waiata*, of an eagle's watchful and circular flight over the Urewera ranges, her rivers, her forests, her gorges, her tracks, and her people past and present.[88]

[83] Salwen et al (n 78) find that belonging to the land is a fundamental tenet of Māori land ethics, and a common theme in Iwi Management Plans.

[84] www.doc.govt.nz/parks-and-recreation/places-to-go/east-coast/places/te-urewera/ (accessed on 28 December 2014). It is also home to the Lake Waikeremoana Great Walk.

[85] http://www.doc.govt.nz/news/media-releases/2014/tuhoe-claims-settlement-and-te-urewera-bills-passed/ (accessed on 2 December 2014).

[86] New York State entrenched its protective contract for the Adirondacks and the Catskills in the State's constitution, requiring they be held 'forever wild', New York Constitution, §14.

[87] S Krech, *The Ecological Indian* (New York, WW Norton & Co, 1999).

[88] J Binney, *Encircled Lands: Te Urewera 1820–1921* (Wellington, Bridget Williams Books, 2009) 18–19.

The eagle sees and sings of a land and people so intertwined that the most human of actions, staking territory, is done by the land, not the people: 'The *rohe* (borders) of Tūhoe's ancestral lands were not measured in lines, but they were known and defended. Its *pou rāhui* (boundary markers) are mountains, waterfalls, marked and unmarked stones, and tall trees.'[89]

This is a remote corner of Earth's last major landmass to see humans.[90] New Zealand was populated by seafaring Polynesians, who became Māori only about 750 years ago.[91] Tales of men with horses drifted in to the Ureweras in the 1820s;[92] Christian missionaries arrived there in the 1830s;[93] the first NZ government visitor arrived in 1862.[94]

On 6 February 1840, the Crown and many Māori chiefs signed the Treaty of Waitangi, a constitutional document to guide the relationship between the Crown and the Māori in the newly founded colony.[95] The Tūhoe did not sign the treaty, an anomaly in which they take much pride.[96] Armed invasions of the Ureweras by the Crown commenced in the mid-1860s,[97] and by January 1866 the Crown had sparked a Tūhoe rebellion when it started confiscating land 'for establishing military settlements to maintain the Queen's authority'.[98] Brutal land wars ensued. In 1867, the Tūhoe announced its sovereign borders, Te Rohe Pōtae o Tūhoe. These boundaries created 'The Encircled Lands' of Te Urewera.[99]

The land wars ended, for a while, in 1872. The Tūhoe announced their autonomous territory and established a board of land guardians, composed of local chiefs. They rejected the Crown authority of the Native Land Court.[100] Extraordinarily in New Zealand history, the Crown eventually agreed. Tūhoe autonomy was enshrined in law with the 1896 passage of the Urewera District Native Reserve Act, which fulfilled the Native Minister's 1872 war-ending pledge (with a few intervening wars for emphasis).[101] This 1896 Act established perhaps the first example worldwide of co-governance, a coexistence of two authorities and two sovereignties—a word that is plural only uncomfortably.

The Crown itself quickly grew uncomfortable with this coexistence, and started less than scrupulous land acquisitions in 1910. By 1927, more than two-thirds of the statutory reserve was back in Crown ownership.[102] Though Parliament had to retroactively validate these purchases in 1916, respected New Zealand historian Judith Binney chronicles persuasively the effect of the colonial acquisition of the peopled land—to dissect and undermine the hard-won autonomy of the landed

[89] ibid 19.
[90] G Gibbs, *Ghosts of Gondwana* (Nelson, Craig Potton Publishing, 2006).
[91] M King, *The Penguin History of New Zealand* (Auckland, Penguin Books, 2003) 156–57.
[92] Binney (n 88) 44.
[93] ibid 45.
[94] ibid 61.
[95] King (n 91) 156–57.
[96] Binney (n 88) 47.
[97] ibid 68–99.
[98] Binney (n 88) 100.
[99] ibid 100.
[100] ibid 5.
[101] ibid 398–404.
[102] ibid 603.

people. Binney shows that the 1896 Act recognised the truth on the ground at the time: there could, and did, exist two separate and parallel sovereignties. The coexistence did not last long, but neither did the idea disappear from Tūhoe consciousness. This encircledness also seeped into the nation's wider imagination, perhaps best captured by noted New Zealand painter Colin McCahon's famous 1975 'Urewera Mural' inscribed with the words:

> **TŪHOE**
> URE WERA
> **THEIR LAND.**[103]

In the same year that McCahon painted his mural, the New Zealand Parliament passed the Treaty of Waitangi Act 1975. The Act established the Waitangi Tribunal, a 'permanent commission of inquiry charged with making recommendations on claims brought by Māori relating to actions or omissions of the Crown that potentially breach the promises made in the Treaty of Waitangi'.[104] When the Waitangi Tribunal turned its gaze to reparations for Treaty violations with the Tūhoe, at issue were landownership and financial compensation, just like the other Tribunal hearings. For the Tūhoe though, another central player was their goal of 'a nation within a nation'.[105] Like other *iwis*, the Tūhoe were awarded land and cash settlements. But the Urewera National Park was different.

Sovereignty of the land that became Urewera National Park in 1954 was of particular poignance to the Tribunal. For many Māori, 'the National Parks Act is a mono-cultural statute premising Western values for preserving land'.[106] Somewhat ironically, one of the selling points Crown agents used to acquire the land in the early 1900s was that it would eventually become a park, and thus would never be 'lost' to its people.[107]

Given its history, the land of Te Urewera was in 2014 considered unkeepable for the Crown. The peopled land had endured, even if the people had been de-landed. And the symbolism of co-sovereignty had endured, as if locked in the mist. Indeed, colourful signs mark 'the ring of fire' encircling Urewera's 'Tūhoe Nation'. One such proclaims: 'For the mist, and the mountains, forests and rivers shall stand witness to your thoughts and deeds'.[108] At the same time, after 60 years as a beloved National Park, the land was just as ungive-backable. Trapped between not keeping and not giving back, and under the watchful eye of the singing eagle and the misted mountains, the New Zealand Parliament created a new form of ownership, understood only within the landed context of a peopled history.

[103] http://www.mccahon.co.nz/cm001411 (accessed on 8 March 2015).
[104] www.justice.govt.nz/tribunals/waitangi-tribunal (accessed on 8 March 2015).
[105] Tame Iti, quoted in Binney (n 88) 14.
[106] Ruru (n 4).
[107] Binney (n 88) 552.
[108] ibid 14.

VII. THE LAND AS OWNER

The Te Urewera Act 2014 (the Act) represented a 'win–win' for both the Crown and the Tūhoe,[109] redressing historical grievances and enshrining 'an apology for the Crown's grievous actions': 'The Crown and Tūhoe intend this Act to contribute to resolving the grief of Tūhoe and to strengthening and maintaining the connection between Tūhoe and Te Urewera.'[110]

The Act was passed on 27 July 2014 and came into force in September of that year. Its centrepiece is the establishment of Te Urewera as a legal entity, with 'all the rights, powers, duties, and liabilities of a legal person',[111] and its vesting of the fee simple estate in Te Urewera.[112] Te Urewera ceased being national park, Crown land, reserve or conservation land, as the case was, effective from the settlement date.[113] Instead, Te Urewera became the land, and the land became Te Urewera.

> Recognising Te Urewera has its own identity confirms Tūhoe's view that it is not something which anyone owns ... Te Urewera exists in its own right, and we as Tūhoe and New Zealanders have the responsibility to recognise its *mana* and commit to its care and protection.[114]

The proposition that land can own itself evolves from the thesis that things of the natural world—trees, rivers, wild valleys—are autonomous right-holders. Famously articulated in Christopher Stone's seminal 1972 article 'Should Trees Have Standing?',[115] this ecocentric perspective is a central organising principle in the emerging fields of wild law or ecological jurisprudence.

Te Urewera is the logical, arguably inevitable, end game of 'trees having standing'. Stone predicted that, to achieve such ends, laws (including property laws) would require a fundamental redesign, such that they had 'two sides ... legal-operational aspects, and ... psychic and socio-psychic aspects'.[116] The Te Urewera Act fulfils, and adds flesh to, Stone's dual prophecies.

In terms of its 'legal-operational aspects', the cornerstone section 11 meets all of Stone's threshold prerequisites from 1972: first, it enables the land to 'institute legal actions at its behest';[117] secondly, it impliedly envisages 'injury' to Te Urewera, rather than simply quantifying loss as a measure of damages for its human resource-users; and thirdly, it provides that 'relief ... run[s] to the benefit of the thing'.[118] Further, the creation of the statutory board tasked 'to act on behalf of, and in the

[109] Ruru (n 4).
[110] Te Urewera Act 2014 (NZ), s 3(10).
[111] ibid s 11(1).
[112] 'The fee simple estate in the establishment land vests in Te Urewera and is held under, and in accordance with, this Act': Te Urewera Act 2014 (NZ), s 12(3). Section 13 provides it is inalienable; section 89(1)(a) provides that the freehold title is registered as a single title in the name of Te Urewera under the Land Transfer Act 1952 (NZ).
[113] Te Urewera Act 2014 (NZ), s 12(2).
[114] www.doc.govt.nz/about-doc/news/media-releases/2014/board-appointed-for-new-era-for-te-urewera/. (accessed on 28 December 2014).
[115] Stone (n 11).
[116] ibid 458.
[117] Te Urewera Act 2014 (NZ), s 11(1).
[118] Stone (n 11) 458.

name of Te Urewera'[119] is the embodiment of Stone's 'guardian *de jure* representative of the natural object'.[120] The board has wide powers,[121] including the implementation of management and operational plans, the passing of by-laws and the granting of activity permits, concessions,[122] covenants and easements.[123] Coupled with mundane, real-world necessities like Te Urewera's tax status[124] and its registration in the Torrens land title register, such matters of procedure and administration are crucial, albeit dry, 'legal-operational aspects' at the heart of the land's self-governance.

More intriguing is the Act's enlivenment of Stone's 'socio-psychic aspects'. Stone observes that natural objects communicate 'in ways that are not terribly ambiguous'.[125] Using his parched lawn as an example, Stone writes of 'the appearance of bald spots, yellowness, and a lack of springiness after being walked on' as telltale, not terribly ambiguous signs of the land speaking for itself, of its obvious need for water. Stone says the law should listen to 'the conscious mind of the Earth',[126] much as it listens to other inanimate entitles, like corporations, through their proxies. The Te Urewera Act enacts Stone's call, accepting as a foundational premise that Te Urewera speaks for itself, through its spirit and culture, its *mana* (loosely translated as authority, influence, status and charisma) and its *mauri* (essence or special nature).[127]

Section 3 of the Act details this collective narrative of Te Urewera, one inclusive of all New Zealanders:

> (4) For Tūhoe, Te Urewera is *Te Manawa o te Ika a Māui*; it is the heart of the great fish of Maui, its name being derived from Murakareke, the son of the ancestor Tūhoe.
>
> (5) For Tūhoe, Te Urewera is their *ewe whenua*, their place of origin and return, their homeland.
>
> (6) Te Urewera expresses and gives meaning to Tūhoe culture, language, customs, and identity. There Tūhoe hold *mana* by *ahikāroa*; they are *tangata whenua* and *kaitiaki* of Te Urewera.
>
> (7) Te Urewera is prized by other *iwi* and *hapū* who have acknowledged special associations with, and customary interests in, parts of Te Urewera.
>
> (8) Te Urewera is also prized by all New Zealanders as a place of outstanding national value and intrinsic worth; it is treasured by all for the distinctive natural values of its vast and rugged primeval forest, and for the integrity of those values; for its indigenous ecological systems and biodiversity, its historical and cultural heritage, its scientific importance, and as a place for outdoor recreation and spiritual reflection.

Te Urewera represents a Kuhnian paradigm shift, 'a profound alternative to the human presumption of sovereignty over the natural world'.[128] Yet, despite its radical

[119] Te Urewera Act 2014 (NZ) s 17(a).
[120] Stone (n 11) 470. Stone envisaged that groups like the Sierra Club or the Environmental Defense Fund would be likely guardians (466).
[121] Te Urewera Act 2014 (NZ), ss 19, 31–37. The board's composition is determined by ss 21–29.
[122] ibid s 18; see also ss 55–62.
[123] ibid ss 98–99.
[124] ibid s 40.
[125] Stone (n 11) 471.
[126] ibid 500.
[127] Te Urewera Act 2014 (NZ), s 3(2).
[128] Pita Sharples, Minister for Māori Affairs, cited in Ruru (n 4).

overhaul of the concept of ownership, public rights to use and enjoy Te Urewera remain undiluted. For example, after initial uncertainty about the permitting of hunters in Te Urewera, the board quickly organised a system of permitting and monitoring that, by all reports, works better than before—for both the hunters and the land. Section 4 reiterates Te Urewera as a 'place for public use and enjoyment, for recreation, learning, and spiritual reflection'. Section 5 requires that 'public freedom of access and entry to Te Urewera'[129] be a guiding principle to 'all persons performing functions and exercising powers under this Act'. To paraphrase the Australian High Court, Te Urewera remains a land over which no 'individual … has [any] greater claim than any other member of the public … [where] all members of the public may have the right to go … and walk freely and resist attempts by anyone to eject them'.[130]

Te Urewera is a stunning, seemingly unbelievable leap in legal logic. Yet, as Stone explains, it is but a natural step in an inexorable progression: '[t]hroughout legal history, each successive extension of rights to some new entity [for example, married women or children] has been, theretofore … unthinkable'.[131] Te Urewera aligns with this trajectory, evolving from the once unthinkable to the legislated here and now.[132]

VIII. EXPANDING THE OWNERSHIP SPECTRUM INTO THE THIRD AND FOURTH DIMENSIONS

Te Urewera reveals that our present constrained thinking of the range of forms of public ownership of land is out of touch. Before the 2014 Act, the land lay in limbo, simultaneously unkeepable and ungive-backable. After 2014, the heresy that land could own itself was laid bare. In this section of the chapter, we cite Te Urewera to propose a way to reconnect public property with the modern multicultural world, by adding to our spectrum a third dimension, of particularised place, and a fourth dimension, of particularised time.[133]

Property as traditionally conceived is two-dimensional, devoid of place and time. As Wesley Hohfield argues, property is a series of disaggregated relations between persons about things. As such, property is placeless, a bundle of go-anywhere rights.[134] For public property in land, the threshold problem with the detachable,

129 Te Urewera Act 2014 (NZ), s 5(2). See also s 56 for the broad list of activities that do not require authorisation.

130 *Stow v Mineral Holdings (Australia) Pty Ltd* (1977) 51 ALJR 672, 679.

131 Stone (n 11) 453.

132 The Minister of Conservation, Nick Smith, described the evolutionary unthinkableness in the following terms, quoted in Ruru (n 4): 'It is surprising for me, as a Minister of Conservation in the 1990s who was involved … in the huge debate that occurred around the provisions of the Ngāi Tahu settlement in respect of conservation land, how far this country and this Parliament have come when we now get to this Tūhoe settlement in respect of the treasured Te Urewera National Park. If you had told me 15 years ago that Parliament would almost unanimously be able to agree to this bill, I would have said "You're dreaming mate". It has been a real journey for New Zealand, iwi, and Parliament.'

133 A Einstein, *Relativity: The Special and General Theory* (R Lawson, tr, Methuen & Co Ltd, 2000).

134 The rise of abstraction in Anglo-American property law is chronicled in S Banner, *American Property: A History of How, Why, and What We Own* (Cambridge, Harvard University Press, 2011) 289–90.

go-anywhere bundle is its inaptness. It may have limited appeal to the individual state as owner, but when we see public ownership as an indistinct everyone's, it becomes less applicable. And when the land itself holds the sticks, the bundle becomes a useless currency. Much like the common law doctrine of merger, the merger of the land and its owner supervenes and redefines all, in the process exposing the artifice of the law's placelessness.

Legal geography is an emerging discipline that recognises that all law is 'worlded'[135] in some way. For legal geographers, 'nearly every aspect of law is located, takes place, is in motion, or has some spatial reference'. To put it simply, 'the *where* of law is not simply some inert site ... but is inextricably implicated in how law happens'.[136]

In the language of space, legal geography adds a third dimension to the spectrum, of contextual topography. Legal geography also adds a fourth dimension, of time, with its more recent engagement with history and the 'multiple aspects of the temporality of legal spaces'.[137] The relationship between space and time in legal geography has been vexed. Many scholars concede that space enjoys an entrenched privilege, a consequence of its centrality to the geography of the law. Thus, space is described as 'theoretically interesting' while time is reduced to a background 'empirical history'.[138] In recent scholarship however, greater inquisitiveness about the effects of time on space has fostered more sophisticated spatio-temporal concepts to develop. Increasingly, each is seen to inform and add substance to the other, such that neither is privileged. As Mariana Valverde argues, 'time can have the effect of thickening space, and space in turn can shape time', the net effect being that 'time thickens and takes on flesh'.[139] Importantly, time imbues space with its many human meanings, turning de-peopled spaces into peopled places.[140]

Indeed, that fourth dimension, of time, is essential to understanding the tale of two parks presented in this chapter. Where Te Urewera embodies the peopled history of the land, the Everlasting Swamp papers over that history with the bare ownership title of the state. The Everlasting Swamp is an ecologically sensitive place, and national park status will preserve its endangered ecology from coastal development. But that preservation locks the place into one time, of the state's choosing, when the land did not happen to be peopled. Preservation risks locking the Everlasting Swamp into Plato's cave, the linear,[141] two-dimensional end of our spectrum, replete with its old constraints and old limitations.

[135] I Braverman et al, 'Introduction: Expanding the Spaces of Law' in I Braverman et al (eds), *The Expanding Spaces of Law: A Timely Legal Geography* (Stanford, Stanford University Press, 2014) 1.

[136] ibid (original emphasis).

[137] ibid 14.

[138] M Valverde, 'Time Thickens, Takes on Flesh: Spatiotemporal Dynamics in Law' in Braverman et al (n 135) 73.

[139] ibid. Valverde uses the courtroom as an example of time adding flesh to space, transforming a four-walled room into a court when the judge enters and sittings commence.

[140] Geographers distinguish space from place by the latter having been invested with human meaning, T Cresswell, *Place: An Introduction* (Chichester, John Wiley & Son, 2004).

[141] 'Property in land tends to be linear': S Keenan, *Subversive Property* (Abingdon, Routledge, 2015) 89–90.

Embracing place as well as time, past and present, as at Te Urewera, makes room for new forms of public property that venture into new dimensions. To focus on the question of ownership only exposes its shortcomings. It reveals a growing awareness that answers to the conundrum of public property may lie elsewhere. Focusing on ownership also risks failing to recognise that belonging can go both ways.

In Te Reo Māori, *tangata whenua* means people of the land, not the other way round. Te Urewera shows that people can belong to the land. This belonging can endure over time even as formal ownership shifts: from no one; to everyone; to the British Crown; to the *iwi*; to the New Zealand government; and finally back to a combined no one and everyone, the Land as Owner. This landed identity of a people will of course change over time and as formal ownership shifts, but it endures.

Sarah Keenan draws links between space, time and belonging in ways that loosely align with *tangata whenua*. Keenan describes property 'as a relationship of belonging held up by space … not a permanent relationship but rather something that happens when a subject becomes embedded in particular spaces'.[142] And time is critical to space, it is 'the repetition, the habit, the accumulation of gestures that shapes the space' so that 'issues of time [become] inseparable from issues of space'.[143] To focus on belonging, on time and space, is to focus on the contextual, 'the space in which the subject is embedded, rather than on the propertied subject herself'.[144]

Adding the third and fourth dimensions allows property to expand from mere ownership to a richer and fuller belonging, which can go in both directions. Recent antipodean developments such as Te Urewera, and New Zealand's 2014 granting of the legal rights of a person to the Wanganui River,[145] make it possible to conceive of a form of public property better suited to its setting than to an ownership-premised model.[146] It thus seems that adding space and time, each equally privileged, allows us to better understand public property and, by inference, property itself. Perhaps more importantly, it allows property to better understand us, and our deeply inter-connected senses of belonging.

IX. CONCLUSION

This chapter suggests that the owner of public property in land could be someone, everyone or no one. The Everlasting Swamp is owned by the someone state. Te Urewera is owned by no one, yet it is everyone's, Tūhoe and non-Tūhoe alike. Understanding public lands through the ownership prism seems only as good as far as it goes. Yet, for the purposes of this chapter, it remains a structure worth building, if only to see its limitations, to see how far it does go.

142 Keenan (n 141) 14.

143 ibid 87.

144 ibid 150.

145 Tutohu Whakatupua (Agreement between Whanganui Iwi and the Crown, 30 August 2012), available at www.govt.nz/treaty-settlement-documents/whanganui-iwi/ (accessed on 8 March 2015).

146 Te Urewera Act 2014, s 6 says as much: 'Tūhoe and the Crown have together taken a unique approach, as set out in this Act, to protecting Te Urewera in a way that reflects New Zealand's culture and values.'

Interpreting property though the legal-geographic frame of space and time is another way of seeing our relationships with public lands, an alternative that might go further. In the case of Te Urewera, this very unorthodox embodiment of property makes placed sense, an iteration of ownership at one with the mists, mountains and mysteries of the land. Most critically, it makes temporal sense, a resolution of nearly two centuries of competing histories. Te Urewera is a propertied response to the exigencies of a modern, bicultural New Zealand. Its enacted form was once unthinkable; now it passes as uncontroversial.

Te Urewera shows the importance of the third and fourth dimensions of space and time in formulating answers to the question: what is public property in land? Space and time extend our spectrum of public ownership, from the individual State as Owner at one extreme to the Land as Owner at the other. In that process of adding yet another point on an expanding spectrum, a distinct shift occurs, both in our understandings of public ownership and what it says about us. For New Zealanders, it explains who they are in ways that bundles of sticks never can, as a landed people sharing, and belonging to, the much-loved public spaces of a peopled land. For the threadbare institution that is public property, space and time add context to an evolving spectrum, such that our legal understandings of ownership better reflect the lands in which they lie.

Index

www.ingramcontent.com/pod-product-compliance
Lightning Source LLC
LaVergne TN
LVHW080021210926
848481LV00011B/3074